Freud's Answer

Martin Wain

Freud's
Answer

The Social Origins of
Our Psychoanalytic Century

CHICAGO

Ivan R. Dee

1998

Library of Congress Cataloging-in-Publication Data:
Wain, Martin, 1932–
    Freud's answer : the social origins of our psychoanalytic century / Martin Wain.
        p.   cm.
    Includes bibliographical references and index.
    ISBN 1-56663-216-1 (alk. paper)
        1. Psychoanalysis—Social aspects—Europe—History—20th century.
    2. Psychoanalysis—Social aspects—Europe—History—19th century.
    3. Psychoanalysis—Social aspects—United States—History—20th century.
    4. Psychoanalysis—Social aspects—United States—History—19th century.
    5. Freud, Sigmund, 1856–1939—Influence.   6. Europe—Intellectual life—20th century.   7. Europe—Intellectual life—19th century.   8. United States—Intellectual life—20th century.   9. United States—Intellectual life—19th century. I. Title.
BF175.W25   1998
150.19'52—dc21   98-20125

In loving memory of my parents

Contents

Beloved, believe not every spirit, but try the spirits whether they are of God: because many false prophets are gone into the world.
—1 John 4:1

A dialectic of rupture, modernity becomes very quickly a dynamism of amalgamation and recycling. In politics, in technology, in art, in culture, modernity defines itself by the rate of change tolerated by the system without really changing anything in the essential order.
—Jean Baudrillard, *Symbolic Exchange and Death*

The play of substitutes fills and marks a determined lack.
—Jacques Derrida, "The Play of Substitutes"

. . . We shall go along with the doctors on the first stage of our journey, but we shall soon part company with them. . . .
—Sigmund Freud, *Five Lectures on Psycho-Analysis*

You have no need to be afraid that any special medical knowledge will be required for following what I have to say.
—Sigmund Freud, *Five Lectures on Psycho-Analysis*

The Hundred-year Mystery

Attempts to clarify Freud's metapsychological
speculations or reduce them to consistency have proved
vain to date and the suggestion has often been made
that they be abandoned.
—*The Oxford Companion to Philosophy* (1995)

Napoleon once said—"Mightier than any army with
banners is an idea whose time has come." This well
describes the advance . . . made by the ideas of Freud
and Jung. . . .
—Alan McGlashan, Preface, *The Freud/Jung Letters*

FOR A HUNDRED YEARS, from the time it was introduced until
today, it has been impossible to determine whether psychoanalysis
was, as presented, a science and therapy for the treatment of individuals suffering from mental illness. Those who were certain that Sigmund Freud, the leader of the psychoanalytic movement, was a genius
never raised the issue. But in recent years he and his disciples have
come under sharper scrutiny than ever, and many experts, popular
media, and laymen have concluded that there was little or no truth in
their theories and no efficacy in their practices. Yet no one has been
able to determine what the pioneer psychoanalysts were actually doing
if they were not creating a successful new psychology and therapy.
That their work might simply be explained as a failed experiment, a
wrong path, seems inadequate in view of the status it achieved in
Western culture—though there are examples of influential scientific errors lasting for a long time, among them Ptolemy's geocentric theory
of the universe, and the eighteenth century's phlogiston theory (as the
explanation for combustion).

The first and easiest answer usually offered by skeptics of psychoanalysis is hoaxing. Yet it is doubtful that Freud, who was developing his theories while he had a growing family and was in most ways a typical middle-class burgher seeking success in his chosen medical profession, would have become a jokester, or would have been followed by trained physicians willing to do the same. Perhaps the hoax explanation means to say that the pioneer psychoanalysts wished to offer magical cures on the model of Cagliostro and Mesmer in the eighteenth century, in the hope of enhancing their fame and income. But Freud and his colleagues in the psychoanalytic movement held degrees from the finest European universities, and most were physicians with the ability to make an adequate or better living. Becoming charlatans would have been a chancy way to increase their income, which at all odds was quite satisfactory but never very great, even after their work was widely accepted.[1] As to ambition for fame, that must be conceded, but not necessarily on the grounds of fame for its own sake.

Another answer sometimes given is cocaine. Freud experimented with it from his late university years to slightly beyond his early forties when he propounded his crowning theory, the Oedipus complex, and completed his essential theoretical framework. Cocaine may have given him a manic confidence that he had discovered the wellsprings of human psychology, but for the rest of his life would he have stuck to ideas that had come to him in drug-induced visions? Some charge that he was self-deluded, perhaps by blind ambition, perhaps by the accomplishments of such predecessors as Jean-Martin Charcot, the famed French neurologist with whom he studied for a time, and the hypnotist-physicians Auguste Liébeault and Hippolyte Bernheim, who were reporting spectacular cures in the late 1880s, so that he would not have known clearly what he was up to.[2]

There is also the question of his Jewish heritage. Might he not have been seeking revenge on a Christian Europe that designated him an outsider? But not all his followers were Jewish—for example, Carl Jung and Eugen Bleuler in Switzerland, James Jackson Putnam in America, Ernest Jones (his future biographer) in England, and others in Holland and Russia, and before long in India, Japan, and Scandinavia; nor were others who were inspirations for the movement or independent creators of psychoanalysis such as Charcot, Liébeault, and Pierre Janet. Some inspirations were in fact "philosophical" anti-Semites, such as Arthur Schopenhauer and Friedrich Nietzsche.[3]

Among other explanations for Freud's work are that he wished to destroy the false values of Victorianism, that he was inspired by a decadent Vienna, that he hoped to strike back at the authoritarian, anti-Semitic Austrian political system, that he was obsessed with his father and sexually attracted to his mother. Several commentators propose that since he could not create a viable scientific psychology, he mimicked one—along the lines of Arthur Conan Doyle's Sherlock Holmes and Edgar Allan Poe's M. Dupin discovering miraculous solutions through amazing feats of deductive reasoning. Marxists have declared that Freud created an illusory theory that helped preserve the status quo, and it has also been suggested that psychoanalysis was aimed at social reform; scattered commentaries even suggest that Freudianism had a proto-fascist streak. The French philosopher Michel Foucault, a master of the origins of theories of mental illness, thought psychoanalysis was designed to support the state and its laws.[4]

Evident elements of religion and philosophy in psychoanalysis have led some to think that the Freudians were priests or philosophers under the skin. Among these interpretations is that Freud suffered from a delusional neurosis focused on religion.[5]

Despite the doubt cast on it for a hundred years, psychoanalysis achieved an unparalleled success in itself and in the many variations it spawned. Among the explanations for this success are that it duplicated past methods for persuading recalcitrant members of society to "go along to get along"; that it provided a means of fashioning a private identity in the modern age; that it provided a coherent belief system; that it answered the need for belief after the loss of religion; that it paralleled the egalitarian, humanistic, and compassionate rules of democratic society; that in America its optimism was appreciated; and that it capitalized on the gullibility of the public and the willingness of many people to follow the lead of authority.[6] Few studies fail to characterize Freud as a supersalesman whose writings were calculated for sensation as well as credibility.

Considered individually or in clusters, none of these explanations has been able to account fully either for the Freudians or for their overwhelming acceptance by Western culture. What, then, were the pioneers doing, and why were they so successful in dominating the field of modern psychology? "It seems to me," Freud wrote in 1923, "that the world has no claim on my person and that it will learn nothing from me so long as my case (for manifold reasons) cannot be made fully transparent."[7] Here I seek to make the case transparent and to provide the "manifold reasons" why Freud did not wish it to be so.

Freud and his colleagues were social, political, and economic therapists in the broadest sense. Their patient was modern Western culture at a time of maximum danger. Their treatment was a set of theoretical concepts and practices that carried deep, suggestive, symbolic messages so effective and desirable that for a hundred years they made psychoanalysis and its many related therapies appealing; raised therapists to the status of magi; led to a multi-billion-dollar therapy industry; influenced psychiatry, education, child-rearing, law, penology, philosophy, the arts, historiography, the social sciences, literary criticism, and biography; and maintained a believability so high that many people still consider it science and therapy.[8]

A few definitions will be helpful at the start. By *gemeinschaft* I mean the character of rural community life before the Industrial Revolution. *Gesellschaft* refers to the life of the individual and mass populations in urban settings and large organizations beginning in the nineteenth century. The terms *common man* and *masses*, very much in use in the period before and after the birth of psychoanalysis, designate the majority populations of Europe that had been outside formal history but appeared on the scene after the French Revolution. The *new age* I use as a cognate for the nineteenth century as a whole.

Liberal, as in *liberal democracy,* refers to the interests and institutions of the middle class after the overthrow of the aristocracy. By *liberal democracy* I mean representative government in the nineteenth century, which by present standards would be considered politically conservative. More particularly I mean that form of representative government reflecting the philosophies of John Locke, Adam Smith, Voltaire, Jean-Jacques Rousseau, and others, which developed first through revolution and evolution in England, then appeared through revolution in America, and after the French Revolution began to spread throughout Europe. In nineteenth-century liberal democracy the middle class is the upper class (its leading members usually called the *haute bourgeoisie*); a parliament is elected by a franchise still narrow for most of the century, excluding whole classes of citizens; the press is generally free but in some nations is censored; the economy is more or less free-market, and there are secularized civil institutions and the beginnings of mass education. The formal liberty guaranteed by law functioned, in the words of Karl Popper (characterizing the view of Karl Marx) "within a social system which destroyed freedom," since the exercise of freedom flowed from the vote and education, which few possessed initially in any of the democratizing countries, and from wealth, which even fewer possessed.[9]

The first three parts of this book are devoted to historical background. The later parts decode the hidden meanings and functions of psychoanalysis. Throughout, references to "he" and "him" rather than "he and she" or "him and her" are for convenience and do not imply a gender preference.

THANKS ARE DUE the many scholars who have contributed to this befuddling field of study; to the Sea Cliff and Glen Cove public libraries and the C. W. Post College Library, all on my home turf, for fulfilling my many requests for specialized books in American collections coast to coast; and to my publisher and editor Ivan R. Dee for his breadth of understanding in recognizing the course I took to bring the discussion of Freud and his colleagues to its effective close.

My portrait of psychoanalysis has this in common with Picasso's portrait of Gertrude Stein: she said it did not look like her; he said it would, in time.

Freud's Answer

Part I

ETIOLOGY: THE TRAUMA OF HISTORY

. . . Everything that had formerly been absolute
became historical. . . . This was the melancholy of a
world passing away—the last world where the security
of myth could still balance history. . . .
—Guy Debord, *The Society of the Spectacle*

Brave in the face of familiar dangers, untutored minds
are as a rule unable to endure surprise and mystery.
—Marc Bloch, *Feudal Society*

To regard [psychology] as rising above the sphere of
history, and establishing the permanent and
unchanging laws of human nature, is . . . possible
only to a person who mistakes the transient
conditions of a certain historical age for the permanent
conditions of human life.
—R. G. Collingwood, *The Idea of History*

There appears to be a direct relationship between the
assault on old fixities and the growth of new myths.
—Modris Ecksteins, *Rites of Spring*

ONE

Before 1800:
The World We Lost

Time was when the whole of life went forward in the
family, in a circle of love, familiar faces, known and
fondled objects, all to human size. That time has gone
forever.
　　　　—Peter Laslett, *The World We Have Lost*

It is easy to romanticize the past.
　　　　—Peter N. Stearns, *European Society in Upheaval*

THERE WAS ONCE a time emotionally more comfortable—in retrospect—than our own. It was a real time; later it was a nostalgia
painted in the colors of the rainbow, like a child's world, a sort of Eden
or Golden Age from the modern perspective. That time was the pre-
industrial world of our ancestors, which came to an end in the years
surrounding 1800. However distant it may seem from the present and
from the work of Sigmund Freud and his colleagues, it constituted at
least half of what became psychoanalysis, quite possibly the weightier
half. Out of a familiar history came many of the essentials of the theories and practices of psychoanalysis.

Before 1800 Europe was largely agricultural, religious, patriarchal. It was hierarchical, with a small elite at the top possessing all the
political power and social status. The elite, the aristocracy, was composed of individuals who were also constituted in families. Most of the
others, in all the European nations, were not individuals; they could
not even be said to be a mass, though they were sometimes called "a
mob" or "the rabble." In some ways they did not exist as full human
beings; they were more like reasoning animals. At least this is how the

higher society looked upon them. And the common folk did not take it amiss, for, as they were taught, it was what God ordained.

Most institutions were constituted as families. Kings and nobles held wealth and power as the members of family dynasties. Those who worked the land for the kings and nobles did so as families, and those who worked in the noble households were considered members of the noble's family. Those who worked for a butcher or baker or candlestick maker were likewise considered members of the proprietor's family. There was no other way of describing such relationships except as family relationships. Even the church constituted a family— the Family of God, with the Father at its head. The common folk did not count as individuals but only as members of familial house-holds.

Households were all patriarchal. Similar ones had existed for thousands of years everywhere. The father's rule was never questioned. A certain number of households, in a lonely, largely empty countryside, formed a village or hamlet. "As a community," writes the social historian Peter Laslett—whose study *The World We Have Lost* is considered by many social historians the best general survey of pre-industrial society—"the village consisted of households in association." Set off in a green countryside of lush meadows and thatched cottages, this was "the lost world which vanished with the coming of industrial, urban life." Even cities then had countryside next to them, and in those cities, Laslett notes, "Everything physical was on a human scale. . . . No object in England was larger than London Bridge or St. Paul's Cathedral. No city in Europe was larger than ancient Rome."[1] There were no hotels, hostels, hospitals, or apartment houses as we know them today.

Few large industries existed that required the labor of more than twenty or thirty men. Aside from the military, large labor forces could be found only in mining, shipping, and the production of armaments. Some of these establishments could rightfully be called factories, but there were only a handful of them, and even those were often referred to as households, though they might employ fifty to several hundred men. Almost everything else was made in a very small household that might consist of a husband, wife, children, helpers, and possibly servants—from three or four souls to perhaps ten or fifteen. This was true for the making of baked goods, clothing, pots and pans, or whatever else could be found at a market. This was the nature of a "business" in the world we lost; there were no firms.

Every farm and artisan shop was a family affair, held in title by a family and operated by the family, with the work performed by the family in the family residence or in an attached shed. Those brought in from the outside as apprentices, journeymen, workers, or servants became part of the business and also part of the family. Food, clothing, living arrangements, and income were provided by the household for all its members. As a result, as Laslett points out, "Working the land, managing, nurturing a family were one and the same thing, and could no more be 'rationalized' than the cherishing of a wife or the bringing up of children."[2] Most relations with the outside world were relations *between* families. The peasant family dealt with the noble family that owned the manor and the land. They had known each other for many generations. At harvest time, farm families cooperated to bring in the crops.

The family household was the site of whatever education most children received. There the sick were nursed, the family's clothes were made, and recreation took place in the form of group singing, for example, accompanied by a family member or neighbor on a musical instrument of the day. Entertainments outside the home consisted of visits to the local alehouse or wine shop, and occasional sports. At Christmas and Easter, miracle plays were on view; before Lent there were carnivals (in the countries that remained Catholic after the Reformation), during which the lords were spoofed; and in spring maypole dances.

Few people traveled to work, for work was usually in the home. For that matter, few traveled very far in a lifetime, except for journeymen who for a time wandered the countryside to select a site in which to set up a new household that replicated the former master's; and except of course for nobles who might travel far and wide and even visit other countries. The few trades and professions could be listed on a small sheet of paper, compared with today's thousands of occupations. A minimal technology was applied to agriculture, but it was not much greater than had been available in Roman times. Only churches in the West, mosques in the East, and military fortifications exceeded in scope what had been known before. Beyond the riding stirrup, which made possible the heavily armored mounted knight, the major military advance was gunpowder and its employment in cannon, bombs, rifles, and revolvers.

The pace of life was what we would call slow, largely dictated by the seasons, the weather, the length of daylight in which to perform work. Work hours were long; as a bonus, workdays were frequently punctuated by holidays, as many as 120 days a year, so that the total hours of work each year might have been fewer than now. Peasant landholdings consisted of dispersed plots, supplemented by common rights to open fields owned by the lord but available for use by all. Except for some rich peasants and landless laborers, most common folk lived a life of "stable poverty." They were not abjectly poor, usually knew where their next meal was coming from, usually had a small amount of capital, and did not aspire to more. Whether farmer or smith or wheelwright, theirs was not a life in which one might grow rich. There was very little of what later came to be called "rising expectations." One generation had no better expectations than its predecessor. "The ancient order of society," Laslett observes, "was felt to be eternal and unchangeable by those who supported, enjoyed and endured it. There was no expectation of reform. How could there be when economic organization was domestic organization, and relationships were rigidly controlled by the social system, by the content of Christianity itself?"[3]

Few among the common folk thought about money, and did not know how to get much of it beyond highway robbery. Money was not how they passed their lives, not even their economic lives, for barter was the common means of exchange. If a peasant needed capital, which was rare, he turned to family, friend, or neighbor. Money, in the form of land and rents, was the chief abiding concern of the nobles, not the majority. The nobles ran opulent manor houses, contributed money and men to armies when needed, and at most times were clothed in the richest fashions of the day.

Little changed beyond the seasons and events in the family. There might occasionally be war, but if one were not in the war zone and not in the army, he would be affected very little; and he would not likely be in the army unless he so chose, for there was no draft. He might not even know that a war was being hotly fought in some distant place by the armies of the lords of society, for communications were primitive and the mass of the population illiterate. Heads of households were concerned with such things as arranging suitable marriages for their children, and those marriages were a matter of family policy, just as they were for the upper class. A child could not marry at will at any time, the son needing assurance of a suitable livelihood before that event could take place. The family saw to that too. And of course they were most concerned with running the family business, be it farm or craft. As Laslett notes, "Social revolution, an irreversible changing of the pattern of social relationships, never happened in traditional, patriarchal, pre-industrial society."[4]

This was a comparatively unpopulated world. In 1541, for example, there were just 2.7 million people in all of England, and over the next 150 years the population never rose above 5 million. One-tenth of the entire population lived in London. Four-fifths lived in villages with an average population of 300, some with as few as 100 or fewer. In such a village, these were all the people one would see and know for most of a lifetime. A few people might be out and around at any one time; groups seldom collected in larger numbers than could fit into a rather small house. More were at church on Sunday, but that was an exception, others being public celebrations and weekly markets and annual fairs where greater crowds would gather. Aside from such events, daily life was lived within the family, within the household. Beyond the community was open countryside, and then another village, and then open countryside, and then another village. Between villages there was only rare contact. For the residents, the village was the world.

This is the way most people lived, the vast majority of the populations throughout Europe. Life and work, present and future were a family affair. The need for the family and its multiple functions was self-evident. The home was not only a place of kinship relationships, it was a business, and all the members were part of the business. This business side of the family anchored the affective, emotional side, and vice versa, so that the family held a totality of meaning for its members. It was a scheme, says Laslett, of "settled family life among a body of men and women who had known one another a long time, from birth perhaps; indeed, their own family forebears may have known each other, too." And "to the facts of geography, being together in one place, were added all the bonds which are forged between human beings when they are permanently alongside each other; bonds of intermarriage and of kinship; of common ancestry and common experience of friendship and cooperation in matters of common concern."[5]

The number of personal decisions that did not have to be made in such a time are uncountable, for this world was organized to receive each new member and to direct him or her into a livelihood and marriage. Disputes within the family were settled by emotional confrontations with the frustrated and the discontented. The ties that bound were superior to reasoned arguments. Conflicts might occur within the family but were rarely perceived to extend to outside institutions or to society as a whole.

Biblical injunctions governed sexual codes for the common folk. The codes were officially strict, however they may have worked in practice. The punishment for incest, adultery, or homosexuality was death. Unwed parents were whipped in the public square. Priests sometimes molested women in their parishes, which they had been doing for centuries, but if exposed they were not usually punished but rather protected by their superiors. Of all sexual taboos, homosexuality was the most deeply abhorred. Libertinism was common in "good society." If anyone could be said to have complete sexual freedom, it was the nobles, and they suffered no censure for it. It was their way; everyone knew it and accepted it as their right. The sexual habits of female nobility were no more subject to public law than those of the males, but the males were considerably more active and flaunting.

Religion was centered on sin, and for the common folk sin was apt to be capsulized as sex. Witchcraft trials from the fifteenth century forward linked sex with idolatry, heresy, and the worship of Satan. Sex was a convenient symbol for pleasure-seeking in a world that was said to be not a place of human satisfactions but a vale of tears. Sex itself was held to be not so much human as animal; through St. Augustine it had become, more than any other "transgression," the sign of Original Sin. Worldly high churchmen in the Middle Ages may have chafed at the overemphasis on sex as sin, but they kept silent.

People were no more saints then than now, but they believed it to be the truth of God that it was better to give than to receive, and that this practice would help the community to prosper. The church labeled selfishness, avarice, gluttony, and the worldly pleasures as vices.

While religion ruled, only one faith was allowed full freedom: Christianity. Judaism was anathematized, and so was Islam. There were few Muslims in the Western nations, but Jews (who numbered perhaps 800,000 in Europe by the thirteenth century) were ghettoized in cities, blamed for plagues and poor harvests, made the objects of riots, tried for superstitious crimes that did not exist, burned at the stake, and from time to time chased en masse from one country to another. Religion was seen very much as a competitive affair; there was only one truth, and only one religion could possess it. But this did not make the Hebrew Bible any less relevant; both testaments were earnestly believed.

This was not a free society as that idea is understood today. Only a small percentage of the population—the minuscule aristocracy (two hundred families in England in 1688, for example, numbering not more than a thousand individuals) and some members of the small middle class—enjoyed political power. They were the only people who could be called independent in mind and heart. The mass of the population, without a vote, without literacy, knew very little of political goings-on. They were in the background. There was an "immense majority of uneducated people," the historian Marc Bloch notes, and a "little handful of educated people."[6] In a few German principalities, compulsory elementary schooling was enacted as early as the sixteenth century, but this was rare for Europe as a whole.

Nobility was thought to be forever. If a noble family lacked male heirs, the king would appoint a distant successor to acquire the titles and lands. That same permanence was felt by all, for people then seemed to occupy "in Time," as Marcel Proust wrote a hundred years after the collapse of the old order, "a place far more considerable than the so restricted one alloted them in space, a place, on the contrary, extending boundless . . . reaching far back into the years. . . ."[7] That sense of permanence and attachment to a long past was an essential feature of the old world.

The nobility owned most of the land and wealth of the country. They were born to their positions, earning their keep by managing local and national affairs, which they did as a consortium of families. Later, in the new age, applying sense and logic to the matter, Tom Paine judged that "an hereditary governor is as inconsistent as an hereditary author,"[8] but in the familial society of the pre-industrial age, that idea had no currency.

Nobles were aided in managing society by the clergy, which in its upper reaches also bore noble titles and came from noble families. Churchmen for a long time did much of the intellectual work in the old world, providing diplomats, ministers of state, historians, philosopher-theologians, and poets. There were gentlemen, too, most of them practicing the professions of the age as architects, lawyers, physicians, university dons, and military officers. They were literate like the lords and clergy, but held much less power than the lords. The literate—the lords, gentlemen, clergy, and some of the middle class—believed they did the thinking for society as a whole. In any case the common people did not worry about running the country, nor were their views regarded outside the village circle. Even toward the end of the old world, a friend of the political philosopher John Locke wrote, "There never was any government where all the promiscuous rabble . . . had votes, as not being capable of it. . . ."[9] The local nobleman was important, the church was important; after that, at the village level, there was a rough equality in the population and a rough form of communal democracy.

Since political, social, and economic power was invested in a small minority, an effective system of obedience was needed to control the large majority. Beyond law this was found in the Bible, and most specifically in the Ten Commandments, which provided the grounding for behavior and relations between people. Biblical beliefs were supported by mandatory attendance at church and the literal faith of most of the common folk. Other societies, in the long past of civilization, had similarly found support in the religion of the day, which conveyed a series of understandings incorporated in law and tradition to help maintain order.

Jesus said that to love thy neighbor as thyself was the essence of the law and the prophets. In the old order that carried weight on the personal level, but for society as a whole the fifth commandment, Honor thy father and mother, was the essence of organization, order, and control. The old world was based on this commandment above all, so intimately connected to the family. Not simply an ethic, it was the guarantor of social order. The father was the master to whom respect and obedience must be given. He might not be much outside the household, but inside he was the law. The father in his turn gave respect and obedience to the lord of the manor, and both father and lord gave respect and obedience to the king and to the Lord and Master of all, Father God. In this way the three institutions that ruled society— the family, the nobility, and the church—were all the same in the sense that each was family, authority, and hierarchy, with a single leader: father, king, God. A line led directly from the father of the family to the father of the country to the Father of all humanity. The father of the country, the king, in the political theory of the day, ruled by divine right, which extended from the king to his nobles; so it was God who had established the political order of the old world.

Paying proper obedience along the hierarchy of rule was the principle of social life at the time, inherited, it was thought, from the Bible. The English *Shorter Catechism* of 1644 asked (Question 64) what the fifth commandment required. The answer: ". . . preserving the honor and performing the duties, belonging to every one in their several places and relations, as Superiors, Inferiors or Equals." Thus was set the nature of relationships within the family and beyond it. And the response to Question 65 forbade "neglecting or doing anything against the duty which belongeth to every one in their several places and relations." Landlord rights and property rights were similarly based on the fifth commandment and also the tenth (not coveting thy neighbor's wife or goods).

All knew their place. The formula ran: "There is degree above degree [in social status]. . . . Take degree away, Untune that string, And hark what discord follows." Chaos and disorder would follow a change in the rigid style of social relations, threatening not only the established order but everyone's psyche as well. During Cromwell's revolution in England, when newer ideas were pushing their way to the fore, Cromwell's son-in-law Ireton answered calls for popular freedom with "Honor thy father and thy mother and that law doth extend to all that are governors." Woe to any who disobeyed that law. The general thought of the time, echoing the Bible, was expressed as: "Short life was the punishment of disobedient children"—disobedience invoked death. "Submission to the powers that be went very well with the habit of obedience to the head of the patriarchal family," Laslett writes, "and it had the extremely effective sanction of the universal fear of damnation to the defiant."[10]

When heretics took disobedience to the final degree, they were burned at the stake or put to death in other ways. This severe punishment was justified because a challenge to established religious belief was also a challenge to the state, for the state was based on Christianity, beginning with the king who ruled by divine right. Church and state were partners. Government, in the words of a medieval French chronicler, was "by the will of God and the ministry of the powerful of this world."[11]

Along with subservience to the powers that be went duties—not only duties of the lowly to the great, but the other way around. Custom, law, and religion dictated how the noble was to treat those under him. The economic relationship of lord and peasant was "the moral economy," E. P. Thompson points out, "as against the economy of the free market." Those who worked the land gave a portion of their bounty to the lord and performed duties for him, but these were not arbitrary; they were contractual. Artisans were protected by guilds which set quality standards, wages, prices, and market share. As bitter as we might view the plight of the common people of those days, the historian G. G. Coulton records that for much of the Middle Ages, "the peasantry were perhaps more prosperous . . . than they have been until almost the memory of living men. They had no voice in the State; their personal services and disabilities [vis-à-vis their lords] were often such as the modern laborer would have found degrading; but it is possible to argue that a large number of them, at any rate, were better fed and had more economic security" than after the old world collapsed and they were freed from serfdom.[12]

Superstition and miracle played a strong role in the mentality of the age. People's minds, says Bloch, "were constantly and almost morbidly attentive to all manner of signs, dreams, or hallucinations." The clergy were "vocationally centered on the problems of the unseen. No psychoanalyst has ever examined dreams more earnestly than the monks of the tenth and eleventh century." Popular religious life was nurtured "on a multitude of beliefs and practices which [were] the legacy of age-old magic or the more recent products of a civilization still extremely fertile in myths." The consequence was an "astonishing sensibility to what were believed to be supernatural manifestations." Almost as if they were Hindus or Buddhists, the Christians of the time viewed the material world as "scarcely more than a sort of mask, behind which took place all the really important things; it seemed to them also a language, intended to express by signs a more profound reality. Since a tissue of appearances can offer but little interest in itself, the result of this view was that observation was generally neglected in favor of interpretation." Here we have a direct glimpse into a Freudian borrowing from the old world. A typical scholar of the time, Rabanus Maurus, sought less the nature of things, he said, than "their mystic meanings."[13] The Freudian equivalent was the quest for unconscious meanings.

THIS WORLD had existed forever, or so it seemed—and in some form had been going on since the fall of Rome. In many ways it replicated older civilizations—kings, nobles, clergy, craftsmen, tradesmen, peasants. All of this was to disappear in Europe and America. This centeredness, rootedness, tradition, slow pace, sense of belonging was the *gemeinschaft* world, the world of the village community—simple, ordered, relatively straightforward—in which "Everyone had a circle of affection and every relationship was a love relationship." Laslett, a sober social historian whose much respected study of the old time is filled with charts, graphs, and tables, grows dreamy contemplating this lost world of "stately castles, spacious manor houses, splendid churches, farmsteads, cottages, mill-houses, bridges, all built for itself by the familial social order. . . ." The psychiatrist A. Gallinek points out that "The ideal man of the Middle Ages was free of all fear because he was sure of salvation, certain of eternal bliss."[14] This is an exaggeration only to be understood with the modifier "ideal"; but something of it was true. It was a world at once human and certain in its ways, ruled by the divine in its institutions and beliefs.

The *gemeinschaft* world is not to be romanticized. It was, by and large, a place of dirty houses and smelly streets, visited by plague since the fourteenth century; a place of great ignorance and superstition from our vantage, given to hunts for witches and heretics. Waves of famine swept through the peasantry, who were ruled by haughty lords. Life was much shorter than now, especially for the common people, and often brutish. Yet with all its faults it *was* the *gemeinschaft* world, centered on town and village, family and church, alehouse and wine shop, with familiarity all round and close, underpinning ties. It might have been impoverished and authoritarian, the social historian Peter N. Stearns points out, but it gave its inhabitants "an automatic sense of identity."[15]

As late as the 1730s in England (and later in other places), households could still be found engaged as of old. But soon the common lands were taken from the peasants and enclosed; machines and foreign competition added to the difficulty of surviving on the land. Many peasants became agricultural laborers. Most, with little choice, fled to the cities and the new factories of the dawning industrial age. Some, Thompson notes, tried not to give way: "Hand-loom weaver, artisan or village craftsman . . . held fast to an alternative culture. As we see them change, so we see how we became what we are. We understand more clearly what was lost, what was driven 'underground,' and what is still unresolved."[16] They were trying to preserve not merely a local way of life but the long past as it had ever and always been known and would soon be abandoned—entirely, like a meadow turned to sand.

In the old world, and probably throughout history, suicides increased when economic times were hard. But they were higher in the eighteenth century, as dramatic change came to the old world, than in any past time for which there are records. In the late eighteenth century, as the old world approached its end, malnourished adolescent poor in London were found to be so short in height that only two in eighty-one ethnic groups are known to have been shorter—two badly malnourished populations in New Guinea. With the appearance of factories came perhaps the first British government reports on poverty, for "When factory life did at last become the dominant feature of industrial activity," Laslett observes, "it condemned the worker . . . to the fate previously reserved for the pauper."[17] These details were the merest signs of a monumental change, the onset of a social, political, economic, cultural, moral trauma—all at once and in a rush.

Some argue that the old time was a dream and never a reality. It was certainly "replete with its own social problems and indignities," as Modris Eksteins concedes. But certain essentials could not be missed: a wholeness and a psychological security that provided the power to explain and accept. In a loving homage, Carl Jung compared the Middle Ages to the childhood of the Western world:

> How totally different did the world appear to medieval man! For him the earth was eternally fixed and at rest in the centre of the universe, encircled by the course of a sun that so solicitously bestowed its warmth. Men were all children of God under the loving care of the Most High, which prepared them for eternal blessedness; and all knew exactly what they should do and how they should conduct themselves in order to rise from a corruptible world to an incorruptible existence. . . . That age lies as far behind as childhood, when one's own father was unquestionably the handsomest and strongest man on earth.

For our purposes it is not important if that was how the men and women of the past actually felt. More notable is, this is the way the modern age looked back on the older one. Reflecting like Jung on those times, the Russian revolutionary Prince Peter Kropotkin thought that "not only many aspirations of our modern radicals were already realized in the middle ages, but much of what is described now as Utopian was accepted then as a matter of fact."[18]

While Freud thought that religion, the backbone of the old world, was a neurosis, he nevertheless sensed "an extraordinary increase in neurosis since the power of religion has waned. . . ." Jung thought the same, and saw the need for a resurgence of religious belief if modern life was to have value and the individual was not to become neurotic. Of course it was more than religion that went out with the old world, and the loss of much that passed from the scene was to have dire effects on the human psyche, almost as dire as what now appeared. But it cannot be said that it was unwise to abandon the old world—as if there were any choice in the matter. It was a restrictive place for most. The dignity it conferred with one hand it took with the other because of its lack of freedom, its confinement of the human personality and human abilities in general. Its abandonment represented the investment in a huge potential, an enormous leap in human freedom. Still, in retrospect, its emotional comforts, and even to some degree its economic security, were envied and missed after they were traded in for the promises of freedom. "Ironically," notes Stearns, "the same transformation that spread an idea of progress also embraced a more traditional notion that somehow the past was better."[19]

The loss of the old world affected every point on the political spectrum. For those in the center of political currents it represented the loss of rigor and order in society. For those on the left it produced the sort of nostalgia Prince Kropotkin expressed for a cooperative society. For those on the right it was most consequential of all. The conservative German-speaking nations of central Europe, Marshall Berman observes, became "prolific in constructing idealized fantasies of life in tradition-bound small towns."[20] Russian thinkers shared some of this wishful longing; French thinkers sought the departed glory of a monarchy backed by religion. Common folk joined in this longing for a lost world, for in the face of the most dramatic changes that would ever come to a civilization, the dream of the old world would not be let go.

The family, the father, the old village community with its slow, uncrowded ways, the king and his nobles, God and his Ten Commandments, sex as the medieval symbol of sin, rule by the few, superstition, the reality behind the surface of things—these characteristics and more from the lost world were guideposts to Freud and his followers. In response to a startling cultural revolution that made society unruly, uncertain, anxious, and, finally, dangerous to itself, the nature of the lost world helped inspire and direct the creation of psychoanalysis. But that is only the beginning of the story.

TWO

To 1850: The World We Gained

History . . . a shout in the street.
  —James Joyce, *Portrait of the Artist as a Young Man*

Before a cluster of ideas can rapidly take control of
people, there must perhaps be a plague upon the land.
    —Ernest Gellner, *The Psychoanalytic Movement*

THE PASSING of the old world unleashed social turmoil on a scale
scarcely seen before. A new world came into being with new rules,
new rulers, new styles of life and work—new everything. The family
changed, the prestige of the father declined, living conditions altered
profoundly, the individual appeared en masse. Faith was challenged;
greed gained the day. Governments aiming to increase their legitimacy
found it weakened, and the need for new levers of control became apparent. Just as the old world inspired many of Freud's theories, so did
this new one. Many of the changes, and the totality of change, found
a resonance in the meanings and functions of psychoanalysis as a
treatment of the culture.

The old world was doomed by conflicts within the church (the Reformation) and between the church and secular authority (the Thirty
Years' War among the European powers); by changes in the economy
(from mercantilism to capitalism), in forms of government (the budding of republicanism in the Dutch Republic and middle-class parliamentary supremacy in England), in philosophy and belief (from
scholasticism to humanism to rationalism to empiricism), and in science and technology (from alchemy to experimental science). These
shifts are well known and need scarcely be reviewed; they were the
looming background. Then, all at once, the world of the fathers was
killed by twin revolutions.

The almost simultaneous Industrial and French revolutions that "murdered" the old world wrought more change, were more astounding in their results, than anything recorded since the fall of Rome. Some historians argue they were even more unsettling—as great as the beginning of agriculture and civilization. They were what the late French philosopher Michel Foucault called a "discontinuity," when "within the space of a few years a culture . . . ceases to think as it had been thinking up till then and begins to think other things in a new way. . . ."[1]

The French Revolution of 1789 marked the end of traditional power relations and therefore of all personal relations based on those traditional patterns. No absolute monarch would be able to stand after it, and since monarchy stretched back to the beginning of civilization, this change was almost unique in the history of the world: the end of government by family (the royal dynasty). England had killed a king in 1649, and that had been a lesson filed away but not forgotten. America had broken with the dynastic system in 1776 to establish a republic. These were national revolutions; the French Revolution made the break with the old order European-wide. The mode of government first seen in England and America, liberal democracy, became a new standard, based on a parliament of elected representatives, freedom of conscience, speech, and assembly, and laissez-faire economics.

To meet this challenge, the conservative rulers of Austria, Russia, and Prussia, under the guidance of the wily Austrian minister Clemens von Metternich, formed the Holy Alliance in 1815, dedicated to reasserting monarchy and its old styles of repression. Metternich remained on the European scene until 1848, when revolutions across Europe led to his dismissal by the newly installed eighteen-year-old Austrian emperor, Franz Joseph. The Metternichean reaction to the new age was the first attempt to roll back political change. Afterward, reaction on the one hand, and visionary efforts to enlarge the margins of freedom and equality on the other, became the political rhythm of the nineteenth century. At the end of the century, Freud, more than any of his colleagues, understood the cultural significance of the loss of the old order and of deposed kings as fallen father figures. He made them, along with the drive toward expanded freedom, into cardinal principles of psychoanalysis.

In unleashing the mass populations of Europe, the French Revolution had emancipated the Jews. Napoleon had seen to it in France, and wherever his armies marched, emancipation followed. In Austria the process had begun earlier with the Enlightenment emperor Joseph II. With emancipation, Jews could find places in the larger society. They were free to attend university, enter professions, own land, operate businesses of their choosing. One effect of this liberation was the rise of modern anti-Semitism—which proved to be yet another influence on the creation of psychoanalysis. And as Napoleon's armies planted the seeds of nationalism throughout Europe, many peoples yearned to be ruled by their own kind, not foreign dynasts as in those vast conglomerations of disparate ethnic groups, the Austrian and Ottoman empires. In the second half of the century, nationalism added fuel to the turmoil of change that was the prime influence on Freud's creation.

The Industrial Revolution that began in the eighteenth century was more disruptive than the political one. It revolutionized "the whole relations of society," Karl Marx wrote, ". . . producing uninterrupted disturbance of all social conditions, everlasting uncertainty and agitation. . . . All fixed, fast frozen relations, with their train of ancient and venerable prejudices and opinions, are swept away, all new-formed ones become antiquated before they can ossify. All that is solid melts into air, all that is holy is profaned. . . ." In with the machine came free enterprise, and out went the "moral economy" of the old world—all those understandings that had helped to mitigate the harshness of life for the mass of men and women. In with free enterprise came a revolution in ethics, as "virtue, love, conviction, knowledge, conscience . . . passed into commerce. It is the time of general corruption," Marx wrote, "of universal venality . . . when everything, moral or physical . . . is brought to the market to be assessed at its true value."[2] Here were changes that became absolutely central to the creation, meanings, and functions of psychoanalysis as a treatment of the culture.

The Industrial Revolution in England, where it first took hold, was announced by a series of Enclosure Acts which took from the peasants the common lands owned by the lord but used by an entire village as part of the "moral economy." The effect was to render farming no longer economical for the masses of the landed population that had too little land of their own to eke out even a subsistence livelihood. Other laws followed which, along with the appearance of machines, foreign competition, and the disruption of the lord-and-master system with its feudal communality, ended an entire ordered way of life. Luddites, former peasants, wandered over England destroying machines, as though the machines—progress—had ruined them. One peasant wrote imperfectly to a Gloucester clothier: "Wee hear Informed that you got shear in mee sheens [shearing machines] and if you Dont Pull Them Down in a Forght Nights Time Wee will pull them down for you Wee Will you Damd infernold dog." Laslett offers this as an example of the "terror which the coming of factories and the machines struck in the hearts of ordinary people. . . ." The Luddites hated more than the machines those forces that had driven them from the land without offering compensation, or a substitute for the moral economy, with which to start a new way of life.[3]

The breakup of the landed life ended the dominance of the family, which was no longer the locus of a livelihood or the guarantor of the future. "We can say that the removal of the economic function from the patriarchal family at the point of industrialization created a mass society," Laslett observes. "It turned the people who worked into a mass of undifferentiated equals, working in a factory or scattered between the factories, the mines and the offices, bereft for ever of the feeling that work was a family affair, done within the household."[4] The splintering of family life took authority from the head of the household, who was no longer an employer in his own right but was now himself a lowly employee suffering paltry wages and wretched working and living conditions with little power to change them. With the loss of the old family went self-identity. The lowly men and women of former times had always known themselves as the members of a family, and through the family, the community. Now they had to know themselves as part of a nation-state, with far looser ties to the family and fewer ties to the community—a community now growing very large and sometimes overtly, sometimes subtly, oppressive.

Children aged five or six were put out to factories in order to increase the pitiful family income; women too worked in the factories, so that the family began to reflect the exploitation of the outside world. Children had labored before, and so had women, but they had done so within the family, with restraints on exploitation.

Adding to the traumatic change from old to new was urban crowding. Where before most people had lived in an open landscape and came in contact with scarcely 100 or 200 souls over a lifetime, now they migrated to cities and lived in relatively barren landscapes among thousands and then millions of other people. Increasing the crowding was stupendous population growth. England in 1800 had a population of 8 million; a hundred years later, 22 million. The city of London grew more than four times in the same period, from 900,000 to 4.7 million. The population of Paris climbed sixfold, from 600,000 to 3.6 million; Berlin sixteenfold, from 170,000 to 2.7 million. In Europe as a whole, population grew from 190 million in 1800 to 452 million in 1900.

Where many towns and villages had been dominated by a church or cathedral spire, expressing certainty, now they featured tall smokestacks belching black clouds, compared by William Blake to hell. Where quiet had once reigned, noise held sway, amid a squalor more evident than in the past. Life in the town, noisy and brawling, was very different from that in the village. In the village one worked according to the season, the weather, and the availability of daylight. Not so now when nature had little effect on factory production. Work went on all the time, in a particular, specified way that demanded strict discipline as to exactly when to start, when to finish, what to do, and how to do it. "These pressures towards discipline and order," Thompson notes, "extended from the factory, on one hand, the Sunday school on the other, into every aspect of life: leisure, personal relationships, speech, manners."[5]

While peasants who had been thrown off the land flocked to the city looking for work, the new factories created jobs much more slowly than they destroyed them on the land. For millions, the transformation was one long economic depression, the longest they had ever known, lasting generations. Europe on the whole was enriching itself, but it was enriching mainly the new leaders of society. Among the mass, a nostalgia soon set in for the old rural life. Poets and painters joined in, recalling the old times of a simpler life on the land. These reminiscences fed the accumulating stream of romanticism which featured a love of the land, the past, and institutions and relationships then in the process of being destroyed. "Times used to be better before [the land] was enclosed," a laborer recalled. Another cursed his new lords and masters: "You have by this time brought us under the heaviest burden and into the hardest yoke we ever knowd." The majority felt abandoned. "Orphans we are," cried a laborer, "and bastards of society."[6]

Workers were now enslaved to machines in factories that never had to stop for dark or seasons or anything else, subjected to "the general pressure of long hours of unsatisfying labor under severe discipline for alien purposes." These conditions D. H. Lawrence would later excoriate as the "ugliness" which "betrayed the spirit of man in the nineteenth century." There came to be, as there was not in former times, a "violent technological differentiation between work and life." An English gentleman many years away from his homeland, returned in 1834 to find that his countrymen had "lost their animation, their vivacity, their field games and their village sports; they have become a sordid, discontented, miserable, anxious, struggling people, without health, gaiety, or happiness." Work itself was longer and harder than it had been before.[7]

The countryside too was turning into a factory as agriculture changed from a craft to an industry. Land became a commodity like any other, like labor and those who did the laboring. Many of those who still worked the land became a rural proletariat as agriculture underwent its own form of technological revolution, pressed to the straining point to feed ever-growing populations. Still, some famine continued—calamitously in Ireland and Russia and from time to time in other European countries.

When the members of the family went to work in the new factories, offices, and industrial farms, they were for the first time confronted with having to win approval from strangers. Factory workers found themselves exploited in an alienating society bereft of the stalwart, loving family and the family society. With strangers now in charge everywhere, with expanding bureaucracies, there was no longer the emotion of the family tying together people and things. A new will, like a chill wind, ran through the industrial cities and the countryside throughout the Western world. Life became colder, in many ways solely "a business proposition."

The nature of political freedom in the new age deepened the trauma of change. Before, the local lord's primary residence had been walking distance from the family cottage. Even when he was away from the district, the common folk could make known their wishes and complaints at the manor house. Now there was a complex bureaucracy with a ruler in a place called the capital; if one did not live there, he was very far away. The ruler could not see his people, they were so distant, and would not see them if they appeared on his doorstep. Local politicians who sprang up in place of the lord might be strangers, and in any case owed the people nothing because the people still did not have the vote—or if they did, they cast it at the behest of the local master. (In America all white males might vote, but not women or slaves.)

Marx's partner in communism, Friedrich Engels, wrote of the situation around 1844 in *The Condition of the English Working-Class.* What he as well as conservative observers described should be seen as journalistic reporting, not propaganda: a life of filth, poverty, disease, deprivation, oppression, and exploitation for the main populations of the cities, and much of the same in the countryside. This was true in England as it was everywhere else in industrializing Europe, England being notable as the first to arrive there. Fearful that these poverty-stricken masses had cause for revolt, the authorities monitored them but otherwise left them to their own devices. Thomas Hardy, a gentleman, in his *Memoirs* of 1832 estimated that "one-fifth of the electorate and most of the unenfranchised [were] pure Jacobins . . . objects of eternal vigilance." The diseases of the body politic demanded in his view "the critical terrors of the cautery and the knife."[8] Rebellion was to be surgically excised by force.

Trauma was intensified by another change that brought something totally new: the creation of the individual. A member of a family, village, class, tribe, religion, kingdom had existed before, but not an individual, and not mass man, the totality of all individuals in this new world. Of course the aristocrats of the old world were individuals as well as members of families, and in the Renaissance so were artists, learned men, and members of the small bourgeoisie. But the mass of people were members of families until they were unleashed and driven from the old world. This new individual took himself and his personal interests to heart in a way never quite taken before. Major values arose for each individual and not just for the leaders of society—money, power, pleasure, advancement, struggle. Everyone had to fight for a place in the sun of society, where before the sun had shone only on the aristocracy, which had inherited its place and had no need to fight for it. Of all the factors in the creation of psychoanalysis, this may have been chief of all, because of its contribution to the turmoil of the new age.

New concepts arose for this new individual—success, happiness, normality, competition. In traditional society one's daily rounds were his success, and he was content when he did his duty. He expected no more than that, and he was normal if he was not the village idiot. No one among the common people had been free to seek his or her heart's desire; now freedom presented the challenge and the ability to do so. As all relationships were new, so were all norms. The creation of the normal was under way, to replace what had been wiped away. Governments no less than individuals sought normality in a time that, from the vantage point of the past, was completely abnormal. To cite competition as a new concept would only adumbrate the obvious. Competition was what money, laissez-faire economics, and democratic politics were all about. Competition and political freedom, among their many effects, opened the marketplace of ideas, so that one could suddenly choose what to believe.

Assigning to individuals en masse, for the first time in history, mastership of the nation, was nothing less than traumatic for people who had never before ruled anywhere except on a small scale in America. Even quasi-popular rule by a portion of the population had been rare in history. The conversion of the people into the masters of the nation—which went on at a different pace in the various western European countries—was a fearful event, since the people had no experience in running anything except a family, farm, or artisan shop. It was just as fearful for the new rulers, who needed rationales for controlling the beast, the mob, mass man, who was now a collection of individuals due respect. The mass similarly needed rationales for accepting control by their rulers after being told that they themselves were the new masters.

Since the first duty of the master of a nation is to protect it, the common man, now free and a sovereign, became subject to military draft. War had been the responsibility of the nobles and those they hired for war; now every man became a knight-errant, a potential warrior in time of need. Prussia, a supremely militaristic state, had had a form of universal draft, but it was mere play-acting compared to the new demands. The French Revolution instituted the *levée en masse*, the drafting of all the men needed to fight the wars of the revolution, and this rapidly became standard practice throughout Europe. If one was not drafted he might be impressed into service, kidnapped by the government to be a warrior. A certain supreme absurdity entered everyday life. The nobles had been recompensed handsomely for the service of war; now common men, with scarcely a shred to their lives, were called on to sacrifice themselves in the name of their newfound putative sovereignty. The West was becoming existential long before existentialism.

Having been given mastership of the self, the individual faced dramatic personal challenges that were as novel as the acquisition of political power. Before, almost everything had been decided by familial decision. Now the individual, become a citizen, had to think for himself about himself. He might have unlimited hopes, dreams, ambitions, but he had no more guidance in achieving them than in the governing of a powerful nation. Even marriage was converted to a personal challenge as arranged marriages passed from the scene.

At the top of the social structure were no longer lords and ladies but a smug and gruff middle class, roughly the size of the old class of lords, that is, about 5 percent of the population. Overawed by money and the power to make it, the new class raised money to the chief value in industrial society. As the Gironde States reported to Paris in 1827: "The basis of all laws is wealth; the condition of all distinction is gold; the reward pursued by everyone is riches." In the old world the poor had lived as best they could according to the ethics of the Bible, backed by a sense of submission and resignation, not spurning money but never having much of it. The lords had always lived by the ethics of Machiavelli; now everyone would live by the ethics of Machiavelli. Under the impact of the money economy, there was little to arbitrate or mediate obedience except guns, and guns became the law between the new upper class and the lower class. In major strikes by workers, the historian George Dangerfield points out, "soldiers, sooner or later, would have to be used, for democratic governments, strange to say, are always on the side of the employers, employers are solicitous for their property, and property is safer when ringed about with bayonets than it is behind barbed wire and police."[9]

Stripped of protection in a society ruled by money (of which they had little), the common man and woman were now socially and economically naked. They were pure economic abstracts, less than the thinking beasts they had been before. Yet in the new understanding they were free, independent beings. A great challenge, for they had no means of independence and barely the means of subsistence. The situation was ripe for messiahs. The radicals of the French Revolution, knowing what was in the air, proposed every conceivable overturning of the existing order: the redistribution of wealth, socialism, anarchist self-government, the dissolution of international borders. Tom Paine, then in Paris, laid out a more rational, solid program that fared no better: taxes on wealth and reduced government spending on bureaucracy and armaments, the savings to go to the poor in the form of family allowances, education, old-age pensions, and benefits for maternity, marriage, and death. By these means, he wrote, "Widows will have a maintenance for their children . . . and children will no longer be considered as encreasing the distresses of their parents. . . . The number

of petty crimes, the offspring of distress and poverty, will be lessened
. . . and the cause and apprehension of riots and tumults will cease. . . .
Ye who sit in ease and solace yourselves in plenty . . . have ye thought
of these things?"[10]

Many had, and had rejected them, giving the play to utopian reformers such as David Owen, Charles Fourier, Pierre-Joseph Proudhon, Saint-Simon, and Karl Marx. Saint-Simon's socialism became a
secular religious movement, sounding a persistent note for the nineteenth century: the quest for a secular religion. His followers raised
him to the status of a savior. Get rid of the old religion, he urged, and
substitute "terrestrial and positive morality" for the former "celestial"
one.[11] Kings, nobles, and priests would be replaced by a meritocracy
of industrialists and scientists (which was already happening). Saint-
Simon imagined a benevolent industrial feudalism featuring a new
Christianity, the religion of Jesus, dedicated to lifting up the lower
classes. If that were not enough there was Proudhon's anarchism and
Marx's communism. In reaction came proposals to return to monarchy, and where monarchy still existed, to strengthen it; and if monarchy could not be the answer, then some form of strong-man rule.

The essential mode of relationship in the new age was instrumentality—the use of others for one's own benefit. This had been the mode
of relationship practiced by the nobles, as recommended by Machiavelli; now it was the mode for all. Instrumentality was the "natural"
counterpart of the new age's materialism; it was the materialization or
commodification of relationship. Not to attain, or to lose, instrumentality was to be alone, cast out, adrift. In the new age, depression leading to suicide was less of a mystery: "The single biggest reason for
suicide among men," Paul Johnson writes about the mid-nineteenth
century, "was debt and business failure"—the loss of instrumentality.[12]
Immanuel Kant, even before the eighteenth century gave out and the
old world fell for good, had famously advised, "Act in such a way that
you treat humanity both in your own person and in the person of all
others, never as a means only but always equally as an end." He saw
that in the new age the temptation would be—as part of the logic of
the new situation—to dispense with ends except regarding one's personal goals, and to operate solely on means.

By the 1830s urban populations were losing their religious allegiance. With the new literacy, and with church attendance no longer
mandatory, they were attracted by other ideas that better described
their life. This loss of religion was a monumental shift, a first-time

event in the experience of civilization, just as universal freedom and industrialization were first-time events. Few societies had ever been without a religious underpinning. God had not passively disappeared in the new age; he had been killed by history. An aspect of the *gemeinschaft* world that had lasted from the beginning of time to 1800, he was not part of the *gesellschaft* world. The loss of faith can be ascribed to more than loss of faith in God. In the old world, religion combined faith in man *and* God, since men and God were on a continuum, from the head of the household to the lord to the priest or minister and to God: all the fathers of the old world. The lowly were taught to have the same faith in the paternalism of the high and mighty as in the goodness of God. God, in this way, was part of their social system.

But in the new age cupidity was "freed from old sanctions," Thompson observes, and "not yet . . . subjected to new means of social control." Relations were "depersonalized . . . no lingering obligations of mutuality . . . are admitted. . . . The worker has become an 'instrument,' or an entry among others items of cost." The talk now among the masses was that "they wish to make us tools," or "implements," or "machines." William Cobbett, an English radical journalist of the early nineteenth century, informed the new laborers that their betters called them "insolent hirelings . . . the mob, the rabble, the scum, the swinish multitude . . . your voice is nothing." They were no longer in the eye of God. Heinrich Heine, the German radical poet and essayist, spoke for all Europe in 1834 when he wrote: "Don't you hear the bell? Down on your knees! The sacrament is being carried to a dying God!"[13] Darwinism drove another stake into religion when it posed humankind as a distant cousin to senseless, grasping animals. New studies of historical Christianity continued the process by casting doubt on the revealed truth of the Bible. What before was gospel was coming to be seen as myth.

Government in all the industrializing countries, no longer endowed by God, no longer a family enterprise composed of respected betters who operated a "moral economy," became oppressive in new, impersonal ways, and lost legitimacy. As William Hazlitt conceded as early as 1820, "Legitimate Governments . . . are 'Gods to punish,' but in other respects 'men of our infirmity.' . . . You will find it easier to keep them a week than a month; and at the end of that time, waking from the sweet dream of legitimacy, you may say with Caliban, 'Why, what a fool was I to take this drunken monster for a God.'" In revolutions of 1830 and 1848 the middle class hoped to seize total power from the aristocrats, and the lower classes wanted concessions from the middle class. A mid-century French socialist recalled that "Even as a child, I said this social order was iniquitous. . . . And I swore a Hannibalic oath against this society which makes so many of our brothers wretched."[14]

To bolster popular submission, Christian ministers such as William Wilberforce in England preached a "grand law of subordination," leaning on the old religious rationales. The poor must be made to see that "their more lowly path has been allotcd to them by the hand of God; that it is their part faithfully to discharge its duties and contentedly to bear its inconveniences; that the present state of things is very short; that the objects, about which worldly men conflict so eagerly, are not the contest." The contest was heavenly salvation. Writing of female education, Hannah More announced that it was a "fundamental error to consider children as innocent beings"; they were to be viewed as possessing "a corrupt nature and evil disposition" (the doctrine of Original Sin). Sunday-school teachers were encouraged to "tame the ferocity" of their charges' "unsubdued passions—to repress the excessive rudeness of their manners—to chasten the disgusting and demoralizing obscenity of their language—to subdue the stubborn rebellion of their wills—to render them honest, obedient, courteous, industrious, submissive, and orderly," thereby turning "rebellion into submission."[15] Similar preachments were a stock in trade throughout Europe, directed to adults no less than to children. The old basis for mass submission having fled, a new one was needed in a society where there were officially no more lords and masters, where religion was losing force, and where everyone was theoretically free and equal. Here the greatest efforts of the Freudians were to be made.

In a peculiar case in early nineteenth-century France, Pierre Rivière, a peasant, murdered his mother, sister, and brother, then wrote an account of his crimes. His acts were especially troubling because killing a parent was still thought of as close to killing a king. Worse, Rivière coolly maintained his right to have to committed the crime. He revealed an earnest anarchy bubbling below the surface of the new societies by calling into question the legitimacy that resided in the new laws of democracy—but not necessarily in the hearts of the people, especially in the new, bewildering, chaotic societies so officially equal but so practically unequal.[16] Still, even as legitimacy weakened, a quasi-religious halo appeared over democracy. The blood of the French Revolution (as the American one before) had consecrated democracy as the fulfillment of biblical wishes. Democracy was seen (by democrats, at least) as a system forecast by prophets from Moses to Christ. Turmoil was the order of the day during the growth of democracy, but it was not without a sense of celebration.

SUCH WERE general conditions in the Western nations during the transition to industry and democracy in the first half of the nineteenth century. Among the new masses, there was alarm over the loss of a landed livelihood in a society without God, certainty, an assured future, or social support; amidst new machines in the factories and on the streets, including new, mechanized modes of transportation and communication; amidst speed in the very tempo of everyday life. "Behind them," wrote the poet Alfred de Musset, "a past forever destroyed; before them, the first gleams of the future and between these two worlds . . . a troubled sea filled with wreckage . . . in a word: the present."[17] Physical, emotional, and moral displacement required that everyone find a new place, a new way of tuning oneself into society. The stress provoked many ideas of what was right and wrong, good and bad, and a growing need for personal decision on such issues, decisions formed within the self and not by mere—not apparent—acceptance from others.

The external world constituted by God, the nobility, the family, even philosophy, were all dying. The new certainty of science had not yet conquered. Disorder was always in the air, and frequently rebellion, leading in England to the evolution of the political system toward full representative government; in other countries, more hidebound, to bloody revolutions, three in France alone during the nineteenth century, and many, across the face of Europe, in the year of revolution, 1848. Slowly political change was forced throughout the West, and in some places was bitterly resisted. "This is an age of the world where nations are trembling and convulsed," wrote Harriet Beecher Stowe. "A mighty influence is abroad, surging and heaving the world, as with an earthquake. . . . Every nation that carries in its bosom great and unredressed injustice has in it the elements of this last convulsion."[18]

Surveying the fall of the *gemeinschaft* world in all its familiarity and closeness, and comparing it to what came after, Laslett concluded: "These changes of scale, that sense of alienation of the worker and his work, that breach in the continuity of emotional experience [constituted] . . . the trauma inflicted at the passing of the old world."[19] In the mid-years of the nineteenth century Matthew Arnold composed in "Dover Beach" perhaps the first existential poem:

Ah, love, let us be true
To one another! for the world, which seems
To lie before us like a land of dreams,
So various, so beautiful, so new,
Hath really neither joy, nor love, nor light,
Nor certitude, nor peace, nor help for pain;
And we are here as on a darkling plain
Swept with confused alarms of struggle and flight,
Where ignorant armies clash by night.

One compensation for the mayhem of the new age was, of all things, sex, which sprang to public life as never before. As Foucault remarked, "We have had sexuality since the eighteenth century and sex since the nineteenth."[20] Quite aside from the nineteenth-century upper-class view that sex and liquor were the amusements afforded the poor, sex came to have deeper social meanings. The people now stood in the place of the aristocracy and accordingly wished to ape the sexual mores of the aristocrats, which they took as a symbol of sovereignty, wealth, and power. The sexual style of the nobility had always been free and easy; the peasant attitude had not been very different but had always been trailed by the censure of the church. What mass man now wanted was a free and comparatively open sexual life without censure, just like that of the upper classes, as a mark of the new sovereignty of the people. But that seemed to those on high only another invitation to mayhem. If it were granted, what would mass man want next? Might he also wish to ape the political power of the former aristocrats, since he was now sovereign? And if he could not do so by law—which was evidently impossible at the time—might he try to do so by further revolutions?

The connection between sex and politics was noticed early on. Wilberforce, Thompson points out, saw "the intimate correlation between moral laxity and political sedition among the lower classes," a perception "characteristic of his class."[21] His Society for the Suppression of Vice denounced obscene pictures and nude sunbathers, perceived as threats to the social order. In 1837 Queen Victoria was raised to the throne and gave official support to prudery. The Victorian ethos found a home in other major European nations beset by freedom, industry, urbanization, growing literacy, and loss of religious morality.

The middle class was now in power and wished to exercise its version of law and order, to put into practice a new legitimacy that could replace the father, the aristocrat, the church. Something that would be vividly noticed, like sexual "purity," so biblical, could represent the decency and morality of the middle class to the lower classes. Thus prudery was selected among other official virtues to represent the legitimacy of the new ruling class. The message: the Bible still lived.

THE FIRST HALF of the nineteenth century provided vital materials for the Freudians. Vast turmoil had swept over Europe. The rise of the individual, the insecurity of mass populations and their new rulers, constant threats of rebellion and reaction, loss of political legitimacy, the loss of God, the new pace of life, the hard, disciplined labor, the despair of many, the disorientation for most, sex as a political statement—this and more in the new age spurred the inspiration of psychoanalysis and its theoretical constructions.

The mayhem of the first half of the nineteenth century was prelude to a mounting hysteria in the second half. Founded in all the changes, wonders, excitements, satisfactions, and dissatisfactions wrought by the twin revolutions, the hysteria was fueled by perhaps one feature above all others. According to the new social philosophy of the West— the philosophy of pleasure—everyone was invited, for the first time in history, to fulfill the heart's desires.

THREE

The Philosophy of Pleasure

I have only one passion, a passion for the knowledge that will alleviate human woe and bring mankind the happiness to which it is entitled.
—Émile Zola, *J'accuse*

. . . the time when . . . social organization gave way to cacophony.
—Daniel N. Robinson, *An Intellectual History of Psychology*

THE SUBJECT of sex, so personal and alluring, first found its way into the heart of psychoanalysis through a long tradition of philosophy. The main theme of psychoanalysis, pleasure, which Freud symbolized as sex, assumed cultural importance in the shift from the medieval to the modern age. It became an integral part of political and economic philosophy under the heading of self-interest. Then, as happiness, it became part of general philosophy (which it had been long before among the Greeks and Romans). As the dominant philosophy of the nineteenth century, it was one of the chief driving forces in the creation, meanings, functions, and acceptance of psychoanalysis.

The seventeenth-century philosopher René Descartes, in one sentence—"I think, therefore I am"—wiped away received medieval beliefs in favor of the freedom to think and to observe what was happening in the material world. Thomas Hobbes, his contemporary, also prized freedom and new thought, but Hobbes found that they clashed with his belief that people were interested only in themselves and would compete endlessly (and murderously) for what they wanted if there were no adjudication by a strong monarch. He proposed a negative social contract in which popular freedom was sacrificed to security. If not, life would revert to the jungle—short, nasty, and brutish.

John Locke believed that nature had placed sovereignty, and therefore freedom and independence, in the hands of the people, not the ruler, and were to be used to seek the good of all through competing self-interests. Bernard Mandeville illustrated the benefits of freedom, self-interest, and competition in his *Fable of the Bees: Private Vices, Public Benefits* (1714) wherein each bee's selfishness in gathering honey benefits all the bees. Self-interest, formerly castigated as a vice, Mandeville proposed as a civic and personal virtue. The only problem in applying the life of bees to humans was that, in Mandeville's view, "To make the Society Happy . . . it is requisite that great numbers should be Ignorant as well as Poor," his reasoning being that many drones were necessary to the profits of manufacturing and trade.[1]

Adam Smith believed the economy should be managed by the people, not the government as it was under the old mercantile system. Regulated by the "invisible hand of nature," it would create untold wealth, which he took for granted was the desire of both individuals and nations. When growing up he might have heard in the business district of his town what was already being said by 1700:

"Every man is naturally covetous."

"No laws are prevalent against gaine."

"Gaine is the Centre of the Circle of Commerce."[2]

French *philosophes* argued (gingerly, since they still lived under an absolute monarch) against king and church. They viewed the king as unjust because the rightful ruler was the people, and the church as the support of the king, using superstition to manage the people. Voltaire's model was England, where economic and political freedom went hand in hand. There, he noticed, money was always treated equally. Rousseau's model was an imagined past when noble savages were naturally good and free, living with integrity by their own rules.

These same philosophers also had new thoughts about psychology: they came to believe that the world was inside the mind. All we know, they said, we know by our individual perception of things through our senses. Eighteenth-century English philosophers such as Berkeley and Hume concluded from this that we could never know anything objectively, so there could never be absolute truth because each of us perceived his or her own truth and world. Reaction to this line of thinking was no less psychological. Leibniz had conceded that everything we knew of the outside world came from our perceptions, but not from them alone; it also came from natural structures in the mind that processed what we perceived into coherence. Kant called these structures *categories*. Whichever way the philosophers turned, the world was in the mind. At the beginning of the nineteenth century, Schopenhauer summed up the matter in the first sentence of his masterpiece, *The World as Will and Representation* (1818): " 'The world is my representation':—this is a truth valid with reference to every living and knowing being. . . ."[3]

Freedom and psychology were intimately connected. A psychology that placed the world in the mind put the spotlight on each individual mind, giving enhanced importance to individual perceptions, needs, and wants, and calling into question their control by priests and monarchs; a particularist, individualistic psychology heralded a politics of the individual. It was clear, as well, that a free society could not be managed by *dictat*. Future governments would have to use psychology in order to achieve a more subtle control because laws would have to be believed internally, within each individual, as proper and justified before they could be accepted by free individuals.

Influencing the thought of the first modern philosophers was the rise of empirical science, and with it a modern form of religious thought called deism. Deism held that God expressed himself through reasonable, rational, natural laws. Insofar as religious dogmas were true, deism taught, they were the reflection of those natural laws. Deism had a strong effect on the way psychoanalysis was formulated, as did many of the thoughts of the early modern philosophers.

THE PHILOSOPHERS' THOUGHTS became prescriptions for the new age. Rousseau taught "liberty, property and security"; the American Declaration of Independence spoke of "life, liberty and the pursuit of happiness"; the French Declaration of the Rights of Man proclaimed "liberty, equality, fraternity." Thinkers after the twin revolutions noted problems with the practical application of these formulas. Political freedom could not be exercised by all because all did not have the vote and therefore could not seek their political self-interest. The economy was free, but most people did not have the means to participate beyond functioning as drudges, a further dissuasion to fulfilling self-interest (or achieving political power).

Freedom, which could mean license, took a toll on morality, since the prevailing value became winning through competition (within the law) rather than doing what was right. In fact, few people any longer could say with certainty what was right. As Mandeville saw, self-interest was the obverse of biblical ethics. People thought they knew right when they saw it, but it was difficult to state as a principle, beyond the usual homilies. Now that everyone had been freed, how were they to be saved from freedom itself? Religion had provided answers in the past, but no longer. Law was an answer, but not completely fulfilling because it did not prevent exploitation or other dehumanizing effects of instrumentality. Nor did it guarantee happiness. It was cold and looked to many suspicious, as if it pursued an agenda of power.

How were men and women to be moral if their nature was to seek self-interest above all else, in an age in which the freedom to do so was provided and self-interest was encouraged as the basic motivation for action? As William Heinse declared in a 1787 novel: "Every creature has a natural right to appropriate all that surrounds it to the limits of its power. . . ." His mind was inflamed with the thought that even "bourgeois order," which sanctioned self-interest, "ruins man."[4] From the old point of view, self-interest seemed heartless, irreligious, immoral, and an invitation to anarchy. The revolutionary slogan of fraternity, working against such tendencies, seemed merely a sop, a hope from the Judeo-Christian tradition which served as a patriotic equivalent of community. It did not, for all its appeal, guarantee community.

Just as the new age dawned, Jeremy Bentham proposed that the purpose of freedom was to seek the good, and since the good was pleasure, the role of government was to assure the greatest good (meaning the greatest pleasure) of the greatest number. Such a philosophy, he thought, would strengthen liberal democracy, which he presented as granting the prime wish of all: pleasure. Bentham became an expert on pleasure, measuring its intensity, duration, certainty, propinquity, fecundity, and purity in order to develop a "moral arithmetic" or "hedonistic calculus." He was also an expert on pain, which he accounted the prime evil to be avoided. He believed, like Mandeville, Smith, and Locke before him, that self-interest, expressed by individuals seeking pleasure, was in harmony with social interest, and he encouraged the extension of the ballot so that all could vote their self-interest.

The pleasure principle, long a cautionary theme of religion and philosophy East and West, had been overthrown eighteen hundred years earlier by Christianity. Now it returned as the reigning principle of modernity. Thinkers who did not like this turn of events included

Joseph de Maistre, a Savoyard diplomat and social philosopher at the time of the French Revolution. He believed that people must practice "individual negation" in order to lose themselves "in the national mind." The goal must be "communal existence" or the new societies would explode.[5] Like Hobbes, who preferred authority over freedom, Maistre swam against the tide surging through Europe, but his views were not forgotten. By the end of the nineteenth century they were part of conservative philosophy.

In the town of Koenigsberg, in the easternmost corner of Prussia, Immanuel Kant, an aging professor of philosophy at the university, was similarly disturbed by the arrival of freedom, self-interest, and competition. He feared the disappearance of the rule of God and consequently of the order that civilization had known for thousands of years. The Scottish philosopher David Hume had proved by logic that nothing was any longer certain, that everything depended on what each individual thought because there was no outer reality to access. There was no such thing as cause and effect, Hume argued; they were only a trick of our reasoning; and yet all we had was our reasoning, so we were lost at sea. How were we to judge right and wrong, good and bad, when there was no objective way—as there was coming to be no agreed-upon religious way—to do it? Kant was exasperated by this line of thought, the more so since Hume taught that reason was rightly to be the slave of the passions.

Hume's philosophy woke Kant from his dreamy, sedentary academic life as if by a thunderclap. It drove him to become a hero of thought. There *are* ways to demonstrate that things exist beyond our senses, Kant was convinced, and he wrote a series of thick, heavy books to prove it: *Critique of Pure Reason* (1781), *Foundations of the Metaphysics of Ethics* (1785), *Critique of Practical Reason* (1788), *Critique of Judgment* (1790), and *Religion Within the Boundaries of Pure Reason* (1793–1794). Along the way he found a principle that became famous throughout Europe. It was true that God did not speak to us and tell us what was right and wrong, good and bad; but implanted in each soul was something that served that purpose—the *categorical imperative,* Kant's version of the conscience. We knew naturally, with no outside help, what was right and wrong; we had it within us from birth. That was the way the world and the human being were designed, whoever did the designing or if no one did the designing.

Kant had found a basis for religious ethics without religion. The

Ten Commandments were true not because they were in the Bible but because they were part of the human condition, how we were made. Act, he said, as if everything you did was a universal law, as applicable to you as to everyone else. This philosophical guidepost repeated a very old injunction found in many ancient cultures: Do unto others as you would have them do unto you. But Kant's formulation was different in that he attempted to prove it by logic. This was among his greatest contributions to the new age, later duplicated by the Freudians: establishing an indisputable moral principle without reference to God, very much along the lines proposed by deism. From that moment, without saying so, philosophers passed from logic to near-religion in an attempt to meet the crisis of morality and legitimacy posed by the new age.

Contemporary with Kant in the same city was a penniless philosopher with a passion for personal freedom, J. G. Hamann, sometimes called the Magus of the North. Hamann thought free people needed no one else's rules. Somewhat like Rousseau, he thought they could rely on childish innocence, irrational motivations, and their personal interpretation of religion to guide them. Rulers either coerce or deceive their subjects, he thought, and reason was a "poisonous snake, the arch-heretic, the great enemy of God and truth. . . ."[6] Science and universal rules imposed someone else's thoughts and limited one's vision. Here was romanticism, with its love of irrationalism, abandon, spontaneous feeling and passion, hatred of rules, and desire for unbridled self-expression and self-assertion, picking up wind for its long course through the nineteenth century. To it Hamann added a disapproval of Jews and democracy.

G. W. F. Hegel and Arthur Schopenhauer, Kant's greatest heirs, were concerned like him with the dangers of freedom, pleasure, and competition. Not to fear, said Hegel, competition is the way the Spirit of the Universe produces progress and truth. Human beings are the expression of that Spirit, and they are traveling an infinite path to heaven on earth. The French Revolution had proved that mass man makes history, unleashes movements, creates opinions; countermovements and opinions arise; in the clash, new ideas appear, and so on until the end of time, the end to be in Perfection and the Final Truth in an Ideal State. It was the philosophical equivalent of a return to the Promised Land. Hegel, who had trained in theology, had made the second attempt after Kant to affirm in secular form, in ways consonant with the new age, the essential truths of Christianity, including that most important one for renewed hope: that there had been a Fall, and there would be a Salvation.

In a kind of reverse Copernicanism, Hegel put mass man back at the center of the universe—a flattering thought for the populations of Europe coming into political and economic freedom: they were *somebodies*. The joining of flattery to optimism (that mass man would lead to the Truth) made for much good feeling; that freedom, pleasure, and competition were not evil enhanced the feeling. Hegel became the most popular philosopher of the first half of the nineteenth century, and his influence lingered long after, for he had optimistically justified the new age while reviving religious tenets of the former age in a new form. But he had a dark side. Because the state for him was the *highest* representative of Spirit on earth, mass man's competitive spirit was to be managed by the state. This was not very different from the church and the nobles managing things in the old world. This authoritarian streak in Hegel contributed to the idea of a "corporate state" in which all interests are ordered by government. Hegelian statism was typical of the anti-democratic ideas the Freudians confronted through the theories of psychoanalysis. But they appropriated Hegelian optimism (as regards cures), flattery of the common man, and the goal of freedom.

If cultural influence is the criterion, Schopenhauer, Hegel's polar opposite, was the most significant philosopher produced by the new age. His ideas became the ideas of modernism. His central concerns were desire, sex, pleasure and pain, the irrational, the latent and the manifest, hidden motivations, subjectivity, our animal nature and the struggle for survival (before Darwin and Herbert Spencer). He introduced a long list of modern signposts, including absolute skepticism, amorality, nihilism, atheism, relativism, pessimism about human nature, existentialism, guilt, and anxiety. Most of these ideas and attitudes the Freudians later shared. But Schopenhauer's greatest contribution to psychoanalysis is to be found in the essentials of his philosophy. At the heart of his philosophy was self-interest as the basic nature of humankind and the universe, which he explained by his master concept, the World as Will. In every individual could be found an instinctive, grasping force whose first goal was sex, in order to continue the race, and whose second goal was every other sort of selfish pleasure. When pleasure was satisfied, boredom set in, and that began a new quest for pleasure—and so on, endlessly, boredom's function being to keep us searching for pleasure so we might avoid pain. There was no right, no truth, no good or bad, only survival, pleasure, and the avoidance of pain. Everyone spoke the same message in Schopenhauer's philosophy: Only *I* am important; the rest can go hang.

With romantic ardor Schopenhauer had revived the long tradition that tied together animal and human nature. In the West it began in ancient Rome but had already existed in Hinduism with the belief in the endless cycle of life and death focused on pleasure and the avoidance of pain (the wheel of karma). In the Bible it was sin against the higher human nature. In the words of the Roman jurist Ulpian, it was *jus naturale*, "that which nature has taught to all animals, for it is not a law specific to mankind but is common to all animals. . . . Out of this comes the union of man and woman, which we call marriage, and the procreation of children and their rearing."[7] In contrast was *jus gentium*, the human law of reason and intellect (which in religion was faith in God). In medieval and Renaissance times, *jus naturale* acquired the sense of the divine. Schopenhauer, teaching that animal law—instinct—was the only law, and that human law was its camouflage, had discovered the modern unconscious: animal will for the means of life and pleasure. It was at the foundation of the social, political, and economic philosophies of the new age and became an essential ingredient of psychoanalysis.

Like the Hindus and Buddhists, Schopenhauer conceived the world as an illusion, with an overside and underside. He was a pioneer in the mysterious land of the underside, the concealed, the masked, the unadmitted. Behind the mask was sex above all, the main content of the unconscious. It was the World as Will incarnate, the hidden motivator, the springboard of action, "the cause of war and the aim and object of peace, the basis of the serious and the aim of the joke, the inexhaustible source of wit, the key to all hints and allusions. . . ."[8] Many philosophers had earlier taken account of sex, but it was left to Schopenhauer to make it the root of existent reality. Freud adopted it as the essence of human psychology, and like Schopenhauer he made piercing the mask of the psyche his chief task.

Schopenhauer was a secular religious philosopher who hated the animal-like World as Will (his version of Original Sin). It had to be controlled and might even be dominated, he thought, by a self-therapy of art, understanding, and good deeds. Otherwise it would be Hobbes forever: the war of each against all, individual against individual, class against class, nation against nation. With no faith in the categorical imperative; in fear of pleasure-seeking mass man; and in disgust at Hegel's solution of the state imposing restraint on desire, Schopenhauer thought it necessary to therapeutize the Will. Where Will was, there would reign the conscious mind. Reason would overcome the unconscious, just as in religion the belief in God was supposed to subdue our animal nature.

Having invented the essential concepts of nineteenth-century therapeutic psychology, Schopenhauer went on to invent the theory and mechanism of neurosis that would later serve as the climax of nineteenth-century abnormal psychology. Mental illness, he reasoned, was caused by forgetting (later called repression). The forgetting was caused by a psychic shock (later called trauma). Ideas or experiences too horrible for an individual to contemplate were dispelled from the conscious mind but did not disappear, returning as the symptoms of mental illness (later called the return of the repressed). Sometimes the symptoms were sublimated and the sexual instinct was redirected to social and artistic works. Schopenhauer also believed, as later psychologists would affirm, that human psychology was heavily influenced by youthful experiences. These concepts passed into psychoanalysis, where they were claimed as scientific theories.

To Schopenhauer, the individual and mass man were nothing but grasping Worlds as Will. He preferred to side with the leaders over the followers. The governors, he said, have the job "of protecting the few who have any possessions against the innumerable numbers of those who own nothing but their physical strength."[9] In the revolution of 1848 he offered his window to government sharpshooters firing at the mob.

Instinctively perceptive, Schopenhauer saw immediately what the factory meant: "At the age of five years to enter a spinning-cotton or other factory, and from that time forth to sit there daily, first ten, then twelve, and ultimately fourteen hours, performing the same mechanical labor, is to purchase dearly the satisfaction of drawing breath. But this is the fate of millions, and that of millions more is analogous to it." He saw the power of money: "People are often reproached for wishing for money above all things, and for loving it more than anything; but it is natural and even inevitable for people to love that which, like an unwearied Proteus, is always ready to turn itself into whatever object their wandering wishes or their manifold desires may fix. Everything else can satisfy only *one* wish; money alone is absolutely good . . . because it is the abstract satisfaction of every wish." He was cynical to the n*th* degree: "A friend in need is not a friend indeed; he is merely a borrower." "Do not tell a friend anything that you would conceal from an enemy."[10] Although he personally rejected the middle-class values of striving and competition in favor of quietism and negation, Schopenhauer encouraged the middle class because he recognized that the only absolute truth was striving and competition, and because he willingly backed power against the desire of the mass.

As Hegel dominated the first half of the nineteenth century, Schopenhauer prevailed in the second half, especially in the German-speaking nations of Europe. Strangely for so brilliant a man, he was a philosophical anti-Semite, believing that Judaism was not a spiritual religion like Christianity and his beloved Hindo-Buddhism. Medieval anti-Semitism hung on as the old age transitioned into the new, even among bright minds. Like Hegel, his self-conceived enemy, Schopenhauer contributed—however unwittingly—to anti-democratic thought through his recognition of Will as the principle of the universe and through his contempt for democracy. (He became Hitler's favorite philosopher; the Führer quoted him as others quote beloved poets.) In converting Schopenhauer's philosophy into scientific theories, the Freudians rejected his anti-democratic bias and his repudiation of pleasure. But they adopted his taste for the leaders over the led.

NOT ALL German thinkers eyed pleasure suspiciously. To Ludwig Feuerbach, "Will is will to happiness . . . every drive is a drive to happiness." Happiness was therefore "everything that life consists in, for life . . . and happiness are in themselves originally one."[11] Sexual pleasure was a part of human happiness, Feuerbach maintained, and he was one of the first to call for "free love." With Feuerbach as with Bentham, pleasure as the goal of life was the necessary end product of politics. Freedom and the truths of science would lead to a better world in which all received their portion of pleasure. Fully aware that his doctrines were in conflict with Christianity, Feuerbach wrote a revolutionary treatise on religion as an illusion, a phantasm conjured up by the human mind. Christianity, he said, was nothing but the projection of human goodness onto God and evil onto the devil. His philosophy was another contribution to the formulation of psychoanalysis—and not incidentally to the atheism of most of its pioneers.

Other German philosophers, rejecting any control on the human will, took an even more exuberantly romantic view of pleasure. Herder, Schlegel, and Fichte saw raw human nature as the expression of God's will. Unconscious drives and primitive emotions were close to nature, their goodness proved by the old German tribes that had lived close to the land and possessed the best virtues. These ideas contributed to European romanticism, which valued the old, the primitive, the pagan, the childlike, the innocent, and the irrational. Schopenhauer had tried to beat back the irrational; now it was presented as a model to be followed. This was a battle Freud took up with relish.

In the mid-nineteenth century Søren Kierkegaard saw that morality in an age of freedom, without God and without objective standards, had become a matter of choice, and he knew what the choice was likely to be: the way of pleasure. Choose duty, he urged—and he could only urge it because he realized that this choice could no longer be demonstrated to be right by any authority. Since he did not wish to seem to be preaching, he recommended that Christian ethics, led by the lovingkindness of the Father and Son, be taught by "indirect communication" through fable, irony, and satire. He despaired of the "proper" Christianity of his day which was, in his opinion, anti-Christian and anti-humanitarian—preachers, for example, who called hunger a God-given blessing that drove the humble to work. His preference for duty over pleasure, and his recommendations for the conveyance of moral lessons, found a place in the theorizing of the Freudians.

Others who contemplated the new age thought that morality and social order might be furthered by a new religion, absent the old God. Hegel and Schopenhauer were examples of this trend. Rousseau had recommended a secular religion, and the French Revolution had invented one based on the worship of humanity, with a new calendar and new holidays; Saint-Simon had fashioned a religion of Jesus. Continuing this effort was Auguste Comte, a disciple of Saint-Simon and founder of both the philosophy of positivism (that the gathering and understanding of facts was salvational) and the discipline of sociology. To bind the new society together he proposed in 1844 a Religion of Humanity celebrating reason, with himself as high priest. A Great Being would be worshiped in female form, in chapels festooned with the busts of humanity's benefactors.

Another religious innovator was the German anti-modernist and anti-Semite Paul de Lagarde. Quite unlike Comte, who sought to accommodate to industry, technology, and the other manifestations of the new age, Lagarde excoriated them as the source of degeneration. He sought to blend a Christianity based solely on the Gospels with a revival of German pagan rites. Along with this he proposed the creation of a new aristocracy through patents of nobility issued to families noted for performing social services; these families would live together in rural communities. It was a plan, says Fritz Stern, for the resurrection of the "old German clan in modern dress; in Lagarde's rhapsodic recital one could hear the forest murmurs of a primitive German past." This new nobility would return strength to the family, which to Lagarde was the "tactical unit which the ethos [of a people] leads into battle against sin and nature."[12] Figures such as Comte and Lagarde, so different in many respects, were important in the formulation of psychoanalysis because they highlighted the tendency to try to revivify lost traditions in new form. The Freudians represented the last major effort to accomplish that in the nineteenth century.

WITH THE APPEARANCE of Darwin, those tendencies of the age that Kant, Schopenhauer, and Kierkegaard feared, were affirmed. Man had an animal heritage; animal desire had no morality, only instincts for coping with the environment, finding food, reproducing. The best would be successful, improving the species; the worst would lose the race. It was Hobbes in biology: strength was all. From Darwinism came Herbert Spencer and social Darwinism: the survival of the fittest. The waxing middle classes throughout Europe understood these doctrines and were pleased, for these beliefs not only described the competitive life they led but justified it. The major nations of Europe, moving to greater belligerency in the second half of the century, found support in these same ideas for hostility and conflict.

Pleasure, the World as Will, the death of God, the freedom to choose one's own path, Darwinism and social Darwinism, love of aristocracy and hatred of the present—all climaxed in Friedrich Nietzsche, the disciple of Schopenhauer who turned his master on his head. It was true that we endlessly seek pleasure, Nietzsche said. That is the way of the world, and it is not to be denied but rather encouraged and celebrated. Choose pleasure and power because might does not make right, it *is* right—a necessary truth beyond the paltry morality of the Christian past. If the weak cannot compete, they deserve to lose; the fairest flower of humanity, "blond beasts" and supermen will create the better tomorrow.

The political implications of Nietzsche's philosophy were not hard to find: he was against democracy, socialism, the middle class, the poor. The new ruling class was not free or fierce or grasping enough for his tastes. A ruling class should be the only class, no one else should count, just as in the Middle Ages and all the aristocracies before. "The strongest and highest Will to Life does not find expression in a miserable struggle for existence," he intoned, "but in a Will to War, a Will to Power, a Will to Overpower." He therefore abominated his master's proposal for treatment of the Will. Expressing little taste for politics, Nietzsche nevertheless presented a totalizing vision of human relationships and power. The "refrain of my practical philosophy," was "who is to be the master of the world?"[13] His answer was that the strong shall inherit the earth. Like Schopenhauer, Nietzsche was a philosophical anti-Semite, disliking mainly what he thought to be the slave religion of Judaism rather than Jews themselves.

The long line of care and restraint from Kant through Kierkegaard ended in Nietzsche's moral anarchy, revealing what had been unleashed by the twin revolutions and needed chaining. In Nietzsche, nostalgia for the lost world of order that controlled the beast within was recast as aggression and will. His was the view from the top; in an age of dying aristocracy, he was the last aristocrat, the foremost individualist, and the fiercest libertarian. Whether his enthusiasts understood him or not, some would think his ideas an attractive addition to fascist philosophy. They were not dissuaded by his last ten years in a state of total insanity, a condition that may well have informed his work before his final breakdown. At the same time it must not be missed that Nietzsche often wrote in the style of a biblical prophet because he was the creator of another nineteenth-century humanistic religion without God, of which he himself was the messiah. Nietzsche was the Caesar of philosophy. Sigmund Freud was the Brutus who sought figuratively to assassinate him.

The philosophy of pleasure, born of freedom, self-interest, and competition, was a dynamic force that shaped the new culture of the West. It was always potentially revolutionary, for if one was not meeting his heart's desires, and if he were not just one individual but the majority of individuals in Europe, and if he thought the path to his heart's desires was barred, he might erupt in anger and seek novel solutions to his plight. That is to say, the philosophy of pleasure was advertised for everyone as good and proper, so it was to be followed; but inevitably it led to social, political, and economic frustrations for those who found the promises of freedom and plenty hollow and binding.

How to get out of the bind came to be the preoccupation of Georges Sorel, a French thinker who devoted himself to the efficacy of violence. The state and the ruling class possessed a power of coercion that could only be met successfully through violence, Sorel believed. If one wanted something badly enough, it was proper to get nasty about it. If one were a class, it was proper to become violent and not worry about the blood spilt (he was clearly philosophizing anarchist terrorism and socialist revolutionary propaganda in the second half of the nineteenth century). Wanting was all to Sorel, and he was not fastidious about who wanted what, initially favoring the people against the government and then monarchy against the people. Unable to decide on the rights of the matter, whether they lay with the people or a king or some ruling class, he was reduced to a tactical, instrumental solution to the problems posed by the philosophy of pleasure: violence by whomever thought they were wronged. And with it Sorel urged the development of new mythologies to cohere groups and societies. His prime model here, he readily admitted, was Catholicism.

Fear of the political violence Sorel contemplated was shared by most European liberal democrats. A new revolution would disrupt what had been established by their forebears. The Freudians, themselves liberal democrats, shared this fear. Yet they were not unaffected by Sorel's plea for new mythologies to bind groups and societies. Sorel's model of Catholicism was not lost on them.

While philosophers theorized, the forces unleashed by the twin revolutions molded a civilization unforeseen and unforetold in scope and wonder. Rush, excitement, achievement, alienation, wealth and poverty—for some the sun was rising, for others the sky was falling. After a hundred years of the twin revolutions, the West found itself in crisis. Those who liked the new order made compelling arguments for it; those who did not found glaring faults in democracy, modernity, industrialism, individualism, the philosophy of pleasure, competition, science, technology, atheism, the Jews. They were not fastidious in their targets. What they featured was ferocity, amply expressed in the second half of the nineteenth century as it waxed, waned, and climaxed in the hysterical fin de siècle, the period in which, and because of which, the Freudians appeared. These heralds of twentieth-century psychology brought with them their new specialty—physician of culture, with expertise in treating social hysteria.

Part II

HYSTERIA IN THE FIN DE SIÈCLE

For a long time now our whole civilization has been
driving, with tortured intensity growing from decade to
decade, as if towards a catastrophe: restlessly,
violently, tempestuously. . . . Where we live, soon
nobody will be able to exist.
—Friedrich Nietzsche, *The Will to Power*

No one is able completely to withdraw himself from
the influence of his time, and under the impression of
events which affect all contemporaries alike, as well as
the scientific views prevailing at a given time, certain
features develop themselves in all the works of an
epoch, which stamp them as of the same date.
—Max Nordau, *Degeneration*

FOUR

Riding for a Fall

I foresee something terrible, Chaos everywhere.
Nothing left which is of any value; nothing which
commands: Thou shalt!
　　　　　—Friedrich Nietzsche, *The Will to Power*

... The hysteria of the time has created these
beings. ...
　　　　　—Max Nordau, *Degeneration*

RUSHING toward crisis, the second half of the nineteenth century contributed even more than the first half to the inspiration and formulation of Freudian theory and practice. This age, in which the Freudians were born and matured, was no longer merely in turmoil. Amidst glistening scientific, engineering, industrial, and artistic achievements that only added to a sense of uncontrolled change, it seemed to go mad. Hatreds and reactions blossomed as the trauma of the twin revolutions gave way to hysteria. Here was an invitation to physicians of culture. In the constant search for solutions to the troubles stirred up by the twin revolutions, social and political techniques did not guarantee success. That accounted for the prescription offered by these new physicians: a new belief system to steady the new age—in effect, to cure it of hysteria.

Happy with neither the philosophy of pleasure nor any of the other fruits of the twin revolutions, Pope Pius IX in 1864 issued a *Syllabus of Errors*, breathing anathema on liberal democracy, socialism, science, individualism, atheism, secularism, rationalism, industrialism, progress, and modernity in general (there were eighty-eight errors in all). As if to confirm the pope's forebodings, Karl Marx a few years later formed the First Communist International, dedicated to world revolution. The pope, perhaps fearing that he was not being heard, in 1870 declared papal infallibility in matters of doctrine. This led some to think that the church was making a bid to share secular power as in the medieval past, as a means of pacifying the accumulating wildness of the new age.

Further confirming the pope's forebodings was an agricultural depression that swept across Europe from 1870 on, felt especially hard in Germany and Austria, where cheap foreign producers dumped farm commodities and undersold domestic sources. The hard times created an embittered class among those remaining small farmers who had not already been ruined by industrialization and driven from the land. In the cities, dispirited industrial workers barely able to support themselves even with cheaper grain were finding leaders and organizing under the banners of socialism. The more radical joined the anarchists to throw bombs at kings, legislators, and industrialists. When a French anarchist was caught red-handed in a theft, he was sufficiently well versed in revolutionary rhetoric to claim "the right of those who have nothing to take from those who have." An anarchist hymn ran:

> Kings, gods, are dead, and we don't care.
> Tomorrow, we'll live free as air,
> No faith, no laws, no slaves, no past.
> We are the iconoclasts.[1]

Socialism was feared by the powerful, not alone because it represented the growing power of vast working populations but because it meant to many a new form of enslavement. "The people" would be on top and all that was cherished in hierarchical societies would be gone, including religion which, while now honored mainly in the breach, was nonetheless a nostalgic and loved reminder of the old world. Socialism's prospect created a fierce reaction which united many conservative and reactionary forces. And bad as it seemed to the new rulers, socialism was eclipsed by anarcho-syndicalism's plan to replace the nation-state with local self-government at worker-owned and -managed factories. Since the anarchists were least likely to gain a hearing for their radical views, they were the most likely to turn violent, which they did.

Even before the turmoil of contending political and economic ideologies took hold, the call to reinstate monarchy where it had been lost, or where it still existed to strengthen it, grew louder. In France, scions of three dynasties waited to take over if the opportunity presented itself. In 1851 the opportunity was forced in a coup d'état in which Louis Napoleon, the great Napoleon's nephew, already the democratically elected president of France, became Emperor Napoleon III. His feat rekindled aristocratic hopes of recovering monarchy as the surer form of government.

Between 1815 and 1854 the battlefields of Europe were quiescent, but when Prussia attacked Denmark to gain the provinces of Schleswig and Holstein, Bismarck's "blood and iron" entered the European imagination in the service of a cause virtually invented by the French Revolution: nationalism. Next Prussia attacked Austria and drove her from the leadership of the German states. Then Italian and French troops defeated Austria, allowing Italy to become a unified nation. Prussia used victory over France in 1871 to unify small and large independent German states into a single nation led by an emperor, introducing Europe to a contentious, authoritarian Great Power.

In reaction the French toppled Napoleon III, and left-wing radicals established the Paris Commune. After the Commune fell to the cannonades of the French army, French generals made bids to take power as strongmen. One such was General Georges Boulanger, whose attempt ended in farce. Marx observed that the tragedies of history repeat themselves as farce; but we know that this drive for a strong leader shedding the restraints of democracy began in farce and ended, in the twentieth century, in unparalleled tragedy.

In Germany, Austria, Italy, and Russia, vestiges of the old world where kings or emperors still ruled, weak parliaments continued to make gains against the dynastic power, even as repression and censorship held sway. In Germany and Austria, where there were fewer outlets for their demands, socialists grew stronger in number, at any time portending to take control of the state. In Russia, where the serfs had been freed in 1867 under a heavy burden of repayment to their former masters, socialist *narodniks* roamed the countryside praising the old way of life of the Russian peasants and damning the government for exploiting them and keeping them in poverty. To dramatize their dissatisfaction, in 1881 they assassinated the reforming Tsar Alexander II. He was followed by his reactionary son Alexander III, one of whose responses to disorder was to persecute religious minorities, especially his Jewish subjects, blaming them for radicalism as much as for liberalism.

To dampen change and disorder by reasserting monarchy, the emperors of Russia, Germany, and Austria formed in 1873 the League of the Three Emperors, successor to the Holy Alliance. It was neither successful nor lasting. Turmoil intensified in all the major nations. Nationalism spread to many of the smaller peoples of Europe who daily threatened war and revolution to free themselves from overlords such as the Austrian and Ottoman empires. Austria, plagued by more than fifteen disruptive nationalities and weakened by defeats, lacked the ability to manage its numerous components effectively. The center was not holding, and as the century wore on Austria looked to disintegrate. The Ottoman Empire, which still controlled lands in the Balkans, was also coming apart. England, the most secure of the liberal democracies and the prized example for democrats throughout Europe, generally stayed out of Continental wars, but in Africa and Asia it fought many small wars to protect and expand its imperial interests. Before long, France, Italy, and Germany joined in the scramble for empire beyond the shores of Europe.

To socialism, anarchism, conservative reaction, nationalism, imperialism, and war was added racism in midcentury. Count Gobineau, in his *Essay on the Inequality of Human Races* (1853–1855), argued that the Nordic races were the ideal type, creative and masterful; all other peoples were inferior, including the Jews. He was surpassed by Houston Stewart Chamberlain, an Englishman who grew up in France, became a German citizen, and wrote the textbook of Germanic racism, *The Foundations of the Nineteenth Century* (1899). To Chamberlain, the ancient Teutonic tribes were the source of all virtues; their only failing was not to have exterminated their inferior neighbors. Flush with social Darwinism and eugenics, he dreamed of breeding a new superior race. One of its goals would be to rid the world of the Jews, said to be racial inferiors who had managed (unaccountably, considering their supposed inferiority) to dominate Europe culturally and financially.

Among the flourishing anti-Semites in Germany were Lagarde, already mentioned, and Julius Langbehn, whose book with the mild-sounding title *Rembrandt as Educator* was a screed against democracy, Jews, modernity, science, socialism, and all the other isms that Pope Pius did not like either. The train of German (and European) reactionary thought was that Europe had taken a misstep, leaving behind blood, religion, and hierarchy for despised cosmopolitanism, by which was meant all the modern ideals, from individualism, self-interest, and the market economy to liberal democracy. Psychoanalysis developed strong responses to this wish to revive a lost past.

According to the historian Fritz Stern, to Langbehn it was an "article of faith that Jews and modernity were one, and the fury of his anti-Semitism sprang from his resentment of everything modern." To Karl von Vogelsang, a German anti-Semite who rose to influence in Austria, "the Christian social order is being dissolved by Jewry."[2] The association of Jews with money was the reactionaries' way of indicting capitalism, a much reviled economic system among them. It was ruining small farmers, artisans, and shopkeepers, creating a mass socialist *lumpenproletariat*, and destroying the beliefs and securities of the old way of life. Thus behind the smoke screen of racial anti-Semitism was cultural anti-Semitism, a mask for the struggle over the values and achievements of the new age as against those of the old.

While modernity was bewildering, often heartless, and filled with turmoil, it had salutary effects appreciated by the Jews of Europe. They had been ghettoized, marginalized, spat upon, inveighed against, and, when opportunity afforded, murdered in the hundreds and thousands or deported wholesale from nation to nation. The new freedom, education, and tolerance were thus much to Jewish taste and benefit, as were liberalism, the secular state (after a thousand years of oppression by the church), and the ability to operate freely in trades and professions. On the Continent, those who disliked the Jews held a similar low opinion of the English, for many of the same reasons: fixtures of modernity who had gotten there first, they were contemptuously said to be a nation of tradesmen. The complex enemy the Freudians would confront through psychoanalysis—including anti-modernists, anti-Semites, racists, monarchists, conservative reactionaries, proto-fascists, socialists, anarchists, and romantic revolutionaries of every stripe—was amalgamating itself.

Anti-Semitism was brought to a head by the false accusations of treason against Alfred Dreyfus, a Jewish captain in the French army. When the case was called to public attention in 1896 through the efforts of his family, it ripped French opinion apart and reverberated throughout Europe. Liberals and left-wing radicals allied with Dreyfus; conservative forces opposed him. The case brought home to Theodor Herzl, an upper-class Austrian Jewish journalist covering the case in Paris, that Christian Europe would never permit the Jews to rest. In a pamphlet he hurriedly composed in 1896, *The Jewish State*, Herzl proposed establishing a nation for the Jews in the Holy Land,

and in the next year founded the Zionist movement to achieve that goal. Max Nordau, a Hungarian Jewish physician, novelist, and journalist living in Paris and covering the Dreyfus case for German newspapers, was attracted by Herzl's appeal and joined the movement. Herzl served as a model and a demon for Freud; Nordau, who attained fame as a cultural critic, was very much a model.

Anti-Semitism was not the full extent of "racial" hatred in nationalistic Europe. Ethnic groups conceived a hatred for each other, spurred by the new imaginary science of racialism spawned by Gobineau and adopted with a fury in the German-speaking lands of Europe. Race came to be as much a matter of science as Cesare Lombroso's study of physiognomy; both were believed to be new revelations about humankind. Warring Western racists joined hands when they regarded their conquered peoples overseas. The British *Anthropological Review* explained that "As the type of the Negro is foetal, so that of the Mongol is infantile"; they were all "beardless children whose . . . chief virtue consists in unquestioning obedience." A ship's captain, one Osborne, advised: "Treat them like children. Make them do what we know is for their benefit as well as our own. . . ."3

In a class application of this attitude, rural populations in Europe were often seen as country cousins of the "savage." They too needed the paternal care of the upper classes. Aside from legitimizing white over dark and rich over poor, such attitudes provided the means, comments the historian E. J. Hobsbawm, by which Europe, a "fundamentally inegalitarian society based upon a fundamentally egalitarian ideology, rationalized its inequalities, and attempted to justify and defend those privileges which the democracy implicit in its institutions must inevitably challenge."4 That concisely states one of the great confounding issues of nineteenth-century liberalism as it drove to defeat all opposition: on its home ground liberalism was often oppressive. Here Freudianism would make a major contribution by shielding some of the ill effects of liberal democracy.

The melding of nationalism, chauvinism, authoritarianism, racism, and nostalgia led to the formation of political organizations pledged to those ideals. They were particularly successful in Germany and Austria, where they took as their special tasks vilifying the Jews, countering the growth of "godless" socialism, and keeping strict restraints on liberal democracy. In 1878 the anti-Semitic German court preacher Adolf Stoecker founded the Christian Socialist Workers party to rally the lower classes around reactionary policies. In 1890 the Pan-German League was formed to further the chauvinist political goals of "Germanism." Four years later came the nationalist Deutschbund, dedicated to Teutonic purity, and in 1897 the Wandervogel, a German youth movement dedicated to nature, mystic worship of the body, and a preference for the passions over the intellect.

In Freud's Austria in 1890 the Christian Social party was formed with an avowed anti-Semite, Karl Lueger, at its head. Opportunistic as much as anti-Semitic, Lueger appealed to mass populations still imbued with medieval superstitions. Repeatedly elected mayor of Vienna, he was not allowed to serve by the emperor until, in 1897, under pressure from the Vatican and the Austrian elites, he took office, backed by even woollier romantic reactionaries such as Georg von Schoenerer, in whom all the later marks of fascism could be seen. Schoenerer formed his own proto-fascist German People's party, appealing to depressed rural districts. Among his typical harangues: "The Jew Bible is not a moral and religious work";[5] his religious ideal was Teutonic paganism. During the heyday of Lueger's and Schoenerer's ideology, the young Hitler took up residence in Vienna—and Freud completed his basic psychological system.

Where reactionary groups could not muster sufficient numbers for parliamentary representation, they formed movements and publications like Action Française, led by the French anti-Semite Charles Maurras, preaching monarchy and the reestablishment of a state religion. Maurras was not a believing Catholic, but he did believe in the order and hierarchy of the old world. Proto-fascism, whether neoroyalist or not, was in formation, later to turn into the real thing. Against these groups were ranked the liberal democrats of the middle class, the social democrats of the lower classes, and the violent anarchists.

AGAINST this background of barely contained political mayhem, the second half of the nineteenth century witnessed a stupefying acceleration of scientific achievement: the germ theory of disease and the isolation of disease bacilli and parasites; the theory of evolution; new chemicals, antitoxins, vaccines, and anesthetics; the discovery of radio waves, electrons, and radioactivity; x-rays to see behind the surface of the body into the physical structure. Pasteur, Koch, Roentgen, Ehrlich, the Curies were regarded as beneficiaries of mankind. Science was establishing itself, in the words of the historian Thomas P. Neill, as "the measure of truth. Every discipline, from philosophy to sociology and history, aspired to be scientific" on the model of physics and chemistry.[6] The Freudians, among many others, made a bid for the prestige of this flowering science.

To science was added the striking achievements of technology: new chemical industries, electricity, telephones, photography, typewriters, bicycles and motor bikes leading to motor cars and improved highway systems. Then steel-frame buildings and skyscrapers, and airplanes planned for the skies. Great engineering feats included the construction of the Suez Canal and the laying of the Atlantic cable. Factories grew from human scale to gigantic. For war-making came rifled guns, breech-loading guns and rifles, the Gattling gun and then the machine gun, ironclad ships, and dynamite and cordite for naval mines and self-propelled torpedoes. Between 1870 and 1914 manufacturing capacity quadrupled as trade expanded worldwide. Public hygiene—sewers, potable water supplies, and drainage—came to towns and cities. The new West was demonstrating an unsurpassed power of thought and achievement, placing in stark relief its distance from the old world.

Cooperation between business and politics led to financial scandals, a notable one being over the French attempt to construct the Panama Canal. Such scandals were proof to some that the mix of democratic politics and capitalist wealth was a brew of the devil. Herzl, covering the French parliamentary debates over the Panama scandal in 1892, thought he was watching the end of the democratic experiment in the land that had introduced it to Europe through revolution: "Whoever saw with his own eyes the last sessions of the Chamber had a vision of the Convention [preceding the Reign of Terror]. . . . Thus it was a hundred years ago and the bloody year ensued. Death knells sound, 'Ninety-Three!' "[7]

With the growth of productive capacity and mass urban populations, advertising applied images, suggestion, repetition, and (as much as was allowed) eroticism to sales and marketing. These elements of persuasion were later applied in psychoanalysis. The advertising supported popular news sheets of the day which became, Neill observes, vehicles for "molding the national mind and obtaining blind support of national governments by the literate masses of the people."[8] So important was the molding of opinion by newspapers that in Germany, Chancellor Bismarck secretly purchased one as his mouthpiece and bribed journalists wholesale to get his views across. Public opinion entered the scene as something to be influenced and juggled by the powerful. Psychoanalysis was not laggard in its effort to influence public opinion.

Throughout the century the laboring masses, seeking to improve their impossible situation, formed workingmen's associations and unions where they were allowed, demonstrated and struck, enlisted in socialist and radical parties. The first May Day celebration took place in Paris in 1889, the same year that saw the formation of the Second International by the Socialists. At a union celebration in France the workers sang:

> It's gonna be okay, be okay, be okay!
> To the lamp-post with the bourgeoisie,
> The bourgeoisie, let's string 'em!
> And if we don't get to hang 'em
> We'll flatten the bastards out.[9]

Authoritarian nations such as Germany moved to outlaw socialism while introducing social insurance programs to quell agitation. Little Switzerland took the same direction in 1890, but most of Europe was content to do as little for the workingman as possible, short of affecting his ability to work. The Catholic church in 1891 finally took official notice of labor in *Rerum Novarum,* its encyclical lamenting the conditions of the working classes.

As exercise, entertainment, and diversion, sports grew apace. Populations working in restricted quarters and no longer engaged in agricultural pursuits sought outlets in soccer, rugby, cricket, bicycling, roller-skating, golf, baseball, football, and basketball. Some team sports professionalized and acquired the flavor of cultural bonding for communities and nations. In 1896 the first modern Olympic Games were organized, combining sports, individualism, teamwork, competition, nationalism, international comity, and diversion. Sports illustrated the linking of teamwork and diversion in the new age. Psychoanalysis, admittedly distant from sports, learned this lesson. Along with sports, public entertainments flourished, featuring two favorite themes, sex and violence, that were also part of high culture in poetry, plays, novels, and operas, and likewise became part of psychoanalysis.

Sex was celebrated by the avant-garde throughout Europe, purveyed by Havelock Ellis, Oscar Wilde, and other leading lights in England; by body culture movements in England and Germany (nudist-*cum*-vegetarian); by the Wandervogel in Germany, which "revel[ed] in a 'return to nature' and a hardly licentious but certainly freer sexuality";[10] and by Eastern gurus traveling the capitals of Europe with a message of mysticism and sex. Avant-garde sex amplified the theme of sex as the will of the masses seeking cultural freedom when they could not find it in politics. That most of the masses cared little about avant-garde sexual themes, movements, and gurus made little difference; much of the middle class did, and sex pervaded the second half of the nineteenth century in Europe from top to bottom. This was one of the impelling factors, along with the philosophy of pleasure and sex's political meanings, for the central role of sex in psychoanalysis.

In the arts, novels turned from romanticism to realism to naturalism ("the slice of life"), showing the underside of modern conditions. From Poe forward, the entertaining detective story presented puzzles solved by the astute discovery of clues analyzed by deductive reasoning (a replica of science). Painters turned to impressionism, brashly illustrating what the seventeenth-century philosophers had discovered, that the world was what it looked like, not what it was. For our story, perhaps the most important turn in the arts was the school of poetry known as symbolism. All art had utilized symbols from earliest times, but now it became an aesthetic in its own right. Symbolist poets spoke their meaning indirectly, through suggestive words, sounds, pauses, seeking to express a mysterious individual interiority. Much of this poetry had to do with the unconscious, with sex, violence, despair, and disgust at modernity, and was often keyed to shock. The poets were asking the new Europe to look itself in the face, an invitation bourgeois Europe declined with the help of the Freudians—and ironically with the help of symbolist methods.

A symbolist manifesto issued in 1886 declared that most of reality was submerged, like the proverbial iceberg. It was best understood by intuition and best invoked by subtle allusion. Subjectivity was the source of truth, the artist was a magician who made the unconscious apparent. Reality, said Émile Bernard in 1888, was nothing more than an imaginative idea. We are all, said one symbolist, followers of Schopenhauer. In music, tonality gave way to a subtle, indefinite surging under the influence of Richard Wagner, another Schopenhauer aficionado. Schopenhauer's influence on the arts was no less than his importance to psychoanalysis.

New religions came to prominence: in America Mormonism and Christian Science, which were variations on Christianity, and Theosophy, a variation on Eastern mysticism. Christian Science and Theosophy were especially notable for what they revealed of the new age. Christian Science, founded by Mary Baker Eddy, grew out of hypnotism. When Mrs. Eddy came to view hypnotism as the work of the devil, she substituted faith in God as a cure-all for diseases of the mind and body. The cause of disease, she said, was wrong thinking, including lack of faith in God. Problems within the body and mind were susceptible to solutions developed by the mind—the old idea of mind over matter. In the mind, ready to solve your problems, was God (an adaptation of German Idealist philosophy and Eastern religion). Neither germs nor society made people sick. They made themselves sick and were themselves the source of cure under the guidance of "Mother Mary" (Baker Eddy). She had gotten her ideas from a hypnotism guru; once she stated them, she found others stealing them as she had stolen his. She ended up in paranoid fear of her followers, friends, and neighbors, whom she accused of trying to filch her glory. Christian Science was a near-perfect middle-class therapeutic that refused to recognize how the new rules and ways of society and culture had affected individuals. It recognized only the lone, struggling individual working out his or her fate as if *in vacuo,* and put the solution on the individual and God within. Mrs. Eddy's beliefs often read like the re-Christianization of German philosophy, as did another of her sources, the American poet and philosopher Ralph Waldo Emerson, whose creed was self-reliance. Mary Baker Eddy's experience, from hypnotism and mind-over-matter to paranoid rejection of disciples and emphasis on the individual as the source of sickness and cure, was largely repeated by Freud.

Theosophy blended anti-Christianity and progressive views on international amity, pacifism, and improved social conditions with an out-of-this-world occultism and racial theories that gave primacy to "Aryan" spirituality. It spawned reactionary groups such as the Ariophists in Vienna, who followed the lead of Guido von List and Jorg Lanz von Liebenfels, prophets of German world power. Like Nietzsche, the Ariophists regarded Christianity as the support of the lower classes. They were more comfortable with racist exclusivity, sun worship, and wisdom emanating from entities called *Armanen.* Slavs and Jews were their pet hatreds. Through Theosophy (probably), they bequeathed the swastika symbol to the Nazis.[11] Spiritualism, with its rapping on tables, was another example of the continuing sensitivity to religious experience as orthodoxy waned. Connecting religion and science was interest in the paranormal, seen as a secret realm which science would one day pierce. This continuing religious impulse was appropriated by the Freudians.

In a Europe that had become psychologized through philosophy and politics, psychology became a much-discussed discipline, splitting into two camps in the second half of the century. Innovators such as Hermann von Helmholtz and Wilhelm Wundt wanted to make it an experimental science while visionaries such as Johann Herbart, G. T. Fechner, and Eduard von Hartmann leaned toward the old association of psychology with philosophy, religion, and mysticism. In Paris the neurologist Charcot studied illnesses that the nineteenth century had seemingly patented (hysteria, neurosis, and neurasthenia), thinking he had found a bridge between the physical sciences and the psyche (he too was a disciple of Schopenhauer). A fully modern man, Charcot nevertheless furnished his palatial Parisian home as if it were a medieval castle, the sort of backward glance the Freudians would exemplify in their theories; to Freud, who studied with him, he was like a medieval priest, his lectures imbued with the same atmosphere Freud felt in Notre Dame. The Freudians enlisted with the visionaries, by far the strongest psychological stream.

In America William James, psychologist and philosopher, popularized the pragmatism of Charles Peirce as an appropriate adjunct to the scientific and materialist thought of the age. Countering pragmatism in Europe was vitalism, which looked to mysterious powers in the universe as the explanation for things large and small, including human motivation and action. An adaptation of Schopenhauer ("the entire mechanistic and atomistic view of nature is approaching bankruptcy"; "the metaphysical appears . . . as the immediate ground of the . . . physical"),[12] vitalism was carried forward by Henri Bergson in his philosophy of the *élan vital* as well as by proto-fascist thinkers who found in it an association with the philosophy of Will and a nostalgic version of medieval mysticism. Vitalism was romanticism in philosophy, an attempt to understand and encompass the almost mad vitality of the nineteenth century. Somehow Western society had gotten itself into a fix and did not know how to exit gracefully. The new psychology of psychoanalysis, both pragmatic and vitalistic, responded when crisis finally exploded.

FIVE

Crisis

Out of . . . the last decades of the nineteenth century,
suddenly throughout Europe, there arose a kindling
fever. Nobody knew exactly what was on the way . . .
perhaps a reshuffling of society.
          —Robert Musil, *The Man Without Qualities*

Collapse society; die . . . !
          —Joris-Karl Huysmans, *A Rebours*

As it approached its end, the nineteenth century was not unlike
Charcot's last, and Freud's first, psychological specialty, hysteria; it
was hysterical. In the 1880s Europe entered what many historians
view as a cultural crisis. It was no longer sure of who or what it was.
Eighty years had been enough to set aside a thousand years and more
of history.

In this period called the fin de siècle, pessimism competed with excitement and climax meant apocalypse. Fear was pervasive. In
1885–1887 alone socialist agitation, strikes, and bloody riots occurred
in France, Belgium, and the United States; war between Bulgaria and
Serbia attracted the interest of Russia, Austria, and Turkey; the British
and the Russians sparred in Central Asia ("the Great Game"), as did
the French and British in Africa, the Spanish and the Germans in the
South Sea Islands, and the Germans and Russians in the Balkans. Germany and its ally Austria drove to connect with the East and threaten
the British Empire; Russia and Austria squabbled over the spoils of the
tottering Ottoman Empire; England invaded Burma, Italy invaded Er-
itrea, and the French moved into Indochina.

But the most troubling characteristic of the times was a loss of confidence among sectors of the population in the direction Europe had

taken since 1800. The losses and gains of a huge cultural revolution were reflected in a perpetual agitation that was personal and social as well as international. Many felt the wish to return to some Golden Age of quiet in the soul, of authenticity, honesty, and spontaneity—everything that was being squeezed out by modernity; or, alternatively, to forge a future that replicated some fabled past, as if the past had really been a Garden of Eden. However unlikely the alliance, avant-garde artists, socialists, Communists, anarchists, neoroyalists, and proto-fascists joined in the conviction earlier sounded by Pius IX that something had gone terribly wrong. Europe's civilization might disappear in a cloud of dust. Amid the growing adaptation of the middle class to new conditions, there came to others an end-of-the-world pessimism. Even in the middle class there were those who feared Europe's direction. As Stearns notes, in every group and class in every one of the new societies there were some who could adapt, however strange the times, and some who refused the invitation.

Like everyone else, those of higher social position were driven forward by the new forces. All were keenly aware of the pace, the clamor, the press of people, the instrumentality, the loss of faith, and, far worse, the consequent loss of certainty. The common man constituting the majority was free, lost, and exploited. The middle class understood neither its luck nor admitted its social and political role as ruler of liberal democracy. It was acquisitive and productive and considered that enough. It knew how to justify itself only by the economic and political formulas upon which the new age was founded. But more in the way of justification was needed for the change and turmoil that had led to a crisis of the culture. A highly notable part of that justification, still famous today, was developed in the mental laboratory of the Freudians.

"The disposition of the times is curiously confused, a compound of feverish restlessness and blind discouragement, of fearful presage and hang-dog renunciation," Max Nordau recorded in *Degeneration* (1892), his remarkable study of the arts and temper of the period. "The prevalent feeling is that of imminent perdition and extinction . . . of a Dusk of Nations, in which all suns and all stars are gradually waning, and mankind with all its institutions and creations is perishing in the midst of a dying world."[1] Nordau felt well-placed to understand the situation: he had studied with Charcot and was adept in the psychologies of the time, including that of the physiognomist and criminologist Lombroso, to whom he dedicated his book.

Nordau had taken note of Benedict-Augustin Morel's *Treatise on Degeneracy* (1857), which argued as scientific gospel that the European "races" had declined from their former standard, becoming lazy, filthy, criminal, and unruly.[2] Morel, with other "degeneration theorists," held the cause to be city life, factory work, noise, rush, poor food, poor housing, polluted air—in other words, the turmoil of the times, against the backdrop of mass culture, imperialism, and socialist and anarchist agitation. The effects of these phenomena supposedly appeared in bodily signs called "stigmata" and in hidden "mental stigmata" betokening psychic illness. Dr. James Cantile of Charing Cross Hospital, London, dubbed the condition "urborobus"; others called it "hysteria" or "nervous exhaustion," products of the stresses of modernity. Pierre Janet, one of Charcot's most able students, would later identify nervous exhaustion as the basic cause of neurosis, when the human nervous system could no longer deal with the load placed upon it.

Unlike Morel, who found degeneration primarily among the lower classes, Nordau found it in modern writers, artists, musicians, and their upper-class admirers. He loosely identified them as Diabolists or Decadents. He believed these people were literally suffering from nervous ailments organically based in degenerated organs and senses. If a painter employed unrealistic colors in a landscape, it was because the painter's eyes were diseased and he could not see correctly the actual scene before him. The same held true for writers who dealt with the undersides of life (their psyches were diseased) and composers who cluttered their work with dissonance (their hearing was diseased). By this means Nordau indicted Gustave Flaubert, Leo Tolstoy, Émile Zola, Charles Baudelaire, Richard Wagner, Stéphane Mallarmé, Paul Verlaine, Henrik Ibsen, Algernon Swinburne, Oscar Wilde, Walt Whitman, Friedrich Nietzsche, and scores of lesser lights, whose themes he declared were sex, violence, mysticism, and egoism. The theme-philosopher of these degenerates, according to Nordau, was Schopenhauer, whose sex obsession, pessimism, nihilism, relativism, and defeatism suffused the arts and sensibility of the age.

Nordau saw himself as a healthy voice speaking for the successful middle classes that had made the new age. Their work and their values and the new age they had spawned were good; the degenerates were too weak in body and mind to appreciate what had been given to them. If the fin de siècle would reassert the good religious-based values of the past, and the good middle-class values of the present, all would be well. It would be seen that the sun wasn't setting at all, but rather that the new Europe was a wonder. Alert to the power of suggestion, Nordau feared that everything wrong advertised by the "degenerates" would be believed by the popular masses, leading to the decline and fall of Western civilization.[3]

In an effort to protect what he valued, Nordau hurled withering abuse at the enemies of modernity in displays of verbal hysteria that anticipated Hitler's propaganda minister, Joseph Goebbels. "Mystics," he wrote, "but especially ego-maniacs and filthy pseudo-realists, are enemies to society of the direst kind. Society must unconditionally defend itself against them." Whoever upholds the values of civilization "must crush under his thumb the anti-social vermin." Modern artists were pornographers to whom a healthy society "must show no mercy."[4] The fin de siècle was developing hysterical symbolic categories of the sick and the well as disguised social criticism. Among the new psychiatric practitioners who were hard on Nordau's heels, notably the Freudians, his intemperate language would be replaced by a cool, assured medicalism, no less damning but far more subtle.

IN THE YEARS surrounding the turn of the century, expressions of hysteria mounted to a climax. In 1900 the novelist Jules Renan advised artists and writers: "Every one of our works must be a crisis, almost a revolution." The Italian Futurist writer Marinetti declared that war was "beautiful because it combines the gunfire, the cannonades, the pauses, the scents, the stench of putrefaction into a symphony." Vladimir Cerina, the intellectual mentor of Gavrilo Princip, assassin of Archduke Franz Ferdinand in 1914, hailed the destruction of "every dogma, every norm, every authority," advocating unrestrained freedom for "critics, subversives, rebels and wreckers."[5]

The German expressionist painter Ludwig Meidner saw on Berlin streets "human rags, advertising signboards and masses of threatening, formless colors . . . a chaos of light . . . tumult." In Edvard Munch's signature painting *The Scream,* a contorted face, between that of a clown and a madman, howls in insupportable agony against a background of violently swirling colors. Egon Schiele's pictures show mutely anguished erotic figures. Vassily Kandinsky painted an abstract picture suggesting cannons and explosions in order to communicate, he said, "a terrible struggle . . . going on in the spiritual sphere."[6]

In "Weltende" ("World's End"), the Viennese expressionist poet Jacob von Hoddis saw the middle class bringing on the apocalypse.

(He went mad in 1914.) The Viennese composer Arnold Schoenberg, creator of the twelve-tone system that produced anguished, unyielding dissonances, recorded a dream: "I had the feeling as if I had fallen into an ocean of boiling water, and not knowing how to swim." Franz Kafka was born in 1883 and grew up in the fin de siècle. In his "Metamorphosis," a young man awakes one morning to find himself turned into a huge insect. Another of his stories ends: "My ship has no rudder, and it is driven by the wind that blows in the uttermost regions of death."[7] Kafka's novel *The Castle* tells of someone receiving an invitation to visit a great castle and arriving to find the owner permanently unavailable, his whereabouts or claims on the visitor unknown: the castle was an abandoned monument of the past, as inaccessible as certainty and God. Kafka's last novel, *Amerika,* is a pilgrimage to the home of the new world incarnate.

The British historian G. M. Trevelyan, reflecting on the change from old to new, felt that life in the old times had been "beautiful and instructive," whereas now it was "ugly and trivial." It had become impossible to "see the earth for the pavement, or the breadth of heaven for the chimney tops." The great cities produced "a wholly artificial life" lived in "endless rows of little prisons." Everywhere there was "intellectual and moral degeneration . . . ugliness, vulgarity, materialism, the insipid negation of everything that has been accounted good in the past history of man." Looking back on these same changes, the Spanish philosopher José Ortega y Gasset argued in *The Revolt of the Masses,* "It will not do, then, to dignify the actual crisis by presenting it as the conflict between two moralities, between two civilizations, one in decay, the other at its dawn. . . . Europe . . . has accepted blindly a culture which is magnificent, but has no roots."[8]

A year before the Great War, Stravinsky's ballet *The Rite of Spring* wedded the primitive to the clanging motor-rhythms of the machine in a dance of death and rebirth.

IN THESE same years the vote was made universal for men in England, with no strings of property or taxation attached, and was extended, if not that far, in other European nations. In the United States, President Grover Cleveland signed the bill creating Labor Day, recognizing that in a hundred years the common man had become a common laborer, and that the discipline of modern work had triumphed in the Western world—even as populists and progressives realized that the legacy of the twin revolutions was neither fair nor reasonable. In this same period Leon Bloy, French novelist and social reformer, was discovering that while newspapers covered "the merest irrelevance . . . there is no one who can tell us any news from God."[9]

When Queen Victoria died in 1901, a quarter of the population of England lived in poverty worse and more widespread, by some estimates, than anything ever known. One Londoner in five could be found in the workhouse, the poor-law hospital, or the lunatic asylum—and would ultimately rest in a potter's field. Others in the lower classes barely scraped by, even as an expanding lower middle class came into view. These conditions were more or less replicated throughout industrializing Europe, and in other places were far worse. Even if, as some argue, the mass of the population was marginally better off than before, the new atmosphere of "rising expectations" made their comparative deprivation that much more galling.

In America conditions were little different. In the words of the historian Alan Ryan:

> . . . The problems of the inner city were appalling. In the early 1890s homelessness in Chicago sometimes reached 20 percent. . . . Disease was rife. . . . The upper classes were apparently indifferent to the fate of the poor and even to the fate of the working near-poor. In the cities the response of the better-off was to remove themselves to the suburbs . . . in Congress it was to legislate to make it harder for the poor to organize, and in the courts it was to make it impossible for the unions to strike.
>
> Nor was it clear what any individual person should or could do about all of this. The political parties of the day were networks of influence-peddling, and local government was corrupt. . . .[10]

According to most economists, "two nations" had taken shape in each of the advanced countries of the West, consisting, not unlike the past, of those few on the top and those many below (plus a small middle). Over the century, conditions marginally improved for those below. For all, life span increased with a better and more varied diet and with medicine for the first time placed on a scientific footing. Nevertheless the "two nations" persisted.

To practical poverty for most was added emotional poverty for all. Gone were the close ties of the past in familiar surroundings, in a natural landscape, a certain identity of self and community, and a certain knowledge about God and the order of society and the world. These poverties joined with all the other disorganizations, including internal ones in the personality, induced by momentous changes in relationships, meanings, activities, morale, ethics. What could return order and meaning, no one knew. It was obvious to many that "If there is no God, everything is permitted." According to Hannah Arendt, European intellectuals "knew instinctively that they lived in a world of hollow pretense and that its stability was the greatest pretense of all. . . . All governments knew that they were secretly disintegrating . . . and that they lived on borrowed time."[11]

The phrase "The Century of the Common Man" came into vogue, more flattery than description since most of the major European nations refused to give complete rule to the majority. They feared that further compromises in political power would lead to compromises in the economic power of the elites and the weakening of social order. Most of all they feared that the common man, who had always been the rabble, the mob, was now without restraints on his wishes and dreams, from the family, the aristocracy, or the church. The common man could not be released into full freedom because, to the elites, he was a pig, lovable when he had been under the heel in the old world, not so lovable now when he was officially free and sovereign.[12] Everywhere he portended revolution. He wanted to eat *your* meal, have *your* house. Fears of Jacobins at the end of the eighteenth century were replaced at the end of the nineteenth century by fears of Marxists and anarchists.

Right-wing reactionaries continued to counter left-wing utopianism with proposals for dispensing with parliaments and returning to powerful monarchs or strongman leaders who, they believed, could settle the new age, now that it had so amply revealed its cracks and strains. "Corporatists," volkists, and proto-fascists called for the revival of traditional religions or the creation of new ones that could shepherd the masses through modernity. Among their other proposals was the elimination of the Jews, the old medieval solution to turmoil. Jews were the symbol chosen by radicals of the right to represent the new age. Marx had once also believed the Jews were guilty, even though some of his later followers were Jewish, among them leaders of socialism in France, Germany, and Austria.

The major nations of Europe were forming into two blocs, on the one side the liberal democracies of England and France (bolstered by authoritarian Russia), on the other the authoritarian powers of Germany and Austria (joined by Italy) which resisted giving the rule to mass man. (There were, of course, many other disputes between them aside from how far liberal democracy should be implemented.) Within all the European nations, an adjective of disdain had entered the vocabulary of avant-garde artists and left-wing and right-wing anti-democratic radicals: *bourgeois,* designating what stood in the middle of the contending polar forces. What was bourgeois was loud, obvious, and spiritually cheap: pure soullessness, the visible form of instrumentality. The bourgeoisie were held to be philistines not only of art but of life, their sign the city and its culture, valueless at bottom beyond the value of money. The leading French sociologist Émile Durkheim saw society as normless, neither regulating the individual nor providing a defined place for him. In *Suicide* (1897) he named the modern condition *anomie.*

In 1887 the French psychiatrist Paul Regnard had predicted that "the decline of the family, aristocracy and religion, the unleashing of uncontrollable social competition and the spreading of revolutionary ideologies" would lead to "the folly of slaughter, the madness of blood and destruction." Six years later, Daniel Paul Schreber, a presiding judge in the city of Dresden, went mad, his insanity taking the form of a firm belief that the world had come to an end and that he had been appointed to start it up again as the new Jesus who would be reborn of a new Mary (himself). Modernity had superimposed on Christianity a sleazy religion of materialism, lust, and happiness, and Schreber was destined to return Europe to its old values. He maintained this belief through long stays at insane asylums, dying at the last one in 1911, still awaiting his rebirth as the new Jesus.[13]

In the 1880s Charcot had aptly reflected the age in his study of hysteria. It may not have been a disease, as he thought. But it called attention to the excitement, fear, apprehension, and anxiety in the air. These were factors in the life of the time that exacerbated feelings, thoughts, relationships, endeavors. They were novel in that they had appeared on a continental scale. Charcot had in effect symbolized social hysteria in a medical diagnosis. His students, Freud among them, must have been as impressed with his acclaimed medical expertise as with the timeliness of his specialty.

Hysteria was not only characteristic of each society, it operated among Western societies, and between them and the rest of the world. Europe and America were in the grip of forces—technology, industrialism, market imperatives, nationalism, imperialism, racism, and the pressures of mass populations—seemingly beyond direct control. The Western world was on a track that might be taking it somewhere outside human will. It was like a permanent roller-coaster ride in a dream that was reality. The new age had proved exciting, promising, and at the same time plaguelike.

Into this atmosphere of hysteria and crisis stepped the Freudians with a message of healing. They were well suited to take up the standard of a middle class that did not think the world was coming to an end but felt itself endangered. In a Europe that since the seventeenth century had become progressively psychologized, their expertise found its definitive application.

SIX

The Freudians:
The Liberal Imagination

I am beginning to perceive . . . large, general, framing
motives, as I should like to call them, and other
motives, fill-ins, which vary according to the
individual's experiences.
                    —Sigmund Freud, Letter to Fliess

The Freudian legend . . . blot[s] out the greatest part of
the scientific and cultural context in which
psychoanalysis developed. . . .
                    —Henri Ellenberger, *The Discovery of the*
                                        Unconscious

CONTRIBUTING TO the creation and formulation of psychoanalysis were the trauma of the old world lost and the new world gained,
the philosophy of pleasure, and the hysteria of the fin de siècle. To
these were added the background and social position of Freud and his
followers.

It may seem a coincidence that the Freudians appeared in the wash
of the twin revolutions and the apogee of fin-de-siècle hysteria; or that
medical science was building toward their discoveries at that particular moment. But the true motive force was the danger to everything the
Freudians valued in the new civilization. They saw danger on many
fronts—political, social, economic, cultural, racial (or what was
thought to be racial at the time). The enemies of the new age wished
to impose alternative political or economic systems with different definitions of freedom, morality, goals, and ways of life. Beyond these
virulent enemies were all those millions who were suffering through a
still unfamiliar life—the uncanniness of things, poverty for many, star-

tling wealth for some, a newness difficult to absorb. "This is your life," the new age said, and it led many people to have second thoughts.

The challenge for those who liked it was to keep it together, against those who wished to tear it apart or see it fall of its own weight. The pioneers were not directed to respond to these dangers; they were inspired, as were other intellectuals of the age, to fight for what they considered to be right. In a culture that had become psychological, they were strategically placed to employ psychology as a weapon in the cultural wars.

On the evidence of the Freudians' achievement, the dangers of the fin de siècle must have induced a crisis of conscience: whether to practice psychology or politics. Striding before them like a tempting devil was the psychological pseudo-science of such figures as Morel, Lombroso, and Nordau. Psychology had been shown to be a way to support opinion, influence mass thought, and inveigh against one's enemies. The Freudians' definitive practice became not psychology but psychological politics. It enjoyed a good chance of success because in democracies power works through the mind; it is more a function of ideas than guns. Sorel's advocacy of violence could be countered by his appreciation of the power of mass myths.

In his definitive history of dynamic psychology, Henri Ellenberger found that "The difficulty in understanding the complex personality of Freud has led many to seek a basic notion that would make him intelligible. Interpretations have been given of Freud as a Jew, as a Viennese professional man of his time, as a Romantic, as a man of letters, as a neurotic, as a genius."[1] Seen in the setting of the fin de siècle, when he formed his basic ideas, Freud must first be identified as a satisfied member of the middle class, in cultural orientation an adherent of modernity, in religion a proud, atheistic Jew well schooled in his heritage, in politics a liberal democrat, and in social outlook an elitist. Except for his Jewish heritage and his aversion to socialism, the others who followed Freud's teachings were much the same as Freud in all of this, and so were such non-Freudian psychoanalysts as Janet and such inspirations of the new psychology as Charcot. All their values were endangered in the conflicting currents of the fin de siècle; all these challenges they elected to fight through psychoanalysis.

In his lifestyle Freud was the complete bourgeois. Ellenberger notes that from his thirty-fifth year he lived "in a large apartment with several servants in one of the best residential quarters in Vienna, took three months' summer vacation in Austria and abroad, read the *Neue Freie Presse* [the leading liberal newspaper of Vienna], and strictly conformed to the obligations of his profession."[2] He conducted his career according to a stringent schedule of his own devising that would have been the envy of a first-class business executive. Every hour was accounted for, from early morning when he wrote, to late morning and afternoon when he saw patients before and after his lunch break and brisk walk, to late at night when he was again at his writing desk, smoke wisping from his ever-present cigar. In the years of success he arrived at sessions of the Vienna Psychoanalytic Society sporting a fur-lined, fur-collared coat, silk hat, and ivory-handled walking stick, as though to the manner born. A devoted husband and father of six children, he lived under the usual burden of money cares, which he cited often in his letters. Otto Rank, who knew him well, saw in his work "a justification for the social and moral standards of the middle class."[3]

The other Freudians followed suit in upholding the standard of the middle class that had allowed them to rise. Jung was born into the modest household of a Protestant minister and married rich; Adler and Rank worked themselves up from below; Janet was a secure member of the middle class; and Charcot came from the upper reaches of society but might be described from today's perspective as a liberal. All of them lived conventional middle-class lives; there was not a cutup among them. The ruination of the world they knew would take everything valuable from them and all others who had achieved middle-class status. Thus they warmly supported the new culture of the West or, as Freud liked to say, "civilization."

Likewise they accepted modernity as a great advance over the past. They were comfortable with its liberal politics, urban life, industry, science, and technology. The meritocracy of the new age was much to their taste. In former times they might never have been allowed into the professions or allowed the opportunity to rise socially. Contemplating these advantages, Freud, according to Erich Fromm, attained "an unquestioning belief" that the new age, "although by no means satisfactory, was the ultimate form of human progress, and could not be improved in any essential feature."[4]

While content with modernity, the Freudians, like Nordau, had little taste for modernism—that is, the art, design, and ideas of the new age.[5] Modernism was at once a reflection and critique of modernity, and the Freudians were not among the critics. They were quite happy with bourgeois style and taste—Renaissance painting and sculpture, through contemporary genre scenes; novels and poetry with recognizable themes; the arts of Greek and Roman antiquity. Freud did not care for music of any sort, but he attended the occasional opera; like Nordau, modern music of the time disturbed him. Herzl, another Viennese bourgeois, liked Wagner, which then was modern music; and once he attended a performance of *Tannhäuser* and found a mystery in the music and a theme of redemption that gave him a sense of the depths of emotion to which a leader must appeal. It was after this performance that he began to set down his ideas about a Jewish state. (The Freudians may not have favored modernism, but like Herzl they were influenced by it.)

For the Jewish Freudians, modernity was close to heaven. As Max Horkheimer observes: "We need only glance at the nineteenth century, to say nothing of earlier times, in order to see how the historical vicissitudes of the Jews made them dependent on a pluralist culture. Whenever such a culture was in danger, whenever injustice began to appear in Europe, the Jews were among the first victims."[6] Freud viewed modernity the way most assimilating Jews did: it was another name for freedom and the ability to achieve. He was inextricably linked to it, as, he had to believe, was the fate of his people. He might have seen that the defamation of the Jews in his time was aimed at modernity and was only another sign of social hysteria.

By lifting the ban of medieval anti-Semitism, modernity had performed a great work for Freud and his co-religionists. Yet the old threat persisted in its new form of cultural anti-Semitism. Freud knew anti-Semitism from his earliest years. He despised it in general and in particular for its effects on Jews like himself in the professions. He recalled a story his father told him. When the father was a boy, all dressed up one Saturday with a new cap on his head, he was walking along a street when suddenly a "Christian came up to me and with a single blow knocked off my cap into the mud and shouted: 'Jew! get off the pavement!'" And what did you do? his son asked. "I went into the roadway and picked up my cap"—thus sidestepping confrontation. Sigmund contrasted this unheroic response with one he liked better: "the scene in which Hannibal's father, Hamilcar Barca, made his boy swear before the household altar to take vengeance on the Romans. Ever since that time Hannibal has had a place in my phantasies."[7] Unlike his father, Freud was eager to fight back, if only in his fantasies.

When Freud entered the University of Vienna in 1873, "I was expected to feel myself inferior and an alien because I was a Jew." As a young man he was reviled on a train by a group of anti-Semites.[8] At university a fellow Jew was taunted into a duel by anti-Semitic remarks. During a summer stay in the Alps Freud's family was menaced by an anti-Semitic mob. Jews were routinely held back from the higher positions in Austria (including the university professorship that Freud desired) because advancement was not by merit alone but by approval of the emperor, to whom not being Catholic was mildly scandalous, Vienna being the second Catholic city after Rome. Freud's appointment came only when one of his patients, with influence at court, advanced his cause with the bribe of a painting.

Through hard experience Freud had learned to hate anti-Semitism as an affront no less to the Jews and Judaism than to common human dignity. It demeaned a whole class of people, his people, and he was outraged by it his whole life. If there was a European unconscious filled with evil, this was one of its prime contents; and it was not, of course, unconscious, except in the sense that many Europeans were its slaves and unaware of when it first appeared and how it grew into a cruel, false, but commanding belief. Valuing Judaism as a tradition if not a religion, Freud viewed anti-Semitism as dignity denied. Like many Europeans, he recognized its modern origins in medieval Christianity and folk beliefs. Though an atheist, he treasured the achievements of the Jews for what he loved most—civilization. Because of his Jewish pride, and the importance anti-Semitism assumed among the anti-moderns, fighting anti-Semitism was integral to the war Freud waged through psychoanalysis.

A partisan of the Napoleon who had liberated Europe from medievalism, Freud was a stout supporter of liberal democracy. He had "contempt for royalty and aristocracy," says Carl Schorske, a leading cultural historian of the Austrian fin de siècle. Throughout his life Freud maintained an "undying admiration for England" and "hostility to religion," the old cohort of feudalism. When at university he read W. E. H. Lecky's *History of the Rise and Influence of the Spirit of Rationalism,* on the recommendation of a friend, he said it gave him "revolutionary feelings" against Austrian autocracy. But Freud's revolutionary fervor stopped at liberal democracy. He was dedicated, in the words of Philip Rieff, "to authority and coercion against Marx or any other ideal of social perfection," being "unstirred by the large possibilities of altering the political order."[9]

As a young physician Freud placed a copy of the Declaration of Independence over his bed, probably the same one that graced a wall of his Berggasse 19 apartment in Vienna until he was expelled by the Nazis. One of his sisters recalls that he could recite Lincoln's Gettysburg Address from memory. Among his childhood idols were Hannibal, Brutus, and Cromwell, fighters against injustice and tyranny. In adolescence he admired the German political journalist Ludwig Boerne, whose collected works he received as a gift and retained to the end of his life. Like Freud, Boerne deplored aristocracy and looked to France as the seedbed of European freedom. He viewed Germany as one vast political ghetto controlled by the aristocracy and himself as a prophet of justice and freedom after his models, the biblical Prophets. Liberalism, Boerne believed, was the modern product of Judaism, and he dedicated himself to changing the oppressive politics of his country.

Freud's partisan political sympathies were with the local liberal democratic party, called in Vienna the Jewish party because so many of its middle-class adherents were of that faith. Like most liberal democrats, he was wary of the Social Democrats (the workers' party) and appalled by the anti-Semitic reactionary parties of the right. By "family background, conviction, and ethnic affiliation," Schorske points out, Freud "belonged to the group most threatened by the new forces" of left and right: Viennese liberal Jewry. He "watched with anxious interest the rise to power of the New Right both in Austria and abroad, especially in the France of the Dreyfus affair. Karl Lueger was his bête noire; Émile Zola, the novelist who championed Dreyfus, his political hero."[10]

The new forces of the fin de siècle were not merely political, as noted earlier. They were cultural in the broadest sense, ranging from stolid conservatives to wild radicals who were disgusted with the new age and wanted to dissolve it—a feeling echoed in many a European heart, not only on the right but on the socialist left. To the extremes, rationalistic liberalism at the center was the enemy, flabby and insincere, an evil to be extirpated. It did not seem to pose a *Thou shalt not!* Instead it seemed to say, Do anything you like! and was therefore accounted weak by the more "virile" nations still led by kings and emperors, and also by the many intellectuals, politicians, professionals, and businessmen in the lands of democracy who prized their middle-class status while recognizing the failings of a scientific, secular culture.

In 1898 Freud accidentally encountered a representative of the forces he despised in politics. On a summer evening, at a Vienna train station, he spied one of the leading conservative politicians of Austria, Count Thun, the minister president. The arrogant and imperious count, who strode to his train without presenting his ticket at the gate, was on his way to visit the emperor at the latter's summer residence in Ischl for discussions of thorny political matters. Freud was leaving on a summer holiday and just at that moment needed to urinate. Seeing the count, he distracted himself by insinuating his liberal political colors, whistling a melody from Mozart's *The Marriage of Figaro* whose words were "If the Count wants to dance, I'll call the tune." Freud was "in a combative mood" all that evening. "I had chaffed [sic] my waiter and my cabdriver" and "all kinds of insolent and revolutionary ideas were going through my head." He was eager to flee Vienna for any place the count was not, yet both were leaving the city for summer destinations for markedly different reasons—the count for serious political business, Freud for a holiday. The disparity in missions was not lost on Freud. Since Thun in German meant "to do," mocking journalists called the count *Nichtsthun*, "Count Do-Nothing," since he was having great difficulty in finding solutions to Austria's political dilemmas. "He [the count] was on the way to a difficult audience with the Emperor," Freud recalled thinking, "while *I* was the real Count Do-Nothing—just off on my holidays."[11]

Freud later dreamed about this encounter. In the dream the count delivers a bombastic speech which so upsets Freud that he strides away in anger. In the next scene Freud encounters an old man whom he assists in urinating by giving him a hospital urinal. Interpreting the dream, Freud reflected on the disrespect he showed by walking out on the count (and perhaps by the image of urinating, and perhaps by picturing him in the second scene as a decrepit patient—decrepit Austria—needing assistance to urinate; Freud's dream images in this case extended to his father's last illness, so that the old man in the dream might also be his father). Freud conflated these scenes with another in which as a young child he enters his parents' bedroom unannounced and urinates on the floor, to which his father angrily responds by shouting that the boy will never amount to anything. Writing of the dream, and adding the scene of domestic embarrassment, Freud concluded that "the whole rebellious content, with its *lèse-majesté* and its derision of the higher authorities, went back to rebellion against my father. A Prince is known as the father of his country; the father is the

oldest, first, and for children the only authority, and from his autocratic power the other social authorities have developed in the course
of the history of human civilization. . . ."[12]

Rebellion against authority was a theme Freud would repeat over
and over, as when in *Leonardo da Vinci and a Memory of Childhood*
(1910) he writes: "Psycho-analysis has made us familiar with the intimate connection between the father-complex and belief in God; it has
shown us that a personal God is, psychologically, nothing other than
an exalted father, and it brings us evidence every day of how young
people lose their religious beliefs as soon as their father's authority
breaks down."[13] This theme of the father authority figure haunted
Freud, his colleagues, and Europe for good reason. Rebellion against
the father represented rebellion against religion, the old ways, the old
family (Europe's course since 1800). It was the source of the society
and culture Freud knew and supported. In a harsh act of *lèse-majesté*,
liberal Europe was born by killing the father/Father/king, an essential
ingredient in the turmoil of the new age. Rebellion therefore entailed
political and moral ambiguities for Freud; the individual no less than
Europe ambivalently confronted a murder that overthrew many cherished standards and yet produced freedom.

In his dream Freud apparently feared that neither he nor Austria
would come to any good end—he the liberal democrat, Austria the autocratic state buckling under unbearable pressure but unwilling to
concede to liberal politics. Yet the dream-Freud mounts a passive challenge to the old politics by angrily leaving the scene of the count's
bombastic speech. In the actual encounter with the count, his challenge was by insinuation—whistling an insolent tune. Earlier he had
shown his political colors by crowding his head with revolutionary
ideas expressed rather inadequately by chafing a waiter and cabdriver.
If the encounter, the dream, and the commentary on the dream are to
be believed, Freud approached politics by indirection, aware that it
was one thing subtly to enact *lèse-majesté*, another to bring it out in
the open by direct action in word or deed, especially in Austria or any
of the other authoritarian nations of Europe. The count feels free to
bluster on in his haughty way, saying directly what he means; to someone not prepared to meet things head on, that style would have been
disturbing, and it may have contributed to the dream-Freud walking
away and embroidering his anger with images of urinating. Perhaps
Freud's father foretold this predilection for avoiding direct confrontation when he said: "My Sigmund's little toe is cleverer than my head,

but he would never dare to contradict me." Years later Freud told Jung that he often presented an outward demeanor of calm to hide his true feelings. His propensity to avoid direct confrontation (not his alone, we can believe) was not always evident in his professional relations. But it had a marked influence on the inspiration of psychoanalysis.[14]

In writing of another dream, Freud clearly drew the political lesson of indirection. A dreamer, he says, is in the position of a "political writer who has disagreeable truths to tell those in authority"; if the writer feels constrained not to speak out directly, he will "conceal his objectionable pronouncement beneath some apparently innocent disguise." Years later, asked what his politics were, Freud responded, "Politically I am just nothing," implying he was glad he had left politics behind for psychoanalysis. Freud, says the historian William M. Johnston, was an "arch-privatist [who] despaired of changing social or political conditions. . . ." Outwardly this is true, but through psychoanalysis Freud did try to change social and political conditions, or at least manage them in favor of the values he and his colleagues preferred. For this purpose he used arch-privatist means, linking everything to the individual and nothing to the society. And he did it in an arch-privatist way, by secrecy—or, as he says of the political writer who fears flaunting his true colors—by disguise. Thus Freud in his theories rarely spoke of the killing of kings but rather of killing the father; he spoke infrequently of history or politics but instead spoke volubly about psychoanalysis.[15]

An illustration of Freud's desire to act but not be seen doing so is provided in the Count Thun dream: *"I thought of a plan for remaining unrecognized; and then saw that this plan had already been put into effect. It was as though thinking and experiencing were one and the same thing."* This closeness between thinking and acting—as though the first were the substitute for, or the same as, the other—Freud later described as an attribute of both the primitive and the neurotic mind. It became perhaps the chief attribute of psychoanalysis, which Freud fashioned as disguised speech and which kept his purposes from being recognized. For psychoanalysis, as we shall see, was not about mental illness but about history and culture—about all those preferences for the modern, the middle class, the liberal that constituted the Freudians' caste of mind.[16]

While liberals all (except for the few socialists), the Freudians were at the same time elitists. This was not a contradiction. The middle class in general had an elitist attitude toward those below them. The Freudians believed like Plato in rule by the best, and like Aristotle that some people were born to rule while others were destined to follow. "It is just as impossible to do without control of the mass by a minority," Freud wrote, "as it is to dispense with coercion in the work of civilization." Just as the old nobility of Europe had viewed the common people as a rabble, a mob, so the new middle class saw them as human animals, without a thought for tomorrow or the ability to rule their passions; unintelligent and perhaps incapable of learning very much; a danger to order and stability, always potentially rebellious and willing to heed demagogues. To Herzl in 1896, "The folk is everywhere a great child, which one admittedly can educate. But this education would, even under the most favorable conditions, demand such enormous spans of time that we . . . can help ourselves long before in other fashion"—which is the same idea that struck the Freudians.[17]

When Gustave Le Bon published his study of mob psychology, *The Crowd*, in 1895, the pioneers would not have disagreed with his portrait of an irrational lower class like an unconscious that had to be dominated by reason (that is, the middle class). The people yearn for strong leaders, Le Bon assumed, and to be effective the leaders must understand the psychology of the mass mind and how to influence it. The masses, he advised, could understand only simple ideas and would adhere to them only through constant repetition (the same principles Hitler later adopted). Leaders did not have to be intelligent or original, according to Le Bon; what they needed was prestige, to which the mass responded. As political theory his ideas were typical of what middle-class intellectuals thought was needed in a modern republic: strong leadership psychologically managed, so that the people being controlled would always appear to be the sovereigns of the nation (and of their own minds). The Freudians carried middle-class elitism and Le Bon's ideas about influencing the mass mind over to their theories of psychoanalysis.

In all these ways—as modern, middle-class liberals, anti-anti-Semites, and elitists—the Freudians were children of their time, members in good standing of the culture of the new age. Perceiving threats to what they held dear, they prepared an offensive, a veritable war—of ideas—against the foes of modernity.

BORN May 6, 1856, the young Freud came to Vienna with his family in 1860, a country cousin from the backwaters of Freiberg, Moravia, then a part of the Austrian Empire. Like all the main urban centers of

Europe, Vienna was growing at a rapid pace. Industry, banking, and railroads had burgeoned, spawning a sizable middle class but one that was nevertheless small in relation to the total population, as everywhere else in Europe. The city teemed with peoples from throughout the empire, including a considerable population of Jews. Freud's father Jacob was a small tradesman who waxed successful enough in Vienna to send Sigmund to private schools, though life for the family was always hard. His mother Amalia was his father's third wife, the immediate family consisting of seven children including two stepbrothers in their twenties who were the age of Freud's young mother. The family acclimated itself well to city life, but Freud never forgot the time he spent frolicking in the forests and meadows around Freiberg, which he later accounted his golden years. His taste for the countryside was later expressed in the choice of a favorite summer place, Berchtesgaden in the Bavarian Alps. Love of the country was common then among intellectuals: Nietzsche spent much time in the Engadine, in the Swiss Alps, and Gustav Mahler summered in the lakeside country of Austria. All shared in the romantic sense of the great outdoors.

The Freud family's origins were among eastern European Jews. The father had begun as a follower of Hasidism but later turned to the Haskalah, the Jewish Enlightenment, following the ways of Reform Judaism pioneered by Moses Mendelssohn. The household celebrated the most important Jewish holidays and at the Passover Seder Jacob recited the service by heart. The family Bible was the popular German translation by Ludwig Philippson, accompanied by the Hebrew text and extensive commentaries of great sophistication. In one place Philippson draws attention to the similarities of myth and religion, noting that religion is revelation but myth is "fetish" and "representation."[18] A major lesson of Philippson was that freedom was achieved through law, and law had to be internalized as a self-imposed inner discipline. The Bible and home instruction from Jacob constituted Freud's early training in Judaism. But contrary to his later statements, his total religious training was extensive, in part because Austria required all students to take courses in their own faith from the first elementary grade right through secondary schooling. Piety was deemed the essential basis of morality and good citizenship by the political authorities and by the Catholic, Protestant, and Jewish clergy.

The formal education of someone like Freud, from a family striving to better their conditions, was in those days extraordinarily comprehensive in both secular and religious content. His elementary schooling took place at a private Jewish Volksshule, where besides the standard courses taught at all Austrian schools he received training in Hebrew language and grammar, the public worship service, the festivals, biblical history, and the laws and doctrines of Judaism. Here began his intensive study of the Pentateuch (the Torah, the Five Books of Moses), to which was added a smattering of the Talmud, the commentaries on the Old Testament. In 1865, graduating with honors in religion, Freud proceeded to his secondary school, the Leopoldstaedter Communalgymnasium, where he studied for the next eight years, during the so-called "liberal era" in Austria when anti-Semitism was at low ebb. At the Leopoldstaedter he mastered Greek and Latin, reading Xenophon, Homer, Sophocles, Plato, Cicero, Tacitus, Virgil, and Horace in the original. He took required courses in the history of the Phoenicians, Babylonians, Medes, Assyrians, Indians, Persians, and Egyptians, and studied their religions and mythologies. He also learned about the geography and cultures of the Far East and Africa. His European history courses covered the Middle Ages to the Peace of Westphalia and modern times from the Reformation to the Congress of Vienna in 1815. Among other subjects, he studied the psychology of the unconscious propounded by one of Austria's favorite philosophers, the German Johann Herbart, who, with Schopenhauer, made a strong argument for the existence of an unconscious mind.

Each student had to continue with instruction in his own religion, and Freud's Jewish studies at the Leopoldstaedter looked deeper into the Pentateuch and added the Prophets and the other books of the Old Testament while continuing with Hebrew language and grammar and Jewish history. The textbook for Jewish studies was by Leopold Breuer, the father of Josef Breuer, who was to be Freud's early colleague in neurology and psychoanalysis. Its first half covered the doctrines and duties of Judaism, the attributes of God, the Ten Commandments, the festivals and prayers, and the Mosaic Law. The root ideas of Judaism, according to Breuer's text, were universal, the hopes of the Prophets expressing the longings of all mankind. Faith in God was innate but in primitive peoples rose only to the level of superstition and childish ideas. When reason developed, it understood a religion of reason, to which revelation added an inner consciousness of the laws of morality created by a Higher Being. Moses gave to the people of Israel a revelation of God that remained valid for all time. Nothing happened in the world that God did not allow to happen. Israel was the witness and preserver of God's revelation to humanity, and the time would come when this revelation would be acknowledged by all as the truth, and God would be worshiped universally. In the Messianic Age, good and evil would receive their just desserts. (These ideas powerfully parallel psychoanalysis.)

The second half of Breuer's textbook explicated the moral and civil aspects of the Mosaic Law, grounded in the Ten Commandments. Religious duties were owed to God, neighbors, and oneself. Personal duties included cultivation of talents, self-respect, autonomy, and the bourgeois virtues of thrift and cleanliness. The civil law of Moses demanded that Jews be good citizens of the state, which was the creation of human reason and sanctified by God (an exact parallel to Hegel), and that they love the fatherland, respect its leaders, and obey its laws. From Freud's favorite teacher of Judaism, Samuel Hammerschlag, the student learned that the Enlightenment ideals of freedom and human rights were the civil application of the Prophets' teachings. Because the nineteenth century was the era of "intellectual absolutism," when rationalism reigned supreme, said Hammerschlag, religion was needed more than ever. In recognition of the blow that the Enlightenment had struck at religion, Adolf Jellinek, the chief rabbi of Viennese Reform Judaism from 1865 to 1893, similarly advocated the continuing relevance of Jewish ethics in the modern age: "Thus is Jewry called to build on the wreckage of religion its third temple of that true religion, which hallows and sanctifies the aspirations of modern society, which brings to sick and disoriented humanity healing and recovery, peace and reconciliation."[19] These views were rather conventional examples of what the Austrian authorities meant by the value of religious piety for good citizenship. Their relevance for the theories of psychoanalysis cannot be overemphasized.

Freud could not help knowing something of Catholicism too, living in a Catholic country, attending a secondary school with heavy Catholic influence, and learning much about Christianity from his history classes. He had a further Catholic influence from his early years—his Freiberg nanny, who on the occasional Sunday would take her little charge to church. Sigmund would return with tales of sweet incense, gorgeous priestly robes, and the ritual of the mass. His mother recalled that on such occasions "he preached and told us all about God Almighty."[20] Freud did not forget the messages of the church he learned then and later. In his dream book he recorded how gaslights at a train station called to mind souls burning in hell, a very Christian, un-Jewish image. Like many Austrian Jews, he was entranced by the panoply of the church and knew of the power it had wielded in the past, which it retained in some measure. After Jacob's death, Freud's mother Amalia celebrated Christmas and the New Year like most Austrians, and in Freud's home Easter was a holiday for the children. From the time of his first writings in the 1880s and 1890s right through the rest of his career, the majority of religious references are Christian rather than Jewish. In contrast, Freud's letters are peppered with Old Testament references.

It was no mystery to Freud, his colleagues, and other European intellectuals that the religion they were taught had lost meaning in the new age. This is why they were almost universally agnostics first, then atheists. The Enlightenment had taken the path of deism in religion, and now even deism's God as First Cause and Great Engineer of the Universe was waning. Yet intellectuals retained a distinct feeling for what they had rejected, and like Saint-Simon, Comte, and Hegel, they found that atheism was not enough; a belief in *something* had to replace the old religion (often a belief in rationalism, positivism, and science). Religion could not be reformed, Freud told his fiancée; it needed a revolution. But he assured her that "something of the core, of the essence of this meaningful and life-affirming Judaism, will not be absent from our home." In a 1923 letter to B'nai B'rith he wrote of Judaism's "many dark emotional powers, all the stronger the less they could be expressed in words. . . ."[21] When Freud, by hidden means, revived the traditional core of the old beliefs, it evinced strong emotional power.

It will not yet be clear to the reader, but if all that influenced Freud's ideas were his religious instruction, the plight of religion in his day, the Enlightenment solution of a deistic universe functioning by rational laws, the nineteenth-century drive to fashion secular religions, and his knowledge and experience of history, that would have been enough to create the main principles of psychoanalysis. Reuben Rainey, to whom I am indebted for much of this background on Freud's education, notes that one of Freud's favorite books, Gotthold von Lessing's *The Education of the Human Being,* maintained that over the span of history religion evolves into rational forms. This, says Rainey, was the antithesis of Freud's "mature attitude" against religion. To the contrary, the drive to create a "rational religion," so much on the mind of nineteenth-century intellectuals, was fulfilled by the Freudians.[22]

Graduating first in his class, Freud entered the University of Vienna in 1873 with the vague idea of studying law as the road to a political career. "Under the influence of a school friendship with a boy rather my senior who grew up to be a well-known politician," he recalled, "I developed a wish to study law like him and to engage in social activities."[23] In the first flush of Austrian liberalism it was just possible for a Jew to aspire to the position of a minister of state. He began by studying philosophy but soon switched to medicine, eventually concentrating on neurology and neuroanatomy, with a few courses in psychology. He shone in neuroanatomy and very likely would have had a brilliant career in that field.

For five years Freud was a member of a lively student organization called the Leseverein der Deutschen Studenten. It sponsored lectures on art history, philosophy, and the history of religion; held poetry readings; staged debates on political, philosophical, and artistic subjects, including Nietzsche, Wagner, and Schopenhauer; and maintained a library of 2,800 volumes on the natural sciences and the humanities. Members were invited to prepare papers for presentation to the group, and the best were honored by publication. Among them in Freud's time were S. Lipiner's "Concerning the Elements of a Renewal of Religious Ideas in the Present" (a topic close to his later theories) and L. Reinische's "The History of the Origin and Development of the Egyptian Hierarchy and the Development of the Teaching of the Oneness of God (Monotheism)." Freud also belonged to a student fraternity whose interests included the further democratization of the country. He once had the opportunity to debate his fellow student, Victor Adler, and decided not to argue ideas but to vilify his opponent so fiercely that he was criticized for his poor conduct. His tendency toward vilification, not unlike Nordau's, remained a characteristic of Freud's that would be subsumed in the medicalism of psychoanalysis.

Among the topics discussed by students at the time was Eduard Von Hartmann's *The Philosophy of the Unconscious* (1868). Hartmann, a retired artillery officer, in an effort to reconcile Hegel and Schopenhauer, had concluded that there were no terrestrial solutions to the problems of the human race. The pagans sought happiness in life, the Christians sought it in the afterlife. These were illusions. The only way out was mass suicide, by which Spirit would conquer Will. Hartmann was an example of the cultural fever that was starting to burn in Austria—and farther afield, in Europe.

By the end of his first year at university Freud had read, among many other authors, Darwin, David Strauss on the historicity of Jesus and the mythic nature of the Gospels, and Feuerbach on the debunking of Christianity. Throughout his school years and into old age he devoured the classics of Goethe, Heine, Schiller, and Shakespeare, as well as Dostoevsky and other contemporary novelists and thinkers, while also showing interest in the detective stories of Edgar Allan Poe and Arthur Conan Doyle. He retained a lifelong interest in archaeology and ancient history, and kept up with the major excavations in Troy, Rome, and Pompeii, encouraged by his friend Emmanuel Loewy, professor of archaeology in Rome and Vienna. On trips to Italy and Greece he visited ancient sites; at the Acropolis, as tourists will, he expressed his wonder at being in the actual presence of so grand a monument. "A feeling of astonishment mingled with my joy," he remembered. "It seemed to say, 'So it really *is* true, just as we learnt at school.' "[24] He was also a great museumgoer, seeking out ancient treasures and the Renaissance painting and sculpture he admired, including works by Michelangelo, Raphael, and Titian. Later he assembled his own small collection of antiquities, which he kept on his desk until it grew too large. The nineteenth century was a great epoch for rediscovering the history and artifacts of the past, an activity in which Freud, his colleagues, and many other Europeans maintained a lively interest.

These interests, too—from philosophy and science to literature, the arts, archaeology, and history—followed Freud into psychoanalysis. His education and background contained very little that was unique, novel, or original. It was duplicated, with local variations, by most of the other Freudians in Austria and elsewhere in Europe. His religious education may have been more thorough than that of others, and that may be one of many reasons why he became *Freud*. Unremarkable for the most part, the attributes of the Freudians became significant only when the pioneers applied them to the creation of their psychological system and turned their practice into cultural therapy.

SEVEN

In the Shadow of Decline: Freud's Miraculous Years

... The city of Vienna ... was the place above all
others whose inhabitants lived a life of inconsistencies
and false appearances. ... Vienna in decline is like a
cracked mirror that cannot reflect a true image and
therefore appears fragmented and inconsistent.
—Billa Zanuso, *The Young Freud*

... I am in the full swing of discovery.
—Sigmund Freud, Letter to Fliess

AUSTRIA in the last decades of the nineteenth century could not fail
to encourage the development of a specialty such as cultural physician.
Unprecedented social chaos and a sense of imminent doom were countered by vain attempts at salvation. By the time Freud graduated university in 1881, Austria had already begun to abandon its experiment
in liberalism in favor of more autocratic rule, out of nostalgia for a
glorious past and in an effort to hold the empire together. Austria's
glory days had lasted for centuries as the seat of the Holy Roman Empire. With Spain and Bavaria it had been the shield of the church in
the Protestant Reformation. In 1683 it joined with Poland to defeat
the Ottoman Turks at the gates of Vienna. Later it tried to "save" Europe from the virus of Napoleon and the "atheistic" French Revolution, then tried to extend the life of monarchy by backing reaction at
home and abroad. Now it could not save itself as it labored under a
burden of being the "United States of Europe," so called because it
contained so many nationalities, most of them, in varying degrees, hating the German Austrians and hating each other.

Because the country seemed under a warrant of doom, everything that affected Europe appeared in Austria in technicolor. Dancing at the precipice, Austrians referred to the fin de siècle, with grim humor, as the Gay Apocalypse. The outward gaiety of this land of waltzes and whipped cream was counterpointed by secrecy, social repression, and unprecedented political turmoil overseen by a forbidding bureaucracy ruled by a superannuated emperor, Franz Joseph, who had come to power in 1848. Franz Joseph was the paradigm of an elderly father-king, strict and upright in all outward appearance, living dutifully by the severe court etiquette of sixteenth-century Spain. He maintained rather officious relations with his paramour, an opera singer, while his wife, a Bavarian princess who could not stand him, spent much of her time traveling in Europe. (She was assassinated in Switzerland by an anarchist protesting autocracy.) It was easy to see in this stiff, aged figure a father, emperor, and God rolled into one, because the Habsburg monarchy had centered for a thousand years on a single family dynasty and its scion, the ruler. Nowhere else in Europe was this singularity more pronounced.

A typical commentary on what is often called Freud's Vienna is offered by Robert C. Solomon:

> Nietzsche's indictment of the age as "decadent" applied to nowhere better than to Vienna at the turn of the century, in the last days of the seemingly eternal Habsburg Empire, a time which Karl Kraus sarcastically referred to as "the last days of humanity." Under the reign of Mayor "Handsome Karl" Lueger and the emperor Franz Joseph, anti-Semitism, universal hypocrisy, and conservative conformism, coupled with the revolt of ethnic and moral minorities, financial crises, and internal instability imposed an inescapable prognosis of doom. The metaphor of the age was that of the "dark side" of brilliance, the golden surface ornament as a façade for anguish, alienation, neurosis, and despair. It was a period and place that has come to define what we now identify as decadence, a way of life that was effete, elegant, lavish, fanciful, and on the brink of total disaster.

The ruling class, according to Zevedei Barbu, strove "not to know the real problems of their state and society in order to solve them, but to deflect them, to deceive the reality which was unmanageable and fearful. . . ."[1]

Karl Kraus, the brightest of Viennese polemicists, accused the Austrians of masking reality with ornament. *Wittgenstein's Vienna* records that "In Habsburg society as a whole, artificiality and pretense were by now the rule rather than the exception, and in every aspect of life the proper appearances and adornments were all that mattered." Many intellectuals, according to William Johnston, took flight in nostalgia, spectacle, the countryside, minutiae. Seeing little hope of positive change, they "withdrew into the arts and sciences. . . ." Johann Nestroy, a popular Viennese playwright earlier in the century—"our Nestroy," Freud liked to call him—gave voice to the Austrian suspicion of change and activism in a *bon mot* that has been heard in many other times and climes: "Progress is characterized by the fact that it appears much greater than it really is."[2]

As earlier noted, at the beginning of the nineteenth century Hegel and Schopenhauer were among the philosophers who presented visions of salvation for Europe. Hegel proposed the nation-state as the key to managing and controlling the passions let loose by the twin revolutions. Schopenhauer urged, like religious mystics before him, individual restraint on desire. They were followed by innumerable philosophical and political proposals until, by the end of the century, manifestos rained down like confetti. In Freud's Vienna avoidance of reality was matched to a salvational strain that, fired by its history, the influence of Gospel teachings, and the fever of decay, was at once practical and unbridled, if often highly theoretical. Proposals abounded for reshaping the Austrian Empire, the economy, politics, religion, law, art, science, medicine, and philosophy.

One of the strangest efforts was by an acquaintance of Freud, the young university graduate Otto Weininger, a renegade Jewish intellectual heavily influenced by Schopenhauer and Hartmann. His book *Sex and Character* (1903) proposed the wisdom of staying away from women and Jews, defilers of the spirit. The end result of avoiding women would be the end of the human race, to which Weininger, like Hartmann, looked forward with equanimity. Humanity meant nothing, he thought, in the eye of the universe, and humanity's end would mark the end of Evil. Six months after his outrageous book was published, he ended his life with a revolver on his chosen ground, the house of Beethoven—suicide being much in fashion then, presumably as a protest and response to angst and disgust. Weininger was a gauge of the fever of the times, but it must be added that suicide was a style among the better classes, some of it caused by the society's rejection of homosexuality (brothers of the philosopher Ludwig Wittgenstein killed themselves apparently for this reason).

"During the last five years of the nineteenth century," Schorske records, "Austria-Hungary [then the name of the empire] seemed to be serving, as one of its poets observed, as 'a little world in which the big one holds its tryouts'—tryouts for Europe's social and political disintegration."[3] In those years, when all of Europe was in the cultural crisis of the fin de siècle, social turmoil in Austria was at its highest pitch until the nation was dissolved after World War I. In 1895 the Liberal party was wiped out at the polls after Lueger called for a united anti-Semitic front among the conservative forces; the extremes, the socialists and proto-fascists, were left to face each other. In that same year ethnic riots erupted throughout Austria, with crowds shouting "Death to the Jews," "Down with the Czechs," "Down with the Slovenes" (and with the Czechs and Slovenes shouting "Down with the Germans"—the Austrian Germans). To Freud these crowds seemed the unconscious in action; he had never thought before, he said, to see it embodied before his eyes in social phenomena. Rioting continued through 1896, prompting the emperor in 1897 to attempt calming the political waters by appointing a minister who wished to allow greater autonomy to the non-German nationalities in the empire. That set off the greatest wave of rioting ever seen in Austria.

When Mark Twain visited Vienna in 1897 he found conditions that "would set any country but Austria on fire from end to end." In the parliament he discovered that "when that House is legislating you can't tell it from an artillery practice." The newly elected Mayor Lueger was greeted in 1897 by surging mobs shouting "Dr. Lueger shall rule, and the Jews shall be destroyed." Lueger was now hailed as King of the Anti-Semites and Führer. Amidst this hysterical slide to the right, Georg von Schoenerer formed his anti-Semitic, proto-fascist German Peoples party, with a plank calling for Austrian incorporation into Germany and German domination of Europe. The next year saw further rioting between Czechs and Germans, the paralysis and adjournment of the parliament over the question of minority rights, and renewed anti-Semitic attacks in outlying provinces.[4] Austria was cascading into chaos, like a creaky raft torn to bits in a mighty storm.

Farther afield, 1895 was the year Roentgen discovered the x-ray, an encouragement to anyone hoping to see beyond the surface of things. Foucault notes that Freud's 1897 discovery of the Oedipus complex was contemporary with laws in France and other countries weakening parental authority.[5] European parliaments in the same period were agitating for the official separation of church and state, another salvo at traditional sources of authority. And in 1897

Durkheim's *Suicide* was published, with its exploration of the alienated modern condition. That same year saw continuing pogroms in
Russia and a downturn in the fortunes of Dreyfus, and in the next
years there were pogroms and trials of Jews for "ritual murder" in Bo-
hemia. Havelock Ellis published *The Psychology of Sex* in 1897, an
encouragement to anyone exploring the powers of sex, and in that
year the term "psychotherapy" came into public circulation with the
meaning it retains today. It was also the year the romantic, somewhat
proto-fascist youth movement, the Wandervogel, was formed, and the
year Herzl founded the Zionist movement.

AMIDST this turmoil, Freud was enjoying an exhilarating sense of accomplishment. In 1895 he published with Breuer *Studies on Hysteria,*
demonstrating to the authors' satisfaction that a talking treatment (as
opposed to more interventionist medical methods) could cure mental
illness. Among the cases they reported was that of a young woman
whom Breuer had treated in the early 1880s, "Anna O." (real name,
Bertha Pappenheim), which was to become celebrated as the first talking cure (though Janet had published the first such case, "Lucie," in
1886). In this same year Freud for the first time interpreted a dream
(one of his own) and drafted (but never published) his "Project for a
Scientific Psychology," proposing that mental traumas were converted
into mental illness through the diversion of chemicals in the body.
Trained as a neurologist, he was finding that psychology was becoming his "consuming passion" and "tyrant." Always a "distant, beck-
oning goal," it was now, "since I have come upon the problem of the
neuroses," drawing "so much nearer." He urged his Berlin friend and
medical colleague, Wilhelm Fliess, to explain the biology of the sexual
etiology of neurosis (which they were both working on): "Then I will
pay my proper respects to your discovery. You would be the strongest
of men, holding in your hands the reins of sexuality, which governs all
mankind: you could do anything and prevent anything."[6]

In the next year Freud's father died, setting off his self-analysis, for
which he coined the term *psychoanalysis*. He was intensively occupied
with understanding hysteria; like Charcot and others, he believed it
was a mental disease. He was coming to think, like Schopenhauer, that
mental illness was caused by an idea or experience that caused fright,
leading to repression, which in turn led to neurotic symptoms. He was
convinced that the repressed idea had to do with sex, and in this year,
1896, he presented his conclusion to the Vienna Society for Psychia-

try and Neurology: hysteria had its source in early sexual experiences. This was, he claimed, "the solution to a more-than-thousand-year-old mystery," equal to discovering the *"caput Nili,"* the source of the Nile. But his finding was greeted by a famous retort from the leading neuropsychiatrist in Vienna, Richard Krafft-Ebing, who said, according to Freud's report, "It sounds like a scientific fairy tale."[7]

Like many other psychologists of the period, Freud did not support his conclusions with experimental data, measurements, calculations, or statistics of any sort. He simply had the general impression that *"everything* is as I surmise it to be and thus that everything will be clarified." For evidence he relied on what he believed his patients told him, even though many physicians of the period warned that such information was influenced, even directed, by suggestions from the doctor. As he theorized, he found that his own physical or psychic pains were an inducement to fresh thought. "I was suffering that degree of pain which brings the optimal condition for my mental activities. . . ." He was much concerned at this point with the way neurosis displaced attention "onto something else that was going on at the same time," and how hysteria was often replaced "by a later obsessional neurosis."[8] These insights were prescient for the formulation of psychoanalysis.

Working at fever pitch, he was coming around to the idea that psychology for him was only a means and not an end. "As a young man I knew no longing other than for philosophical knowledge and now I am about to fulfill it as I move from medicine to psychology. I became a therapist against my will. . . ." He had already told Fliess in 1894 that "Unfortunately, I am not a doctor." A few years later he would assert that he was "actually not at all a man of science, not an observer, not an experimenter, not a thinker. I am by temperament nothing but a conquistador—an adventurer, if you want it translated, with all the curiosity, daring, and tenacity characteristic of a man of this sort."[9]

Early in 1897, at the height of Austrian and European turmoil, Freud assured Fliess that "We shall not be shipwrecked . . . ; if we do not prematurely capsize, if our constitutions can stand it, we shall arrive." To emphasize the point he added, *"Nous y arriverons."* In this same letter of January 3 he exulted *"Habemus papem!"* in the belief that his interpretations were proving clinically valid (even though at this point he believed that sexual abuse was the cause of neurosis and all his interpretations grew from that idea, which he later dropped).

In his next letter he told Fliess he was making remarkable progress. Soon after, he recognized that he was traveling the same road as "the medieval theory of possession held by ecclesiastical courts," rediscovering, he said, "what was published a hundred times over, though several centuries ago."[10] He had decided that those accused as witches were in fact unrecognized hysterics; it was not their accusers who were hysterical.

In September 1897, amidst fresh outbursts of anti-Semitism in Austria and elsewhere in Europe, Freud joined the local chapter of B'nai B'rith, no doubt to express solidarity with his co-religionists. In October he announced to Fliess his crowning theory of the sexual etiology of hysteria, the Oedipus complex, and in November and December he was feeling elated, "as if I had succeeded in something important." He was forming ideas in a state of "euphoria" and had in mind "my high school hero worship of the Semitic Hannibal." He was thinking that myths were "endopsychic," representing inner psychic life projected onto the outer world, "into the future and beyond." Was this a crazy idea? he wondered. Was he developing a theory of "psychomythology" rather than a theory of neurosis?[11] Again he was prescient about the latent meaning and function of psychoanalysis.

By 1897 he was composing *The Interpretation of Dreams* (published in November 1899 but in honor of the new century dated 1900), and when it was near completion he assured Fliess that he would see it published even if Austria should "perish in the next two weeks." His next project, he reported, would bear the title *Sexual Theory and Anxiety*—more than prescient, for this was to be the theme of his life's work: pleasure and the anxiety encountered in getting it. He also told Fliess that "Vienna and the conditions here are almost physically repulsive to me" (which he assigned to growing old and nervous). The miraculous years drew to a close with Freud's plaintive cry, "I hate Vienna almost personally. . . ." The fear that troubled him most in this period, he told his friend, was poverty, which produced an anxiety in him that he could not conquer.[12]

Quickly, from 1897 to 1901, Freud made clear that he was developing psychological principles that concerned not only mental disease. In agreement with the majority of psychologists at the time, he maintained that the theory of the abnormal was also a theory of the normal (an idea derived from Schopenhauer's explanation that the quite normal unconscious was at work twenty-four hours a day plotting to achieve its goals through deception, cheating, lying, jokes, or any other means). Théodore Flournoy, a French psychologist, took a similar view of unconscious functioning in the psyche. Nordau gave another version of this same thought when he said that "one and the same [mental] state may very well be at one time disease and at another health."[13] Their theories, they were saying, were not just for the mentally ill; they were for everyone, a view that made the potential audience for the consumption and influence of psychoanalysis illimitable.

Freud was by now squarely in the ranks of the mind doctors, whose number and prestige had been growing throughout the nineteenth century. As a consequence of several key factors, Europe had become psychological. In part this was through philosophers of the seventeenth century forward ("The world is my idea"); in part through the emphasis on the individual and interiority; and in part through democracy, which could not rule solely through external authority (nor had the medieval world been able to do so) but needed a subtle authority based chiefly internally, in the psyche of the modern citizen. Modern political, social, and economic theory emphasizing the individual made it urgent to know in more detail about him and his psychic health, and this function was assigned primarily to the mind doctors. Accelerating their thinking was the widespread recognition of the disease they identified as hysteria, whose causes and symptoms were hotly debated against the background of a culture that had itself become hysterical. Better answers were needed to the riddles of the individual and of hysteria. At the same time it had become urgent to know how to sway the unruly masses on whom social order depended—the theme of Le Bon and many others. Because Europe had become psychological, the mind doctors were strategically placed to have a major effect on the European mind if the way could be found.

Perhaps it does not need emphasizing that in the larger cultural issues at stake in Europe, Austria was not very different from the rest of the continent. Aware of its glistening achievements, Europe nonetheless felt it was falling apart. The ground was fertile for a redemptive message. Viewing the social catastrophe while experiencing the personal catastrophe of professional neglect and rejection, Freud had every motive to respond. His elation in the Austrian fin de siècle was evidence that he had taken up the challenge.

Part III

FINDING A CURE

. . . Between the old world of things as they used to be,
and the new world of things as they would be instead,
there has always fallen a sort of passage time, a chaos
of unformed possibility in which all sorts of
manifestations could be witnessed.
—John Crowley, *Love and Sleep*

And always, whenever an old life changes into a new
one . . . there was a belief on the part of those
who lived that new life that they were more rational,
less prone to the hysterias and superstitions
which marked the old one.
—Eavan Boland, "When the Spirit Moves"

Freud was not a great healer. He was a great symbolist.
—Philip Rieff, *Freud: The Mind of the Moralist*

EIGHT

A Climate of Ideas

Politics is magic. He who knows how to summon the
forces from the deep, him will they follow.
    —Hugo von Hofmannsthal, "Buch der Freunde"

All humanity, including the clerks, have become
laymen.
    —Julien Benda, *The Treason of the Intellectuals*

THE MIX OF IDEAS in psychoanalysis included elements drawn
from the politicians, intellectuals, artists, writers, sociologists, anthropologists, ethnologists, mythologists, and philosophers of the day.
Added to these influences, for Freud, were cocaine and his Berlin
friend Wilhelm Fliess.

The radical politics practiced in Austria by such figures as
Schoenerer and Lueger was labeled by Carl Schorske "politics in the
new key" and "the politics of phantasy." The historian William J.
McGrath calls it "psychopolitics," and Freud, "the politics of psychosynthesis." The psychopoliticians, says Schorske, were "political
artists" who "expressed a rebellion against reason"; they transcended
"the purely political" by constructing "ideological collages . . . made
of fragments of modernity, glimpses of futurity, and resurrected rem-
nants of a half-forgotten past." To Viennese liberals "these ideological mosaics were mystifying and repulsive." To Freud, those who led
the people in this manner were "a dangerous breed . . . robbers in the
underground of the unconscious world . . . the sharpest opponents of
my scientific work." What he especially disliked about them was that
they specialized "in the realization of dreams." "I deal in psychoanalysis," he said, "they deal in psychosynthesis." He had "the modest profession to simplify dreams, to make them clear and ordinary.

They . . . command the world. . . ."[1] The irony of this complaint is evidenced in the theories and practices of psychoanalysis. Despite his criticism, Freud adopted the collage technique of the psychopoliticians. Like them he blended past, present, and future. And his goal would have had to be as immodest as theirs—dominating the European mind.

Among the psychopoliticians was, perhaps surprisingly, Theodor Herzl, who observed in a diary entry: "Believe me, the politics of an entire people . . . can only be made with imponderables which shimmer high in the air. . . . Do you know how the German empire was made? Out of dreams, songs, phantasies, and black-red-gold ribbon—and in a short time. Bismarck only shook down the fruit of the tree which the masters of phantasy had planted." Gratefully reaping the rewards of fantasy, Herzl "saw and listened as my legend grew. The people are sentimental; the masses do not see clearly. A light haze is beginning to well up around me which will perhaps be the cloud on which I shall go forward. It is perhaps the most interesting thing that I record in these diaries: how my legend grows."[2]

Like Schoenerer and Lueger, Schorske writes, Herzl tapped "the well-springs of a deferential past to satisfy the yearnings for a communitarian future. That he should have espoused the politics of the new key in order to save the Jews from its consequences in the gentile world does not destroy Herzl's affinity with his antagonists." Herzl was aware that liberal culture might satisfy the mind but, in Schorske's words, it "starved the souls of populations still cherishing the memory of a pre-rational social order." When asked by Herzl's son Hans whether to follow in his father's footsteps, Freud warned against the psychopoliticians: "Stay away from them, young man. . . . Stay away even if one of them was your father . . . perhaps because of that." Avner Falk notes: "It is clear that Freud is talking about himself no less than about Hans Herzl."[3] It is also clear that Freud did not take his own advice.

Herzl was an instructive liberal intellectual of his time who, because he was "committed to liberal culture, began to seek new foundations to save its most cherished values."[4] Having watched the apparent decay of liberalism, he first conceived himself as its savior and then swerved toward saving his people, whom he would lead to a new land and there implant the true liberalism that Europe could not support. Like Lueger and Schoenerer, Herzl was an aristocratic messiah, content to believe that leadership from above would weld together those below.

The daughters of Freud and Herzl were good friends, but Freud hardly knew the man (though he would have read his work in the *Neue Freie Presse*). Before ever actually seeing him, he had a dream in which Herzl appeared with a haggard, doom-ridden face and told him in the most dramatic terms about the coming catastrophe of the Jews of Europe. When Freud finally saw him on a tram, he noted that Herzl's face was as he had imagined it in his dream. Freud at that time had no sympathy for Zionism because he feared it would reawaken religious belief among the assimilating Jews of Europe. But he also disliked Herzl's activism, being more comfortable with ideas rather than action, perhaps in the spirit of Herzl's dictum, "Dream is not so different from deed as many believe."[5] To present a vision might be as powerful as leading an army.

According to Schorske, Freud's psychological crisis at the time of his father's death in 1896—when he began his self-analysis—was to "affirm the primacy of politics by removing what was rotten in the state of Denmark (a civic task) or to neutralize politics by reducing it to a psychological category (an intellectual task)."[6] Freud resolved this crisis by rejecting the either/or choice. He affirmed the primacy of politics by projecting it in psychological theories. That was his intellectual task. Its function was to remove, insofar as it could, what he viewed as rotten in the politics of the day—the accumulated resistance and hysterical reaction to the new age. That was his civic task. The civic task was accomplished through the intellectual task.

SURROUNDING the European elites in the fin de siècle was a class of intellectuals later called "the clerks" by the French philosopher Julien Benda. They had taken the place of the clerics (*clercs* in French) who had formerly been the guardians of the spiritual, according to Benda. He wrote about them in a famous book, *La Trahison des Clercs (The Treason of the Intellectuals)* (1927), that has never been forgotten, so keenly did it define the modern temperament. Their treason, Benda said, so much in contrast with intellectuals of the past, lay in discarding the spiritual for the worldly. Nietzsche was a modern clerk in Benda's opinion, and so were Charles Maurras, the French neoroyalist, and Charles Péguy, the left-wing French poet and activist, and Georges Sorel, the philosopher of violence, and the proto-fascist Julius

Langbehn, and Karl Marx, and William James. Such clerks could be found throughout Europe and America, of every political stripe, their chief role, according to Benda, being ideological publicists for the political interests they backed.[7] Little was more consequential for the inspiration and formulation of psychoanalysis than the intellectual clerks. Most of their attitudes were reflected in Freudian theories and practices.

"At the end of the nineteenth century . . . the clerks began to play the game of political passions," Benda records. These political passions, "ready to obey on command," were found even in those "who belong to the so-called liberal professions . . . men of letters and artists, scholars, philosophers, 'ministers' of the divine." The clerk brought to his opinions "the tremendous influence of his sensibility if he is an artist, of his persuasive power if he is a thinker, and in either case his moral prestige." The social class or "race" or nation to which the clerk belonged "was now frankly God." They preached that "the state should be strong and care nothing about being just. . . ." They admired vehemence, hatred, goals, excess, fixed ideas; and they scorned reasoned argument. "Today the clerk has made himself Minister of War." Among their conspicuous characteristics was "an affectation of the political feelings of the aristocracy . . . [and] a cult for the past. . . ."[8] The clerks were thus disguised political operatives. Like many others in the new culture, they retained a feeling for the sentiments of the past. On both these counts the Freudians followed suit.

Like the new culture of the West, most of the clerks were atheists, pragmatists, realists, and materialists who exalted the practical side of existence. They were the "spiritual militia of the material" for whom "the practical is the divine" and "'atheism' consists less in denying God than in shifting Him to man and political work." This *divinizing of politics,*" said Benda, this "displacing of the transcendental," was "the secret of [their] great influence." They worshiped at the altar of "concrete advantages and material power," avowing a morality of realism and circumstances. The clerk bestowed a "mystic personality on the association of which he feels himself a member, and gives it a religious adoration which is simply the deification of his own passion." "From his loftiest pulpit the modern clerk assures man that he is great in proportion as he is practical" and that justice, love and charity are "'metaphysical fogs.'"[9]

In battling for interests, the clerks took a sophistical attitude toward truth, content to view it as poetic, without the need for it to be factual. "The writer of history," announced Theodor Mommsen, a seminal historian of the German school, "is perhaps closer to the artist than to the scholar." Another German historian, Heinrich von Trei- tschke, an avowed racist and anti-Semite, deplored "that anemic ob- jectivity which is contrary to historical sense." According to Fritz Stern, the reactionary Langbehn held the view that "Historians should not only be subjective but also patriotic and 'racial.' " Ecksteins points out that this thinking led to a tendency, especially among German in- tellectuals, "to seek for answers to man's problems not in the outside world but in one's imagination," truth being "more a matter of intu- ition than of rational analysis."[10] Bergson furthered this attitude with his praise of intuition as the source of the most valuable knowledge. Freud too looked for solutions within, largely ignoring the social world (at least according to his own testimony). And he did so mainly by an intuitive grasp of what he had learned and experienced. He trusted his intuition above all sources of knowledge, and was followed in this by his disciples.

In the view of the clerks, said Benda, "to accept an error which is of service to them (the 'myth') is an undertaking which does them honor, while it is shameful to admit a truth which harms them." The novelist Maurice Barrès thought it proper to maintain "necessary prej- udices," and Péguy admired philosophies to the extent that "they are good fighters." To allow oneself "to be guided by the desire for truth alone, apart from any concern with the demands of society, is merely a 'savage and brutal' activity, which 'dishonors the highest human faculties.' "[11]

Truth became whatever the clerks said it was, and it was almost always presented as scientific. Maurras asserted that "Politics are a sci- ence" (and therefore what he wrote about politics was scientific); to others history was a science, and so were sociology and psychology, just like physics and chemistry. Nordau stated he was delivering "a re- ally scientific [arts/social] criticism" based on "psycho-physiological" factors that he had "discovered" to be "scientific truth" and would have been wrong to "withhold" from humanity. "Today," said Benda, "all political ideologies claim to be founded on science, to be the re- sult of a 'precise observation of the facts,' " and this was true even in philosophy, which before had been "the inviolate citadel of disinter- ested speculation."[12]

It was not clear whether the clerks believed they were scientific or "simply want to give the prestige of a scientific appearance to the passions of their hearts." To Langbehn, registering facts was the opposite of good science; the goal of true science was to "pronounce value judgments." All of this to Benda amounted to "the superstition of science, held to be competent in all domains, including that of morality. . . ." It was all right to cheat on the facts, the clerks taught, because "the evil which serves [practical interests] ceases to be evil and becomes good . . . in spite of their insistence in declaring that they profess no morality."[13] Whatever succeeded was moral, what failed deserved contempt. As "scientists," the clerks professed complete objectivity, even though like Nietzsche (and Schopenhauer before him) they often proclaimed that objectivity did not exist. Clerkish science, of which Morel and Nordau were examples in the medical profession, opened the way for science as opinionated moral and social arbiter. Psychoanalysis followed this style. That is why it has been so difficult all these years to find empirical science in psychoanalysis.

The clerks favored cohesion at the expense of independence. Said one clerk: "independent thought is contemptible"; groups that want to be strong have no use "for those who think for themselves." Another thought it utopian "for everyone to think with his own head." The clerks had the truth and would guide the common people who were in the position of "servants abdicating their liberty of mind." In place of personal opinions it was best to adopt what was taught by "vigilant leaders"; and what they taught was the justification of "habits and prejudices." The clerks preached the "abdication of the individual" in favor of "a great impersonal and Eternal whole" (the nation). "To be moral," they said, "is not to wish to be free from one's group." The essence of morality to them was group solidarity, because "the strength of the State depends upon authority. . . ."[14] In their theories and practices the Freudians similarly called on old habits and prejudices. By providing a substitute for thinking for oneself in crucial moral and social areas, they attempted to cohere group thought.

The clerks so much preferred artistry above intellect that they lost the distinction between the two; but when, "towards 1890," they again became conscious of the difference, they "ardently chose" artistry. A work was great not if it made sense but if it was successful; a superb artistic gesture "was as good as an argument"; ideas were appealing if they were "amusing," and if exasperating, all the better. Paradox was a favorite—the clerks took pleasure in "throwing off irritating paradoxes," and like the symbolists they treasured the piquancy of shock. Like many of the intellectuals of that day, they gave primacy in human motivation to instinct, the unconscious, intuition, the will. The philosophy of vitalism accompanied their pragmatism.[15] These attitudes point to the strong aesthetic component in psychoanalysis. In privileging artistry over exactitude, in taking pleasure in what they thought was shocking in their theories, and in stressing instincts and the unconscious, the Freudians followed the clerks. They had all inherited Schopenhauer's legacy of the high position of art in thought and feeling.

These new intellectuals could be seen as a study in collective nostalgia. They pined for a new ruling class bearing the marks of the old one, however the new governing methods might be hidden behind democracy or some other populist formula. They yearned for a rebirth of religion, but one without the old transcendence, to do for modern culture what religion had earlier done. They sought a respectful relationship of groups and classes, as of old, the underlings respecting their betters. It was a touch of genius for Benda to call them "clerks," for these new intellectuals were doing again the work of the old clergy, justifying *ways*. In times past, the work was said to be justifying the ways of God to man; now it was justifying the ways of man to man, an effort of secular theology whose main tenets—realism, materialism, practicality, competition, success, the fungibility of truth, follow-the-leader—were the values of middle-class culture. And its goal, like that of the clerisy of old, was to support the secular power, which in turn protected the clerks.

Not only the Freudians but many other psychologists of the day assumed the attitudes of the clerks. They were Cometean positivists, realists, materialists, elitists, gurus, intuitionists, scientists-*manqué*, atheists with secularized religious ideas, moralists, politicians, and publicists. In the 1890s, when his theories were being rejected by most of the medical profession, Freud felt lonely and unappreciated. That was because—as he was never shy to point out—his was the layman's view of psychology. His enterprise was not pure science or the art-science of medicine. It was the work of the clerks: organizing society around coherent beliefs likely to strike chords among the public. The Freudians became the intellectual clerks of psychology.

AN INFLUENTIAL FORUM for ideas in the nineteenth century was fiction, which Freud thought had a tangential connection with mental illness: "The mechanism of fiction is the same as that of hysterical fantasies."[16] It had a more obvious connection with the great issues of the day, which migrated wholesale from philosophy, religion, and social and political commentary into novels and short stories. While being engrossed in a love story (present in almost all the major novels as a structural element), the reader learned what was afoot in the society of the day, at the same time imbibing huge dollops of history, philosophy, and sociology. Aristotle's injunction to teach while entertaining was alive and well. Literature had the further value that it could indirectly criticize society in a time when a virulent frontal assault was difficult, considering that what the Enlightenment had fought for had arrived: freedom. Novelists could be social critics in disguise.

Freud's intense love of literature expressed itself when the great thoughts of past and present, and the problems that history had rolled up to Europe's door, were symbolized in psychological theories and practices, including the love triangle of a father, mother, and child (the Oedipus complex). The hidden appeal of Freudianism to students of literature rests on its literary strategies. Its main function was as a technique for imagining and conveying psychological stories.

Lesser fiction, such as the detective stories of Edgar Allan Poe and Arthur Conan Doyle, favorites of Freud, proved immensely popular from the middle of the century forward. These stories were built on suspense, with a trail of clues leading to the solution, the writer proceeding like an author of crossword puzzles from the end to the beginning, starting with the answer but keeping it hidden. Detective stories proclaimed that striking solutions were available by the exercise of reason, and that society had a handle on crime. The message was that modern detectives were phenomenally clever, so criminals beware!—the sort of blustering confidence for which the Victorians were famous. And the message went deeper: that deductive reasoning could solve even the most difficult problems. These stories, in their way, were a vindication of science. The Freudian way of understanding the unconscious and finding solutions for patients followed the principles of the detective story. The writer knows the solution (as the pioneers invariably did) and leads the reader to it step by step.

Fiction high and low had the attractive feature of providing emotional coherence for an otherwise disorganized, confused reality, and few realities were more disorganized and confused than the nineteenth century's. That same sense of coherence would be provided by psychoanalysis.

Always a lesson in symbolization, the arts were never more so than in the hands of the symbolist poets of the fin de siècle, masters of nuance and subtlety. As Nordau found to his dismay, the symbolists were also masters of shock, psychological persuasion, and public relations. One of their messages that shocked was that the new age was degenerate and decadent, not in Nordau's sense but in everything that people like Nordau stood for. The avant-garde of the fin de siècle held the middle class to be the end of decency, refinement, and high culture, the end of any sort of livable civilization. That, more than anything, shocked the rulers of the new age. Freud turned the methods of the symbolists against those who found the new age wanting.

Fueling the arts of the nineteenth century was romanticism, much in contrast to the practicality of the middle class. Romanticism loved the past, the mysterious, the Faustian, the evil, the unconscious, the natural, the childlike, the spontaneous, the mad; and it was in love with love. It hated the practical, the commercial, the studied, the reasonable. Its métier was excess and the murky depths of the heart, in opposition to modern rationalism. As the century moved to its close, romanticism climaxed in philosophy and politics. Its chief philosophical proponent was Nietzsche, the romantic hero of emotion and sincerity assaulting middle-class convention. Political radicals sought to recast the entire structure of modernity and liberal democracy with romantic notions about the past and the future. However wild and vicious some of them were, they wanted in their various ways to improve the world, and most especially their moment in history, which they perceived as blighted. Here, more than anywhere else, Freud found the enemies that psychoanalysis engaged.

NEW SPECIALTIES on the academic scene by the end of the nineteenth century included sociology. Having absorbed the collapse and rebuilding of Western culture, it was much concerned with the breakdown of family and community that had left the individual anomic and alienated. The Viennese sociologist Ferdinand Tonnies (1855–1936), in *Gemeinschaft and Gesellschaft* (1887), noted how the guiding principles that had formerly cohered society had been lost in the change from old world to new. The old world, said another leading sociologist, Max Weber, had been ruled by an effective and affective enchantment through God, family, community, and prescribed social relations. When these disappeared, a corrosive and dangerous disenchantment had set in.

Émile Durkheim was similarly concerned that, in the turn to secularism and individualism, the glue that bound societies together had decomposed. Groups, up to whole nations, he theorized, lived by "collective representations," agreed-upon ideas of morality, the world, and social relations, founded in religious ritual. These group ideas, internalized by a society, were always represented as having their source outside society, in a timeless, universal, transcendental sphere. When collective life disintegrated, the need reappeared for beliefs that were morally coercive and incumbent on all because they were sacred. On his deathbed Durkheim was trying to conceive new collective ideas for modernity, using science in place of religion and the family. His faith in collective ideas was not far different from Sorel's faith in collective myths. The sociologists' conclusions were similar to those of the psychopoliticians: that the loss of the past was potentially corrosive for modern culture. Evincing the same conviction, psychoanalysis sought replacements for what had been lost.

Anthropology and ethnology became components of psychoanalysis through the work of Freud and Jung. In *The Descent of Man* (1871) Darwin told of "primal hordes" in which dominant males took to themselves harems of women, sexual jealousy and rivalry ruled relations among the men, and codes of exogamy (marriage outside the clan) developed. After Darwin came a wave of Victorian anthropologists, among them Andrew Lang, whose cousin J. Atkinson was one of Freud's favorites, along with the ethnographer W. Robertson Smith, whom Freud accounted a genius. Freud relied on these anthropologists, notably in the caveman theory he presented in *Totem and Taboo*; Jung drew on them as well.

Comparative mythology had become an interest shared across Europe by such figures as Adolf Bastian in Germany and James Frazer in Great Britain. Bastian believed that mythologies contained universal ideas that were localized in regional folklores. Frazer's *Golden Bough* (1890), a landmark study of myth, was followed by such works as *Totemism and Exogamy* (1910) and *Folklore in the Old Testament* (1919), the latter study showing how the beliefs of earlier cultures had found their way into Christianity. By the end of the nineteenth century it was thought that all mythologies performed an identifiable set of functions: opening up a mystical dimension to reveal what was behind the surface of things; presenting a cosmology and the individual's place in it (the cosmology usually patterned after the science of the times); validating and maintaining the social order; and guiding people through the crises of life by identifying the good, the evil, the safe, and the dangerous. Psychoanalysis fulfilled these functions. In his letter to Fliess of December 12, 1897, in which he wondered if he was developing a psychomythology instead of a psychology, Freud was more than prescient of where he was headed.

A pronounced direction of philosophy in the fin de siècle was language. Earlier philosophers had placed reality in the mind; now it came to be thought that the mind was known, and knew itself, by language. Among the many contributors to this trend was Gottlob Frege (1848–1925), who compared language and mathematics, the latter taken as a source of objective truth. Language could convey objective truth too, Frege thought, if words and syntax could be formulated properly. Words, he said, had two meanings: a dictionary meaning, and the subjective images and associations they called up (one of many entrees, including also Janet, that Freud had to free association). The use of language—as opposed to laboratory experiments—to uncover psychological truths became the methodology of the Freudians; hence, talk therapy.

WHILE FREUD SHARED these and other intellectual sources with his colleagues, he had some stimulants that were particular to him alone. One of these was cocaine. In the 1880s, when he first experimented with it, recommended it to his fiancée, and prescribed it for his patients, it was not known that it could make a humble fellow feel like a conqueror, induce sexual mania and messianic conviction in otherwise silly ideas, if much abused could damage the frontal lobes of the brain and deteriorate the nose cartilage (if sniffed), and could lead to the mimicking of a wide range of diseases from which the addict thinks he is dying. Freud began taking cocaine in relatively pure form when he was a resident physician in Vienna, completing his medical studies. He returned to it when he studied with Charcot (to lower his inhibitions and impress the great man with his acumen) and again in the period when his father died and he began his self-analysis and came upon his theory of the Oedipus complex. In this last period he suffered a series of illnesses and symptoms, most of them, it is now believed, brought on by cocaine but interpreted by him as psychological. He psychoanalyzed himself in the hope of finding relief, thinking he was neurotic, when in fact, according to E. M. Thornton, who made this her special subject, he was trying to rid himself of what was actually in part hypochondria and in part cocaine poisoning. His use of cocaine probably heightened his response to the hysterical events of the day and the faith he had in the theories he was developing about the sexual etiology of neurosis.[17]

Another resource particular to Freud was Fliess, the Berlin ear, nose, and throat specialist who, like Freud, was a friend of Breuer and had studied with Charcot in Paris. On Breuer's recommendation, Fliess attended Freud's university lectures during a visit to Vienna in 1887, and they struck up a friendship, professional collaboration, and correspondence that lasted until 1904, meeting several times a year for "congresses" in which they shared their latest thinking. In regarding himself as less a medical doctor than a conquistador of ideas, Freud could not have chosen a better mentor than Fliess. A lesson in otiose speculation, Fliess believed in the influence of the moon on body and mind, and used the model of menstrual periods for a theory of periodicity in women of twenty-eight days and in men of twenty-three days. He theorized the inherent bisexuality of all individuals, an idea he may have gleaned from Greek myth. Freud knew Otto Weininger, and when Fliess learned that Weininger's book included his concept of bisexuality, he thought Freud had revealed it to the young man without giving him credit.

Fliess's favorite idea was that the bodily organs, including the genitals, were represented by nerve clusters in the nose. This belief led to a surgical procedure performed by Fliess on one of Freud's patients, Emma Eckstein, on the theory that her stomach complaints were due to sexual longings and could be relieved by operating on her nose. Fliess mistakenly left a length of surgical gauze in her nose after sewing up the incision, which caused infection, leading to several more operations and the permanent disfigurement of her face. Freud blamed suppuration from her facial wounds on her sexual longings for him.[18] A hypochondriac at this stage of his life, Freud was having fantasies of death whenever confronted with serious problems, and the failed treatment of Emma Eckstein led him to dire thoughts of his impending demise, for which he could choose from a list of suitable complaints.

Presumably Freud looked to Fliess to establish the biological basis for his psychological ideas; but the relationship had a deeper significance. Fliess encouraged Freud to speculate in broad ways that were essentially symbolic and without strict medical content. A reviewer said of Fliess's 1897 book *The Relationship Between the Nose and the Female Sexual Organs*, "If one nowadays seeks to render such mystical nonsense that aspires to be intellectual wealth capable of discussion, the attempt founders on the realization that it is not the business of science to embark on a critique of the fantasy creations of every author, for such disquisitions can be neither refuted nor confirmed." No one has figured out what the nose meant to Fliess; it was one of his medical specialties, and perhaps he needed to find that whatever he thought important in life and medicine centered on his specialty. But how to make uncanny theoretical connections must have been a lesson to Freud.[19]

Most of Fliess's speculations were peculiar to him and a few other medical men at the time, but his *will* to speculate unfettered by empirical evidence was well within the range of science in the nineteenth century—witness Morel, Nordau, and the other degeneration theorists; the racial theorists; and the phrenologists, graphologists, and physiognomists, all of whom, without acknowledging it or perhaps knowing it, were responding, like the psychopoliticians and the intellectuals, to the roilings and alarums of a mass society.

All these sources and influences, along with the others noted earlier, needed a vessel or mold, something to hold them together and shape them. This the Freudians found in the prevalent psychology of the nineteenth century—romantic soul psychology.

NINE

Soul Psychology: Mind over Matter

Much of what, in retrospect, looks to us as startling novelties in the theories of Bleuler, Freud, and Jung, appeared to their contemporaries as a return to old-fashioned psychiatric conceptions.
—Henri Ellenberger, *The Discovery of the Unconscious*

The oldest ideas are really the most useful ones, as I am finding out belatedly.
—Sigmund Freud, Letter to Fliess

THE THEORIES of psychoanalysis were firmly grounded in the long tradition of soul psychology that found new life among psychologists in the nineteenth century. While such figures as Helmholtz and Wundt (and at the medical level Ernst von Bruecke and Theodor Meynert, two of Freud's teachers), were developing a scientific psychology in the laboratory, most psychologists and psychiatrists favored soul psychology. (There were overlaps in both directions, but that was the rough division.) Soul psychology is the catchphrase for an amalgam of beliefs and practices extending from the earliest cultures to the days of the Greeks, and then to medieval confession and exorcism, the magnetism of Paracelsus, seventeenth-century Protestant *Seelsorge* (the "cure of souls" by the cathartic confession of secrets), eighteenth-century Mesmeric animal magnetism, and nineteenth-century hypnotism, spiritualism, and Christian Science.

The earliest soul psychology featured spirits, traumas, foreign substances in mind and body, psychic frustrations (such as homesickness and lovesickness), and harmful beliefs or mental indisciplines that might upset the human soul, misdirect its energy or whisk it away, causing disease. The cure was to return the soul to its former undisturbed state. This was achieved, according to the period in which it was practiced, by a shaman or medicine man, a group of shamans acting as god-representatives, a philosopher, or a clergyman, and later by psychotherapists. Methods of cure included suggestion, magic stunts to fool the patient,[1] appeals to religious faith, ritual ceremonies, reenactment of traumatic events, and philosophical prescriptions such as the mastery of the passions.

Soul psychology concerned itself with possession by evil spirits (in medieval times the devil, later multiple personalities), the significance of dreams and dream wishes, the reintegration of the formerly alienated patient back into the community. Forgotten encounters between patients and spirits (later called repressed memories) were recalled, and the exercise of will was used to defeat evil in the mind or body. After the appearance of experimental science in the sixteenth and seventeenth centuries, these phantasms began to dissipate. In the eighteenth century, however, they returned in such figures as the impostor Cagliostro and Franz Anton Mesmer.

Cagliostro toured Europe and the Middle East dispensing cures by magic words, philters, and hypnotism. Mesmer, Cagliostro's contemporary, was an Austrian physician who achieved success and scandal by treating a wide array of ailments by what he called animal magnetism. Magnets, he believed (following Paracelsus), could draw disease out of the body or organize energy flows in the body so that they followed prescribed channels and did not go off on their own to produce disease. Later he practiced hypnotism, which he said could control the energy flows, and accompanied this with the laying on of hands. A sensational healer always hounded by conventional medical practitioners, he was run out of Austria only to take up practice in Paris, where he was eventually condemned by a royal commission in 1783 as a charlatan. His cause did not rest and was taken up by a French nobleman, Puységur, the first to realize that hypnotic "cures" were achieved through the belief of the patient. Hypnotism, he saw, worked by the suggestions of the hypnotist and the imagination of the subject.

It is not difficult to find already in these ideas familiar Freudian concepts—trauma, frustration, energy flows, suggestion, abreaction (reliving traumas), dreams, wishes, repressed memories, the cure of mental and physical (psychosomatic) ailments without medicines.

NINETEENTH-CENTURY romantic soul psychologists, influenced by the philosophers of pleasure, sought cures for real and obscure illnesses by means of mental therapies focused on the passions. They observed, hypothesized, and deduced, but they rarely sought knowledge through experimental proof, the measurement of phenomena, or the gathering of statistics, the domains of scientific psychology. The early centers of soul psychology were in the German-speaking lands, where it was reinforced by another incarnation called *Naturphilosophie* (the philosophy of nature), whose main tenet, like shamanism before and Christian Science later, was mind over matter. Goethe, among many other leading German intellectuals, favored the philosophy of nature over strict scientific discipline. A Goethe essay on this subject inspired Freud to study medicine.

Johann Christian Reil (1759–1813), a notable romantic soul psychologist, believed that mental illness could be biological, psychic, or both, in any case loosening the sense of the self in a region below consciousness. His prescription was psychic therapy to reeducate the senses. Johann Christian August Heinroth (1773–1843) considered mental illness to be sin. The psyche progressed from self-consciousness (narcissism, pleasure) to consciousness (reality), he thought, and thence to conscience or divine reason. Mental health was freedom from sin, mental illness the loss of freedom resulting from self-love and the passions. One of the main symptoms of mental illness, delusion, was caused by the passions disturbing the intellect. Heinroth prescribed a psychotherapy that took into account the patient's family and surroundings. In providing it, the therapist was to assume the position of God, being always right and demanding rectitude on the part of the patient. Heinroth leaned toward the belief—which grew throughout the century—that mental illness was caused by wrong ideas in the mind.

Karl Wilhelm Ideler (1795–1860) called attention to the passions and the effects of solitude and lack of gratification. Hysteria was caused by a hereditary predisposition for conflict between desires and a restricting reality. Dissatisfaction with reality led to flight into the fantasy of a childhood dreamworld. The cure was renunciation of desire, replacing the passions with duty (equally the cure of the Bible, Schopenhauer, Kant, and Kierkegaard), which the patient effected under the guidance of the physician. Heinrich Wilhelm Neumann (1814–1884) believed there were no chance happenings in mental life, only mysterious but identifiable causes, chief among them the drives (the passions), by which he meant mainly the sexual instinct. The drives warned of dangers in seeking satisfaction, but when they failed to show how danger could be met, intense anxiety and mental illness resulted, for which he prescribed, like the others, psychic therapy.[2]

A soul psychologist much admired by Freud was Gustav Fechner (1801–1887), founder of "psychophysics," who not untypically straddled romantic and scientific psychology. After receiving a medical degree, Fechner became interested in blending psychology with physical laws. Upon taking up a post in physics at Leipzig University, he fell into a depression from which he arose with an interest in angels, the psychology of plants, and the earth as an organism. Believing he had been given the messianic role of solving the riddle of the universe, he proclaimed the Universal Law of the Spirit World: Pleasure. (Since he theorized years after Bentham, Schopenhauer, and Feuerbach, he was rather late in discovering it.) By applying the laws of physics to the mind, Fechner became one of many nineteenth-century models for elaborate schemes of mental operation, such as those of the Freudians, that followed "scientific" laws; for in this period, as Hobsbawm remarks, " 'Positive' science, operating on objective and ascertained facts, connected by rigid links of cause and effect, and producing uniform, invariant general 'laws' beyond query or willful modification, was the master key to the universe and the nineteenth century [believed that it] possessed it. . . ."[3] Among Fechner's concepts of mind were mental energy and its conservation, the pleasure-pain dichotomy, and the principle of repetition (instincts are programmed to repeat).

Soul psychologists tended to agree that mental illness was, more or less, dissociation from reality (caused, in the thinking of someone like Mesmer, by the deflection of bodily fluids from their rightful paths). That accounted for the professional title of psychiatrists as "alienists," whose job was treating those alienated from reality.

Many of these insights became part of psychoanalysis—psychic causes of mental illnesses, unconscious disturbances, the transmutation of sin into mental illness, the role of narcissism and pleasure in mental illness, the role of a renewed sense of reality in the cure, loss of psychic freedom, delusions, the effect of passions (notably sex) on the mind, the conflict between desire and reality, the flight into fantasy, mental life determined by unconscious drives, danger signs, dissociation from reality, the conservation of mental energy, pleasure-pain, and unconscious repetition. The psychoanalysts also absorbed the belief in wrong ideas causing mental illness, and the efficacy of psychotherapy in the context of the family.

THROUGHOUT the nineteenth century soul psychology concentrated on five interrelated subjects: hypnosis, suggestion, hysteria, sex, and the unconscious. These subjects would find themselves at the heart of psychoanalysis. From the time of Mesmer and Puységur, interest in hypnosis grew as an amateur and stage entertainment, a medical curiosity, and then a medical modality. An 1888 bibliography listed 801 titles on hypnotism and dual personality (another belief of the time). Medical applications appeared in many places, among them in Paris, where Charcot was demonstrating his theory that hysterical symptoms had a psychic source that could be activated by reaching the unconscious through hypnosis. To prove his point, he hypnotized patients in his ward at the Salpêtrière Hospital to bring forth symptoms such as the paralysis of an arm or impaired speech, and then relieved the symptoms by ending the trance.

To explore the psychic source of these queer reactions, Charcot employed an early form of talk therapy to identify traumas that he believed caused hysteria and its consequent symptoms. He was among the first to propose that hysteria was not limited to women (the prevailing medical opinion to that time) and that there could be and were male hysterics. This proposal extended what had been a disease limited to half the human race to the whole of humanity. Freud traveled to Paris for postdoctoral research with Charcot and, much impressed with his theories and methods, offered to translate several of the master's books into German, which he later did.

Another application of hypnosis was in progress in Nancy, France, where a country doctor, Auguste Ambroise Liébeault, was treating patients with physical diseases by placing his hand on the diseased area of the body, hypnotizing the patient, and giving assurance when the trance was over that the disease was cured. The Nancy physician Hippolyte Bernheim expanded this method by using suggestion without hypnosis. He would lay his hands on the diseased area and after a short time tell the patient he was cured (his poor ward patients believed him, his middle-class private patients did not). Soon other doctors joined in what was called the School of Nancy, which put into practice Puységur's insight that hypnotism was suggestion. Bernheim characterized hypnosis as "merely a sleep, produced by suggestion, with therapeutic implications." A visitor to Nancy, Wilhelm Winternitz, reported that "it is not only hysterics who are subject to influence via suggestion."[4]

In his autobiography Freud reported how "news reached us that a school had arisen at Nancy which made an extensive and remarkably successful use of suggestion, with or without hypnosis, for therapeutic purposes." He hastened there in 1889 to consult with Bernheim and, as with Charcot, agreed to translate Bernheim's books on the therapeutic effects of suggestion. Bernheim called his treatments "psychotherapy," and when Freud returned to Vienna he used the methods of the School of Nancy on his patients, first with hypnosis and then with suggestion alone. From that time on he abandoned the treatment of organic nervous diseases and resolved to practice psychic therapy exclusively. Bernheim's methods gave Freud "a sense of having overcome one's helplessness; it was highly flattering to enjoy the reputation of being a miracle worker." The new methods, he found, were "more effective" than giving bald "commands or prohibitions" to the patient.[5]

Freud was learning, he said, that "as far as the neurosis was concerned, psychical reality was of more importance than material reality." Suggestion was leading him and other soul psychologists to an understanding of the power of belief in shaping ideas, actions, and mental states: "I discovered the principle of the 'omnipotence of thoughts,' which lies at the root of magic."[6] Probably advertising was one of many nineteenth-century reinforcements of this doctrine, along with a growing European knowledge of the practices of witch doctors and shamans in regions of Asia, Africa, and Latin America. In the background were those philosophers who held that everything in the mind was our own idea or representation of the outside world. Here perhaps, the last word in the title of Schopenhauer's book gains its greatest significance: *Vorstellung,* an idea or representation of something in the mind. Of all the components of soul psychology, the "omnipotence of thoughts"—the idea of mind over matter earlier emphasized by Heinroth and taken over by fin-de-siècle romantic soul psychologists—was the most consequential for psychoanalysis.

According to Freud, Charcot proved through the hypnotic manipulation of symptoms that hysterical paralyses "were the result of ideas which had dominated the patient's brain." The Christian devil, he wrote, was only another name for this effect. Therefore, he concluded, the medieval priests had had it about right: "By pronouncing possession by a demon to be the cause of hysterical phenomena, the Middle

Ages in fact chose this solution [of domination by ideas]; it would have only been a matter of exchanging the religious terminology of that dark and superstitious age for the scientific language of today." Modern scientific psychologists, he thought (by which he meant such figures as Charcot, Janet, and Breuer), had developed "a theory of neurosis which coincided with the medieval view—when only they replaced the 'demon' of clerical phantasy by a psychological formula."[7] Here again, Freud was prescient about how psychoanalysis would be formulated. Medieval views and practices—and also institutional structure—would play a considerable role.

Freud believed that hypnosis was like love, that yielding to it was like yielding to love. In therapy the therapist was like a lover and also a leader, and all of this was the product of suggestion. "From being in love to hypnosis is evidently only a short step. The respects in which they agree are obvious. There is the same humble subjection, the same compliance, the same absence of criticism, towards the hypnotist as towards the love object. There is the same sapping of the subject's own initiative; no one can doubt that the hypnotist has stepped into the place of the ego ideal" (the leader).[8] These ideas about therapist and patient had a natural application in the mass psychology of leaders and followers, and were applied that way by Freud.

In the fin de siècle, hypnotism clinics throughout Europe treated a wide variety of illnesses. They were joined in 1892 by the first Suggestion Treatment Clinic, opened in Amsterdam. Frederick van Eeden, one of the clinic's two partners, defined the suggestion psychotherapy he practiced as "the cure of the body by the mind, aided by the impulse of one mind [the therapist's] over another [the patient's]." To effect cures, he thought, the therapist could not command the patient to think the right, healing thoughts (as soul psychologists were wont to do earlier in the century) but rather had to guide subtly and instruct by suggestion. As if to ward off doubters, Eeden denied that the healing effects of suggestion were not lasting, a theme that would become insistent as evidence accumulated that psychological cures, if achieved at all, were only temporary.

In that same year, 1892, Adolf von Struempell lectured at Erlangen University on the "Origins and Healing of Diseases Through Mental Representations," expressing the growing conviction among European psychologists that mental illness was brought on by ideas in the mind. To effect a cure, one had to change those ideas. The change was achieved by faith in the treatment and in the healer—in effect, by the power of suggestion. Hypnosis worked, said Struempell, repeating Puységur, because the patient believed in it and not because of its inherent power. If the patient were not "fooled" by his faith in the treatment, he could not be cured. A normal individual, said Struempell, understanding the nature of hypnotism, could not be hypnotized.[9] Doubts about the efficacy of hypnotism and suggestion in psychotherapy continued to grow. The doubters were unaware, apparently, that they might have their true application in a mass psychology disguised as psychotherapy.

Suggestion was becoming a belief about belief: that ideas could be inculcated without the receiver being aware of it, if only, as Puységur and Struempell thought, the receiver had faith. Such faith, according to Le Bon, was encouraged by prestige, which practitioners like Liébeault, Bernheim, and Eeden traded on with their medical expertise. The idea of one mind dominating another, as if by hypnotic trance, was popularized by George du Maurier's novel *Trilby* (1894), in which Svengali mysteriously imposes his will on the heroine. Freud succeeded in wedding suggestion to the prestige of science.

MOST OF Freud's early writings, published and unpublished, concerned hysteria. He reported on Charcot's work, wrote "A Case of Successful Treatment by Hypnotism" and "On the Theory of Hysterical Attacks," and with Breuer published in 1893 a paper "On the Psychic Mechanisms of Hysterical Phenomena." Moebius in Germany defined hysteria as "morbid changes in the body that are caused by representations."[10] Charcot took the view that faith healing at Lourdes was actually ridding individuals of hysterical symptoms through suggestion, demonstrating that religion and neurosis shared the same psychic processes. Freud thought the same, and that he could achieve as many cures as Lourdes if only his patients had the same faith in him as in the Virgin Mary.

When in 1895 Freud and Breuer published *Studies on Hysteria,* about successful cathartic cures of hysterical patients by hypnotism and suggestion, the reaction of Eugen Bleuler, director of the respected Burgholzli mental sanitarium in Switzerland, was that the cures may have been due to suggestion rather than the confession of secrets. Struempell, in his review, expressed distrust of hypnosis as a technique for investigating the psyche, because he had found that in the suggestible state of hypnosis hysterics fabricated elaborate memories. Another reviewer, Michael Clarke, pointed to the danger of crediting the statements of mental patients because of their susceptibility to even the slightest suggestions given to them by the therapist. Krafft-Ebing, the leader of Viennese psychiatry at that time, echoed these caveats, pointing out that the memories of repressive traumatics often emerged mangled, with little connection to the originals. A novelist, perhaps perceiving Freud and Breuer as soul mates behind their medical degrees, in a review titled "Surgery of the Soul" praised the authors for "a piece of ancient writers' psychology."[11] As it must have had for Charcot, hysteria came to have symbolic meaning in psychoanalysis far beyond its medical definition.

From early in the century, sex was of wide psychiatric interest. In the 1860s Moritz Benedikt in Vienna was proposing that daydreams and suppressed sexual passions caused hysteria and neurosis, an adaptation of the medieval belief that sex was sin. He called for psychic treatment to root out sexual secrets as the route to cure (an adaptation of Catholic confession and Protestant *Seelsorge*). Hans Gross, a psychologist and criminologist in Vienna, produced a treatise in 1891 on crime as a mask for frustrated sexual desire. Charcot implied to his students that sex was always at the base of hysteria. The linking of hysteria and sexual desire strengthened belief in earlier soul-psychology theories about the passions. From these sources, and from popular culture, literature, earlier soul psychology, and the philosophy of pleasure, sex found its place in psychoanalysis. It played a major role in Freud's theories and in their symbolic meanings and functions.

The fifth subject to engage the attention of romantic soul psychology was the unconscious, one of the oldest traditions in psychology.[12] Helmholtz viewed the unconscious as the mechanism that shaped perceptions according to one's preconceived ideas. In England Frederick Myers spoke of the "subliminal self" which performed inferior and superior functions and wove fantasies. In France Janet explored what he called the "subliminal" and the "subconscious." Charcot thought the unconscious was the place where traumas lodged and out of which came hysteria. By 1889 the unconscious was declared an established scientific fact by the French psychologist Jules Hericourt, proved, he said, by habits, instincts, forgotten memories returning spontaneously, problem-solving in sleep, unconscious movements, and unaccountable sympathies and antipathies. Usually the conscious and unconscious cooperated, he theorized, but when they warred on each other a mental dissociation from reality occurred, producing symptoms of mental illness ranging from phobias to insane delusions.

Théodore Flournoy (1854–1920), physician, philosopher, and psychologist, furthered his understanding of the unconscious through a five-year study of a fashionable medium named Catherine Muller (professional name, Helen Smith). He concluded that spiritualist revelations represented the normal workings of the subconscious mind weaving wish fulfillments out of forgotten memories. The unconscious, he said, was the source of human creativity, protection (providing warning, comfort, and recovery from blunders), compensation for social or financial frustrations, and play. Mediums and mystics did not mean to deceive but instead were overcome by their unconscious desire to play.

By 1900, according to Ellenberger, the unconscious was said to perform four functions: creating; conserving memories and unconscious perceptions; dissociating disturbed parts of the personality; and fabricating myths and romances which sometimes rose to the level of mythomania, the construction of delusional beliefs. The unconscious was thought to work in such a way, he said, that "We receive suggestions from the environment not only in hypnotic experiences but in the waking state, and transform them into thoughts and feelings that we believe to be our own."[13] An unconscious peculiarly susceptible to suggestion had become an established psychological fact. It went on to become one of the most famous concepts of psychoanalysis.

By now therapists were practicing suggestion (with or without hypnosis); catharsis (modernized Catholic confession and Protestant *Seelsorge*); and a combination of supportive, expressive, and directive techniques that might be called guidance therapy. Janet and Benedikt were treating patients by the *Seelsorge* approach, searching out secret problems, usually with a sexual component, in order to effect cures. Janet's methods included having the patient talk at random (a form of the free association Freud would later adopt) in order to reach subconscious fixed ideas that were presumably affecting the patient's psyche.

When the Freudians appeared, European soul psychology had settled on the formula that an unconscious harboring of guilty secrets, usually sexual, could make a person sick. The indicated treatment was psychotherapy, either to discover the secret (Charcot, Janet, Benedikt) or to suggest with subtlety the "right" ideas that would cure (Eeden and the other Suggestion Therapists). So widespread were such ideas that Langbehn, the anti-modern, anti-Semite proto-fascist, might be considered a romantic soul psychologist. After all, as Stern records, he "championed hypnosis, emphasized the interrelation in most diseases of the mind and body, and called for a partially psychic healing therapy," an indication of how widespread these ideas were, even among nonprofessionals.[14]

Soul psychology had prepared the way for psychoanalysis. Le Bon made a major contribution when he carried suggestion over to mass psychology. Crowds were highly credulous and suggestible, he wrote; ideas spread through them like a contagion, for the "crowd, as a rule, is in a state of expectant attention, which renders suggestion easy. The first suggestion . . . which arises implants itself immediately by a process of contagion in the brains of all assembled, and the identical bent of the sentiments of the crowd is immediately an accomplished fact." One reason for this effect, he theorized, is that the crowd was "perpetually on the borderland of unconsciousness. . . . The improbable does not exist for a crowd." This accounted for "the facility with which are created and propagated the most improbable legends and stories."[15] These ideas were perhaps the final element needed to convert a medical discipline into a mass belief system.

The continuing growth of soul psychology at the end of the nineteenth century occurred precisely when scientific psychology was on the road to experimental, empirical proofs of hypotheses and the exploration of the organic bases of what appeared to be mental diseases. This parallel development has confounded scholars who find it uncanny and perverse. They approach it as a sad mistake: the inability of some scientific thinkers to shake off the old traditions even as science was moving to positivism; or the mistake perhaps of rogues in the garb of medical men eager to be modern shamans; or a well-meaning mistake among men and women who believed romantic soul psychology to be scientifically true. To the contrary, it was neither strange nor perverse. Romantic psychology was to the period and its dangers born. It was not an accidental selection by certain psychologists, merely one of several psychologies from which they might have chosen. It was virtually the only one that could effectively subsume social opinions and represent them as medical science. The degeneration theorists had proved that. It was so broad that it could contain virtually any ideas.

Because the romantic soul psychologists were labeled romantics, it must not be thought that they themselves were romantics. They may have shared in some of the romantic spirit of the times, but by and large the romantic temperament, with its passions, mists, mysticism, and heaven-storming will, is what they opposed. Romantic soul psychology developed to understand and treat the romantic spirit. As if in a hypnotic trance, the romantic psychologists reached for soul psychology to accomplish their goals, as though it had been *suggested* to them by their culture, just as degeneration theory had been "suggested" to Morel and Nordau, or phrenology to Lombroso, as a suitable scientific medium through which to convey social opinions. All these figures in turn suggested back to the culture what the culture had suggested to them would be fitting and useful. Since soul psychology was only tenuously tied to empirical science, it could more easily do that.

Romantic soul psychology, as Ellenberger and others have demonstrated, was the direct antecedent of psychoanalysis. But compared to what Freud added, it was naive, without the power that Freud's ideas possessed for mass acceptance and mass influence. Freudian soul psychology, as events proved, was a masterful instrument of mass suggestion. It gathered from European traditions familiar beliefs, attitudes, and historical experiences, joined them to its many other sources and influences, and conquered the Western world.

Theory and Practice: Desire's Vicissitudes

Woe to him who has begotten children at the turn of
the times.
—Frtiz von Unruh, quoted in *German Men of Letters*

I can indeed only assert, I cannot prove, that it is
always and in every instance so.
—Sigmund Freud, *Introductory Lectures on
Psycho-Analysis*

As the response to practical social issues, psychoanalysis has the
appearance of a conundrum, a theory and therapy about mental illness
couched in a special psychiatric terminology. It seems to have little to
do with social and political concerns. It was said to be about and for
individuals, and that was generally accepted as the fact of the matter.
Freud's manifest motive in creating it was to treat hysteria, the presumed mental illness on which late-nineteenth-century soul psychology concentrated. Other mental conditions were later absorbed into
his system under the inclusive heading of the "neuroses" (which he
also sometimes called the "psychoneuroses"). Even serious psychoses—paranoia, dementia praecox (schizophrenia), manic depression (bipolar disorder), and catatonia—fell under Freud's theories, he
said, but he held them to be unsusceptible to his treatment.

The theory of psychoanalysis as it existed around the turn of the
century, drawing on Schopenhauer and soul psychology, maintained
that human psychology was ruled by the passions. Most specific of
these was the desire for pleasure, already part of the newborn babe
and contained in the sexual instinct, called the libido. "A child," Freud
wrote, "has its sexual instincts and activities from the first; it comes

into the world with them."[1] This became one of his most famous doctrines, infantile sexuality. The libido was conceived as a form of energy that flows toward what it finds pleasurable, a process the Freudians called cathexis (like tropism in plants); rejection of the unpleasurable was called anti-cathexis. The purpose of seeking pleasure was to avoid pain, which, as in Schopenhauer, was the primary motivation.

In infancy the child is said to be polymorphously perverse—seeking pleasure from any conceivable source. It finds it first in its own body—the stage of narcissism. This is followed by the stage of infantilism and beyond when external sources of pleasure are found. In the incessant quest for pleasure the libido may sometimes want to cathect and at the same time refuse to, due to an internal conflict stemming from a sense of danger warning the psyche not to reach for a particular pleasure that might result in pain, such as punishment. "The ego notices that the satisfaction of an emerging instinctual demand would conjure up . . . danger. This instinctual cathexis must therefore be somehow suppressed, stopped, made powerless."[2] When that happens the psyche is traumatized and libido energy may flow into inappropriate channels.

The trauma is immediately hidden by being repressed to the unconscious. This may happen one or more times in childhood but has no immediate effect. Only after a long delay, called a latency period (which in Freudian theory can last until puberty or after), does the repressed trauma produce symptoms of mental illness. This return of the trauma in the form of symptoms, Freud called "the return of the repressed."[3]

The early name for trauma followed by repression and the flow of libido into inappropriate channels, resulting in symptoms, was "dissociation." Specific mental functions, as a current guide to modern psychiatry explains, "become separated (or dissociated) from the mainstream of consciousness and, as a consequence, are lost to the individual's awareness and voluntary control."[4] This theory conformed to the soul-psychology notion—and common observation—that mental illness was dissociation from reality. How the dissociation occurred followed the model of Mesmeric energy flowing into a new path rather than the normal one marked out for it. In Freud's thinking, trauma in this way converted libidinal energy into a sexual noxa or toxin, a poison that affected the mind. The poison might produce either psychological symptoms, physical (that is, psychosomatic) symptoms, or both.

From Freud's belief in the biological conversion of trauma into symptoms—that "psychic pain," for example, "often becomes transformed into physical pain"—came the diagnosis of conversion hysteria, which Charcot and others had brought into vogue. In the 1890s Freud looked to Fliess to map out the biology of this part of his theory. What took place between the psychic and the organic, he told him, "will require a hypothesis." "I hope you will explain the physiological mechanism of my clinical findings by your approach. . . . I still look to you as the messiah. . . ." But after a time Freud realized it was not to be, and the conversion of sexual energy into toxins producing symptoms was thereafter simply assumed, even if it could not be detailed by any known biochemistry. It was never demonstrated to occur but was to Freud "What must in fact be . . . taking place between quotas of energy in some unimaginable substratum."[5] The mind, he was convinced—following the mind-over-matter convictions of the soul psychologists—affected the biochemistry of the body in a way that could produce mental illness.

Symptoms are delusions, according to the theory. The sufferer believes, for example, that a hand is paralyzed and has an apparently paralyzed hand to show for it, the result of no known physical cause. Freud and most soul psychologists believed that they were seeing patients with these delusional symptoms caused by mental trauma. The function of the delusion, it was thought, was to comfort the sufferer by demonstrating that something tangible had gone wrong—a physical paralysis, for example, as terrible as that might be, rather than something horrible and chaotic in the psyche. Patients would rather face the physical deformation than the mental one, taking "flight into illness in order that by its help they may find a satisfaction. . . ."[6] Mental illness, Freud repeats over and over, is the patient's symbolic representation of the trauma and an attempt at self-cure, a way to dismiss the trauma by disguising it. The trauma and the symptoms both represent a frustrated desire and in that sense are perverted and diverted wish fulfillments.

If delusional symptoms do not totally incapacitate, they are said to be neurotic; if they do incapacitate, or if they are accompanied by symptoms such as hallucinations—hearing voices or seeing visions—they are said to be psychotic. In this way neurosis and psychosis were seen to share the same mechanism, but neurosis was the less severe form of mental illness. Accompanying the delusions was said to be an excessive sense of guilt capable of causing fear to the point of paranoia, disintegration of the personality, and loss of identity, to use the terms of psychotherapy. These were further delusional symptoms.

Convinced by the emphasis on sex in soul psychology, Freud (and many others) first thought the cause of trauma was a range of sexual practices including coitus interruptus, contraception, homosexuality, and masturbation. These practices presumably caused shame, trauma, and the remainder of the process leading to mental illness. But since they did not occur in early youth, and Freud was aware of the soul-psychology belief that mental illness was caused by experiences in youth, he theorized that they probably reawakened early traumas and in that way led to mental illness.

When Freud began to think his patients were telling him of sexual seductions in youth, he thought he had hit on the ultimate source of mental illness. This is often referred to as Freud's first seduction theory. But he came to believe that these stories either were made up to please him by confirming his theories, or were fantasized. That last thought, fantasy, led to the final, irreducible cause he said he discovered: the Oedipus complex, the child's imagined wish to seduce the parent of the opposite sex and kill the parent of the same sex, which everyone was said to experience in the young years of life.[7] This is usually referred to as Freud's second seduction theory. Freud said he found this idea in a Greek myth and the plays of Sophocles dealing with Oedipus of Thebes, a prince who is born with an oracle's curse: he is destined to kill his father and marry his mother. On hearing the prophecy, his father, King Laius, abandons his son in a wasteland, to die. A kindly shepherd finds the child and takes him to the royal palace in a neighboring kingdom where the infant is adopted and brought up.

Years later the oracle's curse is repeated, driving Oedipus to seek refuge in the neighboring city of Thebes. On the way he is overtaken by a charioteer who whips him off the road. Angered, the youth kills the charioteer who, he does not know, was his father, King Laius. Continuing on his way, he arrives at Thebes and finds the gate guarded by a monster. By solving a riddle posed by the monster (the Sphinx), he causes the monster's death, which wins him the hand of the city's queen who, he does not know, is his mother, Jocasta, widow of King Laius. When, during a plague in the city, Oedipus's unwitting crimes are discovered, he is condemned to tear out his eyes and wander the countryside until death overtakes him. The myth and the play—which Freud probably read in the original Greek—were included in his formidable education.

Oedipus's lack of awareness of what he had done was thought by Freud to be the equivalent of the unconscious. His acts Freud regarded as examples of infantilism, the desire to fulfill childhood wishes for pleasure at any cost. In the case of Oedipus, the attempt is unwittingly by rebellion against, and murder of, his father and lawful sovereign, and incest with his mother. Freud drew a similar interpretation of the "world-famed neurotic" Hamlet, a young prince who wants to kill his uncle (his stepfather) and, says Freud, satisfy his sexual desire for his mother. "Shakespeare's *Hamlet* is equally rooted in the soil of the incest-complex, but under a better disguise. . . ."[8] Freud had found a way to express in a psychological theory a theme much on his mind: *lèse-majesté,* the son killing the father (the king), which he combined with Schopenhauer's philosophy of pleasure (expressed by Freud as the son's incest with the mother).

The fantasy wish to seduce one parent and kill the other causes immense unconscious guilt, fear, and anxiety, Freud theorized, especially regarding the consequence: punishment. That constitutes the trauma of anticipated danger which is repressed; it returns after the latency period as mental illness if the individual is not able to resolve the Oedipal conflict spontaneously. Even in a successful navigation of the Oedipal conflict, a sense of guilt never leaves because "A threatened external unhappiness—loss of love and punishment [from] the external authority [the parent]—has been exchanged for a permanent internal unhappiness, for the tension of a sense of guilt." The Oedipal conflict results in the permanent implantation of a conscience in the psyche: "Every renunciation of instinct . . . becomes a dynamic source of conscience and every fresh renunciation increases the latter's severity and intolerance [of instinctive will]."[9] In this way one learns to defer pleasure and accept one's rightful duties, becoming, in the terms of one's family and society, "good." This lesson Freud called the reality principle. It had much in common with what the Austrian clergy and his own religious instructors taught. It clearly reflected the clerkish sense of the practical and the realistic, which were principles of middle-class life. And it was the opposite of what the soul psychologists defined as mental illness, dissociation from reality.

Freud believed the Oedipus story, and the theory he derived from it, was the timeless, universal core of human psychology, a fact of science that was "the nuclear complex of every neurosis." He told Fliess how "The Greek legend seizes on a compulsion which everyone recognizes because he feels it within himself. Each member of the audience was once, in germ and phantasy, just such an Oedipus, and each one recoils in horror. . . . I have found, in my own case, too, falling in love with the mother and jealousy of the father, and I now regard it as a universal event of early childhood." Given the nature of his theory, Freud referred to it as "the family romance."[10] The female version acquired the name "the Electra complex," after the myth of the Greek princess yearning for her murdered father and hating her mother who, with a lover, had killed the father. The daughter arranges the killing of both the mother and the lover—her surrogate father.

While other theorists and practitioners would later discard the Oedipus complex (and anthropologists such as Bronislaw Malinowski would demonstrate that it did not seem to operate in cultures outside the West), it became a model for what were called central issues in human psychology (the family, pleasure-seeking, infantilism, guilt, and fantasy wishes, for example) and a singular trigger for the cause of mental illness. From at least the time he first expressed the desire to find a single key to human psychology, Freud had been searching for one. In the Oedipus complex he believed he had found it, and from that moment he never wavered in thinking he had made a major discovery. From then to the end of his life, he embroidered the Oedipus theory but never abandoned it.

The key was easily expressed: "We see that human beings fall ill when, as a result of external obstacles or of an internal lack of adaptation, the satisfaction of their erotic needs *in reality* is frustrated." That human psychology was almost wholly determined by unconscious sexual desires Freud thought to be a novel idea: "people are unaccustomed to reckoning with a strict and universal application of determinism in mental life. . . ." However that may be, determinism, along with the key of erotic desire, was the core of Schopenhauer's philosophy almost a hundred years before Freud.[11]

The frustrated subject, disillusioned with reality, flies into the fantasy of mental illness because he is in rebellion "against the outer world" in which satisfaction cannot be found; he is unwilling to adapt to necessity—that is, the reality principle which sets limits on desire. Neurotics as a consequence regress mentally "to earlier phases of sexual life" when desires were fulfilled. They cling to the past emotionally, Freud found; "they cannot get free of the past and for its sake they neglect what is real and immediate." They view the past as a Golden Age, comforting and reassuring. This flight into fantasy is not a wholly satisfactory solution, but since it is all the neurotic thinks is available, it will have to do. "Remote times have a great attraction—sometimes mysteriously so—for the imagination. As often as mankind is dissatisfied with its present—and that happens often enough—it harks back to the past and hopes at last to win belief in the never forgotten dream of a Golden Age. Probably man still stands under the magic spell of his childhood, which a not unbiased memory presents to him as a time of unalloyed bliss."[12] Nostalgia for a specific historical past—the old world before the twin revolutions—was a commonplace by the time Freud conceived of making the longing for a lost Golden Age into a psychological theory. Freud's version had a religious ring to it, implying the recovery of paradise.

Every child, Freud theorized, lives through a real Golden Age up to about the age of five or six, when wants are responded to. After that the Golden Age is lost, and the individual is left with a nostalgia for it. The well adapt to the loss; the sick are those with too powerful a longing for the past. They continue to seek fulfillment of childish desires in spite of danger signals. At the age of puberty or after, when the satisfactions of the Golden Age are most sharply contrasted with the needs and wants and frustrations of the present, sickness may enter as a compensation for those needs, wants, and frustrations. The delusional symptoms are substitute wish fulfillments, that is, substitutes for what is desired but unattainable in reality. In this sense mental illness is an artistic creation composed of symbols. The sickness has the value of diverting the mind from its problems and conflicts by means of the delusional symptoms, and that is one of the comforts it affords; another is the false sense that the wishes are being fulfilled by the delusions, however inadequately.

Freud described mental illness as a compromise formation. In the conflict between desires and the forces of repression that want to keep them hidden, the neurotic solution is to develop delusional symptoms that express the desires and the contrary need to stifle them. What is missing and wanted, but cannot be admitted, is replaced by neurosis. Delusion, Freud notes, is "found like a patch over the place where originally there was a rent in the relation of ego and outer world." The patch (the symptoms) are manufactured out of "residues . . . of former relations with reality" and "materials from the present" mixed together.[13] These familiar elements drawn from the neurotic's own life make the neurosis less strange than it would otherwise be. This mix of past and present had a far wider application than neurosis in the hidden meanings and functions of psychoanalysis.

The cure, according to the theory, is for the patient to remember that period when he found his satisfactions slipping away (say, when he began to be punished); or perhaps to remember a single incident that summarizes the experience of thwarted desire and loss. That was the trauma. Once remembered, the patient can be shown that what happened was natural, and that he took too strong a view of the matter rather than incorporating the loss as a part of growing up. If one forgets the past (represses it), says the theory, one retains it in the unconscious and repeats it in the form of symptoms; if one remembers it, he can dispel its power to make him sick—the psychological equivalent of George Santayana's dictum about history: those who forget the past are doomed to repeat it.

Exactly why one individual became ill and another did not, considering that the experiences that caused neurosis were common to all, Freud could not exactly say. It might have to do with a particular individual's constitution. He did know why some individuals who had cause to be sick were not: he theorized that they sublimated their sexual energy in productive work, artistic or otherwise, an idea that had appeared before in Schopenhauer and Nietzsche. In any case, it was not only neurotics who repressed ideas to the unconscious and converted them into symbolic gestures; normal people did it too, in a process Freud called "the psychopathology of everyday life" (the title of his 1901 study of "Freudian slips" and other unconscious missteps called parapraxes). They also converted repressed ideas into jokes, a further form of normal symbolic representation of unconscious conflicts, which he explored in *Jokes and Their Relation to the Unconscious* (1905).

Years after developing the Oedipus theory, Freud supplemented it with the caveman story he told in *Totem and Taboo* (1913), based on views of the ethnographer Robertson Smith and writings by Darwin and Jung on the "primal horde." This was another expression of the themes of *lèse-majesté* and the quest for pleasure. Back in the far eons of prehistory, ran Freud's version of the story, fathers monopolized the available women. The sons' only recourse was to kill the fathers in order to get some of the women. If the sons failed in the attempt, the fathers punished them by castration. The young girls in this cave society, watching the castration, believed they too must have rebelled at one time in the past and been castrated, and that was why they did not have a penis—hence penis envy.

If the sons succeeded in killing the fathers, they ate their flesh in a totem meal designed to "appease the father by deferred obedience to him." The sons further expressed their deferred obedience by reinstituting the social order that led them to kill the fathers, stipulating that what they had done was wrong, and that it was also wrong to kill brothers and mate with women of the clan. "What had up to then been prevented by [the father's] actual existence was thenceforward prohibited by the sons themselves, in accordance with the psychological procedure so familiar to us in psycho-analysis under the name 'deferred obedience.' They revoked their deed by forbidding the killing of the totem, the substitute for their father; and they renounced its fruits by resigning their claim to the women who had now been set free."[14] "Deferred obedience" had great resonance for the hidden meanings and functions of psychoanalysis.

This caveman experience, Freud proposed, was the source of conscience, guilt, and the potential for mental illness in all succeeding generations of humankind throughout the world, via the Lamarckian inheritance of acquired characteristics. It also impelled the beginning of civilization, religion, and the arts through the sublimation of the sexual drive to social order. When scholars demonstrated that Robertson Smith's reconstruction of prehistory was untenable, Freud responded as he did on other occasions when he was shown to be relying on faulty information. Since the information supported his theoretical structure, he retained it: "It was my good right to select from ethnological data what would serve me for my analytic work."[15]

To explain his scheme of psychology more fully, about 1923 Freud postulated three components of the mind: id, ego, and superego, each of them an aspect of the ego. This was a refiguring of Plato's fable about a chariot driver with two horses. One horse was unruly (which became the id in the theory); the other was cooperative (becoming the superego); the driver was the ego. The id (a new version of the libido) was instincts, wants, aggressions, the sex drive. It was about satisfying the self above all, in spite of all. The ego was reason. The superego was the rules that manage the id and the ego. The superego develops when, as we saw, during the Oedipal conflict (as in the conflict in the caves) the child is so fearful of the father that he internalizes the father's morality. The father's morality says, *You* must not kill the father and have sex with the mother. The child incorporates this as, *I* must not kill the father and have sex with the mother, and in this way begins to become socialized within the family and in a larger sense within society.[16]

Freudian theory strikes many familiar notes: conflict with parents, which every child experiences; the efforts of parents to discipline children; the father (or, gender-free, the parent) as the first rule-giver; guilt, a common enough feeling which everyone is bound to experience some time or other. Even those who did not accept the reality of infantile sexuality could acquiesce in these common, everyday elements. Over time the Oedipus complex with its additions and reexplanations proved inordinately attractive, even in the years when it was officially scoffed at in some quarters.

ACCORDING TO FREUD, an individual requires treatment when, after the latency period, trauma flares into symptoms upon the return of the repressed memory of transgression. The patient has regressed to that childhood Eden when anxiety was introduced through fear of the parent. The goal of treatment, then, is to exorcise the Oedipus complex and its attendant guilt—or whatever other cause of mental illness a particular school of treatment believed in. Classical treatment begins with the patient lying on the famous Freudian couch with the therapist behind, out of sight of the patient. The therapist questions the patient about his problems in order to form a diagnosis and program of treatment. By virtue of Freudian theory he already believes that the problems, if they are neurotic, have a sexual cause in the patient's past.

Treatment proceeds by questioning the patient about memories, often but not exclusively of childhood, in order to locate the trauma through memory traces in the unconscious. Information is sought in dreams, which Freud thought were "the royal road to the unconscious";[17] in word associations ("free association") that might release or refer to unconscious memories, usually about family members; in current experiences that might relate to the neurosis; and also in such details as the patient's clothes or gestures. Except for more recent forms of therapy, the patient does not much deal with the present, using it only for examples of problems whose cause, in the theories derived from Freud, are in the past. Therefore the patient explores the past. The injunction of the therapist is, Remember!

The therapist maintains a cold, impersonal demeanor, speaking very little, mainly asking questions and occasionally interpreting responses. The responses are usually interpreted to have two meanings, a conscious, manifest, surface, false one, and an unconscious, latent, true one below the surface. The true meanings are found, according to the theory, by understanding what the patient says as symbolic reflections of sexual thoughts and experiences. Freud wrote in *The Interpretation of Dreams* that even "ideas centering around plant-life or the kitchen may just as readily be chosen [by the patient's unconscious] to conceal sexual images" which the therapist must interpret to reveal their latent meaning.[18]

In this book Freud lists among these symbols: animals, asparagus, bags, balloons, boxes, branches of trees, brothers and sisters, burglars, children, clarinets, clothing, departures, doors, eggs, eyes, fish, flowers, fruits, fur, gardens, ghosts, gigantic figures, hats, houses, keys and locks, landscapes, left and right, luggage, maps, money, nail files, narrow spaces, neckties, numbers, ovens, phallic shapes (pillars, pipes), prehistoric origins, relatives, rooms, royal persons, ships, snakes, staircases, tables, teeth, tools, urinals, vermin, water, weapons, whips, wood, and zeppelins. In other books he extended the list.[19]

In the case history of a teenager named "Dora," published in 1905, Freud found that a little handbag called a reticule, pinned to her skirt, which she sometimes fingered during treatment, was a symbol of the vagina, and the fingering represented masturbation. In a psychobiographical analysis of a dream of Leonardo da Vinci, Freud found that a bird represented a phallic symbol, evidence that the painter was a latent homosexual. Freud's disciple Melanie Klein found that a train in a dream symbolized a penis and a train tunnel was the vagina. Such symbols had to be decoded in order to reveal the disguised sexual conflicts they were hiding.

Freud sometimes referred to symbols, whether in dreams or in what his patients told him, as screen memories. They were masks hiding the real memories the patient resisted revealing. The reason for the resistance, and why the therapist had to dig so hard, was the patient's inclination, according to the theory, to resist treatment for the same reason that led to repression of the trauma and the resulting mental illness: treatment threatened to bring back the trauma and the patient feared facing it. This reaction was called resistance, or the defense mechanism, and was considered by Freud to be one of the main challenges in treatment because it was proof that patients were afraid of getting well, that is, facing their traumas, those secret, "disgusting" thoughts causing the illness. "The whole theory of psychoanalysis . . . is built up on the perception of the resistance offered to us by the patient when we attempt to make his unconscious conscious to him."[20]

At some point in treatment the patient enters into a "transference," in which the therapist becomes a member of the patient's family in the imagination—the emotions—of the patient. The patient then transfers or projects onto the therapist feelings about various family members, especially the mother and/or father. If this does not happen spontaneously, the therapist may induce it (the so-called transference neurosis) in order to force the patient to get back to the trauma hidden in the unconscious. Freud viewed the transference neurosis as a secondary illness designed to cure the primary one. Transference may be intense, the patient at one time loving the therapist and on another occasion expressing hatred, anger, aggression, and a whole range of other emotions interpreted in classical therapy as reexperiencing the feelings once associated with the parents during the Oedipal conflict. Countertransference may take place as well, the therapist imagining the patient as a member of *his* family and reacting as though the patient were a son or daughter, or possibly a parent or sibling. The concept of transference performed multiple services in the hidden meanings and functions of psychoanalysis.

Since therapy evokes painful emotions, at many points it will become highly charged. The patient experiences feelings of distrust, loss, isolation, fear of being abandoned by the family or by the whole world, of becoming overwhelmed, engulfed, weak, defenseless. The patient passes through this vale of tears, according to the theory, in order to come out the other side, to the positive, the real, the balanced, the poised, the optimistic (however guarded). The powerful emotions evoked are theoretically under the management of the therapist; otherwise they might be dangerous. They are almost invariably viewed as aspects of the patient's illness, devoid of any content beyond early familial conflict, and are eventually to be quieted with the assistance of the therapist and placed under the command of the patient.

Treatment may go on for months, years, decades, until the patient remembers and understands the unconscious wish for illegitimate pleasures and the parent's threat of punishment, these elements that constituted the trauma and later turned into illness. Since neurosis is viewed as the unconscious suppression of "criminal" truths—the infantile desire for illegitimate pleasures—its corollary or obverse is, Know the truth and the truth shall make you free, or the Delphic oracle's injunction, Know thyself! Abreaction, the mental "reliving" of the trauma, leads to a cathartic discharge of the illness. To Freud, "understanding and cure coincide . . . a transversable road leads from one to the other."[21] This was the same doctrine as *Seelsorge* treatment.

When cured, the patient will no longer depend emotionally on parents or therapist and will be able to carve out a fully independent life. "Men cannot remain children forever; they must in the end go out into 'hostile life.' We may call this *'education in reality.'*" Describing the desirable outcome of treatment, Freud wrote:

> The freeing of an individual, as he grows up, from the authority of his parents is one of the most necessary though one of the most painful results brought about by the course of his development. It is quite essential that that liberation should occur and it may be presumed that it has been to some extent achieved by everyone who has reached a normal state. Indeed, the whole progress of society rests upon the opposition between successive generations.[22]

The liberation from past wounds, compulsions, and emotions, originally experienced with one's parents, leads to independence—a hopeful scenario built around freedom.

Freud's theories and methods were paralleled by those of his most famous disciples and later competitors. In place of the Oedipus complex Jung spoke of individuation, the process by which a person achieves independence. Adler theorized the inferiority complex and its resultant sense of powerlessness, which kept a person from assuming his rightful place in society. Janet, like Freud, looked for past wounds or guilty wishes that could not be expressed but had to come to the surface if there was to be a cure. All concurred in the theories of unconscious drives, cathexis and anti-cathexis, trauma, the production of delusional symptoms, the source of mental illness in a crisis over desire, and the cure achieved through cathartic memory.

As time passed, these various systems of the most important pioneers diverged further. To some the present had more weight than the past, or the mother had importance equal to or greater than the father in human psychology, or the therapist had to be more voluble and less withdrawn, or the couch was eliminated and therapist and patient faced each other across a desk. But at the turn of the century all the psychoanalysts were quite similar. By the first decade of the new century the Freudian school of psychology had established an international standing based on shared doctrines.[23]

It has been observed more than once that the swiftness of psychoanalysis's success was virtually unprecedented in the annals of science. That was because the unique theoretical ensemble Freud culled from his sources was so responsive to the culture and the time that it put everything that came before—and much that came after—into the shadows. For the latent functions it served, little if anything could have worked as well.

IN THE second half of his life, as he took on the trappings of a sage who had uncovered vital, timeless, universal knowledge of the mind, Freud applied his theories to larger entities than neurotic patients. In *Totem and Taboo* (1913) he turned to the subjects of religion, society, and civilization. He explored political science in *Group Psychology and the Analysis of the Ego* (1921), concluding, like Le Bon, that while individuals might be willing to give up unsatisfied desires, groups compulsively overlooked the reality principle. The social uses of religion was his subject in *The Future of an Illusion* (1927). *Civilization and Its Discontents* (1930) was his rather pessimistic commentary on the fate of human instincts in their battle with social order. *Moses and Monotheism* (1939) returned to the theme of religion and how it is constructed. By the end of his life there was scarcely a social issue that Freud did not touch on somewhere. The other Freudians, notably Adler, Rank, and Jung, similarly wrote on such broad topics in later life. Anyone wishing to deal with the social, political, economic, and cultural aspects of Freudianism would be expected to appeal to these works. But the political and social meanings and functions of Freudianism are not to be found chiefly in these overt commentaries; they are in the theories and practices concerning *individual psychology*. Freud's scheme of individual psychology was actually a system for influencing mass psychology.

For most his life Freud was in mental conflict over the individual and social aspects of his thought, unsure of how they fit together. At times he saw himself as a doctor treating patients, at other times as a philosopher or social scientist analyzing the roots of civilization. And yet he was not unaware of the connection between the two: "In the individual's mental life someone else is invariably involved, as a model, as an object, as a helper, as an opponent; and so from the very first individual psychology . . . is at the same time social psychology. . . ." His last estimate of himself was that

> after forty-one years of medical activity, my self-knowledge tells me that I have never really been a doctor in the proper sense. I became a doctor through being compelled to deviate from my original purpose; and the triumph of my life lies in my having, after a long and roundabout journey, found my way back to my earliest path.[24]

That path led to the great issues of humankind and civilization. Freud thought he refound it late in life, but in fact his thinking was always of a piece, functioning ironically but smoothly as a single system. He and the other soul psychologists found the core of mental illness and its treatment to be symbolic ideas or representations in the mind that had to be dispelled or changed. That is what connected Freud's theorizing in all its parts. Symbolism was his high road to cultural therapy and the domination of modern psychology.

ELEVEN

The Art of the Symbol

In our time we have not finished doing away with idols
and we have barely begun to listen to symbols.
 —Paul Ricoeur, *Freud and Philosophy*

It is a hard matter to persuade people to adventure into
strange countries.
 —Richard Whitbourne, *A Discovery and
Discourse of Newfoundland*

FREUD'S ASSOCIATION of mental illness with symbols was inherited from Schopenhauer and Charcot, for whom mental illness was the
symbolic repetition or representation of past traumas. To Freud, mental illness was the recreation of past and present experience in a new,
symbolic form shaped by the need of the unconscious to disguise its
purposes and provide comfort by shielding the conscious mind from
dread. The process was determined, Freud wrote, by the fact that

> we humans . . . find reality unsatisfying quite generally, and for that
> reason entertain a life of phantasy in which we like to make up for the
> insufficiencies of reality by the production of wish-fulfillments. These
> phantasies include a great deal of the true constitutional essence of the
> subject's personality as well as those of his impulses which are re-
> pressed where reality is concerned.[1]

Neurotic symbol formation was called by Freud "censorship," or the
"dream-work," by which he meant that the unconscious did not let its
pure thoughts rise to consciousness; it censored them by symbolizing
them. Neurotics were in effect symbolist poets, and their symptoms
and dreams were symbolist poems. The job of the analyst was to translate the symbols back into the ideas or memories they represented.

Among the ways symbolic representations are created by the unconscious, according to Freud, are condensation: for example, a single authority figure stands for many others; displacement: a desire for one thing appears as the desire for another, apparently unrelated to it; symbolization: a desire or anxiety is represented figuratively rather than directly; and secondary revision: logic is applied in recalling a dream in the waking state, so that it seems a connected, rational narrative with the loose ends tied together. Secondary revision "behaves in the manner which the poet [Heine] maliciously ascribes to philosophers: it fills up the gaps in the dream-structure with shreds and patches." Another form of unconscious symbolization is reversal: the appearance of an idea or memory in its opposite form, so that if an object in a dream is white, it can be presumed, under the conditions of interpretation, that it may well be representing something black. This led Freud to the conclusion that when a patient said No the meaning was usually Yes.[2] Still other forms of symbolic representation were diminution, reducing the size or significance of a thing, and elimination, the removal of something too revealing.

Freud vividly described the creation of fantasy symbols in the case of the mad judge I cited earlier, who believed that the world had come to an end and that he, the lone survivor, was destined to revive it. The end of the world, Freud theorized, was the patient's symbol for his illness: his real world had come to an end. The other symbols he produced in his illness were attempts to recreate this fallen world in a form that could be lived with more easily than could the trauma that caused the symptoms. The patient goes about recreating his new, symbolic world "by the work of his delusions. *The delusion-formation, which we take to be a pathological product, is in reality an attempt at recovery, a process of reconstruction.*" To illustrate, Freud quotes from *Faust,* Part I, when, after Faust curses the world, a Chorus of Spirits sings:

> Woe! Woe!
> Thou has destroyed it,
> The beautiful world,
> With mighty fist!
> It tumbles, it falls to pieces!
> A demigod has shattered it! . . .
> Mighty
> Among the songs of the earth,

More splendid
Build it up again,
Build it up in thy bosom![3]

That is what the mentally ill do, says Freud, build up in the mind through symbolic fantasies what they have lost and can no longer find in reality, in an attempt at self-cure (by hiding the trauma).

This imaginary world is endowed "with a special meaning and secret significance which we, not always correctly, call *symbolical.* . . . Thus we see that there arises . . . the question not only of the *loss of reality,* but of a *substitute for reality also.*" Among the features of reality for which the mentally ill individual manufactures symbolic substitutes are "the great group formations from which he is excluded. He creates his own world of the imagination in himself, his own religion, his own system of delusions, and this recapitulates the institutions of humanity. . . ."[4] These symbolic substitutions, which the patient thinks are real and true, fill in the gaps left by the repressed trauma. As in Schopenhauer, they ward off frustration, what hurts one's pride, injures one's interests, interferes with one's wishes, what is shameful or guilt-ridden. In a perverse way the result is comforting, because the psyche prefers not to admit fear and guilt, or failure in the outer world, or that it has had to create substitutes. This resistance to knowledge of what the psyche has done is part of what creates mental illness and makes it so difficult to treat, according to Freudian theory.

The Freudian theory of trauma leading to symptoms is itself a symbolic representation of the Fall in the Bible—the collapse of Paradise and the inheritance of a new world distorted from its original conditions, to which Freud alludes on several occasions.[5] This same symbolization of collapse and rebuilding applied to the single most significant fact of the nineteenth century: the collapse of the preindustrial world (the trauma) and the inheritance of the world we gained, which after a "latency period" of a hundred years led to the social hysteria (symptoms) of the fin de siècle. The world we gained "forgot" much of the old world, repressed it, and at the same time was ashamed of having banished it and having welcomed the new, lustful age. There was violent reaction to the loss and what was substituted—urban life, mass poverty and powerlessness, anomie, atheism, and the other manifestations of the new age.

Critics of the new age, says the historian Jerrold Seigel, deplored "a culture that does not protect people from their own animal natures as eighteenth-century society had. . . . The nineteenth century released all the low currents against which the social bulwarks of the Old Regime stood fast: economic materialism, the primitive social impulses of the lower classes, the debilitating and spiritless domesticity of modern woman." These "denatured social forms," the critics felt, opened society to "domination by those foreign and barbarous elements waiting to overtake it from within: the Jews." Tocqueville had said that equality, by challenging the distinction between rich and poor, opened the way to socialism, selfishness, and unrestrained passion for material satisfaction—all of it the result of abolishing traditional social distinctions.[6]

That the missing past and what replaced it could lead to catastrophe was dramatically presented by the French psychiatrist Regnard, cited earlier, and by Judge Schreber's psychotic dismissal of his present reality in favor of a new world fashioned after the old one. It was of huge concern to sociologists and psychopoliticians of the new age, and was in good measure what the artists and intellectuals of the age were reacting to. From the loss of the past and the shock of the new came nostalgia, nowhere stronger than in Austria, where vestiges of the old world were still potent but were daily expected to be wiped out in an apocalypse. One of the ways the Austrians dealt with the situation, we saw, was to hide their problems and live with an ornamental veneer that reflected the past, as though nothing had happened and nothing was wrong, which is the same reaction Freud maintained led to neurosis. It was a reaction shared by many in the nineteenth century.

In the 1920s a standing prize was offered anyone who would fly solo across the Atlantic Ocean. In the years surrounding 1900 there was a "standing prize," real but not embodied that way, for anyone who could revive the *gemeinschaft* in some suitable modern way, or could reempower its central symbols and institutions as a way of saving Western civilization from itself. Such an attempt inevitably must employ imitation, repetition, reminiscence, symbolization, parable, allegory, fetish, substitution, revival, renovation, wish fulfillment, delusion, reparation, and reclamation—all attributes that the Freudians assigned to neurosis.

Here began the hidden, secret, mimetic, symbolical work of psychoanalysis, whose symbols included science, mental illness, mental health, theories of psychology, and practices of treatment. Its goal was to comfort the culture in which psychoanalysis operated, just in the way neurotics were said to respond to trauma. If this characterizes psychoanalysis as a delusion, and the pioneers as mentally ill by their own standards, it must be remembered that Freud theorized from very early on that quite normal people seek satisfying substitutes for frustrated wishes. They create these substitutes by "the psychopathology of everyday life" and by sublimation, "some achievement in the outside world." Throughout his work Freud assured that "neuroses have no psychical content that is peculiar to them and that might not equally be found in healthy people."[7] What has therefore been labeled by critics the delusion of the Freudians in creating their system (and perhaps the mental illness assigned to Freud by E. M. Thornton and others), the Freudians had already countered by explaining that quite normal people create delusions. Indeed, said Freud, societies do the same, among their delusions being religion as a comfort and protection.

As evidence of unconscious processes, Hartmann in his 1868 bestseller underscored a doctrine familiar to the medical profession: *vis medicatrix,* the reparative power of nature, which worked unconsciously in the mind and body. He also called attention, like other soul psychologists, to the "purposiveness of the creative impulse in the unconscious";[8] and many soul psychologists, including the Freudians, believed that the unconscious worked to detect danger, warn of it, and, in the healthy individual, propose realistic solutions—and in the sick individual inadequate, fantasy ones. While agreeing with these theories, Freud warned that the attempt of the unconscious to repair wounds and ward off dangers was never completely successful. Only the real world and real experience in it can provide a really satisfactory solution. Still, if the real world cannot provide antidotes to danger, dissatisfaction, and frustration, the normal individual can employ the psychopathology of everyday life and sublimation. Thus if Freud's system was not perfect in its theories or its effects, he had already explained that substitutes were useful, if not as good as the real thing.

In Freudian terms, and in the common terms of everyday life, psychoanalysis decodes as a delusional response to the crisis of Western culture in the fin de siècle. It was formulated and accepted to provide comfort and protection, resistance to some truths, and a clearer view of other truths. Its ultimate goal was to provide understanding—a new understanding of and for a new age—understanding being itself one of the great components of comfort, and in psychoanalysis the nature of the cure. As a delusion, psychoanalysis was quite normal on the model of the psychopathology of everyday life and sublimation. It is difficult to picture the intelligent, middle-class members of Freud's circle as anything but normal, satisfied with themselves and their construction.

Freud explained himself in 1895, right at the beginning of his miraculous years, in the "Draft H" he sent to Fliess under the title "Paranoia." "Transposition or projection," he wrote, is "a psychic mechanism that is very commonly employed in normal life," merely "normal delusions and normal projections. . . . The mechanism of substitution is also a normal one. . . ." Then, describing himself when he meant to be describing paranoia, he concluded: "Paranoia and hallucinatory confusion are the two *psychoses of spite or contrariness.* The 'reference to oneself' in paranoia is analogous to the hallucinations in confessional states, for these seek to assert the exact contrary of the fact that has been warded off. Thus the reference to oneself always seeks to prove the correctness of the projection."⁹ Psychoanalysis was a confession of what Freud was actually doing, if it could only be read aright; the reference to the individual (as in "individual psychology") was the exact contrary of the idea being warded off. Psychoanalysis was not about the individual but about history and culture. ("Draft H" is in many ways the best short symbolic explanation of what Freud did.)

In its public, surface form, Freudianism was about the interpretation of symbols in the unconscious mind of the mentally ill and the mentally healthy; in its secret, latent form it was about the creation of symbols placed in the mind of a hysterical culture as suggestions or representations of what to believe in order to achieve comfort. When Freud described neurosis as a substitute for wish fulfillments, and dreams as embodiments of wish fulfillments, he was also describing psychoanalysis. When his much admired disciple Georg Groddeck wrote that "Illness has a purpose; it has to resolve the conflict, to repress it, or to prevent what is already repressed from entering consciousness . . . ," he too was describing psychoanalysis.¹⁰ When the sparkling controversialist of Freud's Vienna, Karl Kraus, famously remarked that psychoanalysis was the illness it purported to cure, he incisively divined its essence. And when Freud described transference neurosis as a new illness imposed by the therapist to treat an old one, he was once again on the mark, for psychoanalysis was a vast transference of the social onto the personal.

When Freud spoke of the deferred obedience of the caveman sons, he was giving a parable of what he and his culture were doing. The culture had put in place a new politics and new relationships that in important ways replicated what had come before. For that reason they were in more danger than they had been before because they no longer possessed the absolute justifications of a God-ordained hierarchy, and for that reason they required new totems and rituals for support. When Freud said that neurotic symptoms were created out of the "constitutional essence" of the sick individual, he was again offering a parable about psychoanalysis: it was created out of the constitutional essence of the Western tradition and out of social reactions and repressions that at the time needed to be explained and rationalized or hidden as well as might be.

With this in mind, the tapestry of nineteenth-century history and what came before can be unraveled as psychoanalysis. In fact, one may weave another tapestry from the same materials of history and demonstrate it to be psychoanalysis. The history and thought of Western culture, up to and including the fin de siècle, is what the Freudians imitated, countered, or addressed in some other way—in disguise—in line with their values and goals, which were essentially those of the reigning Western culture. Fantasy symbols, Freud emphasized, come out of familiar materials very close to the neurotic and are substitutes for what is repressed. The same features may be seen in psychoanalysis as the proposed curative for the trauma and hysteria of the West.

In an example of the unconscious symbol techniques Freud described, what would not have been expected—the presentation of a medical psychology which was in fact a cultural and social therapy—is what happened. Among the many technical Freudian terms for this process was *reaction formation* (similar to reversal), hiding something by its opposite. Because of this camouflaging, many commentators think Freud retreated into a career in psychology out of a frustration with politics. They fail to notice that Freudian psychology was more than a substitute for politics; it was politics by other means, in the same sense that Clausewitz said war was diplomacy by other means. Herzl, the activist politician, wished to lead the Jews back to the Promised Land. Other activists wished to lead Europe to a new and different future based on the past or on dreams of imagined new possibilities. Freud, the quietist psychologist who disliked putting dreams into action, as he said—who whistled tunes to express his political opinions and chafed cabdrivers and waiters in his unease—helped to keep Europe on the path of liberal democracy and modernity by advancing symbolic representations designed to affect the mind.

The Freudian symbolic representations constituting psychoanalysis were of four types. One was the revival of the past in a new form, exactly what the theory maintained about the neurotic. The second was the demonization of cultural enemies, something psychotics did with those they conceived as their personal enemies. The third was a diversional editing or revision of the European mind. The fourth was the wall of protection the Freudians built into their theories so that their latent work might not be found out (what in Freudian theory was called resistance).

Freud tells Fliess that dreams and neurosis are one and the same—wish fulfillment in both being the cause of both; and that dreams and neurosis are "falsifications of memory and fantasies—the latter relating to the past or future."[11] The reader should be aware that from this point on, what Freud says—and what I quote—about dreams, neurosis, falsification, fantasy, and delusion, what he says about fetishes, substitutes, imitations, and repetitions of past and present realities, is actually about psychoanalysis in its latent meanings and functions. And what he says about psychoanalysis is actually about history and society, including what he is living through. The hidden commentaries on his labors throughout Freud's work are not his only statements about his latent work. The best commentary is the work itself. The proof is not so much in what Freud said, however intriguing, but in what he did, evident in what he and his colleagues settled on for their theories and practices.

In 1589, encouraging the settlement of the New World, the English pamphleteer Sir George Peckham weighed "whether it were as well pleasing to almighty God, as profitable to men: as lawful as it seems honourable: as well grateful to the Savages, as gainful to the Christians. And upon mature deliberation, I found the action to be honest and profitable." That can be taken as the motto of the Freudians. Freud himself provided another that is just as apt: "Let me give you an analogy; analogies, it is true, decide nothing; but they can make one feel more at home."[12] The latent, symbolical work of psychoanalysis as a system of belief was to give encouragement to the voyagers who were navigating the new age, against all those who wished to turn back or find a still better world in the mists of conjecture. It was an attempt, through analogies (symbolic representations), to make them feel more at home. Travel on, the Freudians urged, do not fear.

In sublimating the troubles of Europe in a symbolic system of suggestion, psychoanalysis mimetically reconstructed the past and modernity according to the old wedding formula, "something old, something new, something borrowed, something blue." By imitating the reigning Western culture in a literary form (said to be scientific), psychoanalysis made all the loose ends, the despairs and discouragements, the contradictions and offenses, along with the wonders, a single, comprehensible, and absolving story. It was a Freudian patch over the rent that had appeared in Western culture. As Freud wrote in *Moses and Monotheism,* perhaps looking back on his great creation, "in the meantime the use of analogies must help us out."[13]

Symbolism had compelling advantages for someone like Freud, who preferred not to confront the general public or his political enemies directly—the more so in an authoritarian country such as Austria. Politicians spoke more directly, and so did public activists; everyday citizens would feel constrained. Professionals such as physicians, serving a public with differing opinions, would put themselves at a disadvantage by voicing strong political opinions. Nor was it safe, without some protection such as a disguise, to denounce political enemies on the far right who practiced bullyboy tactics.

Under any political system, disguised persuasion is often far more effective. Obvious persuasion can be more readily confronted; hidden persuasion is more difficult to grapple with and therefore potentially more effective. In any event, it would have been absurd for the Freudians to advertise as their medical specialty the treatment of a society or a culture.

Being something other than what you were publicly advertised to be was already popular. Intellectual clerks in many fields were doing it. Nordau demonstrated how to voice social views while hiding behind a medical vocabulary. Maurice Barrès, the novelist, succeeded as a right-wing agitator while doing little more than writing his novels. To the public, Treitschke was a historian, not an agitator for anti-Semitism and Germanism. Houston Chamberlain presented himself as a racial theorist, not a first-rate bigot. The Freudians did not present themselves as guardians of liberal democratic modernity; yet that was their definitive role. In performing it, they employed what their understanding of psychology told them was one of the most effective means of persuasion: suggestion.

Part IV

TREATMENT: REVIVING THE PAST

Then death, so call'd, is but old Matter dress'd
In some new Figure, and a vary'd Vest:
Thus all Things are but alter'd, nothing dies;
And here and there th' unbody'd Spirit flies. . . .
—Ovid, *Metamorphoses*

What is "past" tempts us to reconstruct a world rather
like a walled city, finite and contained and in
the most literal sense predictable.
—Joyce Carol Oates, "The King of Weird"

When it's dark ahead, you feel like turning back. . . .
—Tatyana Tolstaya, "The Way They Live Now"

TWELVE

The Old in the New

For man sets store by recognition, he likes to find the
old in the new. . . . From that recognition he draws a
sense of the familiar in life, whereas if it painted itself
as entirely new . . . it could only bewilder and alarm.
　　　　　　　　　—Thomas Mann, *Three Essays*

. . . Memory traces [are] subjected from time to time to
a *rearrangement* in accordance with fresh
circumstances—to a *retranscription*.
　　　　　　　　　—Sigmund Freud, Letter to Fliess

PSYCHOANALYSIS "treated" the European mind primarily through
ideas placed inside psychological theories about the mental illness of
individuals. The ideas thus symbolized as psychology functioned in
toto as a belief system. We can begin to decode the Freudian symbolization of ideas by considering those elements of the theory that drew
attention to the family, the individual, the community, and the emotions.

From the start, modern psychology was centrally concerned with
the dire effects of parents on their children. According to Freud, "the
chief part in the mental life of all children who later became psy-
choneurotics is played by their parents." A near-parody of this view is
recounted by Jeffrey Masson in the case of a therapist telling a psychotic patient, "I am trying to find out what made you crazy. I think
your mother did it."[1] Since, with little scientific evidence available to
the pioneers, virtually anything could have been designated as the
locus of mental health and mental illness, how did it come to be that
the family was selected for this role? Why did the "family romance"
find itself at the core of modern psychology?

The conviction of the pioneers was that something went wrong in the family—in Freud's view, the unsuccessful navigation of the Oedipus complex. What was actually wrong was obvious but unspoken: around 1800 Western culture had abandoned the family, and the family had consequently abandoned its members. The family as functioning household had been traded in for the individual. For all those who lived in the modern age, Jacques Ellul observed, the family was "broken up. It no longer has the power to envelop the individual, it is no longer the place where the individual is formed and has his root." In the allegory of caveman society, Freud described what had happened: after killing the father, the sons themselves became fathers, but much weakened: "the new family was only a shadow of the old one . . . ; the father became again the head of the family, but he was no longer omnipotent."[2] Freud imagined that happening in the long ago, but in fact it had happened after the twin revolutions.

The threat to security posed by the dissolving family was felt by all, seen by all. The focus on the family in modern psychology was impelled by the sense of—for the first time in history—the loss of the family as the central institution. There was a satisfying nostalgia in having the family highlighted in therapy, even with pain, because the real family, outside the therapist's office, was disappearing. And the family, important as it was, was a reflection of something else that was lost: the old world of certainty and permanence, and the assured place of each member within it. Psychoanalysis had got hold of history (that is to say, major social trends) and was impelled by history to select its main symbols. It was filling a gap that had appeared with the loss of the old world.

Part of the appeal of psychoanalysis was the hope of refinding the family and thereby ending the alienation of modernity. This accounted for one of the main concepts of therapy: transference. According to Freudian therapy, transference turned the therapist into the patient's father or mother in the patient's imagination. But the true case was that history and the psychological theorists placed the therapist in the position of the parents and the patient in the position of the child. The patient did not later, during the course of therapy, enter into the transference process, as the theory held; the patient began with the quest for the lost family, which was the quest of an entire culture, and therapy fulfilled it. The Oedipus complex did not accidentally emphasize the role of the father as moral guide or the mother as comforter; the therapist *was* Dad again (or Mom), a safe haven. Therapy was designed, wittingly or not, that this should be so—because of history, not because of the imperatives of theory.[3]

Transference, Freud thought, helped establish the therapist's authority and smoothed the exploration for the source of the patient's neurosis. Out of sight of these theoretical justifications was its reinstallation of the family hierarchy with the powerful, feared father at the top, a reflection of the old world family. The patient was again part of the old family hierarchy, and so was the therapist, through countertransference. In the therapist's office, as in the old world, as Laslett wrote, "Everyone had a circle of affection, and every relationship was a love relationship." The patient wanted to believe that here, for pay, would be refound the family, or at least a replica of authentic relationships. This could naturally develop into a fantasy of trust, even sometimes of love, as though the therapist's shingle read, "Find Love Here."

The increasing length of treatment was part of the "family feeling" of therapy. At first Freud thought that six weeks would be sufficient for diagnosis, treatment, and cure. In time that became six months and then, not infrequently, six years, and still later an indefinite, elastic period which could last most of the life of the patient and/or the therapist. One famous patient, called the Wolf-Man, was in treatment on and off for sixty years.[4] Freud eventually came to believe that therapy was an interminable process with no end, finally realizing perhaps what he had done by turning the consequences of history and modernity into theory and practice. The family was a permanent institution, lasting for the life of its members; *therapy functioned as a simulacrum of the family's permanence,* a substitute for the disappearing/disappeared family. Analysts such as Adler, Jung, Rank, Ferenczi, and Franz Alexander (and later Jacques Lacan) tried to shorten the treatment process, but they swam against the tide. Shortening the length of treatment abrogated one of the root functions of therapy: the representation of the family. As a result, short therapies gained less currency than long ones.[5]

Once having created a spectral image of the family, therapy taught that it was right and proper that the old family should have been dissolved. It had been a restrictive, irrational formation, ruled by a tyrant in the same way the old world had been. Therapy was the better substitute, for it was rational, and in that way a parallel to the new democratic institutions, so different from the authoritarian institutions of the old world. The therapist as the rational father could *with author-*

ity say what the father wanted to say, and he might be heeded in a way the father was not, for parents were no longer respected as they had been. The therapist, on the other hand, was a doctor (a scientist), who could elicit the sort of respect that might have been given to the father of old.

Therapy theories that assailed the parents not only recognized the loss of the old family but posited the blessing of that loss, in the same way that the killing of the caveman father opened the way to civilization.[6] The same advancement and improvement over the old models were to be seen in the impelling forces behind psychoanalysis, which it was copying: political freedom and industry, superior to the old ways of tyranny and serfdom. The liberation from the family preached by Freud was the liberation from what was to be understood as the hated, bigoted, superstitious, ignorant, arrogant, irrational past of aristocrats and priests lording it over the commons and keeping them from being free and equal individuals. We must be released from our parents, Freud taught, by which he was saying symbolically that we must be released from the despotic historical past to which Western culture still clung as a nostalgic haven from modern hysteria.

Through nostalgia and the relief it offered from alienation, therapy possessed both irresistibility and verisimilitude. All at once it was the family revivified; the rationale for the rejection of the family consequent on the twin revolutions; the justification for the rejection; and a much improved replacement. That is why the family found itself at the center of therapy theory. Freud tells what he is accomplishing when he writes of the insane Judge Schreber.

> Such a reconstruction after the catastrophe is more or less successful, but never wholly so; in Schreber's words, there has been a "profound internal change" in the world. But the man has recaptured a relation, and often a very intense one, to the people and things in the world, although the relation may be a hostile one now, where formerly it was sympathetic and affectionate. We may conclude, then, that the process of repression proper consists in a detachment of the libido from people—and things—that were previously loved. It happens silently; we receive no intelligence of it, but can only infer it from subsequent events. What forces itself so noisily upon our attention is the process of recovery, which undoes the work of repression and brings back the libido again on to the people it had abandoned. In paranoia this process is carried out by the work of projection.[7]

When Freud spoke in *Moses and Monotheism* of the "reanimation of primeval experience," he was talking symbolically about his own reanimation of Europe's preindustrial experience in the modern context.[8] It was not happenstance that guidance in living became a major function of therapy. Guidance, once the province of the family, was taken over wholesale by therapy.

IN ADDITION TO the family, therapy placed the personality, cares, and deficiencies of the individual at the heart of the proceedings. People as they once had been were now lost in a mass, and it was only due their dignity as free men and women in an impersonal, modern, *gesellschaft* world that they be refound as meaningful, not anonymous, not evicted from the lost family and the old community. By focusing on the patient, therapy affirmed the individual created by the twin revolutions as a person of worth (even in demanding payment that demonstrated worldly worth in the medium of the modern age). For that fifty minutes, only that patient's life and cares were the subject. While affirming the modern individual, concentrating on the patient as a person of worth known to the Other (the therapist, representative of the whole "well" world) replicated the *gemeinschaft* style of relationship in which all were known to all in the small village setting. It might be a poor reflection, but it was something, and therefore appealing as a counter to anomie and alienation.[9]

Freud's name for therapy, psychoanalysis, was a warrant that the individual's psyche—*your* psyche—was worth analyzing. The general name, depth psychology, was another warrant of individual worth: the individual patient had depths worth plumbing. Adler's name for his school was individual psychology, another homage to the new man and woman. Adler chiefly, but also Freud and Jung, paid heed to a characteristic of the new individual they thought necessary to recognize and overcome—the sense of inferiority (which Freud interpreted as a weak ego). This was vitally true in a historical sense, for the new individual en masse was recognized by his superiors, the elites, as inferior, former peasants, rabble. Therapy held out the promise of reversing that feeling by emphasizing an individual who could—potentially—feel superior or at least equal. That was one of the cures modernity needed but did not yet supply: recognition of the individual in his or her full dignity. "The myth, then," Freud explained in *Group Psychology,* "is the step by which the individual emerges from group psychology."[10]

Mythically, psychoanalysis was attempting to affirm the individual who had arisen from the old group and was now lost in the new mass. Focusing on the patient confirmed the romantic and democratic affirmation of the individual. Mass man got his attention from where he did not want it—impersonal bureaucracies, company managers, tax collectors. The focus was off him or her as a person, an individual. Psychoanalysis gave it back while theorizing that the need for attention was a sign of illness. It then fulfilled the need through a therapy that acknowledged what the patient wanted and missed but would have to do without except in the "supportive," "nonjudgmental" atmosphere of therapy. Therapy taught that in the modern world, attention was no longer readily available: learn to live without much of it; everyone was busy. In this way it functioned as an aversion process that taught the wisdom of staying away from the need or desire for attention.

The psychoanalytic attention paid to the individual, even if painful, was appealing. "You are somebody," the therapist was saying. "I am somebody," the patient silently responded. This may seem simplistic, but set in the frame of modernity, with its masses and crowding, it had an altogether greater meaning. In response to critics of the new society who took the emergence of the mass as an indictment, came the Freudian answer: the return of the individual in psychoanalytic theory. And then came the Freudian twist: healthy individuals in the modern setting did not demand childish attention; they went about their business.

The Jungian concept of *individuation* was only another of the many psychotherapeutic warrants of the new individual, the term itself a play on democratic individualism. That was its positive message; the negative side was that the patient, in the new age, was created in anomie, and it was time for him to get out on his own, to make his own way since there was no support system any longer to enmesh him in care and ritual. He was not only on his own in the modern world, was the message, by being cut away from the old family and individuated in that way; he was also cut off from the very idea of the old family and the meanings and functions it used to have. The patient was to live with the substitutes provided, one of them being therapy.

IT IS NO mystery that modernity is not hospitable to the idea of community. In the liberal democracies there was no longer a community so much as an atmosphere in which individual wills could express their desires and talents. There they could pursue, as the original modern liberal democracy put it, life, liberty, and happiness by competition political, economic, and social. How to foster feelings for this new national entity whose very premises were anti-community and yet whose survival depended, as does that of any institution, on coherence and adherence? Here once again the Freudians entered the breech with theories about the conflict that gave rise to mental illness. Given the needs of the time, it should not be surprising that these theories concerned what was missing from the sociopolitical and economic philosophies of the day: community.

Freud taught a psychic conflict between the unconscious libido and the conscious ego (later among id, ego, and superego), the unconscious libido/id wanting, wishing, grasping for personal satisfaction, the conscious ego (reason) placing restraints on the libido/id. The restraining ego was already a community concept, for it taught that we could not be free to do whatever we wished when living in a larger world than our psyche. But Freud underscored the point when he added the superego, embedding family and community standards in the psyche. The superego became the substitute for the community, now revivified in the mind as psychology. Outside this psychic community in the mind, Freudian theory taught, lay mental illness—a commanding motivation for adhering to community standards.

For Jung, overindividuation led to separation from the community in favor of the self, resulting in an anxiety-ridden isolation. Again, that way lay mental illness, was the message; health was within the community. For Adler, community appeared in its most blatant psychological form: mental health was "the community feeling"; separation from the community was the root of mental disease, expressed in feelings of powerlessness, persecution, and rebelliousness. Separation from the human community, to Adler, was also separation from the largest community of all, the cosmic order, for like all the theorists he had incorporated the lesson of German Idealist philosophy—garnered from the world religions—in which the individual was part of a vast universal whole.

These theories fostered the return of an idea whose time had passed: community, which was needed again to counteract the centrifugal forces of modernity. Since individualism was apt to be anarchic, or could become so, all three theorists, according to Otto Rank, "reached a similar conclusion, namely, that the evil from which our personality suffers is over-individualization, hence, they agree in the remedy consisting of an emotional unity with something beyond the self. . . . In this sense, psychology is searching for a substitute for the cosmic unity which the man of Antiquity enjoyed in life and expressed in his religion, but which modern man has lost. . . ."[11]

It was not however, I suggest, the cosmic that was being sought in these psychoanalytic theories. It was something smaller, but still large: the community of modern society, culture, and the nation-state. Rank recognized this, seeing in the new psychology "the same force which is striving for the maintenance of the existing social order." The concept of a universal unconscious, one of the main features of all versions of the new psychology, bolstered the community idea. Jung's "collective unconscious" underscored the point by finding primordial, universal images and beliefs in the mind common to all. The goal, according to Rank, was to reconnect "the isolated individual with a bigger whole of which he can feel an essential part."[12] The old community having been lost, a new one was created within the self by the psychological theorists.

THE GREEKS knew the importance of the emotions in psychology; nineteenth-century soul psychologists, influenced by romanticism, likewise gave the emotions great attention. In the view of the psychiatrist Jerome Frank, all therapies are emotional because the sufferer is in a tug-of-war between what he believes and what he must come to believe if he is to be cured. According to the social anthropologist Ernest Gellner, a psychic treatment without high emotional involvement would not be compelling, for belief must be "able to invoke . . . inner anxiety as evidence of its own authenticity."[13] The Freudians could scarcely avoid the emotions in the familial conflicts they were exploring. But these explanations do not touch on the prime reason for the high place of the emotions in psychoanalytic theory and practice.

"Emotion" derives from the Latin *emovare* (or *emovere*), meaning "to move" or "move out." In Freudian theory emotional energy attaches to what is desired (cathexis). According to the *Baker Encyclopedia of Psychology:* "Ideas are of no value until emotions are attached to them, since the emotion provides the force of action. It is imperative, then, that as one accumulates a body of knowledge, appropriate emotions be cathected to ideas in order that they have value. Values are ideas—with cathected emotions—that make a favorable difference in life."[14] In the society of Freud's day, human emotions no longer had several significant objects with which they had formerly cathected—not religion, or the family as it once had been, or the community, or the king or local lord.

Through its evocation of emotions, psychoanalysis functioned as a process of *emovare* or transference from old world to new, from one set of affective objects to a new set. Wittingly or unwittingly, Jung explained the process: "The secret of the development of culture lies in the mobility of the libido, and its capacity for transference." When that happened, as Freud explained in *Moses and Monotheism,* "the emotions belonging to [the old God, the old world] could now be repeated" with new objects of veneration.[15] Therapy sought to *transfer* the emotions once given to religion, family, king, and community, to the president, the prime minister, the bureaucracy, the therapist, the new "fathers." The need just then was to solidify affective attachment to the state, its machinery, one's place in it, and the modes of the modern world; to say, after a hundred years, that the change from the old world to the new was over, successfully navigated. It needed to be not just said but felt. Emotional engagement assured that what was being revived from the old world and explicated about the new would not be received as merely symbolical, or worse, dry-as-dust ideas, but as the integuments of a present, living reality.

It was necessary now to tell the patient—and the culture—that the weaknesses in the new order were not the problem; the problem had been the evils of the old world, now ended—a memory and not a present reality. The patient was no longer in feudal bondage, either to lords or fathers, said Freudian theory. He was only remembering it and believing it was still going on, and that was what made him sick. At fault was his memory and his present state of mind, not the present state of society. Hence Freud's dictum that transference is overcome when the patient learns that his feelings do not arise from present conditions or events but are based on what happened in the past. Until the transference is broken, according to the theory, the patient believes he is still living under the conditions of the past. That was too close a reflection of social conditions in the present for the Freudians to tolerate. There had to be a vast improvement in the present, even though many did not experience it that way.

TO SERVE AS a secular substitute for traditional religion, psychoanalysis offered a ready-made theology: its body of theories, including sex as the invariant cause of mental illness, a fair rendering of medieval sex-as-sin;[16] a ritual, the fifty-minute treatment session; a ritual site, the therapist's office; a ritual fixture, the Freudian couch; a priest, the therapist; and a high priest, Freud (or all the pioneers taken together). Initially it recommended prayer—treatment—daily; then, like Western religions, it became content with less than daily attendance. Freud the founder bore the signs of miraculous self-cure (his self-analysis), achieved solely by psychological understanding. The treatment bore signs of miraculous cures which could be achieved in no other way, without medicines, medical apparatus, or any similar aids, only words, like the practice of the guru. The theology was built around the central religious myth of Judaism, rebellion against God, and the central myth of Christianity, the killing of God—in Freud's day replicated by the killing of the old world. Of all the belief systems offered by earlier philosophers and intellectual clerks trying to fashion a secular religion after the twin revolutions, Freud's was the most finely tuned to the needs of the day.

The other-worldly charisma of psychoanalysis, which it possessed amply in contrast to science, enhanced its appeal. Its largest subject—the fall and resurrection of Western culture (the same as the rebellion against God, and his murder)—was readily recognizable to Europeans and comported well with past belief. Freud as a dying and reborn god ("dying" from neurosis and "reborn" by psychoanalysis) reawakened beliefs going back to prehistory. The Freudians as miracle workers—a reputation which Freud said he enjoyed—had the same appeal, reawakening the long tradition of soul psychology. In an age of fact, measurement, and the denuding of nature by science, psychoanalysis joined romantic art and adaptations of Eastern mysticism as an appeal to what was lost but still desired, even as Freud criticized the mystical in favor of the rational and pitted science against religion and the romantic spirit.

Psychoanalysis was constructing, in a phrase John Cuddihy applies to Hegel, "an illusory gemeinschaft,"[17] as if the old village life still existed within modernity, the old emotions were still present or at least potential, belief and certainty were still present. As if through psychological theories, the past could live again, the present could be reenchanted. Psychoanalysis reaffirmed the possibility of finding in the world we gained what had been lost from the old world. It identified the new world with old world components, while marking the new world versions as improvements.

Hegel, says Cuddihy, supported the new *gesellschaft* through illusion while the Freudians tried to tear it down. Not so. It is ironic that the pioneer psychologists should be viewed as hostile to the new order when they were exhausting themselves to save it, build it, repair it, justify it—in part by appealing to the old order. The nineteenth century was, despite its stupendous newness, an age of reinvention and obsessive, protective illusions. It was a time—ironic from the point of view of Freudian theory—of defense mechanisms responding to social hysteria, nostalgia, still-surviving elements of the old world, including the old religion, and newfangled ideas for reinventing the new world, as though the first invention had been a failure. Freudianism, liking neither what was past nor what might lay ahead, made its contribution to defense by lifting elements out of the past, modifying them, and placing them in the present.

"The first stage of hysteria may be described as 'fright hysteria,'" Freud had explained to Fliess in the "Draft K" of 1895; "its primary symptom is the manifestation of fright accompanied by a gap in the psyche."[18] The Freudians were filling gaps in the cultural psyche, in a modern way consonant with the culture in which they operated.

THIRTEEN

Themes

In a psychosis the remodelling of reality is effected by
means of the residues in the mind of former relations
with reality . . . perpetually enriched by . . . perceptions
of a kind corresponding with the new reality. . . .
　　—Sigmund Freud, "The Loss of Reality in Neurosis
and Psychosis"

. . . To take from the traditional material what seems
useful and to reject what is unsuitable. . . .
　　　　—Sigmund Freud, *Moses and Monotheism*

AMONG THE psychoanalytic themes that blended old and new was
identity. One's self-identity had once come from the family and the established social order; there had been comfort in an identity well
known to one's self and all others. In the new world many people did
not know what their identity was. The quest for it, and the strength-
ening of it in therapy, carried a message extending far beyond individual patients; it announced identity as a modern requirement, not
unlike an identity card. Just when one was no longer sure of who he
was, he was being told that he had better find out. When he did, he
was to learn that identity was an aspect of conformity and community.
It was, Freud taught, "the assimilation of one ego to another, as a result of which the first ego behaves like the second in certain respects,
imitates it and in a sense takes it up into itself."[1] The lesson of the
Oedipus complex: you must act like your father; followers must follow the leader.

　　Linked to identity was personality. Modern personality had not
existed in any important sense for the common people of the old
world. They had had personalities, but that was insignificant because

most people were insignificant then; they were not individuals. The only individuals with personalities were the leaders of society—the nobles, and to a lesser degree the professionals and the burghers. But now that everyone was theoretically free, all needed a personality as a mark of freedom and equality. Therapy's emphasis on it, like the emphasis on identity, was an instruction to find one. Both identity and personality would become useful for introducing oneself to strangers, since everyone now lived in a world of strangers.

Two other popular themes of therapy were love and relationships, memories of the love relationships of the pre-industrial family. One did not need lessons in them then, for they were natural, naturally significant, and grew out of the family and the family society. With their former basis gone, love relationships became central to the new psychology, a recognition of what had been lost, was missed, and had to be replaced. As if displaying a second shingle on the lawn, psychoanalysis announced: "Relationships Found Here."

Love relationships in the old world had been based on the reigning doctrine of Christian universal love, drawn from Christ's instruction to love one another. The new world had discarded that doctrine in favor of competition, turning what was once vice (self-love, self-interest) into virtue. On its face this new social doctrine seemed poorly calculated for social order. Best obscured in the same way the church had occluded everyday reality with the doctrine of love, the base nature of the new age was hidden, in psychoanalytical theory, behind the intensive investigation of love under such headings as sex, desire, pleasure, and cathexis. Love might be difficult to find, but not as a subject in therapy.

Relationships had once invoked not only love but the social order of "degree on degree" by which one recognized one's betters. It was now necessary to recognize a new order, in a new world, of obedience and subservience to betters who no longer had the same official status as of old because the rationales and clear class distinctions of former days had been wiped away. Psychoanalysis recognized the new situation and the anxiety it produced, in the theme of dependence/independence. Here was the majority population of Europe thrown into a dependence as severe in its own way as serfdom, but in an atmosphere that said serfdom had been wrong, which made the new conditions not only economically and politically but psychologically galling.

Independence was the intended outcome of therapy; one was to be free and on his own, exactly what John Locke and Adam Smith prescribed. It made no difference to the ideology of independence (in the culture or in therapy) that one might not have the economic or political means for independence. Therapy was not concerned with that; it focused on emotional means, convincing the patient that he would gain them at the conclusion of the therapy process, after much hard work, the hard work of therapy itself being parallel to the literal hard work that might—or might not—release the patient into independence in the new culture.

The small percentage of the population that escaped economic and political dependence now relied on a larger array of forces than ever before: the activities of thousands and millions of others on whom one's prosperity and well-being depended, right down to the milkman. Everyone was a cog in the new system, so that even the new rulers had their own dependence/independence crisis. In old times the small middle class had depended on the lords to make its world and organize and define its place in it. Now the lords said to the middle class, "You are independent; *you* run the world." The members of the middle class did not have a firm idea of how that was done. They had run businesses, not countries. In this way, dependence/independence was a problem for everyone, even after a hundred years of trial and error following the twin revolutions.

The theme of infantilism, the psychoanalytic synonym for selfish desire, was close to the heart of democratic life not only because it was a variant name for the philosophy of pleasure but because democracy, having first cast the citizenry as individuals, and then as a mass, next cast them as children. The new childishness, a repeat of the old world in modern garb, was founded in people's dependence on the social system to meet their needs, from simple to complex; on an opaque state apparatus something like a distant god or the owner of the castle in Kafka's novel; and on a representative government in which the citizen turned over to political leaders the important national issues of the day, periodically confirming or disconfirming great decisions of state by the vote and providing daily input through "public opinion," which like the vote could be cleverly shaped by propaganda.

"Infantilism" recognized that the new, democratic individual created by the twin revolutions was guided by nothing but the philosophy of pleasure, and needed new guidance in order to subdue desire. If not, the new rulers might react to their own growing desires as against the desires of the mass by instituting an authoritarian regime replicating the old world; or the mass might rebel against the success of the rulers in amassing money, pleasures, and power.

The theme of the father was therapy's symbol for social order, authority, and the pre-industrial world when the father/Father/king had ruled. Brought back by Freud to embody the plight of the new age, in which authority and legitimacy appeared weakened in comparison with the past (in part because they had become democratized), the theme described the following situation accurately: Europe (like the caveman sons) had killed the Father, missed him as a guide to life, law, and order, and was ashamed of why it had killed him—that is, to pursue exactly what the Father had condemned: self-interest, self-love, and vanity (in psychoanalysis, infantilism, narcissism, and the pleasure principle). The new age was patently blasphemous, its rules were blasphemous. It was against the Father, could not fail to know it, and could not fail to resent being known to be so. It was the Rebel Age in which what the Father had condoned—submission, humility, love for others—was condemned as old-fashioned. Europe wanted the Father back while fearing the Father's judgments on its new ways. It was urgent that a modern substitute be found.

Freud's relationship with his own father (or anyone's relationship with one's father) is a mere detail within this theme, which was world-historical in its significance. In Nietzsche's *Gay Science* the Madman cries out: "Whither is God . . . I shall tell you. We have killed him— you and I. All of us are his murderers. What festivals of atonement, what sacred games shall we have to invent?" When Freud imaged the murder of the old world in the caveman sons killing their father—his repetition of the martyrdom of Christ—he called it the event "with which civilization began and which, since it occurred, has not allowed mankind a moment's rest."² This parable represented the social guilt of ending the old world, instituting liberal democracy and modernity, and, not incidentally, replacing old, cherished beliefs with such ideas as those contained in dynamic psychology. As Nietzsche knew, this was one of the sacred games invented by modernity as both atonement and evasion.

The theme of desire—Freud's pleasure principle and sex theme— was Freud's symbolic representation of the philosophy of pleasure, the paramount theme of the nineteenth century. For the first time in millennia (if ever), desire as self-interest became the condoned philosophy of a whole culture, top to bottom. Associated with desire was the Freudian theme of the Golden Age, the lost Eden of endless satisfaction from which we are expelled after infancy, which pointed to the lost, enchanted, pre-industrial world before the Father was killed. Expulsion from the imagined Eden of the old world was the price paid by Western culture for killing the old Father. The culture, not satisfied with this expulsion, sought a return to imagined comforts and some means of wiping away the guilt of the new age so that it could live untroubled with its philosophy of pleasure.

How the yearning for the Golden Age might be met, Freud described in this way:

> Incomplete and dim memories of the past, which we call tradition, are a great incentive to the artist, for he is free to fill in the gaps in the memories according to the behests of his imagination, and to form after his own purpose the image of the time he has undertaken to reproduce. One might almost say that the more shadowy tradition has become, the more meet it is for the poet's use.[3]

No keener presentation has ever been offered of how the theories, practices, and themes of psychoanalysis were formed with the poet's eye for tradition and for turning tradition to the poet's (the pioneers') uses.

The theme of frustration (the impelling force in neurosis) recognized that day-to-day competitive life in the new age produced frustrations for all and major frustrations for the masses who had little hope of satisfying their needs, let alone their wants. Psychoanalysis recognized the frustration by making release from frustration the cure in therapy (a secular version of the Christian hope for a better day). The accompanying theme of fantasy, the response to frustration in the theory, recognized the problematic, combative nature of the new society from which individuals might be tempted to withdraw, perhaps to a fantasy of the past or the future (which in fact was happening on a comparatively large scale in the politics of the day).

In a Janus-like backtracking, the theme of fantasy had a further use: it reintroduced old world enchantment by invoking miraculous religiosity and fantastic superstitions about spirits, witches, mysterious diseases, and miraculous cures. Thus fantasy, through its association with neurosis, was generally bad in Freudian theory; yet it had a positive side: it was good to know that fantasy still lived, that it had found its way through the morass of the twin revolutions. As in the old world, that was an analog to hope.

Other themes of treatment adopted by the pioneers and their descendants were loss, separation anxiety (from the mother or the love object), abandonment (like the abandonment by the family and the culture), the crisis of individuality (like individuation and the later "identity crisis"), inferiority/superiority, striving for power, asserting the will, character structure and character analysis, concepts of self, inhibitions, self-realization and self-actualization, the need for security, and building up the ego and self-esteem. All of these were imposed by the loss of the old world and the necessities of the new world when the individual appeared, lost and struggling for success.

Adler, the most socially conscious of the pioneers, settled on powerlessness (the inferiority complex) as the chief element in his scheme, for good reason. It was the chief problem of most individuals in the new industrial states, an inhibiting factor in the quest for success, and a chief cause of social commotion. From his own observations, and probably from Marx and the sociologists, Adler had got hold of a prime social problem of the new age. Like Freud and all the other pioneers, he converted it into an individual problem derived from biology, early experiences, and the personality structure of the patient. That was one of many examples of the psychoanalytic diversion from the social to the individual that reduced the social problems of the nineteenth century to personal problems.

EMBRACING all these themes was the theme of freedom, the ultimate promise and claim of the democracies and the psychotherapies together. To earlier soul psychologists, mental health had been freedom from the passions, and it became so again in psychoanalysis. Freud spoke of freeing the libido from its obsessive attachments and so placing it "at the disposal of the ego"; of therapy freeing the neurotic "from the chains of his sexuality"; of "the liberation of the human being from his neurotic symptoms." This emphasis on freedom in psychoanalysis, wrote Otto Rank, supplemented and justified "the democratic ideal of self-determination."[4]

In psychoanalysis and democracy, freedom was the payment for all the losses of the old world. All the helter-skelter of modernity, the sharp inequalities of person to person and class to class, the scramble to satisfy needs and wants, were justified by it. Unless that were common belief, the new age could continue nothing with assurance. Freedom was not only political and psychoanalytic; it was one of the great abiding messages of the West, with a religious content that could not be missed. In the Old Testament freedom was the release of the Jews from Egyptian bondage and the bondage of pagan ways—it meant, as it did in democracy and psychoanalysis, the entree into a new civilization. In the New Testament it was release from sin and ultimately from the flesh. In psychoanalysis it meant, among other things, release from the demands of the sexual instinct. At the same time it echoed Schopenhauer and the Hindu release from the wheel of karma. In all these ways it resonated.

By teaching how to steer between social demands and personal desires so that one might develop according to the dictates of his rational will, therapy paralleled liberal democratic government, which in political theory operated on the rational will of an educated, informed populace expressed through the vote and public opinion. The people had been freed, and so would the patient be, through therapy. As an ensemble, the theme of freedom, the proposal of a universal psychology applicable to all (repeating "the dogma of equality," according to Rank), and the terror of a theory that turned the disdaining of community into madness, symbolically fulfilled the promises of the French Revolution, the liberal democratic states, and traditional religion—*liberté, égalité, fraternité.*[5]

Further representing democracy in psychoanalysis was Freud's restatement of the social contract: "The whole course of . . . civilization is no more than an account of the various methods adopted by mankind for 'binding' their unsatisfied wishes." By "binding" he meant keeping wishes in check and rejecting "wrongful" ones as the way to socialize the psyche. This was little different from John Stuart Mill in his 1836 essay "Civilization": "All combination is compromise: it is the sacrifice of some portion of individual will for a common purpose."[6] Both Freud and Mill were saying that to combine, to socialize, required renunciation in the form of compromise, reflecting the spread of parliamentary democracy in the Western nations and teaching a lesson to those among them, including Austria, still reluctant to grant full political freedom.

Freedom's twin in the new age was competition, reflected in the Freudian theme of psychic conflict. Most striking in Freud's doctrine, according to V. N. Voloshinov, is *"the strife, the chaos, the adversity of our psychical life. . . ."*[7] Interpersonal competition is suggested in the Oedipus complex, in which the son enters into an unequal struggle with the father for the mother's affections. It is contained in Adler's idea of sibling rivalry. But in psychoanalysis as a whole, the conflict is instead intrapersonal (called intrapsychic), "man against himself," libido and ego in conflict, or id, ego, and superego in conflict. Dynamic psychology was in this way a psychology of *dynamic competition,* like the society of the day. By projecting competition as normative, natural, and perhaps the leading reality in human psychology, psychoanalysis endorsed laissez-faire economics and social Darwinism as equally normative and natural. By projecting competition as intrapsychic, the pioneers muted the fierce competitive nature of the new age, changing its direction from outward to inward.

By the fin de siècle, freedom and competition had produced too many ideas, too bitterly contested (just as the libido was attracted by too many pleasures). Order was needed and wanted in the marketplace of ideas, with agreed-upon boundaries (just as it was needed in the psyche). After the twin revolutions, government censorship of speech gradually eased and disappeared in the liberal democracies. But around 1900 it returned to vogue psychologically through Freud's theory that the psyche censored itself by sending unacceptable thoughts to the unconscious. This inner censorship was a lesson to the rulers of still-authoritarian nations in central Europe, such as Germany and Freud's own Austria: do not fear democracy, it can contain powerful restraints, and they can be implemented not by the ruler but by the ruled, as belief. We have a better way of managing things, was Freud's message, and nowhere did he more earnestly fulfill his promises.

Part of all these themes was one so pervasive that it was integral to almost all Freudian theories and practices: the past, that makes the individual sick, contrasted with the present, that makes him well.

FOURTEEN

The Return of God and King

In those days there was no king in Israel; every man did what was right in his own eyes.

—Judges 21:25

Only a God can save us.
—Martin Heidegger, *Der Spiegel* interview, 1966

THE OLD MORALITY was missing from the modern world. It was reconstituted by—and as—psychoanalytic theory. Concerned that a future without Christian morality would need a suitable substitute, Rousseau had given renewed respectability to the innate conscience that told people what was right and wrong. Kant, worried that a new age bereft of ethics and bent on pleasure would give right-action short shrift, had turned the conscience into the categorical imperative, which placed biblical ethics in the mind as a necessarily existing, almost biological moral director. Hegel and Schopenhauer had placed the principles of the whole universe in the mind, and since Schopenhauer accounted them evil, he proposed Buddhist ethics (rather like Rousseau's and Kant's godless, philosophic solutions) to counter the will to pleasure and evil. Kierkegaard, vitally aware that goodness and duty might lose out to pleasure, and that the new age might thus fall into chaos, had taught how to convey ethics not by direct preachments but through fables and parodies that might be more appealing to the modern mind.

By the end of the nineteenth century these fears to which the philosophers had responded grew to crisis proportions. Moral certitude had crumbled under modernity's demonstrated ability to destroy every last citadel of past belief and order. The family was a vestige, religion was a vestige, the end of monarchy was in view. Nietzsche gloated over the opportunity to transvalue values now that God was dead: "There are altogether no moral facts. Moral judgments agree with religious ones in believing in realities which are no realities."[1] Onto this scene of moral malaise stepped the definitive Freud. Through nostalgia and past beliefs, he discovered a way of making duty scientific and pleasure scientifically infantile, thereby wedding psychoanalysis to the dominant culture of the nineteenth century.

In place of God, king, father, conscience, and the categorical imperative, Freud theorized the Oedipus complex as the way to tell us what was right and wrong. It was an inner law implanted in the psyche from birth according to the science of psychoanalysis, and therefore timeless and universal. By this means the God-idea, or at least the God-morality, was placed in the mind. Freud gave it a new, objective warrant, made it a scientific "fact" that revived the Kantian categorical imperative as what might be called the *objective* categorical imperative (objective because scientific). Philosophy in the new age was going the way of religion; it was not considered objective and therefore not "truthful"; science was. Freud rendered morality "real" through a psychological father in the mind who was not to be disobeyed and a mother who was not to be traduced.[2]

In a stroke, leaping over more than a century of moral and religious doubt, the Oedipus complex reinstated *as science* the fifth commandment—Honor thy father and thy mother—which had ruled the old world. In its train were all the other commandments, hidden in a Greek myth reinforced by a Kantian proposition. In just the way the Ten Commandments operated in the old world, the Oedipus complex could function in the new one, as both personal and social injunction, representing what the *individual* was supposed to believe and what the *whole society* was supposed to believe. Freud's theory conflated Honor thy father and mother with Thou shalt not kill (the father), nor commit adultery (have sex with another's wife, in this case your father's), nor covet your neighbor's house or wife or goods (that is, you were to seek fulfillment through your own rightful possessions, not your father's, your neighbor's, or your countrymen's). It was the Decalog in a "complex," and a complex it therefore was, reasserting the sanctity of law, property, and social relations.

Out of the old religions he professed to despise and the philosophies he said he ill regarded, Freud had begotten a theory of modern morality which he proposed was scientific. His theory reiterated God's message while replacing God, making him once and for all a supernumerary in the moral order, the same feat Kant had accomplished philosophically. Freud's method, just as Kierkegaard had recommended, was fable—a fable from the past (Oedipus) and a fable of science (psychoanalysis); and parody, a parody of both science and the past—all of it deployed in a symbolic psychological theory that presented morality by indirection, as science. As punishment the new morality proposed not burning in hell but madness, an adaptation of soul psychology in which mental illness equaled sin.

Freud's theory gave psychological practitioners the means to know what was good or bad, right or wrong according to such standards as healthy/unhealthy, normal/abnormal, infantile/mature, putting the practitioners in the place of the old priests. When his theory was later replaced by the notions of other theorists, the formal meaning remained: certain ideas and approaches to life were wrong (called unsuccessful, inappropriate, or some other code word for bad thought or conduct) and led to madness, and if not to madness then some other form of mental disease and suffering. "Though the intent of therapy is to ostensibly show how to live without belief," Rieff writes, "the ideological effect of psychoanalysis and the wider therapy of Freudian doctrine is surely to replace the moral irresoluteness fostered by the decline of religion with a new theoretical resolution." Five months before telling Fliess about his Oedipus theory, Freud had mentioned a "presentiment . . . that I shall very soon uncover the source of morality."[3]

Marie Balmary quotes Nicolevski and Bukharin around the turn of the century: "Have we reached the point where the commandments of Moses must be rediscovered as a new truth?"[4] Just so; we had arrived at that point around the year 1900, in response to what Kant, Schopenhauer, and Kierkegaard had already seen; what Tolstoy, Dostoevsky, and Nietzsche saw later; and what was plainly evident to most people in the new age: God was gone, a moral replacement was needed. Freud's theory said a law existed from all time and was implanted in the human psyche, the law of transgression and retribution, rebellion and defeat, guilt and punishment, punishment and forgiveness. It was like the United States Cavalry speeding to the rescue of a culture deeply unsure of itself, a clarion call as sharp as a bugler's that demanded attention.

Even though there was no more king, no more noblemen, no more God, no more priests, no more old order, authority still existed to mete out retribution. It was not to be found in old books or beliefs but in human psychology—universal, timeless, unavoidable. For transgression (even imagined transgression), the individual meted out punishment to himself through psychological laws. This self-punishment was the democratic equivalent to sovereign punishment in the former age. Since *you* were now the sovereign, who else was to punish you for your transgressions but yourself? You did it by making yourself mad (or neurotic).

Freud had succeeded in converting into a scientific belief no more radical a view than Lord Acton's in 1895: "Opinions alter, manners change, creeds rise and fall, but the moral law is written on the tablets of eternity."[5] Such a comment seems preachy coming from a layman, but when Science says it, in a new language, in heavy disguise, it acquires an entirely different cast, becoming a candidate for acceptance in the way the rules of traditional religion or the logical proofs of philosophy no longer could. Freud's formulation mirrored secular law: punishment for disobedience, and added a new punishment outside the law: madness, just as religion had added damnation. As obedience and punishment were science, the secular law of the modern nation-state could now be based on natural "fact," thereby possessing legitimacy.

As it was wrong to rebel against the father, so it was wrong to rebel against authority: that was the burden of the Bible, the Oedipus complex, and the caveman story. Freud's theory wanted you to honor your society, however unjust it might seem, as those in the old world had honored theirs, and it wanted you to do that in obedience to what it said were the value-free, scientific findings of psychology. The evolving liberal, industrial nation-state was now father/(Father) and king, and you were to honor it, whatever its vagaries insofar as it touched on the quality of your life personally. This lesson countered both Marx and Nietzsche, representatives of the most radical tendencies of the age.

Marx wanted you to rebel; Freud wanted you to accept and had a psychological formula for that very purpose.[6] For middle-class society, still getting its bearings and preaching the virtue of exploitation, Freud seemed to provide a welcome formulation, protective of the new order. He would "free" you personally into a "normally unhappy" life. Beyond that, nothing could be done; there was nothing to rebel against since freedom was the legal doctrine of the day. A Nietzschean solution was no longer needed either. There was no need to return to the Middle Ages and even further back, to the Roman legions; no need to ride over society with prancing horsemen eager to reenslave or dispatch all the *Uentermenschen* freed by the twin revolutions. Control could be built into the new society by lodging a theory of restraint, as science, into the new society's belief system.

EVENHANDEDLY, or so it would seem, the Oedipus theory applied also to the leaders of the new society. Why should they wish to express their desire—which could now operate in untrammeled freedom—to exploit others to the hilt? That too was not right. If you had a million, it said to the industrialists, why did you want—need—to have two million? That thought was only right and fair, and it was good that someone was expressing it, the leaders of society could think. It did not hamper them that such a preachment was in the air, a preachment for goodness and forbearance which they could say they were trying to follow against all odds. Similar preachments, from the Bible, had been in the air of the old world for centuries and millennia and had never stopped anyone from lording it over others under the color of law, order, and rectitude.

A hundred years after the middle class inherited the rule of society, it was still suffering from a Don Juan complex, allowing its pleasure-seeking to run riot in all that represented pleasure in the nineteenth century: money, houses, land, women, art, jewels, grand cuisine, fancy clothes—just like the old aristocrats. Such pleasure-seeking no longer had a sanction in the divine right of the ruling class, as it had enjoyed in the old world. Then, the sharp demarcation between the great and the humble had made it clear that the pleasures of this world were quite evidently for the great. But now the right to those pleasures could only be asserted de facto; there was no de jure legitimacy for it. All had become equal de jure, all had the same rights. That was certainly a problem for the newly great, who needed an appropriate rationale for their assumed rights; and it was a problem for the humble as well, who needed some way to bear their new condition, to yield once more to the "lords" after being told they were free.

The "right-thinking" among the new ruling class, however high or low in the order of things, could not call attention to the new de facto right to pleasure, or question it, on pain of being read out of their class. For this right was simply the theme of liberal democracy and free-market economics: Get what you can while you can. Scads of nineteenth-century novels—not to speak of vocal reformers—led by the works of Dickens, Zola, and Hugo, were based on the idea that to the plain sight of a feeling person liberal democracy was wrong. It was good, definitely an advance politically, but inhuman in its practice. But if the Bible could do no more to restrain the desires of the powerful, what could the criticisms of the day accomplish? *A Christmas Carol?* The powerful loved it; in Dickens's view a "sledgehammer," it fell like a feather. For all his labors, what could Lord Shaftesbury, lifelong crusader for the poor, accomplish? Something, but not a great deal.[7]

The Oedipus complex, which said it was wrong to rebel in the pursuit of pleasure, could be accepted by the well-to-do of the day with equanimity since they had no cause or wish to rebel. The new social system worked nicely for them, quite different than for most others. So the evenhandedness of Freud's theory, its objectivity and value-free insight, were suspect. Thomas Szasz saw clearly seventy years after the fact (and I am not suggesting that he was alone) that it was "a hidden source of comfort and security against the threat of unforeseen and unpredictable change . . . [a] means of obscuring and disguising moral and political conflicts as mere personal problems."[8]

The caveman story, even more than the Oedipus theory, revealed the new psychiatry in its definitive role. The sons accept the ethics of the fathers; they pay homage to the old ways, slightly modified, in ritual (which on the political level can be translated as *in theory*), after having killed the old fathers; and they call it a new order. In the same way, the new culture of modernity, having killed the old world, appealed to its meanings while abrogating many of them, and called it a new, much improved order, which in theory it was, however unjust and oppressive. In this effort Freud was a major player, even if his work seemed peripheral to the West's main lines of technology, industry, and political democracy. He was eventually, and properly, elevated to the heights of Genius and Culture Hero because he was, first of all, a Middle-Class Hero for the middle class of his day. "In many ways [he was] the son, and the voice of a bourgeois age," says Gellner, "and the first part of the Freudian message . . . was—in the republic of the soul, *strengthen the middle class*!"[9] The way to be normal, according to the new Freudian psychology, was to heed the middle class, the current source of community standards.

What then of the freedom psychoanalysis offered as its end product? Freud assured that it was not to be feared. Freedom, Kant had explained (and Spinoza before and Hegel after), was to live in and with constraints, in and with necessity, which became Freud's "reality principle" and his *Civilization and Its Discontents*. Defining successful treatment, he told the audience at his Clark University lectures in 1909 how

> the final outcome that is so much dreaded—the destruction of the pa-tient's cultural character by the instincts which have been set free from repression—is totally impossible. For alarm on this score takes no account of what our experiences have taught us with certainty—namely that the mental and somatic power of a wishful impulse, when once its repression has failed, is far stronger if it is unconscious than if it is conscious; so that to make it conscious can only be to weaken it. An unconscious wish cannot be influenced and it is independent of any contrary tendencies, whereas a conscious one is inhibited by whatever else is conscious and opposed to it. Thus the work of psycho-analysis puts itself at the orders of precisely the highest and most valuable cultural trends, as a better substitute for the unsuc-cessful repression.[10]

Freud openly recognized, as he told his Clark audience, that his work was performed on "orders," conformed to "the highest and most valuable cultural trends," and was a "better" substitute for "un-successful" repression. As the representation of what was wanted at that time by the kind of people in his audience, projected on society at large, his words were reassuring, announcing what was expected in desire and comportment. He and his colleagues had fashioned a mass psychology of the normal which, if not followed, invoked a suitable stigma accompanied by a scientific justification. The presence at Clark of Jung, Ferenczi, Jones, and A. A. Brill indicated that this was not Freud's view alone; it was the gospel of the new psychology movement being recognized throughout the world. Clark's own president, Dr. Stanley Hall, had given it the stamp of approval.

In spite of its appeal to the middle class, the emerging Freudian sys-tem, as a mass belief for millions, cannot be understood purely in terms of class, economics, or politics. The Oedipus complex did not just say *I must not rebel;* it also said *I am in control,* for I possess rules and meanings that are certain, so certain they are scientific. And the *I* was not just the members of the middle class; it was everybody. The new system of psychology proposed a knowledge and therefore a cer-tainty that the new world was not out of control. It had been com-prehended and therefore could be controlled. Experimental science to that time (and after) could not make such an assertion about the world of human affairs. It had much to say about molecules but not about people. Now, with Freud, science obtruded into human affairs, the same human affairs in which religion and philosophy had trod, and gave a new surety. This was comforting and much appreciated by all, those on top and those below. While those below did not hear of it immediately, those on top would let them know in due course, and all would be more emotionally satisfied than before.

In the period he was writing to Fliess about discovering the Oedipus complex, Freud related a dream of an old hag—his nanny of yesteryear—"who told me a great deal about God Almighty and hell and who instilled in me a high opinion of my own capacities." The old woman was predicting Freud's future enterprise, which is to say he was revealing it to himself. Who was God Almighty? Freud reinventing the Judeo-Christian tradition through psychoanalysis. What was hell? The hysteria of the time depicted as neurosis and psychosis. And who was the hag? Old Europe pleading to be saved from its newness. He would do it, God Almighty and all, and the Western world would respond, as in his dream, with a high opinion of his capacities. "What in effect they [the psychoanalysts] have done . . . ," Gellner remarks, "is simply to restore, and in an astonishingly modern idiom to boot, the old condition of humanity, such as it was prior to pervasive scepticism. . . ."[11] They restored all at once the king, a disguised God (disguised as science), and thereby a revivified father, to reenchant and rediscipline modernity through symbolic theories of human psychology.

In the last decade of his life, perhaps realizing what he had accomplished with the Oedipus complex, Freud remarked: "The ethical demands on which religion seeks to lay stress need, rather, to be given another basis; for they are indispensable to human society and it is dangerous to link obedience to them with religious faith."[12]

FREUD FOUGHT so hard for the Oedipus complex and against all competing theories because he wanted to assure One Morality for modernity, just as the Jews had done in the past, just as the Christians had done (and Islam too, for that matter, which absorbed the two earlier religions and declared they were all Islam but not as pure as Muhammad's version of the truth). Even if the Oedipus complex was not a summation of Judeo-Christian ethics (which it was), through Freud it fit the pattern of a new morality: it was not to be challenged or yoked to others. All others were to be Golden Calves. Freud's slogan might well have been, "One culture, one politics, one psychology, one morality."[13] He could not stop others from producing their own versions of the new psychology, but all the versions reflected his methodology, which in turn reflected Judeo-Christianity, Kant, and other philosophers.

Observing that "the King remains the essential personage in the whole legal edifice of the West," Foucault continued: "The essential role of the theory of right, from medieval times onwards, was to fix the legitimacy of power. . . . [Right] is . . . the instrument of domination."[14] That is to say, if a principle of right can be established, it can be used to dominate others, even those who may not wish to follow the principle. In developing the Oedipus theory (and its variations), Freud and his colleagues reconstituted the right of the sovereign as psychology, after religion had done it as theology—the one for liberal democracy, the other for monarchy.

Rebellion against God was the essential narrative of the Bible. In heaven, Satan rebels; on earth Adam and Eve rebel. In the nineteenth century rebellion was again the narrative of history, just when God was disappearing and there was no transcendent hand to hold rebellion back. The Oedipus complex returned to modern consciousness the Judeo-Christian father/king/Father against whom the post-1800 world had rebelled en masse. We had gotten rid of him; now we were to honor him again. "They are rid of the Christian God," Nietzsche noticed, "and now believe all the more firmly that they must cling to Christian morality."[15] In Freud's thought the cavemen, devising a totem and a ritual around the murdered father, had performed a similar maneuver, reinstituting the father's morality (with improvements) after killing him. Why should we be different? Freud had implicitly concluded. It was, after all, a universal story; it was good to destroy the past but just as incumbent to revitalize its symbols.

"Kingship," Peter Murphy tells us, "is the culmination of the familial, clannish, tribal principle of social organization. Household heads, clan bosses, tribal chiefs and kings are all 'the fathers of their people' and the crux of pre-civil society in which identification with lineage, blood ties, and family signifiers are all pre-eminent. . . . *Libertas* [is] life without kings."[16] And yet for the still new civil society of the West, the Freudians reintroduced the king symbolically and scientifically, in the mind. This may seem ironic, but it was not so to Freud. He explained that the child (like a new society forming itself) may grow up with the idea of rejecting those traits in the parent it finds objectionable, but it soon discovers that against its wishes it is turning into the parent. This was human psychology, Freud maintained, to be seen as much in the life of individuals as of societies. He called this another instance of the return of the repressed.

Bernhard Alexander, a Kantian philosopher and father of Franz Alexander, Freud's disciple, thought he had overcome two thousand years of Western civilization when he finally accepted the Oedipus complex as true. Had he looked more closely he would have seen that Freud had revived the past two thousand years and more of Western belief. Had Freud lived in the depths of the Middle Ages he would never have developed his theory of Oedipus. Then it was already in place: civic law backed by religious belief, a total system of submission to higher powers. He would have been told that his very concept of the Oedipus complex, as Honor thy father and mother, had been enshrined in Europe since the fall of Rome as official doctrine. Reflection would show that it already dominated the culture of East Asia through Confucius. Had he returned to ancient Greece, home of the Oedipus myth, he would again have found an adequate system of control in place: law backed by religion, myth, and the arts. Had he returned to the turmoil of seventeenth-century Europe, when Catholic and Protestant elites were challenging each other for dominance and the allegiance of the people in the Wars of the Reformation, his system might have found a place, except that others were in full bloom sanctioning the Inquisition and the witch-hunts as assertions of right and control.

But in the modern age Freud found himself in a chaotic social laboratory short on restraint. "Ethics," he would say, "are remote from me. . . . I do not break my head much about good and evil."[17] Yet that was his greatest effort in the laboratory of liberalism, as Szasz and others have shown. They have spied out the middle-class morality in psychoanalysis conveyed by Freud and his colleagues through the countervailing terms mental health and neurosis. In Freud's hands Oedipus was another "story from the Bible," conveyed neither as old-fashioned religion nor as outmoded philosophy, but as science.

What then of sex, the medieval symbol of sin, which Freud gave every appearance of wanting to free from its old restraints? Was that not a contradiction to his revivalistic Oedipus theory, which seemed to restrain the sexual urge? Early on the elites saw the political sedition implicit in the sex theme, but later they viewed sex more as an opiate of the people, realizing its usefulness while feigning prohibition.

The masses in the same period pressed this issue in lieu of more practical ones, sex becoming the mode of expressing freedom that was to be allowed as long as others, political and economic, were repressed. The Freudian participation in these trends worked in favor of the psychoanalytic movement. "Where transgression becomes virtue," Jacques Ellul points out, "the lifter of the ban becomes a hero, a demigod, and we consecrate ourselves to serve him because he has liberated our repressed passions."[18]

The Freudians were agents and not originators of this cultural trend, but they were among its chief beneficiaries. The credit given to them as sexual liberators translated into greater popularity for psychoanalysis, and that translated into the greater ability of the new psychology to perform its latent functions. The church naturally deplored this shift away from the medieval condemnation of sex, but it came to see that beneath the surface Freudianism was in total a new call to the old morality. In time, churches adopted counseling techniques based on Freudianism, and even evangelical churches bitterly opposed to the "freeing" of sex offered Christian psychological counseling that was a version of Freudianism (without free love).

The Oedipus theory was offered in that period when the Western nations were beginning to sever their legal ties to religion. They were more comfortable in doing so with the appearance of new versions of religious or semireligious doctrines and wisdom, including Freudianism. Freud was comfortable in advocating the shucking of religion without fearing an ensuing chaos, because his psychological system was providing substitutes for it in a form the new age could absorb. Whether that could be sustained was of course open to question. Schopenhauer had seen that Kant's categorical imperative must fail. It was "a scepter of wooden iron" that "without further credentials . . . leaps into the world, in order to command there. . . ." Meant to be as strong and long-lasting as iron, it was soft and impermanent as wood; and meant to have a palpable paternity in unavoidable logic, it had no "further credentials" beyond its self-assertion. "As a basis of political science it would be excellent; as the basis of ethics it is worthless."[19] The Oedipus complex similarly proved useful for politics and social order but less so for therapy and, perhaps least of all in the long run, for ethics.

TAKING INTO ACCOUNT the Freudians' tendency to blame crime on psychopathology rather than conscious will, their public attitude of leniency toward sex, and their atheism, certain critics came to believe that the Freudians were attacking the moral foundations of Western culture. For example, Hans Eysenck, a behavioral psychologist, charges Freud with "ethical nihilism" and "scientific worthlessness" aimed at undermining "the values on which western civilization is based."[20] The Oedipus theory, as we have seen, was not designed to do that. Quite to the contrary, it was formed for the opposite effect, to shore up against loss the fragments that could be preserved of values and ethics from the old world. Nihilism had been produced not by Freudian theory but by the twin revolutions, with their rationales in philosophy, economics, and political science that undermined traditional values and ethics. In conceiving the Oedipus complex as a theory of discipline and control, Freud was the child with his finger in the dike, trying to make the best out of the modern materials before him—the freedom, the sex, the instrumentality, the hysteria. He was trying to quiet modern madness and return a moral tone as a means of supporting Western civilization, not despoiling it.

Thomas Szasz charges Freud with seeking to undermine individuals he did not like, unbelievers in his "science" and believers in Christianity, whom Freud supposedly felt shut him and his fellow Jews out. Like Eysenck, Szasz concludes that Freud was trying to undermine European culture. It is true that Freud wished to undermine most Europeans in their desire to rebel against the new age, but not because they were Christian insiders while he was an outsider. His role was to support the minority in the democracies, that is, the leaders—almost all Christian—against their followers, the many, who threatened riot, rebellion, reaction, or visionary dictatorships. "We know how to follow," Freud wanted to announce for liberal democracy. "We are an orderly society no less than authoritarian nations, and we have more freedoms at the same time."

John Cuddihy views Freud as an avant-garde rebel against the European order and its sham Victorian standards. This was the more so, thinks Cuddihy, because Freud was a Jew who felt himself out in the cold. True, Freud was an enemy of the reactionary Austrian social order, but that was because he was a friend of the democratic order of Europe. As part of his effort to support liberal Europe, Freud wanted to free his nation from its dedication to the past. He offered the means to do so: reformulations of the past in the context of the present, including his modern Ten Commandments. If there was a Jewish component in this, it was, as noted in an earlier chapter, the realization common to most Jews in Europe that they were under renewed pressure and that liberalism was good for them, authoritarianism was not. Liberalism, with its tolerance and secular institutions, was calculated to let the Jews live and let live. Freud was not mistaken in this political estimate, and it was certainly one of his motives—but only one among many—in creating psychoanalysis.

In *The Interpretation of Dreams* Freud explained that "The lesson which, it is said, the deeply moved spectator should learn from the tragedy [of Oedipus] is submission to the divine will and realization of his own impotence." This is the lesson Freud wanted the European public to take from his theory of the Oedipus complex: submission to the new social will and the realization that it was impossible to fight it successfully. "Modern tragedies of destiny," he continued, "have failed in this effect." This was one of many nutshell explanations for his use of the Oedipus myth. He used Oedipus to achieve the same effect as of old, an effect he could not find in other solutions for the crisis of the new age. The play, he points out, is not about "the contrast between destiny and will" but about the audience's realization that Oedipus's destiny "might have been our own—because the oracle laid the same curse upon us before our birth as upon him."[21] The decoded meaning here is not difficult to find: the twin revolutions placed a burden upon all—curse or otherwise, each citizen could judge. In either case, psychoanalysis was a cure that meant to place a burden of restraint on the mass populations of Europe.

Freud says that the action of *Oedipus Rex* "consists in nothing other than the process of revealing, with cunning delays and ever-mounting excitement—a process that can be likened to the work of a psycho-analysis—that Oedipus himself is the murderer of Laius, but further that he is the son of the murdered man and of Jocasta."[22] In the same way, with ever-mounting excitement and frequent despair at the delays he encountered in finding *the* solution, the key to it all, Freud finally revealed in his completed system that we were all the children of the murderers of the old world and the desirers of pleasure in the new. Symbolically considered, we all bore the guilt of Oedipus, whose mythic fate Freud and his colleagues tried to keep at bay by the creation of their own drama, called variously *human psychology* and *psychoanalysis*. They wanted the new age to live, as others wanted it to tear out its eyes and die.

Freud's contemporary, Alfred Jarry, the French absurdist playwright, novelist, and all-round bohemian who, like Freud, had a scientific background, proposed "a science of imaginary solutions." This is what Freud was engaged in. Neurosis was about protection, said Freud, and here he was providing the Oedipus theory as protection for the new culture of the West though the recreation of the Ten Commandments. Freud had already recreated the family, personal identity, community, and emotional ties through imaginative symbolic substitutes in support of the new age. Oedipus was the symbolic recreation of morality. It answered those who charged that modernity was bereft of order, God, ethics, and decency. Jarry both spoofed and loved science. So did Freud. In one of Jarry's books *(Caesar-Christ)* a character is asked if he is a Christian and responds: "I am God." So was the Sigmund Freud who created the God-in-the-mind called the Oedipus complex.[23]

Considering the evident revitalization of God and king in the Oedipus complex, it would be difficult to imagine that Freud was ignorant of the alchemical transubstantiation he had performed. He had created a standard for value, judgment, and law by converting philosophy (which had converted religion) into science. It was a means of forging order out of chaos for the new sociopolitical organization of modernity. "Civilization," he wrote, ". . . obtains mastery over the individual's . . . desire for aggression by weakening and disarming it and by *setting up an agency within him to watch over it,* like a garrison in a conquered city."[24] This is a concise description of what the Oedipus theory sought to accomplish.

The fantasy element in the Oedipus complex contained a powerful effect that would travel throughout the course of psychoanalysis. It made the point that fantasy is what mattered in mental illness, over and above reality. On the social scene it suggested that the deficiencies of the modern age were being largely fantasized by Europe. What Europe needed was discipline to carry it through its false, fantastic mental constructions of decline and fall. Freud was in effect displacing the reality of social hysteria into fantasy. Nordau had found his master; in place of hysterical harangues stood a cool medicalism.

FIFTEEN

That Old-time Religion

... Freud became the most influential symbolist of the
return of sacred order in the twentieth century.
—Philip Rieff, *Freud: The Mind of the Moralist*

... The religious is reactivated at weak points of the
social. ...
—Claude Lefort, *Democracy and Political Theory*

OF ALL THE revivals in psychoanalysis, traditional religion was
among the most ample. In deferred obedience, the Freudians virtually
reconstructed Judeo-Christianity in their theories and practices.[1] Next
to the Oedipus complex as the Ten Commandments stood the doctrine
of Original Sin, the story of the Fall, salvation, the Eucharist, the doctrine of the Fortunate Fall, guilt, confession, exorcism, tithing, redemption, sacrifice, repentance, fear of the Lord and obedience to his
word, hell, sin and the medieval Christian symbol of sin, sex—to cite
only the most prominent features of what was presented symbolically
not as religion but as scientific psychology.

Original Sin was why the trauma leading to mental illness had to
take place early in life, even at birth, according to some pioneers, or
before birth, said Freud, when we were cursed—just as Oedipus was
and as the doctrine of Original Sin maintained. This particular de-
rivation from Christian theology was no mystery to Freud; he acknowledged it, claiming only the distinction of having recognized it as
a scientific fact arising originally from the caveman sons killing their
father and introducing guilt into humanity. "... Are not Freud's theories with their emphasis on infantile incestuous desires ... bizarre?"
Thornton wondered.[2] They were not; they were direct restatements of
Original Sin as inborn moral depravity, whether the source was the

curse of God in the Bible, the curse of an oracle in *Oedipus Rex,* or the consequence of killing the caveman father. The Christian West had believed something like this for two thousand years; Schopenhauer had given it a dramatic restatement.

"This belief in infantile sexuality, perhaps as much as any of his other views, caused Freud to be ostracized," according to the Harvard psychologist Howard Gardner. "How could innocent children living in the prim-and-proper Victorian-Hapsburg era, possibly harbor strong sexual feelings, even if these were only operating at an unconscious level?" As exemplars of Original Sin in Freud's theory, they had to. This belief did not cause Freud to be ostracized (if at all, only temporarily), but quite the opposite made a large contribution to his success. "If Freud simply wanted to gain converts," Gardner adds, "he might well have tempered his claims on this point."[3] This point was crucial to maintain; it would have been a disaster for him to abandon it, which is why he clung to it always.

In the caveman version of Original Sin, all succeeding generations of humanity bear the guilt of the caveman sons for killing their father, passing it on through the Lamarckian inheritance of acquired characteristics. So closely did Freud adhere to his biblical model, that just as sin entered the world through this first *act* of disobedience, in exactly the same way Freudian guilt enters the world through the *act* of killing the father and is inherited as a permanent feature of the human makeup. In both cases, an act of will becomes a biological inheritance. How much more closely could Freud have followed his model?[4] According to theology, Original Sin is in the newborn babe from the start but does not reveal itself until maturity. This paralleled the Freudian belief (held in common by most soul psychologists in the fin de siècle, including Charcot) that there is a latency period between the time of a trauma such as the Oedipus complex and the appearance of symptoms after puberty.

The symptoms that appear when mental illness takes hold are the Freudian equivalent of the biblical Fall from Grace and expulsion from the Garden of Eden. They also have a historical parallel to which both neurosis and the Fall symbolically refer. After the fall of the old world there was a "latency" period during which all the ills of the twin revolutions accumulated, until the fin de siècle when Freud developed his theory. What brings on neurosis after the latency period, according to Freud, is puberty, when pleasure as sex runs rampant in the hormones, an interpretation similar to Christian theology. What brought on the social hysteria that Freud was trying to treat was in large part the philosophy of pleasure which the new age adopted, and which can be seen as a parallel to puberty in the individual.

Thus all at once Freudian theory summarized what happened in the Garden of Eden after the eating of the forbidden fruit, what happens to the individual after the fall into trauma and then hysteria, and what happened to the culture of the West through the fall of the old world. Before the biblical Fall, no morality was needed; Adam and Eve lived in the lap of God. Before the fall of the old world, no *new* morality or substitutive institutions and religious beliefs were needed. Before the fall (trauma) of the patient, no treatment was needed. But after, when all were needed, psychoanalysis appeared, the redemptive cure.

Redemption is brought about in all these cases by a singular figure: Christ in Christianity, the therapist in therapy, Freud (or the Freudians as a unit) in the provision of new beliefs for Western culture. Christ brings spiritual purity, the condition before the Fall; the therapist brings psychic health, the condition before the trauma; the Freudians bring comfort to heal cultural disaster. The condition before the Fall in the Garden was sinless, guiltless; before the onset of mental trauma, normal; before the collapse of the old world, emotionally comforting. The stated role of therapy was to return the patient as close to the original state (guiltless, healthy in secular terms) as possible; the role of Freudian belief was to return European culture to its imagined stability before the collapse of the old world.

The psychoanalytic belief in the potential of mental illness in all human beings was another transposition of Original Sin. In both Christianity and psychoanalysis it was the basis for universalism, covering all people in all times and climes with a single theory or doctrine. Copying the biblical model, Freud asserted in effect that Original Sin (as guilt and neurosis) was a true doctrine, just as Christianity did. We are all a little neurotic, he said, and this was why: we were all more or less sinful on the model of Judeo-Christianity, which Freud adopted and his audience readily understood. And of course we *were* all more or less sinful because of our animal nature, the model that the Bible, Freud, and Schopenhauer held in common (reinforced in Freud by Darwin).[5]

The agent of disgrace in the Garden is the serpent, the devil. The Freudian equivalent, as in Schopenhauer, is the unconscious, our animal nature, our desire: "the devil is certainly nothing else than the personification of the repressed unconscious instinctual life."[6] In this parallel, the new age let loose the unconscious desire for pleasure; it had listened to the devil; Faust had appeared.

Redemption invokes another Christian doctrine that pervades Freud's thought: the Fortunate Fall, which holds that the sin that led to the misfortune of humankind, eviction from the Garden of Eden, led to the greatest blessing, salvation through Christ. Through a circuitous route evil was thus turned to good. Mental illness, according to this model, led to the salvational creed (science) of psychoanalysis by which the mentally ill could be restored to health. Freud was the savior, a status conferred by his biblical source. On the same model, the fall of the old world led to the institution of democracy, redeeming the new world's killing of the old (good again stemming from evil).

In *Totem and Taboo,* the sons depicted as eating the flesh of their father in the totem meal created a parallel to the Eucharist,[7] which in turn provided Freud with an application of the Fortunate Fall that justified the new age. Killing (or disobeying) the father (God) is evil, both Freud and Christianity taught, but eating the flesh of the murdered God/father (expressing deferred obedience) is salvational in Christianity and civilizational in Freudianism. In this light, Freud's caveman parable taught that killing the father (overthrowing the old world) was evil and at the same time character-building and civilization-building, increasing independence and rights, which was the Enlightenment view of the French Revolution. Freud's parable also put a brake on future imitations by the sons (that is, incessant revolutions) since the sons did not wish their own sons to kill them in turn. As Freud explained, after killing the father the sons establish a new rule, the "granting of equal rights to all members of the brother horde (that is, the restriction of the impulse to settle their rivalry by brute force)." The sense of this new rule, he says, "lies in the need of preserving permanently the new order which was established after the death of the father. Otherwise reversion to the former state would have been inevitable."[8]

Europe had recently experienced the granting of equal rights to all, and Freud and millions of others did not wish to see them taken away or revised by further revolutions. The sons, like Freud, were content to benefit from the final revolution, just as in theology, humanity benefited from the final salvation through Jesus Christ (until the Second Coming). Freud was providing the absolution the new world sought for its bloody deed in killing the old world, and doing it along perfectly orthodox Christian lines. In rejecting the old religion, Freud himself bore guilt; in reviving it in a new form, he washed himself clean (again exemplifying the Fortunate Fall). If the grain does not die, said the Bible, there can be no new harvest.

Freud's parable recapitulated the experience of nineteenth-century Europe struggling to put in place a new polity as stable as the old one, and confirmed it as good. Meanwhile the parable validated the atheism of the new age as a natural outgrowth of civilizational maturity. The sons reaccepting the old order with variations, in the name of a new order, was not distant in many ways from what the new age had done with the old age, and what psychoanalysis, a new belief system, did with the old belief system.

The Oedipal fear and anxiety invoked in the fantasy killing of the father, like the guilt felt by the caveman sons, had a transparent meaning in connection with the Christ image and the new age: the new father—whether as the new culture of the West, or the president or prime minister, or the priestlike, shamanistic theorist or therapist, or even the father of the family—was not to be killed (disobeyed, rebelled against) as had happened to God, Christ, the caveman father, and the old world. Absolution having been achieved, a moratorium was placed on bloody deeds. The new father in all his modern forms was to be loved, feared, respected, and followed; no more rebellions. The religious messiah had come in Christ, the political messiah in liberal democracy, the psychological messiah in Freud. The Oedipal conflict being dissolved in this way was not in children, as Freud proposed; it was in the new fathers of the culture of the West who worried that a new revolution might overturn them.

The fear we should have of the father/Father, taught by the Bible, the Oedipus complex, and the caveman story, became in Freudianism the fear of mental illness as the price of disobedience. Mental illness was sin leading to hell; if we departed from the right way—that is, if we sinned, disobeying the father—we received the ultimate modernist punishment: mental illness. In the Freudian, Jungian, and Adlerian systems alike, this illness resulted from disregarding community standards or separating from the community (and in Jung and Adler, disregarding the cosmic will). The greater the disregard, the greater the punishment, unto madness. The model was: Believe on me and ye shall be saved; doubt and ye shall be damned. These religious memories reinforced the thought that to reject the cache of ideas in theoretical psychology was to reject the church of scientific psychology and invite damnation. The political implications were clear: invoking fear of madness, and having madness represent separation from the community, satisfied the needs of the new rulers of society who sought acceptance from the masses. Rejection would send the message that something was wrong with the new society. With the help of psychoanalysis, society wished to hide anything wrong and assert everything right. You had to be crazy to reject modernity.

The father complex—that fear and shame before the father can lead to mental illness—was a simple translation of biblical transgression against the word of God leading to sin and damnation. But it was not an individual who was suffering from this complex, even though that was said to be the case in psychoanalysis. It was the nineteenth century, which had lost the Father, in fact killed him, and wanted him back; and if not the Father, then some principle of authority that could serve in his place, which was the function of the Oedipus complex. Through the father of the family, made powerful again through the new psychology, could be reenvisioned (if only dimly) the universal power of God the Father behind the father of the family, and in that case also behind the state which had replaced the old nobility that used to run the nation. And behind the father now was also the therapist, the new father, like the old father in religion, the priest. The severest sufferers of the father complex in the fin de siècle, it might be said, were the pioneers. They were indelibly burdened by it, though it was not an illness in them; it was recognition of what their culture knew and wanted: a new father, a new God, a new control, which they sought to supply.

The psychoanalytic threat of hell found a response in the nineteenth-century citizen because of the biblical resonance and because a new hell had appeared in modern society: alienation to the point of isolation if one did not follow along (isolation being, in Freud, Jung, and Adler, and the soul psychologists before, a, perhaps *the* prime source of madness, and madness being a source of suffering and the mark of failure to accept, adapt, adjust). The threat of the therapist or the patient to break off therapy made this danger immediate, especially since the therapist was a symbolic representation of the family, and beyond that, society (and beyond that, the priest). Therapy of course did not create the threat of isolation unto madness; the culture did this by being modern, individualistic, alienated, and alienating. If one rebelled against this society and asserted his right to a fresh interpretation of freedom beyond what already existed, the fear of isolation unto madness was what he should feel, Freud's system assured, just as in the past one feared damnation if he went outside traditional religious beliefs.

The failing of humankind in the Judeo-Christian tradition lies in resisting God's message. With knowledge of God, the priest hopes, comes the end of resistance; we are then joined to God's purposes, fulfilling what Freud called the main doctrine of Judeo-Christianity, "reconciliation with God the Father."[9] In precisely this way the doctrine of resistance worked in therapy. We resisted the truth that we had sinned in the mind; we would not be at peace without admitting the truth, cleansing ourselves, repenting. With psychological knowledge, the therapist hopes, comes the end of resistance to the therapist's message (said to be the truth of the unconscious). Through acceptance of the message we are made free and rejoined to the community. Traditional religion could no longer deliver such messages with confidence. The shedding of religion and authoritarianism, together with new modes of living, new truths and facts, had fatally debilitated the old speech, removing its practical serviceability: adherence to a higher authority, to orders, to discipline. Now the voice of God was heard again in psychoanalysis, and it said: Do not resist my message.

The doctrine of resistance in therapy was joined by another doctrine flowing from the heeding of God's message, its twin and outcome: obedience. The enduring message at the heart of the Oedipus complex, like that at heart of the Bible, was obedience to the word of the father. All therapies, in one way or another, taught obedience to a reality principle whose essence was what a particular therapist thought was reality, which was almost always the existing order of his or her society. We were to obey because we were children again, heeding the voice of the father, which was the voice of the Father, which was now the voice of the new order. The obedience taught by psychoanalysis was not unlike the attitude among the aristocrats in the old world, similarly based on the Bible. It was chief of all obedience to one's betters, beginning with Honor thy father and mother and extending up the hierarchical ladder. Psychoanalysis presented this idea not as law or tradition but as scientific psychology, at the very moment the message was needed.

Transference, in its pseudo-religious mode, was the transference of the therapist (and the patient) into God (Christ), a repetition of the noble medieval theme of the imitation of Christ. That was the stance Freud took in therapy—that the therapist was *the* authority figure whom the patient should love, fear, and ultimately emulate. Transference was thus also the transference from wickedness to health through the biblical model, which was now the psychoanalytic model, achieved through obedience to the word from on high (God/father/therapist).

The Freudian reality principle was nothing less than the truth to which we were to conform. The truth was the Way; the pleasure principle was sin, the devil's way. In Christian theology, sin is defined as passing through life ignoring God. This was the same as the injunction of psychoanalysis not to ignore the knowledge and ministrations of the therapist. Even those outside therapy were to know that the therapist possessed the truth (that is, the law, the theory, the science), the modern Way. The therapist occupied the place of the father/Father, as the priest had, and in this way the therapist's message, repeating the biblical one, could support the political message of order and stability. It was therefore important that neither the patient nor the culture ignore Freudianism, which was one reason why it was propagated by the culture that spawned it.

The Bible, and nineteenth-century thinking based on it, more than anything else dictated the source of neurosis in infantilism and narcissism—the pleasure principle from birth forward. The biblical parallel is a famous passage in Corinthians 13:11: "When I was a child, I spoke as a child, I understood as a child, but when I became a man, I put away childish things." Freud's version was: "unconscious wishes are destroyed [and] replaced by a condemning judgment."[10] In the Bible as in psychoanalysis, children are rebellious: "For my people is foolish, they have not known me, they are sottish children, and they have none understanding: they are wise to do evil, but to do good they have no knowledge . . ." (Jeremiah 4:22). They must be cured, made good, through the knowledge provided by psychoanalysis. The cure through knowledge is the same as the biblical cure, knowledge of sin leading to repentance, obedience, salvation. We must be good children again after having killed the father.

This infantilization of the modern citizen by psychoanalysis reportrayed the child humbled before God and noble in the old world. To recall this role—and present it, paradoxically, as the cure—a second mode of the child was invoked by the Freudians, one preached by Christianity, liberal democracy, and psychoanalysis alike—the naive, believing child: "And now little children, abide in him" (1 John 2:28). This was the patient encouraged to believe in the therapist and the precepts of therapy; and the citizen encouraged to believe in the state and its promises of freedom. Such belief was not difficult to muster because the promises and the theories were so evidently based on what had been believed before in Judeo-Christianity.

The impelling reason for this imitation of the rebellious child and the believing child was not alone the Bible. Citizens of the liberal democratic nations, in being freed, had in fact become childlike again. Modern society rendered virtually everyone dependent and rendered some sectors rebellious, which in Freudianism became infantilism. Meanwhile the official philosophy of the new age was this same infantilism (self-interest, the philosophy of pleasure), precisely what the Bible (and psychoanalysis) spoke against as childish ignorance or willfulness. For this reason the patient was portrayed as plagued by the inappropriate wish for pleasure, satisfaction *now,* not delayed, gained, or earned: a biblical lesson as much as a political and psychoanalytic one. As Judeo-Christianity was not difficult for children to absorb, neither was psychoanalysis for the new citizens-as-children of the democratic nation-states, who were to be good, "religious," heedful of higher authority (in psychoanalysis, the scientific god that Freud had placed in the mind).

To St. Paul, a sinful thought was as evil as a sinful act. Similarly, in the Freudian system an *act* of transgression was not under discussion. What was being sought was a guilty *thought,* a psychological guilt. Unlike Pauline guilt, this thought was not conscious; it was an unconscious fantasy. Nevertheless the biblical model and the theory were the same: one was guilty for a thought, which is one reason why Jerome Frank, a psychiatrist at Johns Hopkins University, associated therapy with thought control of both the medieval and modern variety. Another aspect of Freudian guilt appears in Leviticus 5:17—guilt as the result of an unwitting sin, which approximates Freudian unconscious guilt and also reflects a precept of law: ignorance of the law is no defense (in psychoanalysis, ignorance of an unconscious thought is no defense against your having made yourself sick as a result of it; you are guilty though you do not know it).

Whether the source of guilt is Original Sin, the Oedipus complex, or the caveman murder, guilt is the motive power in psychoanalysis as it is in Judeo-Christianity. What psychoanalysis means to offer the patient is clearly expressed in such a biblical source as Psalm 32:

> Blessed is he whose transgression is forgiven; whose sin is covered.
> Blessed is the man unto whom the Lord imputeth not iniquity, and in whose spirit there is no guilt.

> When I kept silence, my bones waxed old through my roaring all the day long [psychosomatic reaction].
>
> For day and night thy hand was heavy upon me; my moisture is turned into the drought of summer. Sellah.
>
> I acknowledged my sin unto thee, and mine iniquity have I not hid. I said, I will confess my transgressions unto the Lord and thou forgavest the iniquity of my sin. Sellah.

What God does, the therapist will do:

> Thou art my hiding place; thou shalt compass me about with songs of deliverance. Sellah.
>
> I will instruct thee and teach thee in the way which thou shalt go; I will guide thee with mine eye.

God (and the therapist) protect against the animal instinct (the unconscious):

> Be ye not as the horse, or as the mule, which have no understanding: whose mouth must be held in with bit and bridle, lest they come near unto thee.

This was the program of psychoanalysis, as it was of soul psychology and *Seelsorge*, conveyed in the words of the Bible. I do not think Freud would have repudiated the comparison, except to point out that the Bible's wisdom was mythic, his was scientific.

Catholic confession and Protestant *Seelsorge*, under the old Greek label of catharsis, were what the new psychoanalytic cure now offered. Neurosis as the condition of the damned, a suffering imposed for transgression and relieved by confession—this was comfortable, traditional, and well known in all Western countries. That catharsis (confession) did not in fact cure mental illness was not problematic for the latent functions of the Freudian system, for it was only the theoretical or manifest cure. The real cure was biblical repentance. The patient repents infantilism, narcissism, and self-love, turns from them, gives them up. The reality principle (giving up infantilism for maturity) was in this way an adaptation of biblical sacrifice, giving something up to gain something else. Freud understood it as the "social contract," both personal and political.[11] It was, par excellence, the Freudian principle of conversion to new belief.

The sexual theme in psychoanalysis was a transparent repetition of medieval Christianity, where sex was the sufficient symbol for sin, the arch representation of Original Sin. The church steered away from the root of all evil, money, which few possessed, and highlighted sex, which all possessed. Freudianism did the same, using sex as a sufficient symbol for the mind gone wrong and as a means of steering away from money (power), which to Freud was a purely social and economic factor insufficient to explain what he analyzed as neurosis and psychosis. In both cases the lesson was the same: Do not be concerned with the social system but only with your sin. You are sinful; the social order is proper, ordained.

In the medieval period, the psychologist Joe Kennedy Adams points out, "One great advantage of such a sex-centered ideology was that it did not interfere with the indecent and tyrannical treatment of other people, as it provided a way of being 'good' that had nothing directly to do with decent or fair treatment of others."[12] Sex (pleasure) as sin supported the medieval control of the serfs, the church's message being: You're not supposed to be having a good time; life is a vale of tears. Freud's freer attitude toward sex made a divergence in line with the modern temperament and the needs of the time, while retaining sex (pleasure) as sin. Adler saw social concerns from a different perspective, which was why he rejected the sexual etiology of mental illness. Jung also took a different view and turned away from the sexual etiology. Freud agreed with the priests of old: sex was the best symbol for sin and an excellent suggestive means of controlling mass populations.

Sex as sin was a handy, persuasive symbol for the church because it transcended class, gender, and every other conceivable separation. It was universal, the voice of the devil to be countered by the voice of God. The message of the church concerning sin therefore included everyone, couched in a symbol understandable to everyone. The same was true for sex as the ne plus ultra of psychoanalytic theory. Following his model so closely in most matters, Freud willingly adopted the medieval church's special condemnation of three great sins, idolatry, homicide, and unchastity, each specifically proscribed by the Ten Commandments. In psychoanalysis the sin of idolatry became a turning away from the truth of psychoanalysis, the new timeless, universal knowledge; the sins of homicide and unchastity became Oedipal rebellion.

Freudian dream interpretation and the reading of unconscious signs were further appeals to the Bible. Joseph and Daniel rose high in the eyes of kings because of their divining abilities. Daniel is praised for a "surpassing spirit, and knowledge, and understanding, interpreting of dreams and declaring of riddles and loosing of knots" (Daniel 5:12), the manifest ambition of psychoanalysis in reading dreams and the unconscious. When Daniel is asked to interpret the writing on the wall concerning the fall of a kingdom, he is told the reward of such knowledge. "But I have heard of thee," says the king, "that thou canst give interpretations, and loose knots; now if thou canst read the writing, and make known to me the interpretation thereof, thou shalt be clothed with purple, and have a chain of gold about thy neck, and shalt rule as one of three in the kingdom" (5:16). A passage such as this must have rung in the ears of the Freudians, for it is not too much to say that the latent ambition of psychoanalysis was to rule as one of three: government, law, and belief (psychoanalysis), with psychoanalysis as the affective aspect and secular holiness, or divinity, of the other two. Buried in the Freudian revival of dream interpretation and the "declaring of riddles" was the desire to command, as in Freud's statement to Fliess that finding the key to mental illness and mental health would give the discoverer command over everything.

Freud's *Civilization and Its Discontents,* a late work about the impossibility of civilization satisfying instinctual desires, reprojected biblical pessimism concerning the base nature of the flesh. This was Freudian doctrine from the beginning of his definitive work. The Golden Calf, fornication and its attendant guilt and punishment, sodomy, childish disobedience, haughty mankind's will to disobey—these were fashioned by Freud into a new language repeating the old condemnations. His judgment on his book—"While I was engaged in this work I have discovered the most banal truths"—can be regarded as recognition of the banal nature of the latent truths behind manifest psychoanalysis. He was purveying old wisdom in new garb. He also said, "It seems to be my fate to discover only the obvious," and he gave as examples "that children have sexual feelings, which every nursemaid knows; and that night dreams are just as much a wish fulfillment as day dreams."[13] Freud's latent vocation, shared with his colleagues, required, just as he stated here, the rediscovery and reformulation of obvious truths that had long been believed as gospel, religious or secular.

Freud's pessimistic determinism, that human acts and motives are triggered by a force within called the unconscious, was as traditional as his optimistic belief that the unconscious could be controlled. His source again was the Bible (reinforced by the *philosophes*, Schopenhauer, and other German Idealist philosophers who were also influenced by the Bible and/or Hindo-Buddhism). The pessimism said we were all sinners, we could do little to escape damnation; the world was a vale of tears. The optimism countered with the promise of salvation, which in psychoanalysis became cure. There was a better future: you could get better, salvation was in view. Any reader of religious texts will recognize the pattern: damnation countered by salvation.

The therapeutic justification for timely payment of treatment sessions—that it was part of the therapy process and would help make you better; that it demonstrated growing maturity and a desire for independence—had its latent source in biblical tithing, and for good reason. Tithing served not only materially to support the church and the priest; it inculcated an attitude of seriousness and dedication toward the church's mission. In therapy, payment confirmed that the patient and the therapist were doing something important. The patient made it important in his life by paying the therapist. He made it important to the therapist by bolstering confidence in what the professional was doing. By recognizing the validity of therapy and the work being done, payment functioned as a mutual reassurance, like tithing.

Underlying the science claim of the pioneers was again the Ten Commandments. The claim functioned on the model of the first four commandments concerning belief and respect. The succeeding six commandments contained no necessary reason for belief without the first four having incited absolute certainty in, respect for, and fear of God and his holy day, the Sabbath. Therapy too needed an antecedent warrant, science, for its hypotheses to command belief. Underlying the "timeless, universal" claim of psychoanalysis was again the Bible, shored up with the claim of science. Freud's habit of damning other schools of psychology had a similar religious corollary. In the Western tradition a new religion as a matter of course attacked the old one, saying the old one did not have the true or full message. This was equally the practice of Judaism, Christianity, and Islam, and Freud followed suit, damning the old religion and thereby making space for the new one.

Freud's insistence on the validity of what his intuition told him, his demand for orthodox belief, and that look (to Jung) of *numinosum* that came over him when he was delivering his rockbed theories, were again an imitation of the Bible, as though he were paying heed to the voice of God. This could not have failed to please a society that wanted a "true" substitute for the old religion, justified in the same fanatic way as a religion of old. Regularly noting that his fanaticism was resisted in many scientific quarters, Freud nevertheless refused to give it up. Bleuler wrote him that his style of doing science was unseemly: "In my opinion, this 'who is not for us is against us,' this 'all or nothing,' is necessary for religious communities and useful for political parties . . . but for science I consider it harmful."[14] Bleuler was calling attention to the social field in which psychoanalysis would operate, but he did not know it, crediting Freud with a scientific impulse. This confusion of enterprises would be long-lasting, the scientific obscuring the political.

Reflecting himself and denying it at the same time, Freud objected to "fanaticism" in the Jewish "psychological structure." When his dissenting disciples accused him of it, he said it was because he had the truth. But he had already explained himself in the "Draft H" of 1895 when theorizing about neurotics: "In every instance the delusional idea is maintained with the same energy which another, intolerably distressing, idea is warded off from the ego. Thus they [neurotics] *love their delusions as they love themselves.* That is the secret."[15] Freud's fanaticism was equal to the intolerable ideas he and the new Europe confronted and sought to ward off. His substitute, which Europe came to love as it loved itself, was the secret of Freud's success.

For Freud to have written a paper on "The Resistances to Psycho-Analysis" was equivalent to a medieval priest writing about "The Resistances to God" or "to Revealed Religion." The message was the same: you resisted knowing your sin (in Freud, your unconscious); you resisted repenting (in Freud, being cured). You lived for your pleasures and would be damned. Freud symbolically re-presented religion in his theories while at the same time devaluing it and developing a new wish fulfillment based on it. Insightfully he told Fliess in 1899, as he was striving to complete his system, "Perhaps the wish-fulfilling dream is wrestling itself out of the darkness."[16]

THE RELIGIOUS FACE of dynamic psychology, however obscured by science, myth, and anthropology, lent familiarity to its message. It identified psychoanalysis with the functions religion had performed— order, rationalization, justification, solace, guidance. These functions it transferred to political, economic, and social concerns, just as religion had done. The biblical borrowings reformulated for the modern age the essentials of Judeo-Christianity as the philosopher Alasdair

MacIntyre gives them: "God is our father. God commands us to obey him. We ought to obey God because he knows what is best for us, and what is best for us is to obey him. We fail to obey him and so become estranged from him. We therefore need to learn how to be reconciled to God so that we can once more live in a familial relationship with him." That is a fair summary of the Oedipus complex, the impulse of theoretical psychology at the time it was created, the relationship of therapist to patient, and of patient—all citizens—to the state. The effort was to reconcile child to parent, citizen to state in a "modern" way. Now we were to obey Freud and his followers, and the social system and state behind them.[17]

"What thou hast inherited from thy fathers, acquire it to make it thine" is a quotation from Goethe's *Faust* that Freud so liked he cited it twice, in *Totem and Taboo* and again in *An Outline of Psycho-Analysis*. He might have known, but did not say, that it was an apt commentary on his work and that of his colleagues. Fredric Jameson believes that Freudianism is a dialogue between two poles, the psychoanalytic and the theological.[18] There were not two poles; one was a reprise of the other. Freudianism was a naturalization of the Bible and a justification of its principles in the same way Thomas Aquinas and then deism had rendered the principles of the Bible rational and the intellectual clerks had naturalized divinity.

The application of Freudianism to education, child-rearing, criminology, penology, law, and other fields concerned with conduct, right and wrong, judgment, and the analysis of human personality was necessary and predictable on its parallel to religion. Psychology was applied to these areas as it replaced religion, which had once operated there. From this point of view, the widespread influence of psychoanalysis was implicit and inevitable on the model of Judeo-Christianity which, besides being religion, was also the psychology of the Western world before psychoanalysis. If many fields of knowledge (and the arts) felt the effects of psychoanalysis, it was because they had once similarly felt the effects of Judeo-Christianity.

In one way chiefly the Freudians did not adopt biblical wisdom. The Prophets and Jesus preached a social idealism, a *caritas* or *agape* of disinterested love of others with which the new age, and therefore the new psychology, did not agree. It was replaced in psychoanalysis by the cold, solopsistic reality principle: Do what is good for *you*. To "Thou shalt love thy neighbor as thyself," Freud responded: "Why should we do it? What good would it do us? . . . What is the point of an injunction promulgated with such solemnity, if reason does not recommend it to us?" Of Christ's corollary he said: "And there is a second commandment, which seems to me even more incomprehensible and arouses still stronger opposition in me. It is 'Love thine enemies.' "[19]

Like the insane Judge Schreber, the quite normal, middle-class Freudians provided a new religion for modernity modified but patterned on the old one. As Freud explained in "Draft H": "The delusional idea is either a copy of the idea warded off or its opposite (megalomania)." He copied main concepts of Judeo-Christianity (the idea he was warding off) *and* its opposite ("science" and "atheism"). "There are things," he assured his readers in *Moses and Monotheism*, "that should be said more than once and cannot be repeated often enough."[20]

Part V

TREATMENT: DEMONIZING THE ENEMY

And now to politics and the right of self-defense!
—Sigmund Freud, *Freud/Jung Letters*

My emotional life has always insisted that I should
have an intimate friend and a hated enemy. I have
always been able to provide myself afresh with both.
—Sigmund Freud, *The Interpretation of Dreams*

. . . Freud's views . . . [are] a generalized technique for
explaining the evil ways of the opposition . . . the
unmasking technique . . . a way of deflating
the things we dislike.
—Charles Frankel, "The Status of Freud's Ideas"

. . . A public that is neither led nor counselled by its
ancients, nor protected by its critical police, becomes
the predestined prey of all charlatans and impostors.
—Max Nordau, *Degeneration*

But the command of this truth-speaking god, and his
proclamation of what *is,* are really deceptive and
fallacious. For this knowledge is, in its very principle,
directly not knowledge. . . .
—G. W. F. Hegel, *The Phenomenology of Mind*

SIXTEEN

Infantilism: Heroes, Villains, Sermons

The specific political distinction to which political
actions and motives can be reduced is that between
friend and enemy.
—Carl Schmitt, *The Concept of the Political*

Freud was always at war.
—Nat Morris, *A Man Possessed*

Having revived the past and modified it in the context of the
present, psychoanalysis next damned the enemies of modernity. It did
this, again, through psychological ideas that functioned as suggestions
of what to believe. Benda called the intellectual clerk a "minister of
war." Psychoanalysis was a ministry of cultural war, with Freud at its
head.

Freud often presented himself in war imagery, confronting enemies, attacking, defending, struggling, fighting, resisting, and con-
quering. At eighty he was hailed by Thomas Mann in words Nietzsche
had applied to Schopenhauer: "a man and knight, grim and stern of
visage."[1] The members of his movement recognized him as their maximum leader, their generalissimo. None of this was misconceived.
Freud truly was a conquistador (as he thought), a knight-errant, a field
marshal, with a strategy and tactics he put into practice—not through
political activism but through ideas. His admiration for Hannibal,
Cromwell, and Napoleon was not just a childhood enthusiasm; he implemented it as a philosophical fighter in the best tradition of the intellectual clerks.

Freudian concepts such as infantilism, sex, the unconscious, and
neurosis were codes for opprobrium, identifying and demonizing en-

emies—not enemies of psychoanalysis but enemies of the new age. Presented as scientifically neutral, they were morally specific, spelling out what the pioneers disliked and viewed as bad. Infantilism, for example, one of Freud's bedrock concepts, meant unruly, ignorant, lustful, disobedient, rebellious, uncivilized. The final meaning was *evil,* which he stated explicitly: *"What is unconscious in mental life is also what is infantile.* . . . This frightful evil is simply the initial, primitive, infantile part of mental life. . . ."[2] When his daughter Anna misbehaved, Freud called her a black devil, a lighthearted expression of parental disapproval but at the same time a window into his thoughts about the evil child.

What was infantile was neurotic, according to the theory, and what was neurotic was infantile. Both concepts pointed to desire, and more particularly illegitimate desire. This was true as well of *narcissism* and *primitive,* and also of *libido, id,* and *unconscious,* all terms having the root meaning of sin or the work of the devil (in more neutral terms, the work of nature). Their obverse in the Freudian lexicon was maturity, reason, the reality principle, and civilization. In this symbolism Freud was the Enlightenment hero at war with romantic idealism. The romantics glorified the primitive, the past, the imaginative and creative child, the spontaneous, the unconscious, what was close to nature. Freud, like Schopenhauer, condemned them—symbolically, through the image of the evil child.

The child was evil first of all by being the source of mental illness. The "powerful impulses of childhood" caused mental illness, Freud wrote, the "imperishable, repressed wishful impulses of childhood hav[ing] alone provided the power for the construction of symptoms." Every neurosis "invariably goes back to the patient's puberty and early childhood . . . which determine the later onset of the illness." This view echoed Schopenhauer, soul psychology, the pre-nineteenth-century equation of madmen and children, and such common maxims as "The child is father to the man." The cause of neurosis was infantile desire (as in the Oedipus complex), another symbolization of what was to be condemned. As the child eventually experiences frustrated desires (leading to neurosis), infantilism also represented frustration. As frustration in the theory led to rebellion, infantilism meant that as well, as when Freud says that neurosis is characterized by a "persistent rebellion against the real world." And as the child is the adult's past, and child and past are the source of neurosis, infantilism also meant the past in Freudian theory, signifying both a lost Golden Age and the longing for it, as when he writes that "the symptoms of hysterical patients are founded upon highly significant, but forgotten, scenes in their past lives (traumas). . . ."[3]

The child also stood for fantasy, and especially fantastical beliefs from and about the past, among them, notably, religion. Freud felt religion "is so patently infantile, so foreign to reality, that to anyone with a friendly attitude to humanity it is painful to think that the majority of mortals will never be able to rise above this view of life."[4] What was wrong with religion was wrong with the child, in Freud's view: dependence and a craving for comfort provided by an illusion. As the child was ignorant (given to illusion and guided in Freud's view solely by instincts), infantilism represented that too in psychoanalysis. And as the child grew and passed through a stage of innocent idealism, infantilism also represented that, based on an ignorance or avoidance of reality that the Freudians deplored and found replicated in neurosis and psychosis (under the theoretical category *dissociation*).

The early disciples followed Freud in these negative meanings of infantilism. Jung associated the child with egoism, archaism (primitive mentality), subjectivity, the unconscious. Infantilism "goes beyond mere childish selfishness," he wrote at one point; "it even verges upon the wicked and brutal."[5] He saw earlier stages of civilization as the childlike state of modern man, just as Freud did. For Adler, the inferiority complex, source of mental illness, was grounded in infancy, like inborn Original Sin. The Freudians consistently contrasted the evil child with the adult, the hero living at the command of the tempered ego. The adult can wait to satisfy desire, the child cannot; the adult knows the ways of the world, the child cares nothing about them; the adult lives in present reality, the child lives in an imagined reality that recalls the past. The mentally healthy, mature adult is therefore the reality principle incarnate; the child is the opposite.

Selecting the child as the unlikely villain of their drama *Human Psychology* (which was otherwise the drama of human history) was absurd, perverse, sensationalist, symbolical, and familiar—and therefore was highly useful in attracting attention and teaching lessons. Most people would think that what infants want is food, sleep, and a change of diapers. Not the Freudians. While the child gave every indication of simple wants, the Freudians thought they knew better, knew a secret not apparent on the surface. Indeed they did know a secret: what psychoanalysis was, how it was to be used, what it was to accomplish, and how it did so through its symbolic concepts.

What was actually infantile to the Freudians were the thoughts and actions of metaphoric infants who required authority (the father) to manage them and teach them what was right. "Infantilism" created a class of psychological malefactors against whom treatment (thought control, mass belief) could be unleashed. It was rather like, at a different level, painting an enemy as subhuman and therefore responsible for the treatment meted out to him. Nietzsche overtly created such a class of subhumans, *Uentermenschen,* comprising most of society, and nothing was bad enough for them. Since it was against the humanity of the Freudians to create *Uentermenschen* of so lowly a nature, and against democracy to countenance such a category, they settled on the class of the infantile as their *Uentermenschen,* people without couth, uncivilized, primitive—"nuts," Freud called them—who had to be educated into civility.

To indict the child as the villain of the Freudian drama was easier and less dangerous than indicting the adult. The child was unlikely to complain or even know it had been made the villain of the piece. Indicting the mass of adults for desire, self-interest, rebelliousness, and nostalgia would have taken on the new world head-on, and moreover taken on the philosophy of that world, which was not the purpose of the pioneers. Attacking adults was altogether too revealing; attacking them under the guise of children was deflective, pleasing, and comforting. It paid due attention to the social graces and for that reason was no doubt appreciated. The child was simply a symbol for everything in the adult world that the Freudians wished to criticize. Once they created their villain and contrasted it with maturity—their hero and psychoanalytic standard of goodness—they could proceed to deliver a series of sermons, which was one of the essential functions of the Freudian enterprise.

The Oedipal child—desiring, lustful, rebellious—and the need to discipline youthful ways were quite familiar in the Western tradition, repeating admonitions throughout the Bible: "Flee also youthful lusts; but follow righteousness, faith, charity, peace, with them that call on the Lord out of a pure heart" (2 Timothy 2:22). "A fool despiseth his father's instructions: but he that regardeth reproof is prudent" (Proverbs 15:5). "If man have a stubborn and rebellious son, which will not obey the voice of his father, or the voice of his mother . . . they shall say unto the elders of his city, This our son is stubborn and rebellious. . . . And all the men of his city shall stone him with stones, that he die" (Deuteronomy 21:18–21).

The first villain was Satan, whose rebellion against God is reflected in the Freudian child, arch symbol of desire, disobedience, and rebellion. Satan, the child, the primitive, the neurotic, the madman—all bore the same sins in psychoanalysis: desire, disobedience, and rebellion. Their symbolism was also the same—they represented the beginning, the past, the untutored, the uncivilized. No one in the West in Freud's day needed more than a reminder about Satan's rebellion, the Fall as the result of disobedience, or the prodigal, pleasure-seeking, rebellious, stubborn child depicted in the Bible.

The Freudian view of the child also reflected—repeated—the prevalent nineteenth-century view in child psychology (similarly derived from the Bible). Carl Emminghaus, for example, in an 1887 study of what he believed were emotional disturbances, deplored the child's "instinctual inclination to the obscene" and "to the base in particular." This was not very different from the attitude of the Reverend Wilberforce in England and later Victorian moralists, not only toward children but toward the lower classes being "tamed" into civil society. Nor was it distinctly different from the psychiatric view. "Nervous children," according to Krafft-Ebing, needed to be taught "renunciation, order, cleanliness, simplicity and freedom from desire."[6]

These were not directions for children alone, I suggest; they were instructions in citizenship in an age of mass desire, and they became the platform for one of the many sermons embedded in the Freudian concept of infantilism. In nineteenth-century psychology, as in psychoanalysis, the preeminent signs of the new age were childish: self-interest and desire. For most these were directed toward the fulfillment of basic needs, for some the fulfillment of Lucullan wishes. Throughout the century, self-interest and desire were difficult to manage because they were revolutionary (virtual Satanic rebellion, seen in riots, uprisings, political revolutions, coups d'état, the hysterical politics of the last decade of the nineteenth century, and early in the next century the Russian Revolution and later, fascist revolutions). Precisely for this reason, they were demonized in psychoanalysis through the formula that infantilism equaled neurosis, maturity equaled health; infantilism was uncontrolled desire, maturity desire under control and gratification postponed (the privileged reality principle). This sermon was addressed to the common people, who were to postpone their gratifications to a time when they could be fulfilled. The message was to be spread far and wide as the norm of the culture and a counter to revolution: patience was of the essence; grabbing (as by revolution) was uncouth and mad, at least neurotic. This was calculated to orga-nize and stabilize the society of the day and allow the prevalent liberal political philosophy and economy to reign.

The irony in theoretical psychology being addressed initially to the middle class, which it was, is immediately apparent in this preach-ment. For infantilism and its cohort narcissism were not primarily the attributes of the common man, who was sometimes threatening but usually powerless. They were rather the expression, in full cry in Freud's day, of the wealthy minority, and they *were* a form of normal madness, a psychopathology of that minority's everyday life. "The problem with this new *economic* man," states Michael Crozier, "was not his hard-nosed rationality but his *hysteria;* government and poli-tics [were] at the mercy of passions and appetites that fed on them-selves *without moral limit.*"[7]

Through the regressions and repressions of the Freudian system, as for example in the reinvocation of God-in-the-mind as the Oedipus complex, Freud recalled the old times of order and stability precisely to conserve and let flourish the infantilism and narcissism of this hys-terical ruling minority. For this, and because of the destabilizing, cen-trifugal effects of modernity, Freud and his colleagues regressed to the old world family, community, emotions, and religious vision, in order to provide an anchor and rationale for the maddening, successful self-interest of the few whose power anchored the new age. Usually quite evil and restrictive in psychoanalysis, here the old world was good, the old ways were good, for they were the ways of order.

Freudianism on the one hand expressed the reality of the day as the elites lived it and everyone knew it to be: sex=desire=infantilism/narcissism=Original Sin/the World as Will=liberal democratic, indus-trial, free-market society. On the other hand, Freudianism was a con-version/diversion of that reality into an illness that warned the masses of the consequences of childish desire. Psychoanalysis served as a so-lace to those who could not readily satisfy their desires but who could understand that a revolutionary reaction to their condition would be childish and sick.

What justified the bifurcation of desire into health for some and sickness for others was the Freudian formula that if one could fulfill his wishes, wishing was not harmful. Disease would attack only those who could not fulfill their wishes. "The energetic and successful man," Freud pointed out, "is one who succeeds by his efforts in turning his wishful phantasies into reality. Where this fails, as a result of the resistances of the external world and of the subject's own weakness, he begins to turn away from reality and withdraws into his more satisfying world of phantasy, the content of which is transformed into symptoms should he fall ill."[8] Wishing was dangerous for those without power and uncertain of successful gambits in reaching for desired objects, he was saying. At the very least, desiring was a gamble needing second and third thoughts. The end result might be neurosis or madness—another warning and another sermon.

Rank explains that modern culture turned to the psychoanalytic ideology of restraint on infantilism and narcissism to disguise the genuine psychology of the new age, which was grasping and pleasure-seeking, bent on gratification. "We come here upon the strangest paradox of cultural symbiose [sic], a state of affairs in which one type of people," the narcissistic, grasping type, accepts restraint "as a therapeutic ideology, and this therapeutic ideology is then proclaimed to be the general psychology . . . of mankind, regardless of time and place."[9] By this Rank meant that not to rebel was the ideology of the elites, which they wished the masses to accept, while not to grasp was the ideology that the mass wished the elites to accept. The elites accepted with equanimity both the proscription against rebellion (much to their interest) and the indictment of desire (except for desire which could be fulfilled, which was their type of desire). In some ways this might be confusing, but the Freudian system had to touch many, often conflicted bases, in this as at many other points, in replicating religion and the complexities of the new age.

Rank believes that Western culture took to the new psychology in the same way "a desperate humanity had accepted Jewish morality in Christianity, as an ideology of deliverance." The difference was that "Christianity signified . . . a revitalization of an outlived ideology in terms of the needs of the present; whereas psychoanalysis merely offers a consolation and justification of the existent type of man."[10] To the contrary, the new psychology appears to have accomplished precisely what Christianity did: it revitalized outlived ideologies in terms of the needs of the present. Here, for example, it replaced Satan with the child and rebellion by childish desire, thus fulfilling functions attractive to both the Freudians and the culture by giving support to some and solace to others.

Infantilism (self-love, self-interest) as rebellion was much to be feared (perhaps all that was to be feared) at a time when pleasure was the reigning philosophy, and when everyone wanted his share and more of the pie—but the shares were restricted. The demand for shares was potentially destabilizing and might bring middle-class civilization as it was then understood to ruin. Here, then, infantilism carried the same message as the Oedipus complex and the Bible: Do not be children, do not rebel, heed the father. This summed up civilization as Freud understood it: leaders and led, the structure of hierarchy which he saw as the structure of order in his time and as the structure, or predicate, of modern freedoms. Everyone had to be responsible in his own way or the nineteenth-century experiment in freedom would come apart.

What had to be feared was that the new social, political, and economic scheme the West had embarked on would not be allowed to mature. It created so much tension, anxiety, and discontent that it might provoke rebellion and be overthrown. Rebellion had to be protected against, and one method was to paint it as infantile. Who wanted to be characterized as infantile? Or primitive? Or narcissistic? Or mad? Freud had successfully developed a method of name-calling that worked in tandem with the culture at large. "Sticks and stones will break my bones but names will never harm me," children sang at school. Not so. The Freudians and Western culture—any culture— counted on the power of names to discipline and control, and they were not disappointed. It was by names above all—the naming system inherent in the goods and bads of psychoanalytic theory—that the Freudians sought to succeed. The names invoked shame at least and madness at worst—just one example of Freud's adherence to the soul-psychology belief about ideas (representations) in the mind and how much could be gained by shaping them.

The rebellious child was none other than the common man and woman, abandoned and lost, released into freedom, industry, and modernity by the twin revolutions, dependent, and ruled, whether willing or not, by the child's ignorant passions which were the passions of the day, desire and self-love. This was the child who was warned not to rebel, at a time when rebellious political forces were vocal and when the new order of liberal democracy was threatened. Because of this resonance, "infantilism" had great acceptance in the West, representing both the potentially rebellious mass populations and the middle class amassing its pleasures and wants. It seemed true, and it was.

In frustration, the rebellious child in the person of the mass populations of Europe looked back on the old world when the nobility were the fathers. That old world, the child-place of modern man which later became a nostalgia and a longing, in therapy theory was the same as the Golden Age to which the neurotic seeks to return and to which many Europeans gave every indication of desiring to return. The evils in that old past were not to be valued, psychoanalysis taught, in favor of the present shorn of religion, tyranny, superstition, and ignorance. God in heaven was the bad old time, God in the mind was the good new time, accompanied by freedom, elected representatives, free speech, and the other adornments of democracy. The past, according to this sermon, was infantile; the present was mature. This was the exact parallel to Freudian clinical theory in which the patient had to be educated into maturity and weaned off the past. The past was evil but was now over, the analysts taught in their theories and practices. You had no reason to be wedded to it any longer, because it no longer existed. What existed now was freedom, if you would recognize it, appreciate it, and respect its norms, especially to be responsible and not rebel.

BY A TWIST built into psychoanalysis (*reversal, unconscious contradiction*), a second type of the child well known to Western consciousness appeared in Freudianism: the obedient child who follows the righteous path, being closest to God. This is the child whom Christ urged his listeners to imitate (and who in Western memory had a historical analog, the serf population of Europe).[11] This child, tamed by the Oedipus complex, brought to light a positive aspect of the past (which the Freudians most often vilified), for there were again exceptions to what was otherwise villainy and evil. Through its regressions to olden times, Freudianism preached that to follow dutifully along, even if that seemed a repeat of the medieval past, was not to be rejected but respected, for every society needed leaders and followers, the followers now being the "children" of democracy.

People, Freud assured his audience, "fall into the two classes of leaders and led. The latter constitute the vast majority; they stand in need of an authority which will make decisions for them and to which they for the most part offer unqualified submission." The leaders are from "the upper stratum of men with independent minds," whose function is "to give direction to the dependent masses."[12] This may be taken as both Freud's elitist view of society and his commentary on his latent work—he and colleagues, in their minds, belonging to this upper stratum destined to lead the masses (and doing so through the beliefs embedded in psychoanalysis). The preachment about democratic children following along appealed not only because it depicted the role of the elites in the new society and the evident condition of the masses, but also because it painted the inevitable frustrations of modern society, in which dependence and discipline were imposed on all.

Infantilism as the past thus served three latent purposes in psychoanalysis: it condemned the past as a false paradise for individuals and the culture; it recalled the order and certainty of the past, much to be desired in the modern age; and it recommended a new order and certainty for modernity under the aegis of liberal democracy, psychoanalysis, and the nuclear family—the better alternatives to the old feudalism, Christianity, and the tyrannical family. Like Lot's wife, the mass populations of Europe were not to look back. Unlike her, they were to take a peek, make a comparison, and accept the present as a much improved order in which stability had been regained, hierarchy had been reimposed, yet everyone was free.

The function of treatment was to redirect "infantile wishful impulses,"[13] according to Freud, and that was what he did culturally with the condemnations and preachments residing in the concept of infantilism.

SEVENTEEN

More Heroes, Villains, Sermons

. . . The ego, driven by the id, confined by the superego, repulsed by reality, struggles . . . [for]
harmony. . . .
　　　—Sigmund Freud, *New Introductory Lectures*

Where id was, there shall ego be. It is a work of
culture—not unlike the draining of the Zuider Zee.
　　　—Sigmund Freud, *New Introductory Lectures*

IN FREUD'S two-part scheme of conscious ego and unconscious libido, the ego is the hero and the libido is the villain. In his later three-
part scheme of id, ego, and superego, the villain is the childish id
(libido, unconscious), the hero is again the ego, and the superego is social morality supporting the hero against the villain, sometimes so
strenuously that it too becomes a villain.

Among the id-villains, Freud counted primitive humankind: " 'In
dreams and in neuroses,' so our principle has run, 'we come once
more upon the *child* and the peculiarities which characterize his modes
of thought and emotional life. And we come upon the *savage*
too . . . upon the primitive man, as he stands revealed to us in the light
of the researches of archaeology and of ethnology.' " In the child Freud
saw "incestuous lustfulness, pleasure seeking and murderous wishes as
primary and basic, on a collision course with the culture and society
in which the human infant has to be civilized. . . . This taming, controlling and proper channeling of the drives occurs against the infant's
and child's wish and self interests. The results are at best an acquisition of a thin veneer of civilization that can, and frequently does, easily peel off, laying bare the original lustfulness and bestiality
beneath. . . ."[1]

These views had resonance and verisimilitude at a time when European imperialism had encountered tribal societies in Africa, Asia, and Latin America as never before, and had projected them as wild, savage, and uncaringly cruel: mayhem crystallized. The Europeans wished to fashion the "primitives" into an image of themselves, they being, par excellence, the ego and superego of the world, bearing "the white man's burden." "Primitive" infantilism pointed to the West as the hero of civilization, a touch of flattery that could not fail to be appreciated since it supported the world hegemony of the West and downplayed the irrational and warlike attributes of European civilization.

Closer to home, id-ego-superego recalled the old world of pre-industrial Europe (the id primitive, unknowing, paying unconscious obedience to God). It was a reminder that the old ego was ruled by overpowering beliefs, the new ego by reason implanted through a rational ideology. In this way the old nation was to be contrasted with the rationalistic nation-state of the new age—further flattery. The id of the mass populations of Europe was to be managed by the ego and superego of the new ruling class (still more flattery) which, mundane and practical, was to be seen as normative, as was their culture—even though Europe had made the id, as desire and pleasure, its ruling principle.

On the political scene, id-ego-superego paralleled Freud's attitudes toward the parties of left, right, and center. The left was the id, creative and disruptive; the right was the superego, deeply conservative and also disruptive because it would not let go of the past or wished to eliminate the present violently; the liberal democratic center was the ego, measured and rational. In the national ideologies of the day, the authoritarian state (like the medieval states of old) was both the id, where the desires of the few ruled without question, and the harsh superego. The democracies were the rational ego.

Echoing Rousseau, fin-de-siècle romantic radicals found the infantile, the primitive, and the unconscious authentic, unlike the false mask worn by maturity and civilization. Since the primitive was in touch with nature and the original impulses of the race, the romantics believed that the proper direction for society was back to the past. The consequences of this thinking had their greatest impact in the German-speaking lands, where the people were attracted by a lost past that extended beyond the pre-industrial, Christian world to the pagan time of wandering Germanic tribes, when humankind was thought to be in touch with the vital forces of nature and the universe. That time and those people were seen as a source of pride and emulation, feeding the accumulating stream of anti-modernity and proto-fascism.

The childlike (*Kinderlichkeit*) was a German romantic ideal. Langbehn viewed it as "the panacea for the evils of the present." Stern notes that Langbehn's hope was that "In the new Germany the talents and joys of the child would be preserved in the adult; even now the 'genuine and pure' Germans retained more of the childlike in their nature than other peoples. . . ." This plea for childhood was attractive, Stern notes, "especially in an age when ignorance and prejudice about childhood ran strong; but the reverse of this idyllic glorification was Langbehn's unrelenting warfare against intellect. Certainly his cult of the child conveyed in yet another form his commitment to a new mystical primitiveness."[2]

Against this trend came Freudianism, its trumpets blaring. The European audience was to absorb the Freudian condemnation of the infantile and the primitive as evil. That was not what was wanted, was Freud's sermon; reason was wanted, and what came after the infantile and primitive: civilization—the message of the Enlightenment. That was what the European was all about, the pioneers hoped, and that the atavistic tendencies of their day were only a passing phenomenon. At a stroke, just as Freud had reinstalled Western morality with the Oedipus complex, he sought to obliterate the enemies of democracy through the concepts of infantilism and the primitive.

Rousseau, whose philosophy contributed to freeing the common man, had tied the noble savage and freedom together, forming a dangerous combustible. German thinkers adapted Rousseau's stance to a view of freedom as anarchic exuberance and wildness, the exact opposite of rationality. To Freud, these Germanic doctrines represented the opposite of civilization, and if triumphant, the end of civilization (he was already fully aware that they were also of vital danger to the Jews of Europe). While such ideas were the work of middle-class intellectuals, and the middle class flirted with them throughout the nineteenth century, the general preference was for the theories of social Darwinism, which made predation (which the Germanic primitivists lauded) a social good based on rational self-interest rather than primitive savagery. The middle class did not wish to seem savage predators; better, rational businessmen. And they knew that the primitivists hated every form of unheroic, modern commercialism.

Closest to home, the villainous id was represented by the first primitive that Freud encountered in his thought: the nineteenth-century child. Punishment by parents was the superego, and the resulting well-disciplined child was the ego. Id-ego-superego was in this way the story of a child's upbringing in Freud's day, parental punishment being how the nasty id of childhood, for whom the Bible recommended not sparing the rod, informed the ego of the "primitive" child how far he or she might go. In this reading of the triptych, the social ignorance and unformed discipline of the child constituted the id, and father (and/or mother) was the superego imposing the reality principle.

This source in everyday life, merely a common observation as it was a common experience, was hidden in science because for Freud's psychology to do its personal and cultural work, it had to represent interior emotions as opposed to exterior force (punishment), a natural internal process as opposed to an external one. This was consonant with liberal democracy, which needed internal controls, not enhanced external ones, to work effectively; hence a theory of the psyche in conflict with itself, rather than a theory of punishment. It was best if one became his own censor, for authoritarian censorship was something from the past that must be discarded.

TO FREUD, sexual "perversions" such as homosexuality, masturbation, coitus interruptus, and contraception were founded in childhood maladaptations that caused neurosis. (This was before he settled on sexual seduction in youth and then the Oedipus complex.) They represented "the general infantilism in sexual life."[3] All the pioneers and virtually all the psychologists and physicians of the day pinpointed these "perversions" as symptoms or causes of nervous illnesses. The initial inspiration was Judeo-Christianity and the Middle Ages, when such practices were roundly condemned, none more than homosexuality. Another inspiration was the practice of doctors in Freud's day never to show ignorance and always to medicalize sex, so that they were determined to find a place for "perversions." Everyone in medicine and psychology at the time was expected to have an opinion on these practices, and the opinion was almost always dire: there was something radically wrong with them.

But that does not fully explain medicalizing these sexual practices and damning them as infantile. The general purpose was the management of sex as desire and pleasure, both with eminently social entailments because sex had become popular politics, arising directly from pleasure as a social "good" unequally distributed in the society of the time. Further, medicalizing sex simulated medical science, providing another cover for the latent work of the pioneers. More significant, however, was that the theory of perversions identified "sins" and thereby acted as moral instruction. One of the chief modalities of psychoanalysis was the No! of not rebelling, in this case not being sexually deviant.

No! regarding "perverse" sexual practices reduced rather than enlarged sexual expression, leading sexuality toward the path of monogamy and the nuclear family, the preeminently normative institutions of the day. This was precisely what was wanted; it conformed to the Judeo-Christian model and conduced to the benefit of modern economics, orders, and the state. It was urgent to view divergent sexual experiences as abnormal and, with the advent of the psychological experts, sick. That coitus interruptus and contraceptives barred pregnancies was not congenial to nations that were seeking to increase populations both for business (as markets) and for war (deeply on the mind of European statesmen). The other two "abnormalities," homosexuality and masturbation, were substitutes for heterosexual sex and were also to be discouraged because they did not lead to children.

The state wanted children and wanted them cared for; the economy wanted fruitful nuclear families as laborers, markets for goods and services, and fodder for war. But neither the state nor industry was in the business of rearing children or reducing the economic burden on the families doing so. To the contrary, according to the theorists of the new economy, children and poor wages conduced to the work ethic: the less you had and the more you needed, the harder you would be willing to work. Stigmatizing "perverse" sexual practices helped to ensure the effectiveness of this philosophy.

For these quite utilitarian reasons, monogamous heterosexual sex was good, the more conventional the better. Some play on the side was understandable for the mature man, most especially the man of means; all else was infantile. In this way the sexual liberators of the psychological revolution preached in medicalese the sexual ethics that were culturally desirable. Definitions of what was sexually proper (mostly carried over from the old world) were put back in place as science. As with much else in psychoanalysis, the theorists strove to meet the specifications of the culture of the day, which is mainly why sexual "perversions" became one of their specialties under the label of infantilism. The Freudians and the culture preached "mature" sex.

THERAPY ENCOURAGED the patient to confront the inner truth of the child who wanted only pleasure. The patient, getting the message, would take over the search. The therapist was telling the patient (and the culture) that what was childish and narcissistic had to be abandoned in favor of the reality principle. This process, like all the condemnations contained in "infantilism," had the same purpose as psychoanalysis in general: reculturation (that is, education in the new times). The old, traditional ways were childish and had to be traded in for modernity. In Europe and America, everyone born after 1800 was brought up in two cultures at once—the vestigial culture of the family and the Father, and the new culture of the organization, in which many of the functions of the father were transferred to the organization and the Stranger, which had to be accepted as new and unavoidable conditions. The "child" in the political, economic, and social configuration of the new age was not only the citizen but the culture at large, born out of the temper of the old world, to be tempered by the new. Everyone, as far as possible, through the messages of theoretical psychology, was to undergo this tempering. Psychoanalysis was the Freudian method of child-rearing and education for the culture as a whole.

The necessary reculturation—the passage from the infantilism of the old world to the adulthood of the new, from id to ego and superego—to which not everyone was amenable, produced one source of patients for psychotherapy and one way of marking deviants against the new age. Some individuals clung to the old world order—especially to nostalgic concepts of love, community, and identity—or had alternative views on what and how relationships and life should be constituted in the new order. They were "deviants," infantilists in the new context, even though the new age made alternate views and experimentation possible by officially removing the mantle of the family and the Father. But the new culture's wish was not for a new style or multiple styles. It was not for freedom in that sense, but rather for a repetition of the old style by transferring what could be salvaged to totally new conditions.

The need was to hem in the impulses of the new age; for above all the new age, readily aware of the revolutionary chaos bubbling below the surface, wanted order. Freudian infantilism was needed as the premise for the ultimate hero of psychoanalysis, the father (more effective for coercion than even the state), who had to be refound so that he could once again lead a coherent social structure. All the effort that went into creating the psychoanalytic theory of the child—the id, the infantile, the narcissistic, the primitive, the neurotic—had as its main purpose the re-creation of the father, who could lead. Not Sophocles or Greek myth but the idea of infantilism spawned the Oedipus complex in particular and psychoanalysis in general, in order to reinstall the father in modern culture.

Oedipal conflict, decoded, described the following situation precisely: Beginning in the nineteenth century the father was no longer revered and followed. He had been once, but his power had been shorn by history (*he* was the castrated one). Freud and all Europe possessed the Judeo-Christian tradition of the revered father/Father and wished to follow the father. The conflict was whether to follow the father, who was now shorn of legitimacy, or to rebel. The culture of the modern age had rebelled while continuing to profess faith in the father. Freud's was an effort to resolve this "Oedipal conflict."

To adopt for a moment Freudian terminology, the effort of psychoanalysis in its prime, cultural function was to refit the father with a penis, to return authority to him, however ersatz. And this rehabilitation must be widely recognized in order to lodge authority and legitimacy in the new democratic societies through the same understanding that older societies had employed—that the father ruled. In capsule, that was Freud's contribution and one of the main reasons for his acceptance. Freud's evocation of the father was more practical and less mystical than anything Jung offered; at the same time it was more concealed in its purpose than anything Adler supplied. It was both covert and deeply significant.

In the re-creation of the father leading the child, the final meaning of Freudian infantilism comes clear: submission, the term of former times, or, as was familiarly said in modern times, conformity—what Freud called identification. This was the most urgent message of the masters of society who sought to create a new culture in the midst of turmoil. Such symbolic concepts as the Oedipus complex, infantilism, narcissism, and the primitive represent how brilliantly Freud above all formed his ideas within the texture of Western tradition and contemporary belief, and at times against the urgings of his closest disciples. His message was little different from the message of the Bible and the Ten Commandments, which was one measure of its brilliance; and the submission he preached was to be not very different from the old variety, in the old world, but it was to be in new garb, the garb of democracy and industrialism.

The most hopeful form of submission outlined by psychoanalysis was sublimation—turning unacceptable childish wishes into acceptable adult achievement; or, in more general terms, the healthful conversion of the primitive, infantile sexual instinct into cultural work (or, said still another way, turning rebellious children into dutiful followers). Nothing better describes what was wanted at the time by the culture's elites as a lesson for all: turn desire into achievement, turn illegitimate desire away. And nothing better describes the process by which Freud created psychoanalysis, not through sublimating his sexual instinct but through suppressing the raw, harsh data of his age and turning it into the cultural achievement he called psychoanalysis.

Democracy, the nuclear family, and psychoanalysis wanted children who could clear the course of maturation through society's hazards. They all wanted desperately to be the new father, the new superego, to be listened to as the divinity in place of God, to overcome their rebellious children, achieve order in their household, meekness in their citizens, the willingness to listen and follow—in short, dutiful children in a dutiful world order. "You can, if you like," Freud wrote, "regard psycho-analytic treatment as no more than a prolongation of education for the purpose of overcoming the residues of childhood."[4] You can regard psychoanalysis, if you will, as the education of mass populations in overcoming the residues of the past while adopting some of them as positive, aimed at producing good citizens of liberal democracy, not grasping, rebellious, or disruptively desirous.

When the sociologist David Riesman referred to Freud as justifying "contemporary authority by throwing over it the mantle of the primal father," Paul Roazen declared him wrong. Yet he was speaking the plainest truth. When Roazen maintains that "It can . . . be said of Freud's theory that it does little to explain day-to-day politics," he is forming a heavy irony. When he cites Robert Waelder approvingly as explaining that psychoanalysis shifted from "the early preoccupation with pathology . . . to the contemporary preoccupation with normal developmental processes,"[5] he and Waelder are recognizing what Freud sought to fashion *from the beginning,* what could, should, and would be believed: *a psychology of the normal for the democratic age.*

In all its variations, psychoanalysis was a sublimation of liberal democracy in all its manifestations. Freud was proud to believe that his ideas and observations were tied to the practicality of helping patients: "I was driven forward above all by practical necessity."[6] That there was a ponderous social practicality at the bottom of his endeavor cannot be denied, nowhere more evident than in the construction and deployment of the concept of infantilism.

EIGHTEEN

The Lessons of Sex

Do you believe with Sigmund Freud that sex is at the
root of everything?
—Vincent Canby, *New York Times*

It is necessary to distinguish sharply between the
concepts of "sexual" and "genital." The former is the
wider concept and includes many activities that having
nothing to do with the genitals.
—Sigmund Freud, *An Outline of Psycho-Analysis*

SEX IN FREUDIANISM was the symbolic representation of the philosophy of pleasure, the single most recognizable theme of the nineteenth century. Sex was pleasure, pleasure was self-interest, and
self-interest assured success and happiness, according to the politics,
economics, and culture of the day. In this way sex as pleasure fit the
liberal philosophy of utilitarianism, which made pleasure the source
of happiness and thereby supported self-interest. It was right to be free
to seek the heart's desire; free-market liberal democracy was based on,
and justified by, freeing the individual to seek the heart's desire. So in
giving pleasure primacy in human psychology, Freud was not merely
repeating philosophical models but was supporting the philosophy
that nineteenth-century liberalism had adopted for all. We can suppose
that the other psychologists of the time who were emphasizing sex
were doing much the same.

Having converted Hobbes, Adam Smith, and John Locke (let alone
Bentham, Schopenhauer, Feuerbach, and Fechner) into modern psychology with his dictum that "our total mental activity is directed towards pleasure and avoiding unpleasure,"[1] Freud translated the
philosophy of pleasure into the symbol of sex. He then enhanced the

democratic credentials of sex as his symbol for pleasure by making it, not intelligence, not reason, the crucial meaning of the mind. Everyone, or practically everyone, has sexuality; and it requires little tutoring, so that an individual might miss out on conscious, reasoning mind power but naturally possess the more—the most—important unconscious mind power, represented in Freudian theory as sex. Sexual universality was democratic universality was psychoanalytic universality.

Placing pleasure at the center of human psychology validated the reigning philosophy of self-interest *as science*. Pleasure was confirmed not merely as the cultural preference of the new age, which it was, but as the underlying preference of *all* times and places, unavoidable and therefore a given. Freedom and individualism, linked to self-interest in philosophy and economic theory, were shown in this way to be the fated course of civilization, with liberal democracy their appropriate expression. That was Freud's answer to the hysterical critics of modernity who claimed that the old ways drawn from medievalism represented the truth of human nature.

When Freud announced in a talk on "The Etiology of Hysteria" (at an 1896 meeting of the Vienna Society for Psychiatry and Neurology) that "Whatever cause and whatever symptom we take as our point of departure, in the end we infallibly come to the field of sexual experience," he was identifying, under the rubric of sex, the human will to pleasure and the social contention over it—who would get it, who would not. This was a political question that in the past had been settled by the rigid separation of classes. When Freud attributed to "the powerful factor of sexuality . . . the origin of the nervous disorders which it was my aim to cure,"[2] he was saying that the whole issue of sex (and mental illness) was people getting the good things they wanted and avoiding the bad things they did not want. He had come to cure the disorders to which the struggle for pleasure and against pain led. When he proposed the theory of "polymorphous perversity," he was representing the will to pleasure let loose as the right of all in the nineteenth century. But it was not children who were polymorphously perverse, it was adults, it was the age, reflected by Freud in a psychological theory.

THROUGHOUT the nineteenth century, with the intertwining of pleasure, self-interest, the market economy, and liberal democracy, sexual liberation became the popular means of calling for greater political and economic liberation. The elites feared that the common people, wishing to ape their betters in sexual style, might extend their goals to acquiring the power and pleasures of the elites, or, that being impossible, usurping them. That was why sex was so problematic for Queen Victoria and the other rulers of Europe, so much so that it can be said to be responsible, almost alone, for Victorianism. Conversely, the explosion of sex in the Victorian era did not necessarily disturb the politically powerful. It happens that a political system sometimes endows a social action that it disapproves of in order to endow another that it desires. That was the case with sex in the Victorian era. The elites preferred to pout about immorality rather than about loss of their power, so sex was officially restrained even as it ran wild throughout the culture. It became the opiate of the people, in which they could recognize their freedom culturally when they could not find it politically or economically. Here sex served in both politics and psychoanalysis as a diversion from the political and economic, and as a lesson in giving something up: the desire for power, in favor of a substitute, a freer social attitude toward sex.

At the end of the *Five Lectures,* trying to make his audience understand that "if the restriction upon sexuality were to be carried too far it would inevitably" lead to great evils, Freud recounted the experience of the legendary citizens of Schilda. They possessed a fine, healthy horse with "whose feats of strength they were highly pleased [with] and against which they had only one objection—that it consumed such a large quantity of expensive oats." So they conceived a plan of daily reducing the oats ration, finally getting down to one stalk a day and then eliminating even that, whereupon "the spiteful animal was found dead; and the citizens of Schilda could not make out what it had died of." Nothing "could be expected of an animal without a certain modicum of oats" was the moral of the story.[3] In other words, you could not take every pleasure from the workhorses of Western society. You had to yield something—for example, a freer attitude toward sex. Although Freud thought he was teaching the elites a lesson here, turning them in a desirable direction, they already knew it, and had known it for most of the nineteenth century. This is what gave reactionaries one of many leads into radical politics, through the assertion that Europe had become immoral and that they, the reactionaries, knew the way back to better standards.

In later years Freud continued to put forward his proposal for a freer attitude toward sex. Psychoanalysis, he insisted in 1927, "proposes that there should be a reduction in the strictness with which instincts are repressed. . . . Certain instinctual impulses [sex], with whose suppression society had gone too far, should be permitted a greater amount of satisfaction; in the case of others the inefficient method of suppressing them by means of repression should be replaced by a better and securer procedure." He had just such a procedure: psychoanalysis as a mass belief. As if to hide its social utility, he claimed to be the butt of critics who saw his work as "inimical to authority" and a "social danger." Stark conservatives saw it that way; but most leaders of society knew better, agreeing with Freud that if something were not given up there would be danger, just as the citizens of Schilda should have known. "The ruler's throne rests upon fettered slaves," Freud warned. "Woe if they should be set loose. The throne would be overturned and the ruler trampled under foot."[4]

Psychoanalysis, he argued, "has never said a word about unfettering instincts that would injure our community. On the contrary, [the instincts] of most people are tamed insufficiently and in a manner which is psychologically wrong and are therefore readier than the rest to break out." Hence his proposal for an easing of restraints on sex, which can be said—not because of Freud but because of the elites, the masses, and the nature of the culture as a whole—to be the course adopted by every liberal democratic society from the nineteenth century forward. Freud proved useful in this effort by rationalizing as science what was already happening, where before it had been sin and therefore beyond the pale of respectability.

While associated with popular freedom in Europe and therefore always potentially destabilizing, in Germany and Austria sex-as-politics was associated with those ideas the nativists and primitivists were encouraging: the naturalism of the *volk* and a new kind of freedom, the freedom to go back to what was perceived as a more satisfying past in which everyone knew their place and life was simpler, more authentic, and therefore far better. These impulses—longings—had become purified and crystallized in central Europe. There they were turned into political programs in which everything Freud meant by the infantile and the primitive being at war with civilization was to be seen. The reactionary forces had adopted sex as a new kind of irrationalism, and the far-left forces were not far behind in interpreting it as an emblem of the freedom and naturalness Europe could never achieve under present conditions.

The imperishable, repressed wishes of modern man for a simpler, more certain time, which trailed back to his pre-industrial beginnings, had demonstrated the power, in the nineteenth century, to construct social symptoms. Without those wishes, the reaction to the trauma of modernity might have taken a normal course. But with them came social malformations—conflicted longing for the past and for the pleasures of the present not available to everyone in the new world. Freud's answer was to provide a diversion from those longings in the form of a morality tale about them, clothed in sex. Thus not only the symptoms of Western longing and dissatisfaction could be described as derived from sex, but the cure, the new mass-belief system, preaching restraint on desire, could be too.

People, Freud wrote, "do not show their sexuality freely, but to conceal it they wear a heavy overcoat woven of a tissue of lies, as though the weather were bad in the world of sexuality. Nor are they mistaken. It is a fact that sun and wind are not favorable to sexual activity in this civilized world of ours; none of us can reveal his eroticism freely to others." Freudianism was just such a heavy overcoat, covering not sexuality but the bitter disappointments and hysteria of modernity, especially as they related to the achievement of pleasure (success, happiness, and so forth). "We liberate sexuality through our treatment," Freud told the Vienna Psychoanalytic Society, "not in order that man may from now on be dominated by sexuality, but in order to make a suppression possible—a rejection of the instincts under the guidance of a higher agency. . . . We try to replace the pathological process with rejection." In *Five Lectures* (and many other writings) he explained that rejection led to three outcomes. First, "the destruction of infantile wishes. *Repression is replaced by a condemning judgment.*" Second, sublimation, the redirection of libido to personally and socially useful work. Third—and this, he said, was for society as a whole—recognition of the need to reduce restraints on sex, which he urged from first to last.[5]

These three outcomes were, in disguise, the social goals of psychoanalysis as a belief system. First, the destruction of agitating thoughts of plenty among the mass populations of Europe, a consequent reduction or elimination of rebelliousness, and the possible but much less likely similar effect on the heterodox thoughts of radical socialists and conservatives. Second, the sublimation of the hurts, fears, and hysteria of modernity into personal, not social concerns. And, last, the substitution of the beliefs of psychoanalysis (for example, easing restraints on sex) for all that could not be achieved by the mass populations of Europe after a hundred years of the twin revolutions. If Freud and his colleagues thought to accomplish all of this, they were vainglorious and totally unrealistic. All they could do, they would have known, was to make what contribution was possible, along with all those others working to shore up liberal democracy and modernity.

The political leader was a sexual object to his followers, according to Freud, the followers cathecting with the leader as a source of pleasure. Whether this is true or not (and it must be true in the sense that the leader is empowered by the followers precisely because he promises them the satisfaction of their desires), it was true for Freud. He could see that the theme of sex would cathect with the culture and help make him what in fact he became, a culture hero of the West.

LURKING IN Freud's theme of sex was another, higher motif: love. Freud routinely discredited romantic and Christian love and their corollary, idealism, he and Janet proposing that love was neurotic; yet all the dynamic psychologists placed it in their formulas. Analysts, Freud explained in 1919, "had to deal with emotions and passions, and most of all with those which the poets never tire of depicting and celebrating—the emotions of love."[6] So strong was this theme that love became the proof against madness in the implicit equation: sex=love, lack of love=isolation/frustration=madness. After a time, almost all the manifest threads of therapy theory led back to love. Why?

We read in the second epistle of John: "He that loveth not knoweth not God; for God is love" (2 John 4:8). The message that changed the Western world, it might be said, finally overthrowing the cultural power of Greece and Rome, was love; not sexual, not needful, but full of grace, the love called *agape*. It was in part out of this dispensation that love, if now as forbidden lust, found itself right at the center of the Oedipus complex. What was the source of Christianity but a family—Joseph, Mary, and Jesus? And what was the eternal theme of this family? Love, the same theme that originated the "family romance" that Freud welded into modern psychology.

But as with everything else in psychoanalysis, love had a twist. However valuable and desirable it might be, it was hard to find in the competitive, instrumental new age, when self-love outbid the love of others. The impossibility of fully gratifying the sexual instinct, since it was insatiable (which the Hindus, Schopenhauer, and Freud preached), was to be found again in the difficulty of finding true love of others in the new age, according to the analysts. That was the reality principle in the age of competitive freedom, against which the romantics had reacted with a mystical, oceanic sense of love of all. The Freudians in turn reacted against the romantics by making the lack of love in the new world a timeless, universal condition which Christianity had disguised. Universal love was associated in the theory of psychoanalysis with the old world, which the new world found urgent to discredit. The romantic "return of love" was impossible, psychoanalysis meant to demonstrate scientifically, because it had never existed—another blow to the nativists and primitivists who insisted that modern culture had taken a wrong turn.

By refinding and then disparaging love as unreal, psychoanalysis repeated what was felt to be true as a cultural fact—that love was no longer readily available. At the same time, said the Freudians, its absence was not to be regretted because it was essentially neurotic, something that had never really existed but was only coveted. The family, and by extension the society, were no longer sites of love, if they had ever been. They were sites of conflict and competition, as they had always been in reality, said psychoanalysis, and this was also true in the individual. Freud reduced love to the benefits people sought from each other; it was nothing more than self-love (which was pure Schopenhauer).

Freud converted love into "objects" (his word) of desire. We love what we want and what will give us pleasure, he said, and what we want are objects of satisfaction. The objects could be people, things, events—all roughly equal in the mind as wants, as though we were all three-year-olds crying over and over throughout life, "I want that! Give it to me!" This was a dramatically different understanding of what love had once been, whether personal or social. Freud was comfortable with this conclusion to the theme of love, because he disagreed with the ascetic dispensation from the Bible through Schopenhauer and Feuerbach. He refused to mix human sympathy and empathy with the quest for pleasure. To him they were idealisms in conflict with the reality principle.

Against some of his sources, therefore, Freud had little use for the connection between love and social justice. In this he was in total agreement with the outcome of the twin revolutions by the end of the nineteenth century. Among so many others of a romantic temperament, Feuerbach had been as eloquent as the Prophets: "Happiness.

No, justice! But justice is simply mutual or reciprocal happiness in contrast with the one-sided, egotistic or sectional [class] happiness of the old world!" Freud, always the realist, would have none of it. He recognized what his culture, which he revered, was and not what it should or might be. When confronted late in life by Romain Rolland, the French novelist, with the "oceanic feeling" of human solidarity, Freud wrote him of "the most precious of all illusions, that of love extended to all mankind." He had spent his life, he explained, destroying "illusions of my own and those of mankind." This was true, but it had become the main line of the modern West long before Freud was born.[7]

Sex was Freud's *substitute* for love, its materialization (in the same way Schopenhauer had naturalized or materialized God). In the Freudian formula it *became* love and whatever pleasures could be obtained from others. This was one of the most important reflections and rationalizations Freud provided of the new age's ethos. By recognizing in sex the materialization of love, he supported the age's materialism. In psychoanalysis love became the tangible act of sex, having lost its spiritual robe. This was in large measure the truth in the modern world, and Freud was not wrong in pointing it out, recording the codes of modernity with the same accuracy as the sociologists of his day. In the modern age materialism had replaced spirit; the way to satisfy desire was through something tangible; materialism was good in and of itself and did not need love to give it value.

Because sex was the materialization of love, it acquired something of the heavenly about it by Freud's time. The direction of spirituality had by now reversed, emanating from the human. With the flight of the spiritual, the material—as sex, pleasure, worldly success—was all that remained. It took the place of the spiritual. As the social theorist Guy Debord has explained, "A fallacious paradise . . . is no longer projected onto the heavens, but finds its place within material life itself."[8] Material goods having become the meaning of life and the measure of success, all the seeking soul in the modern age was apt to find was the material, which had been enthroned in place of the spiritual, the latter having been banished or dissolved or proved never to have existed. Worth and satisfaction now depended on how much of the material was achieved: you won if you had the most toys. As the struggle for the material became the struggle for the only heaven available, pleasure became a spiritual quest, recognized and fortified by Freud through sex as the materialization of love.

WITH THE FLIGHT of love as the most exalted doctrine of the West, suspicion entered as a new doctrine. Psychoanalysis reflected, rationalized, and justified this change by making its essential goal to find out what was beneath the surface of things, to find the ill will in human nature that was thought to be motivating patients as it was motivating everyone else. In doing so it claimed that it was not taking account of a cultural change, for such a change had never occurred; the truth had only been occluded by the illusions of Christianity. Real life had always been conflicted, competitive, and deceitful. When you speak of high aims, Freud informed his patients and the culture at large, you are telling lies. Tell me rather about what is base and therefore true in you. Or as he said, comparing himself to a judge: "When someone charged with an offense confesses his deed to the judge, the judge believes his confession; but if he denies it, the judge does not believe him. . . ."[9]

Freud once explained the lustful, deceitful unconscious to his daughter Anna as they strolled through an exclusive section of Vienna crowded with stately homes. "You see these houses with their lovely façades? Things are not necessarily so lovely behind the façades. And so it is with human beings too." Of course everyone learns this lesson, and of course Freud was repeating here what Schopenhauer had taught, reflecting what had become a severe, central message in the new age. Adler's father Leopold had another way of expressing it, repeating over and over to his son, "Never believe what anyone tells you."[10] This was not a psychoanalytic insight but a response to everyday life at the time, aptly reflected by psychoanalysis.

Skepticism about motive—that there is evil hidden in the unconscious, in contrast to a pleasant outward demeanor—like any other major Freudian construct, is at once very old and very new. In the West it can be found in the Bible: "One speaketh peaceably to his neighbor with his mouth, but in heart he layeth his wait" (Jeremiah 9:8). It can be found in the Renaissance in general, in the Italian Renaissance with Machiavelli, and in the English Renaissance with Bacon and Shakespeare.[11] It might be said to be Schopenhauer's rediscovery for the modern age as it was the theme of Nietzsche. By Freud's day it had become a necessary lesson for all that people were generally dishonest. If you had been a peasant and a believer, and illiterate and ignorant, you now had to recognize this and act accordingly, because you were no longer a country bumpkin. You were becoming pragmatic and scientific and were now to learn that self-interest and suspicion were science, not to be avoided by wishful dreams or theories about the honest old *volk*. In order to blur the difference between the new age and the old (when very different doctrines reigned), Freud projected this understanding as being the timeless and universal one, the other being a cultural lie of the past.

THE FREUDIANS by and large were sour, realistic representatives of their times, which were themselves sour, competitive, realistic, materialistic, and suspicious—and simultaneously exciting and promising. Overall the theoretical function of the sex theme and its many meanings, as with so many of the theories of psychoanalysis, was to recognize with millions of others what the world had been, what it had become, and to affirm what it had become, difficult though that might be. Affirmation was the acceptance of reality, the way to mental health, according to the Freudian formula. The Freudians in this way were not only covert politicians; they were also, as Freud affirmed, teachers ("psychoanalysis," he said, "wishes to educate the ego").[12] They knew the modern world and were resolved that everyone should come to understand it and then accept it. In this they were truth-tellers about their age, even if the truth was delivered by a fiction—a fictive psychological system—just as the serious novels of the day were doing.

The Freudian system taught that the nature of the modern world was the scientific truth of human psychology, and therefore to be *unavoidably* accepted. Freud's enemies, democracy's enemies—the monarchists, radical conservatives, volkists and proto-fascists, socialists and anarchists, all the mad political romantics of the end of the century—were teaching that the way of the world in the modern age was a false turning, a mirage that had to be dispelled (exactly what Freud thought about Judeo-Christianity). Many people without a strong political ideology believed this too, for they had been made vitally uneasy by the new age. Freud's response was that the way of the new world was timeless and universal and had to be borne. This strengthened the only system of civilization he honored as just and perhaps permanent from hence forward, liberal democracy.

The Freudians strove to construct a reasonable, believable story about human psychology. They wove together what the age was experiencing and made it seem normal, not totally objectionable as their enemies did, and therefore to be lived with as common, unavoidable reality. Rebellion against scientific reality, they said, was impossible, futile and infantile, thereby justifying and stabilizing society. The function of the pleasure principle (sex) was to teach the reality principle, including pleasure and self-interest, materialism, the flight of love, restraint for the millions of desiring souls, and success for the lucky. So it had ever been, was psychoanalysis's story, and so it may well have ever been.

Jung believed that the immediate needs of survival, such as food, clothing, and shelter, counted for more than sex on the scale of human concerns, conscious and unconscious. Adler thought the same about power. Freud confidently replied, Consider the imaginative power of sex. He became the pope of psychoanalysis and theoretical psychology generally because he knew best the work to be done and how to do it. Like the Oedipus complex, on a scale of one to ten, sex was a ten. Whyte says that Freud did not like sexuality, and it took its revenge by "obsessing his thinking to the exclusion of the biological order which sexuality serves, and to which it is normally subordinate."[13] He misses the point that Freud was obsessing about the nineteenth-century philosophy of pleasure which ruled politics and economics and was subordinate to *nothing*. Out of that, and not out of sex (which was only a symbol), Freud developed his sermons, lessons, rationales, and justifications.

NINETEEN

The Uses of the Unconscious

In the struggle with nature and with men, the intellect
serves as a weapon by providing rationalizations with
which individuals, interest groups, and nations try to
accommodate their demands to the moral precepts in
force.
    —Max Horkheimer, *Critique of Instrumental Reason*

The world scoffs at old ideas. It distrusts new ideas. It
loves tricks.
    —Roger Shattuck, "Nineteen Theses on Literature"

To FREUD the unconscious was "the enemy," "this eternal enemy of
the ego," the "evil of the human mind," the "dark inaccessible part of
our personality," "a chaos, a cauldron of seething excitations."[1] To
Jung it was the devil ("the shadow") and also, blending high and low,
God (the Christian Trinity to him being not that but a Quarternity
containing the devil as the fourth member). Adler thought it was the
repository of powerlessness and inferiority out of which grew the striving to overcome inadequacy. Janet thought it was the source and
repository of shameful motivations purposely forgotten or not admitted. They all believed, like the Bible, that "man looketh on the outward appearance but God looketh on the heart" (1 Samuel 16:7), and
that they were in place of God looking in on the secrets of the heart.
    For all of them, the unconscious was certainly the hidden depths
of the mysterious psyche, the pathogenic secrets of *Seelsorge* treatment
and all of that tradition of soul psychology and religion the Freudians
appropriated. It was also, as the soul psychologists thought, the source
of creativity and warnings of danger. But in its particular setting it was
first and foremost what Schopenhauer had discovered right at the be-

ginning of the new age: romantic irrationalism—the childlike, the primitive, the natural, the spontaneous, the uninhibited, the creative, the authentic, everything the romantics liked over the staid, learned values of eighteenth-century neo-classicism, everything they attributed to the natural mind untainted by a corrupting civilization.

The romantic vision of primeval forests filled with happy, honest, enthusiastic natural men and women was one of the many Golden Ages and Gardens of Eden the Freudians attacked. They used such concepts as the neurotic appeal of the past, infantile desire as the source of neurosis, the primitive as the infantile, and the need to control desire by installing civilization in the mind. Into these fighting concepts fit the unconscious as another version of the romantic ideal, bane of civilization. The pioneers were repeating their monotonous message born of the Enlightenment and European experience in their century: civilization against the savage. As L. L. Whyte, the leading historian of the idea of the unconscious, points out, for 150 years up to and including Freud's time, the unconscious was regarded "as the realm of irrational forces threatening the social and intellectual order which the rational consciousness . . . had built up over generations."[2]

Because the pioneers were among the chief opponents of this unconscious, because they more than others capsulized their enemy under its heading and popularized it by placing what it stood for at the center of their psychology, they appeared to have discovered it. In fact, what they did was to appropriate a name for what they did not like—the irrational, disruption, disorder, inappropriate (in their judgment) desires and pleasures, in short the romantic disposition let loose in the nineteenth century as a dispensation of freedom and as a reaction to the disappointments freedom led in its train. They were out to destroy it if possible, certainly to tame it. As Freud said, where the id was, there would be the rational ego—their answer (and their culture's answer) to the ills of the new world as it was Voltaire's for the ills of the old world.

In the reactionary politics of the day, the unconscious was associated with tribalism, anti-Semitism, the past; domination of the many by the select few; hatred of democracy; love of the simple, dutiful, undemanding *volk*; glorification of individual genius and individual passion; hatred of science, rationalized government, business and commerce, of modernity root and branch. From the other side of the political spectrum, this same willful unconscious expressed the maximal freedom of socialism and anarchism. In the nationalist politics of

European peoples caught in the grip of great empires (Austrian, Russian, Turkish), this unconscious was associated again with freedom; and in the chauvinistic nationalism of the great powers it was linked to militarism, arms races, and an international social Darwinism.

This dangerous romantic unconscious had arisen out of deep disappointments, inequalities, dissatisfactions, losses: yes, out of multiple frustrations in the new age (just as Freud thought about individual neurosis, that it was a reaction to frustration). Not only mad demagogues and semicrazed portions of the population felt these despairs; so did many in the mass populations of Europe. Among these masses the dream of an unconscious representing something better, something past or something future, was at its most volatile, always in actual or potential conflict with the order of things in the new societies.

Freud analogized the unconscious to a mob: "Our mind . . . is no peacefully self-contained unity. It is rather to be compared with a modern State in which a mob, eager for enjoyment and destruction, has to be held down forcibly by a prudent superior class."[3] That was penned as a metaphor for individual psychology, but it was pure light into the system Freud was constructing as a defense against palpable mobs, the mobocracy that elitist republicans hated from the very beginning of the liberal nation-state. The mob (the mass) was viewed as disorderly, decadent, and degenerate, poised not to serve democracy but to bring it down. Roman nobles, feudal lords, and now the new ruling elites feared the mob, saw every reason to suppress it, and despaired of its conversion to gentility and unforced obedience. It was, as Ernest Gellner said, "the mob of the id," which needed taming.

ALIVE TO the negative power of what they called the unconscious, the Freudians did not neglect its positive aspects as recognized by their culture. The unconscious represented hope to the romantics, a way of getting out of the rational bind imposed by the Enlightenment, science, and the twin revolutions, when enchantment fled with God, love, and spirit. It gave back conceptually what was missing actually, the promise and excitement that life had lost for many. Applied to conventional middle-class individuals seen by therapists in that day, the unconscious was a measure of flattery: you're more exciting than you think, it said. There were many excitements being produced by science, technology, war, revolution, the city, crowding, and other manifestations of modernity, but also much rational, regimented dullness about life in the new age, much of it desperate and dispiriting. The irrational unconscious, situated in everyone, promised excitement for everyone, at least potentially, even if that did not seem to be the true case of life as experienced at the time. It took attention away from the disenchantment of the modern world; or, put another way, it reintroduced enchantment, which was what romanticism was doing on the cultural scene, trying to give back to the modern age a dimension of experience that seemed to have been destroyed in the change from old to new.

For this reason alone, the unconscious had broad resonance within the culture and deep appeal as an ideal, like a signpost reading "Escape—This Way." While the Freudians welded themselves into a force against escape and in favor of rubbing everyone's nose in reality, they could not fail to know the appeal of escape in their age (which was why it was one of the meanings of neurosis and infantilism). It was not beneath them or the political, business, scientific, and technological elites to co-opt romantic irrationalism. They appreciated it even while disliking it, because it gave a more human, promising appearance to things. The romantic irrationalism captured in the concept of the unconscious functioned as a relief valve for what the elites, working out the forces of the twin revolutions, were imposing on Western culture. At the same time it gave to themselves the color of new men of genius, romantic heroes, as though they were the Fausts of modernity. A robber baron such as John D. Rockefeller in the United States might be otherwise difficult to portray as a hero, but romanticism—in his case romantic commercial excess—lent him some of that quality. There was a furiousness in romanticism that the robber barons translated into business enterprise, and it was understood as much because it was business as because it was romantic.

The Freudian unconscious, borrowed from romantic irrationalism, was also a way to explain and justify the absence of charitable feelings in the new age, thereby reinforcing the sour reality principle. Freud said it was natural for people to be uncharitable, always for themselves, always self-regarding, self-loving, self-interested. That, essentially, was what the unconscious was in everyone, said therapy theory, and since the theory was scientific, this explanation served as a justification for the way people behaved in the new age. That made lack of charity a scientific truth and therefore an unavoidable if unpleasant fact. There was no way of getting around it, so there was every reason to accept it (the same justification given for suspicion and the flight of love). Such a justification for evil and the devil, impossible in the old world, still required getting used to in the new one. For all those who deplored the new commercial life, telling them it was unavoidable and eternal (even though it had never existed before on so large a scale) was a clever rejoinder. Commercial life, stemming from self-interest, was rendered just as scientific as the instinct of desire: a piece of one-upmanship against the anti-commercial romantics.

Emphasizing individual will, "the unconscious" had the positive effect of supporting democratic individualism in its quest for life, liberty, and the pursuit of happiness. And it propagandized what the individual needed to get ahead in the new society—a commanding, dominating will, which anyone who had the taste for it was now free to exercise. Here libido as the prime content of the unconscious had its familiar role in Freud's scheme. Everyone knew that the new age was about getting things, the satisfaction of desires, so the resonance in "the unconscious" as the acquisitive faculty was unmistakable, even as Freud marked it unmistakably dangerous because anarchic.

As evil and the devil, the unconscious again had a positive role to play in its very negativity. It provided a singular diversion on which to focus, a monster against which a holy war could be waged. On the individual level the Freudians portrayed it as the very purpose of psychoanalysis: waging war against the dominance of the savage, primitive, infantile unconscious in the psyche. Various nations and portions of nations just then were finding other, much more dangerous diversions for their troubles: nationalist chauvinism, anti-Semitism, capitalism; in some places Catholicism and in others, Protestantism; in most places, local ethnic groups. All these diversions were reactions to dissatisfaction and change, reflecting problems that the new age had ushered in and that were being deflected by a kind of cultural legerdemain.

Instead of particularizing the diversion in a group, a type of economy, or a national goal, the Freudians placed it in everyone, made it internal. This diversion said it was no use fighting forces outside yourself; the evil force was within (a repetition of biblical wisdom that became a watchword for liberal democracy as it had been earlier for feudalism). This mode of thought emphasized democratic individualism: worry about yourself, not the world. But the real problems of Europe just then were pent-up forces eager to explode against each other, for which individuals formed into armies were later to pay dearly. "Explode against the unconscious" (and infantilism and narcissism) was the implicit direction of the pioneers. "Don't fight among yourselves; fight within yourselves. Let us all go to war against the unconscious." This was one of the ways psychoanalysis functioned as a salvational creed; the defeat of the unconscious augured the millennium (the same hope earlier expressed for the defeat of sin).

THE UNCONSCIOUS as the constant and the eternal, as though it were God in the soul, enhanced the aura of psychoanalysis as a science, and support, of eternal truths. But its eternal characteristics had a greater function. Permanence had been banished by the new age, now the site of spectacular impermanence, with changes in practically everything. The new reality was challenged by the romantic "quest for permanence," as it has been called. Freud co-opted this romantic quest as an essential part of his system by resurrecting past symbols of permanence such as family, father, king, community, morality. He continued this effort by making the unconscious the site of permanence through repetition, finding in the instincts "an impulsion towards the restoration of a situation which once existed but was brought to an end by some external disturbance. This essentially conservative character of instincts is exemplified by the phenomena of the *compulsion to repeat*."[4] "The unconscious" fulfilled the romantic love of the past and permanence ("the impulsion towards the restoration of a situation which once existed") while disputing their sole possession by romantic enthusiasts.

Jung represented permanence by a "collective unconscious" containing animas/animuses (male/female principles) and archetypes (ancient, permanent images in the mind such as the Creation myth, the virgin birth, the symbol of the snake, Paradise, the number three, and so forth). The archetypes, which were influenced conceptually by Plato's pure forms and Kant's mental categories, posited in Jung's scheme a constant-state world, society, politics, ever changing but ever, beneath the surface, the same. The world perceived by humans was archetypal, he was saying, and while it bore many visages, the archetypes did not change; they moved below (as in the unconscious), jiggling the surface as if it were a kaleidoscope. As in Freud, Jung's new world was not unlike the old one, however differently configured to the eye.

Like a priest, Jung promised that opposing the archetypes made one ill (sinful), while conforming to them was healthy: another hero/villain, good/bad set of categories along the lines of sick/healthy, infantile/mature, desire/restraint. His dichotomy of anima/animus conveyed the dangers of independent thought. These images of the other gender (we were each both in principle, said Jung), when integrated, resulted in the familiar goal of therapy, independence. For Jung this goal came with a warning: it meant isolation and loneliness, yielding the lesson that true freedom cut one off from one's fellows. By this magical manipulation of theory, independence became the modernist equivalent of anomie, isolation, and therefore madness, desirable as an ideal but best not sought—another version of the Freudian prison that barred advance or retreat, encouraging stasis and satisfaction with stasis, even as the culture was anything but static. Not that the Freudians were against the liveliness of the new culture; they were against the impulse to wipe it away because of its deficiencies, which was the hope of the radicals. In response, the pioneers fortified the new age by associating it with the eternal.

So the very unconscious the pioneers excoriated as the source of excess, madness, the romantic spirit, and rebellion, they managed to turn around so that it came out to be, at the same time, the spirit of conservatism. Combining these two poles was not a problem, for Freud explained many times that the unconscious contained opposites without knowing the meaning of contradiction. Rank, more realistic, saw where the tendency of the conservative unconscious led: "our psychology is inadequate to explain change because it can only justify the type representing the existing social order of which it is an expression."[5]

By emphasizing that most of human life was determined by permanent unconscious drives, the pioneers pointed to that area of life that concerned them most in their theories (and for which the mind was a metaphor): history. Especially they recognized a determinism in history that always produced hierarchy and inequality, whatever the system of government and whatever the political rhetoric—a permanent hierarchical system that might even be wired into the brain (as it appears to be in certain animal groups). The unconscious was a not inconsiderable representation of what was unknown but consequential about the springs of human history.

FREUD ARGUED from early on that the unconscious was a deception machine, "turning trauma into apparently unrelated symptoms." Unconscious self-deception, he said, operated in the sick and the well, converting the "alarming and disagreeable or shameful" into denials, rationalizations, and justifications. He called this the psychopathology of everyday life, and one among many social applications for it is not difficult to find. Freud was keenly aware of the dangers of an unsatisfied, powerful mass:

> It is to be expected that . . . underprivileged classes will envy the favored ones their privileges and will do all they can to free themselves from their own surplus of privation. Where this is not possible, a permanent measure of discontent will persist within the culture concerned and this can lead to dangerous revolts. If . . . a culture has not got beyond a point at which the satisfaction of one portion of its participants depends upon the suppression of another, perhaps larger, portion—*and this is the case in all present-day cultures*—it is understandable that the suppressed people should develop an intense hostility. . . . In such conditions an internalization of the cultural prohibitions among the suppressed peoples is not to be expected. On the contrary, they are not prepared to acknowledge prohibitions, they are intent on destroying the culture itself, and possibly even of doing away with the postulates on which it is based.[6]

The obvious social injustice of the new age could not be blatantly justified by the ruling elites in the nineteenth century. That would be perceived as morally reprehensible in an age of freedom and equality, the more so in contrast to the moral economy in the old age of tyranny, when mass conditions could be remembered as better. With no psychological protection against accusations of cruelty, greed, and excessive power, the elites needed cultural adjuncts or assets that might add convincing justifications to the political and economic theories of the day. We have already seen several of these provided by the Freudians: a new morality derived from the old morality, militating toward conformance and against rebellion; the stress, fear, and anxiety related to the dangers of those without power desiring power, pleasure, and things; emphasis on the permanent qualities in cultures, including hierarchy, the few leading the many, and the deep desire of the mass to follow the leader.

To these was added the psychopathology of everyday life. The elites could say in good conscience that they could not bear their cruelty, greed, and fear, and so they repressed them to the unconscious, resulting in symptoms of denial and rationalization. In effect, they were not responsible; they too were victims.[7] Through the middle-class rulers of the new society ran a mantra: *We are supposed to feel guilty, and to some degree we do. Well and good. Let us say this guilt is so severe it is unconscious and pathological. We are not responsible. We can't face it.* To which theoretical psychology responded, *You are forgiven then, it is not your fault. Go in peace.* The psychopathology of everyday life allowed the elites to acknowledge wrong without admitting conscious intent. With this useful social mechanism, the unequal groups within a society could relate to one another with civility, which might not be the case if they relied on the bare, unvarnished truth. By the same token, the dissatisfied masses could find in the unconscious psychopathology of everyday life (as they could in the Oedipus complex) rationales and justifications for not rebelling and accepting order over potential chaos.

Among the early Greek philosophers were sophists, who taught the rhetorical art of using ideas for one's benefit without regard to their truth or one's honesty. Psychoanalysis and the new sociopolitical system it sought to support cannot be said to have been pathological in their denials, rationales, and justifications; they were sophistical, using what was available, including novel psychological theories, to suppress the truths of the new age or cast them in a better light. Nietzsche asks his reader, have you "ever reflected upon the price that had to be paid for the introduction of every new ideal on earth? *On how much of reality, in each instance, had to be slandered and misconceived, how much falsehood ennobled, how many consciences disturbed, how many gods sacrificed.* The raising of an altar requires the breaking of an altar: this is a law—let anyone who can prove me wrong."[8] With "the unconscious" there was no more evil and no more sin, only actions and reactions conscious or, usefully, unconscious and pathological. In this way the unconscious found its modern application as Christian forgiveness, becoming a literal translation of Christ's words: "Forgive them, Father, for they know not what they do."

In myth, deceit is often represented by the figure of the trickster who gets what he wants by cleverness and deception. Reflecting on depth psychology and political discourse, Andrew Samuels, a present-day British analyst, observes that the Western nations were "caught in a collective love affair with a rotten social order and an unfeeling culture . . . and however much we may know intellectually that it does not work for us on the ethical level, however much we may know about the psychodynamics of greed and envy, we cannot seem to break our tie to our lover: economic inequality." In solving this dilemma we engage the trickster, because "A collective psychology that is infused with a tricky but related mercantile spirit may help a society avoid tyranny and enjoy an active and diverse political and social life." In engaging the trickster we "engage with the warring sides [of ourselves]: . . . On the one hand, our fraud, our criminality, our belief in magic, our love of economic inequality, our own depression-inducing violence. On the other hand, our capacity for exchange, integrity, relatedness, flexibility, our own love of dignity and freedom, our desire to reject coercion and bullying, our skill at making peace."[9]

The choice facing the pioneers and the still young, vitally threatened modern culture of their day, was to play it straight and perhaps lose—or engage that amount of fakery that could contribute to winning. The stakes were high, as many knew at the time and as the future proved. Winston Churchill got to the heart of the matter: democracy might not be the best system, but compared to what? In the minds of the pioneers and the culture, democracy was worth some fakery. Those who did not accept that belief caused world-shattering havoc and the deaths of many millions in the twentieth century, fulfilling threats announced in the century before.

Critics were content to observe that psychoanalysis was fictitious without ever considering the purposes the fiction might have served beyond the personal aggrandizement of the Freudians. Rank had the answer: pathological mechanisms of deceit and self-deceit are "psychically necessary for living and [are] wholesome," he wrote. The "creative searcher after truth" creates his own truth "which he then wants to make general—that is, real."[10] Bruno Bettelheim was wont to say that deceit was necessary to give meaning to life and to make it bearable. The phrase "pathological liar" would seem to be wholly negative, but it was not so with the Freudians. Even if they had been fully aware of what they were doing, it might not have seemed disreputable to them.

Much can be said against social deceptions, but something for them as well. "The unconscious" fortified liberal democracy by concentrating its enemies into a concept and rallying the troops against it; it pumped air into the social atmosphere by co-opting what was attractive in romantic irrationalism; it internalized morality and censorship and stamped them as science; and it buffered the conflict of groups under the impact of modernity. Paul Roazen tells us that "it is beyond doubt that [Freud] uncovered the world of the unconscious."[11] But it was not so. A hundred years after the twin revolutions, the Freudians and the Western world were ready to accept the Schopenhauerian unconscious as dogma because the West had developed as

Schopenhauer had predicted. Hobbesian man had been unleashed rather than Rousseauean man. At the lower reaches this man not only wanted to get all he could, but had to on pain of death or isolation or madness; at the upper reaches this man felt the need to fulfill the destiny of the twin revolutions and live the life of a king. It was then that the Western world recognized itself in the unconscious and recognized the need for enhanced disciplines that could reconcile the many contradictions inherent in the twin revolutions. For these reasons more than any others, the unconscious came to be seen overtly as a real entity and covertly as a real service to state and society.

Social order was maintained by force and law, Freud reminded Einstein late in life, but major political change was apt to come through violence. Yet there was another, "invariably peaceful" way to manage things: "it lies in the cultural transformation of the members of the community."[12] He meant to explore that in detail some other time, he said, but he never did—at least not directly, having already done so indirectly over the entire course of his career. Here the unconscious was an essential part of the psychoanalytic fabric and played its greatest social role, which was its greatest role; and here Freud had least to say about it in direct speech. What he did say was disarming. For example, aware that he had reduced the conscious mind to a mask for the unconscious, he asked: "But what part is there left to be played in our scheme by consciousness, which was once so omnipotent and hid all else from view?"[13] The case was the other way around: the role of the Freudian unconscious was to hide the conscious, what was known and was inconvenient to deal with.

Part VI

TREATMENT:
REVISING THE MIND

. . . In the account given of our contemporary
circumstances, I resented seeing Nature and History
confused at every turn, and I wanted to track down, in
the decorative display of *what-goes-without-saying,* the
ideological abuse which, in my view, is hidden there.
—Roland Barthès, *Mythologies*

I am now prepared to hear you ask me scornfully
whether our ego-psychology comes down to nothing
more than taking commonly used abstractions
literally. . . . To this I would reply that in ego-
psychology it will be difficult to escape what is
universally known; it will rather be a question of new
ways of looking at things and new ways of arranging
them than of new discoveries.
—Sigmund Freud, *New Introductory Lectures
on Psycho-Analysis*

There is not only a *method* in madness . . . but also a
fragment of historic truth.
—Sigmund Freud, "Constructions in Analysis"

. . . I defined the etiology too narrowly; the share of
fantasy in it is far greater than I had thought
in the beginning.
—Sigmund Freud, Letter to Fliess

TWENTY

Neurosis: Diverting Social Hysteria

The repressed ideas—so we must believe—are present
in and enter without inhibition into the most rational
trains of thought; and the memory of them is aroused,
too, by the merest allusions.
                    —Sigmund Freud, Letter to Fliess

. . . To take arms against a sea of troubles, / And by
opposing end them.
                    —William Shakespeare, *Hamlet*

THE TREATMENT provided by psychoanalysis for the ailments of
Western culture—suggestive psychological theories that functioned together as a belief system—gave comfort to the new age. It hid real
sources of personal and social anxiety, provided rationalizations and
justifications, and combated beliefs that were inimical (often violently
so) to liberal democracy and modernity. One of the most imposing examples of this suggestive treatment by ideas (what Freud called the
"omnipotence of thoughts") was the concept of neurosis. This was
Freud's total system in a single concept.

According to Freud, neurosis was a diversion produced by the patient to draw attention away from trauma and hysteria. Yet its latent
content could be understood because "neurotic symptoms have a
sense, like parapraxes and dreams, and, like them, have a connection
with the life of those who produce them." The concept of neurosis had
a similar sense and connection with the life of the Freudians and the
Western culture that produced it. Freud went on (in the *Introductory
Lectures*): "I should now like to make this important discovery plainer
to you by a few examples."[1] We can do the same by decoding neuro-

sis—the largest of all Freudian concepts as it was the largest of all Freudian diversions and displacements except for psychoanalysis itself.

"Neurosis" was the symbolic representation of the social hysteria of the fin de siècle and the many reactions to it which were themselves hysterical, including psychoanalysis. In Freud's theory, neurosis begins with a trauma caused by a fantasy crime. The chief crime or trauma depicted symbolically in psychoanalysis was not individual or familial, it was social and historical: the killing of the old world, ending in the social hysteria of the fin de siècle. Psychic trauma was said to be induced by threat, anxiety, fear, danger, conflict, guilt—these were what the Freudians and many Europeans felt, and what sparked the creation of the Freudian concept of neurosis and the other theories of psychoanalysis. Discussing the elements of neurosis in the *New Introductory Lectures,* Freud said he had a feeling "that something is missing here which could bring all of these pieces together into a whole."[2] What was missing was the latent social, political, economic, and cultural context that was the hidden cause and explanation of the theory.

As in the theory, social hysteria sparked the urge to flee to a nostalgic past, but the Freudians barred, censored, and neutered this urge by transferring hysteria from the social to the personal and psychological. Only neurotics, their theory assured, wished to return to the past as the mistaken attempt at a cure. Anything that took the citizen away from the present, or led to rejection of the present, was neurotic in the Freudian system because it looked away from reality to seek comfort in dreams and fantasies. You could not escape, was the Freudian message, except by flying into mental illness—or, Freud did not say aloud, into another fantasy now being provided, psychoanalysis, the treatment for the wish to escape.

The difference between a neurotic anxiety and a realistic one, he explained, "lies in two points: that the danger is an internal instead of an external one and that it is not consciously recognized." The real danger to which the Freudians were responding was external, but that was not consciously recognized—at least not admitted—by the pioneers. "In phobias," Freud went on, "it is very easy to observe the way in which this internal danger is transformed into an external one—that is to say, how neurotic anxiety is changed into an apparently realistic one." But in formulating the concept of neurosis it was easy to see how an external danger was changed into an apparently internal medical condition. Further, says Freud, a neurotic symptom results from transferring anxiety over the father to some substitute. Freud was transferring anxiety over cultural crisis to some substitute, the theory of neurosis—and more generally to psychoanalysis as a whole, which was about the crisis induced by anxiety over the loss of the father/ Father/king and the old world in which they had lived. When he says that anxiety is caused by "unemployed libido and repression," he is latently explaining that it was caused culturally by unemployed (disallowed) freedom and the repression of mass wishes and needs, and also by "unemployed" wishes for the old world. The unemployed libidinal charge is repressed to the unconscious, according to the theory, where it is "destroyed."³ It was actually repressed to psychological theories that attempted to pull the teeth of the age's social dangers.

Freud held that the neurotic symptom representing the repressed trauma always bore "some kind of indirect resemblance to the idea that was originally repressed." The theory of neurosis, precisely following that guideline, reduced social hysteria to the "local" level of personal hysteria while retaining an unmistakable resemblance to its original—a more telling resemblance than Freud was apt to find between a bird and homosexuality in Leonardo's dream, or in the case of the patient Dora between fingering her little handbag and stroking her genitals. (*Toujours la genitale,* Charcot's lesson, was, as we have seen, one of Freud's most insistent symbolizations and displacements.) When Freud says that the "symptom is a new, artificial and ephemeral substitute for what has been repressed," he is symbolizing the theory of neurosis as the substitute for the reality of social hysteria. When he says that symptoms are the "results of a compromise"⁴ he is symbolizing the compromises psychoanalysis represented: not allowing reality to reign in its evident, social form but instead representing it symbolically in theories and practices; and providing beliefs in place of the failings of the new age.

In a textbook of the period on the treatment of nervous disorders, by one W. Erb, Freud found that what was presented as "an epitome of exact observations was merely the construction of a phantasy." He asserted that he had proceeded differently from Erb. "It was only necessary to translate into words what I myself had observed" and he was in possession of psychological truth. That was true in the sense that it was only necessary to translate into the indirect speech of symbols (his theories and practices) what he and millions of others observed of European experience in order to achieve his symbolic system.⁵

The pioneers' emphasis on the psychological cause of neurotic symptoms (what Freud called "psychogenesis in neurotic distur-bances")[6] served many purposes. For example, it obviated the need to find biological evidence that was not available to them, and justified a treatment of words, not medicines. But the greatest utility by far was that it led away from any biological—that is to say, physically real—component in what Freud found to be a main cause and symptom of neurosis: rebellion in pursuit of lustful desires, his metaphor for the re-bellious atmosphere of the fin de siècle. If the biological thesis held, the impulse to rebel could not be affected—treated—by a belief system such as psychoanalysis, or by any other psychological comforts of-fered in lieu of systemic (on the model of biological) changes in the so-cial order. If neurosis and what it symbolized (hysterical, rebellious dissatisfaction and disaffiliation) were psychological, that made them manageable by mental manipulations and no greater exertions or re-sources of therapists, the society, or the citizens of the new age. What was at issue could then be made out to seem fantastical psychic de-sires, not physical needs and quite reasonable desires. Suggestion Ther-apy for physical illnesses, beginning with Liébeault and Bernheim, duplicated as medical practice European liberal social policy and be-came psychoanalytic doctrine. Therapy was a symbol for what was *not* to be socially provided—something real, a practical therapy, that is, political policies aimed at combating social ills. Instead there would be a therapy for the personal ills of neurosis.

Explaining himself symbolically, Freud wrote: "It is only a step from the phantasies of individual neurotics to the imaginative cre-ations of groups and peoples as we find them in myths, legends and fairy tales." Freud and his colleagues were imaginative creators for groups and peoples (the populations of Europe), weaving unifying, healing, and instructive myths and legends. "Neurosis" was only one instance of this imaginative creativity. In *Five Lectures* he had al-ready made the point: "The deeper you penetrate into the pathogene-sis of neurotic illness, the more you will find revealed the connection between the neurosis and other productions of the human mind, in-cluding the most valuable."[7] For the Freudians, one of those most valuable productions was psychoanalysis and its leading theory, neu-rosis.

Mental illness, Freud told Fliess, wards off "an idea that is in-compatible with the ego, by projecting its substance onto the external world."[8] Freud was trying to accomplish the same goal in exactly the opposite direction, and not as it concerned individuals but Western culture. He wanted to ward off, hide, make seem insignificant what was incompatible with the ego of middle-class, liberal Europe, specifically the many conflicts brought on by the twin revolutions. He did so by projecting their substance into the internal world of the individual, thereby absolving the new culture and placing the blame on individuals and families. There had to be nothing structurally wrong with the new Western culture to account for any deleterious effects on individuals and society or to justify calls for its overthrow. The fault lay in ourselves, our psyches, not in such higher powers as state, society, or the philosophies on which the new age was organized.

INDIVIDUAL ELEMENTS of the theory of neurosis—such as conflict, guilt, and resistance—were themselves symbolizations and deflections of social realities. The cause of neurotic trauma was said to be a psychic conflict. This explanation deflected from the true conflict to which it alluded and which it sought to soothe. The true conflict was not intrapsychic, within the psyche of an individual, but between individuals, groups, classes, and nations. In a draft scientific paper Freud included with a letter to Fliess of January 12, 1895, he reported discovering that paranoia had the same cause as delusional, obsessional, and hysterical neuroses, the key in every case being an internal conflict. That was not the view of most psychiatrists, he admitted, but laymen accepted it because they "are inclined to attribute insanity to shattering emotional events," which he illustrated by a line from the romantic playwright Gotthold von Lessing: "A man who does not lose his reason over certain things can have no reason to lose."[9] That Freud sided with the laymen's view was just, for he was symbolizing the experience of laymen—the populations of Europe—in the new age.

The Oedipus complex became the most famous way of depicting psychic conflict because it symbolized with precision the cultural crisis of Europe in the fin de siècle, when it was clear what bargain had been made with the "devil" of history and what were its consequences. Freud has been criticized for his reductionism, and he criticized himself for the one-note monotony of his ideas; there was justice in this criticism, for he had one big idea above all others: the death of the Father and the need for the Father's replacement. He filled that cultural gap a hundred years after the twin revolutions by replacing the Father indirectly, as a scientific belief, a Father without the former transcendence, a Father in the mind.

The guilt experienced in connection with neurosis (borrowed from the Bible, Schopenhauer, the law, and everyday life) was a reflection or reportrayal of the guilt of the new age. It had murdered the old world and the old God, abandoned the old ideas, beliefs, and rationales along with the old family, and instituted a new, utterly unorthodox social system initially as oppressive or more oppressive for the majority than the old one, and more unruly for everyone. This guilt the Freudians deflected onto the family and the individual, who were made decoys for great historical events. *"In that way,"* Freud wrote, *"the judgment, the reproach, was kept away from [the] ego"*[10]—the ego he was truly concerned about being the culture of the West.

The family was guilty for having abandoned its members—not willingly, and only under the pressure of great historical events, but effectively nonetheless. The indictment of the parents for being instrumental in the mental illness of their children was thus not directed at actual parents but at the symbolic "parents" of the twin revolutions. They had unhinged the populations of Europe by abandoning their "children" to empty, alienated, anomic, anxious, materialistic, overstimulating, unjust modernity.

NEUROTIC RESISTANCE—the defense mechanism—was the symbolic representation of the Freudian defense of the new age by displacing social conflicts onto an illness of individuals. Europe, especially democratic Europe, was sound, the Freudian defense system was saying, at a time when Europe gave every indication of the opposite. Like neurotic patients in the theory, the Freudians took the course of denial. If the condition of Europe was not sound, they were saying, it was not to be noticed.

Or were they, with a good deal of subtlety, saying that Europe was not sound? Were they calling attention to trouble and conflict by means of their concept of neurosis rather than trying to hide it? I think they wished to do both, just as they said neurosis wished to hide and reveal at the same time. They may have wished to give a warning, a signal, that things were not well (which they and millions of Europeans knew) by their symbol, neurosis. At the same time they wished to assert bravely that in spite of appearances, things were well or could be made to seem well by their symbol, treatment. By attending to a panoply of mental illnesses, the Freudians had come upon a particularly apt symbolization for the wellness of Europe they wished to project. The new Europe could appear to be sound by its very ability to understand and treat illnesses that had plagued humanity from the beginning of time. This same claim was being made for the many authentic medical and scientific discoveries of the age, and so Freudianism as a new, world-historical discovery fit quite well.

The proposal that neurosis was treatable and curable symbolically stated that though Europe might be hysterical and sick over desire, loss, and the gain of an uncontrollable reality, the illness could be treated. The reality principle could be taught to all and the good of the new age thereby allowed to remain while the bad was discarded. Madness was not a death sentence and could be treated; similarly it was proper to "treat" Europe for its debilities rather than assign it to doom as its ferocious critics urged. This ameliorative view, a liberal vindication of the new order, was a standard justification for the deformities and injustices of all political systems, so the Freudians did not have to look far to find it. Every group and every nation says it sometimes suffers from (curable) deformities.

Among specific neurotic defenses were said to be projection and transference—casting one's feelings onto others. Psychoanalysis did this by projecting history and social ills onto science, the family, and the individual, deflecting light away from real events, even to the extent of making not real events but fantasy events the subject of exploration. That ill feelings about authority were said to be transferred onto the therapist could minimize ill feelings about society, making them psychological projections of personal feelings about family members or other figures of authority.

The theory of transference nicely served another function. It described Western culture transferring the hierarchies and inequalities of the old world into the new. The Freudians, in support, transferred old world beliefs and fears, dressed up in sometimes unrecognizable forms, into the new world. Just as the theory held that the patient was transferring fear of the father onto the therapist, so Western culture was transferring the fear of God, king, and noble to the prime minister, the president, and the state. The Freudians gave a powerful assist by placing this same fear in the mind as the scientific Oedipus complex. Just as Freudian theory held that the patient was no longer to be in thrall to the past, so Western culture encouraged citizens to give up old allegiances and transfer them to present avatars (one of which was the psychoanalytic belief system).

The theory of transference had the additional function of demonstrating that the problems and ill feelings experienced by the patient—

and the culture—did not have their source in the present (symbolized by the therapist) but were derived from the past (the parents), which was the parable of both the new culture and psychoanalysis. The past was the evil old time of nobles, serfdom, religion, and tyrannical parents, all of which was to become a discarded memory for mass man in the new age. The new age was to be seen not as a repetition of the old one but different, more precious and advanced, even as in the first hundred years it was an eerie repetition of some of the old world's worst traits. Freud recognized the repetition of the old in his theory of "deferred obedience," by which the caveman sons repeated the past but at a new level: "The persons who were united in this group of brothers gradually came towards a revival of the old state of things at a new level."[11]

The concept of neurotic resistance was thus first of all the symbolic representation of psychoanalysis preventing the emergence to view of the negative side of the twin revolutions, its effects, debilities, and perils. Second, it was resistance to allowing the emergence to view of psychoanalysis's methods for achieving that purpose. Third, it symbolically invoked the resistance of those portions of Western society unwilling to give up the fight against injustice, mayhem, and meaninglessness. The Freudian battle cry was, "Throw down your arms." In time, many were convinced to do so. Liberal modernity provided many compensating blandishments and was, quite in line with the Freudian reality principle, the most realistic way to proceed to a better future. All the other ways proposed in the nineteenth century were conjectural. When they were attempted in the following century they proved disastrous.

BY REVITALIZING biblical sin, "neurosis" proved useful for mass discipline and the service it could render as a weapon against inappropriate desire. To paraphrase Freud, "Where sin was, there stands neurosis." The free use of "neurosis" as a diagnosis helped manage desire by impugning it widely, just as "sin" had done in the past. It was another demonization like infantilism and the unconscious, another "sticks and stones" way in which a name might do harm, and thereby, by restraining, do good. Labeling ambitions, passions, obsessions, or needs neurotic kept them within defined bounds. Each citizen became a useful, informal spy and control mechanism against all others when reporting one to another that "he/she is neurotic," at the same time reinforcing the diversion away from the social onto the personal and internal.

Since the terms *neurotic* and *neurosis* were symbolic, they were all the more useful for collecting an array of mental associations that could be attached to varied manifestations of human thought or action. No longer able to accuse others of being blasphemous unbelievers, since that had lost meaning, one could accuse others of being neurotic or, more dramatically, psychotic. Freud and his colleagues used these very terms against each other to express disapproval, for it could be seen that they were calls to order. It was good to have this way of judging others, provided by a new father/Father, considering that the old ways, religious and philosophic, had been cast overboard. The watchful eye of the sovereign was no longer unceasingly needed, in part because the sovereign had delegated authority to the psychologists, whose theories functioned as mass disciplines.

"Think of a whole society dominated by psychotherapeutic ideals," Philip Rieff, an insightful Freud commentator, invites the reader.

> Considered not from the individual's but from a sociological point of view, psychology is an expression of popular tyranny such as not even de Tocqueville adequately imagined. . . . The democratic tyranny which is the typical social form of our era will not have a hierarchy of confessors and confessants. Rather . . . everyone must be a confessant, everyone must aspire to be a confessor. . . .

In this way the hospital succeeded the church and the parliament, he writes, as "the archetypal institution of Western culture."[12] The block wardens of twentieth-century tyrannies were novelly implemented in democracy, as it was right for democracy to do, by internalized psychological beliefs.

The psychologist Joe Kennedy Adams explains that "societies of Western civilization"

> have tended to set up rules (laws, economic and other social sanctions) which are too restrictive and infringe upon the rights of the individual to live in accordance with his basic nature; such rules lead to a vulture-like society in which a large percentage of people watch each other carefully, though furtively, to see who is breaking the rules, crucifying those who get caught (in some instances, glorifying them), and

privately cursing the stupidity of the official restrictions and the dullness of their existence.[13]

Aside from sex, Freud did not care deeply that the rules of the new age
were restrictive or infringing; he thought they should be, else the culture of the West might disintegrate. Given the dangers of the time, and
what the future proved, these fears cannot be lightly brushed aside.

"Neurosis" in this context was a chief element in what Freud
thought of as the fortifications civilization sets up in the minds of its
members, even though it functioned as a subtle, coercive suggestion in
a way he criticized when he first saw Bernheim in action. When the
Nancy doctor impatiently shouted at patients resisting his treatment,
"What are you doing? *Vous vous contresuggestionnez!,*" Freud recalled feeling "a muffled hostility to this tyranny of suggestion. . . . I
said to myself that this was an evident injustice and an act of violence.
For the [patient] certainly had a right to counter-suggestions if people
were trying to subdue him with suggestions."[14] But in the end Freud
was driven to the same approach, except that he employed it with an
unsurpassed subtlety and delicacy on a mass scale. He suggested his
ideas of discipline and control to an entire culture by means of symbolic theories and practices that were presented as science.

Neurosis as sin functioned also as insult (evident in the way the pioneers used it against each other and covertly against the enemies of
the new age). In that form it had the democratic utility of tarring great
figures of the past such as Leonardo. While labeling them neurotic or
pathological might be a calumny on greatness, it was at the same time
a comforting salve to the new democratic man and woman because genius and greatness were no longer admired. Geniuses who produced
positive results, say in science, technology, industry, medicine, or art,
might be sufferable, even mildly admirable, but otherwise they were
distasteful signs of *difference* and therefore an insult to the *amour pro-
pre* of the common man and woman. They recalled the greatness of
kings and nobles, a propertied and heritage greatness that was anathema to democracy. With Freud's weapon, genius and greatness could
be labeled neurotic. But given the appealing meanings and functions
of psychoanalysis, the label was extended to Freud gratefully, in its
most positive sense.[15]

TWENTY-ONE

Wishes, Dreams, Repression, Regression

Thus symptoms, like dreams, are the fulfillment of a wish.

—Sigmund Freud, Letter to Fliess

The flight from unsatisfactory reality . . . takes place along the path of involution, of regression, of a return to earlier phases. . . .

—Sigmund Freud, *Five Lectures*

THAT NEUROSIS was due, in Freudian theory, to the repression of illegitimate wishes invoked one of the most famous and insistent concepts in psychoanalysis, wish fulfillment (familiar from Hobbes's idea of appetites, Schopenhauer's idea of wants, and other sources in the philosophy of pleasure). In this concept Freud summarized the dangers and hopes of the nineteenth century. Normal adults, portrayed in the theory as narcissistic infants, were unavoidably thinking about themselves and the new imperatives of happiness and success, because self-interest was the philosophy of the new age and a life-and-death necessity.

In a historical period that began for most people with largely unmet basic needs, personal needs and wants became paramount in a way they had never been before. Needs had been simple, tended to not just by oneself but by kin and village. Now one needed everything, because he was much more on his own. Beyond needs, there was much wanting (wishing) in the first hundred years of the twin revolutions, when the freeing of social mobility sanctioned dreams of rising in status.

These burdensome needs and wishful wants were appropriated by

psychoanalysis and made into an aspect of neurosis under the rubric
of wish fulfillment. By stressing wish fulfillment instead of need fulfillment, Freud created a diversion. Needs were not the issue in psychology, wishes were, and they were associated with infantilism and
neurosis.[1] Like the Oedipus complex, wish fulfillment instructed the
mass not to wish and not to rebel, while hiding real needs behind what
were said to be wishes. For the elites, the theory of wish fulfillment
was *their* wish fulfillment, the truth as they liked to see it, dampening
the wishing of the many and validating it for the successful few.

The concept of wish fulfillment was also directed at the reactionary forces that imagined going back to a time of legally imposed
hierarchies, strong religious beliefs, and a life built around small communities. These ideals went against the liberal ideology of the Freudians, and that was one reason why Freud had provided substitutes for
them. Wishing for anything but the present, as it was, was a pipe
dream and a danger to the pioneers.

Like neurosis, desire, sex, pleasure, the primitive, the infantile, the
spontaneous, the unconscious, and rebellion, the pioneers disliked
wish fulfillment. They saw it as destabilizing and destructive. It was
therefore portrayed as the essence of neurotic symptoms in one of
those "monotonous" Freudian formulas in which concepts repeat
each other: "Thus symptoms, like dreams, are *the fulfillment of a
wish*."[2] Wishing up to the level of a Faustian desire to master the
world had unhinged the European elites and the great nations they
ruled in the nineteenth century. That could be clearly seen, and by recognizing it covertly in theory the Freudians achieved a ready verisimilitude. But the most dangerous wishing took place among the mass
populations caught between a nostalgia for the past and a ravening desire for the fruits of the present, in the midst of a bitter struggle merely
to survive.

The etiology of neurosis in wishing for pleasure symbolized the
wants and needs unfulfilled for the majority in material terms in the
new age, and for both the majority and minority in spiritual terms.
That is the meaning, for example, when Freud writes that "symptoms
represent the patient's sexual activity," and when he writes that "hysteria is the expression of a peculiar behavior of the sexual function in
the person concerned . . . and is already decisively determined by the
first impressive influences and experiences during infancy." The infancy here is symbolically the old world, and the peculiar behavior is
the reactions that set in after the twin revolutions, reactions predicated

on desires, needs, and their fulfillment or nonfulfillment. An excellent covert analysis of what he means is his assertion that neurosis is "usually brought about by the convergence of several traumas, and often by the repetition of a great number of similar ones." These were the multiple material and spiritual traumas of loss and gain resulting from the twin revolutions.[3]

When Freud goes on to say that through psychoanalysis "it is quite possible to get back more quickly to the first [trauma], which was often the most potent one," he is symbolizing the twin revolutions themselves, the great trauma of modernity that set the stage for many others. When, referring to conflicts in the psyche caused by the striving for wishes, he says that illness or health "depends upon economic conditions, upon the relative strength of the conflicting forces," he means to be talking about the "economics" of psychic energy. Actually he is talking about the relative strength of contending groups and classes in the new age; the losers become "sick" (discontented, rebellious) out of frustration while the winners achieve health through success. When he states that the neurotic's gambit of repression fails because it breaks out in another form, symptoms, he is reflecting the failure of social repression alone to manage social ills because symptoms of discontent and rebellion will break out in another form, social hysteria. He and his colleagues were offering a superior form of suppression that treated the mind of the culture.[4]

One of the many tantalizing—and accurate—statements in Freud's papers occurs in "Neurosis and Psychosis" (from which I have been quoting). Wondering how the ego survives its wish conflicts, in which it encounters so much opposition, without becoming ill, Freud writes: "Now this is a new field for research in which the most various factors will certainly demand consideration." These "various factors" characterized the struggle for success in the nineteenth century. Freud's economic tropes were well selected, because in talking about the economics of the psyche he was talking about the economics and politics of nineteenth-century Europe and America.[5]

He goes on to say that "it is always possible for the ego to avoid a rupture in any of its relations by deforming itself, submitting to forfeit something of its unity, or in the long run even to be gashed and rent." That is, the ego can maintain its relations with the world by surrendering its wishes and, if necessary, becoming sick. "Thus," says Freud—commenting on society by commenting on his ersatz subject, the psyche—if his theory is right, "the illogicalities, eccentricities and follies of mankind would fall into a category similar to their sexual perversions, for by accepting them they spare themselves repressions."[6] In giving up the struggle one acquires characteristics—eccentricities—that may seem strange, but not mad. This is a tacit invitation to give up the struggle against powerful forces and assume the acceptable charm of the eccentric.

For all the negatives the Freudians meant to forestall by the concept of wish fulfillment, it also had a positive aspect that cannot go unmentioned. In science, technology, and productive capacity, in its theories of life, liberty, and the pursuit of happiness, the modern age looked like the fulfillment of wishes and dreams. It was fantastic, literally undreamed of before except perhaps by a few, and now it could be dreamed by all. The dreams of Saint-Simon and the positivism of Comte seemed to be coming true, and little could be more satisfying to the positivist psychoanalysts. This resonance was a further addition to psychoanalysis's verisimilitude, as it was a pat on the back to the leaders of the new age.

DREAMS WERE SAID to be nighttime revelations of the desire for wish fulfillments, not very different from daytime wishes buried in the unconscious. They were easy to interpret, Freud said, for "the patient will always provide the text."[7] In the case of Freud and the decoding of his system, that was true when the patient was viewed as the culture.

The initial source of dreams and dream interpretation in psychoanalysis is not hard to find. Considered in most ancient traditions to be suprarational mysterious omens, pregnant with meaning, dreams made a spectacular return in the nineteenth century after their allure had disappeared with the old world. Both the literal and figurative meanings of dreams were dear to the romantic heart. The mystical, peasant, romantic tradition of dreams, evoking the nostalgic *gemeinschaft* with its biblical tales of Joseph and Daniel interpreting the dreams of kings, appealed to the imagination of an age drawn to the past out of fear of the present and future. Jung, who regarded peasant traditions more highly than Freud, could see that "the day's life is for many people such a bad dream that they long for the night when the spirit awakes. . . ."[8] What became significant after the fall of the *gemeinschaft,* and why dream interpretation was brought down from the heights of kings to the level of patients, was that interpretation was now to be applied to the dreams (wishes) of citizens who in political theory were the new kings and queens.

Ellenberger demonstrates that "investigators of dreams from 1860 to 1899 [the year *The Interpretation of Dreams* was published] had already discovered almost all the notions that were to be synthesized by Freud and Jung. . . ."[9] That explains some of the resonance in the theory of dreams and how it was available for use, lack of originality being a blessing in disguise. But the main resonance did not derive from romantic soul psychology, which most people would have known little about. It came rather from the Bible, the *gemeinschaft,* and folk belief, and from people living by the philosophy of pleasure in the new age who yearned to fulfill their desires, that is, their dreams.

Freud's theory of dreams, repeating and reinforcing his main ideas, was one of the clearest symbolic representations of why and how psychoanalysis was made. Dreams, he told Fliess, "contain *in nuce* [in a nutshell] the psychology of the neuroses in general." He knew, he wrote, that the scientific view in his time was that dreams had no meaning, but that lay opinion, "led by some obscure feeling . . . seems to assume that, in spite of everything, every dream has a meaning, though a hidden one. . . ." It was to this lay sense of the matter, stretching back to prehistory, that the dream ideas—and most of the other theories of psychoanalysis—appealed.[10]

Freud recognized two categories of dreams, those from above (the upper, conscious level of the psyche) and those from below (the lower, unconscious level). Dreams from above, he said, were related to conscious ideas; dreams from below were formed out of unconscious material. The Freudians said they were only interested in dreams from below, but they were actually (latently) concerned with dreams from above, and not in nighttime dreams at all but only in dreams in the sense of wanting things. Nighttime dreaming in the Freudian system symbolically represented the practical, everyday dreams of people in their daytime, conscious state. These were dreams in the sense of the old fairy tales—"You have three wishes, what would you like?" As such, interpreting dreams was precisely what Freud thought it was— wish interpretation, only it was about real daytime wishes and daytime needs, not nighttime wishes couched in dream symbols. The theory of dream interpretation was a royal road, as Freud thought, but not to the unconscious; it led to some of the chief concerns of the age in which the Freudians lived, just as the theory of wish fulfillment did.

The majority was dreaming of the *gemeinschaft* with its moral economy; and of money and power with which to maneuver in the new age. Rich and poor alike dreamed of coherence, integration, certainty, some peace in the soul in an age of mounting anxiety. Money was a protection against the worst excesses of the new age, but it did not protect the soul, and neither did the culture. Instead, a substitute was presented with a comforting name: dream interpretation. We will try to understand you, the pioneers said *sotto voce,* though we can do very little about it. In fact, they said, we already understand your situation, just as sociologists, historians, and political scientists do; it is after all not a great mystery but merely the reality we see immediately and with clarity.

Displacing daytime dreams, wishes, and hopes onto fabulous, hermetic, and often exciting sexual interpretations of nighttime dreams pointed within, away from the outside world. The emphasis was always on wish, not need. The analysts assured people that meaning lay in the internal and private—sex and emotions instead of money and power. Human psychology might reflect a conflict with power, the pioneers admitted, in which case their lesson was: bend to power, accept that the father's *You must not do* means *I must not do* as the way to mental health. For the elites in society, that spelled social health—the continuation of the present social system in which they performed the functions of the former nobility.

Dreams were one of Freud's most incisive coded explanations of, all at once, social conditions, psychoanalysis, and neurosis. They contained, he wrote, "delusional or obsessional ideas" best understood by rejecting "their apparent content" and looking below the surface for their latent meaning. In just this way negative reactions to modernity could be made to seem delusional and obsessional by ignoring their real content and converting them to the "unexplained neurotic symptoms" of individuals. A "manifest dream," Freud continued, "was [exactly like manifest neurosis and psychoanalysis] no more than a distorted, abbreviated, and misunderstood translation" of wishes and needs. The "latent dreams-thoughts contained the true meaning of the dreams," just as the latent meanings of psychoanalysis and neurosis were their true meanings. The "manifest content" (meaning) of dreams (as of neurosis and psychoanalysis) "was simply a make-believe, a façade. . . ."[11]

When Freud wrote that the dream is invariably about "an impulse in the form of a wish, often of a very repellent kind," he rolled into a single image the catalog of desires confronted, disguised, and demonized by the pioneers. The dream "represents a situation in which the impulse is satisfied, it is the fulfillment of the wish which the impulse contains." That was psychoanalysis itself and its latent method of treating the hysteria of the age under the label of neurosis. It satisfied the culture's wish to replace repellent social and political impulses by displacing them—in the case of psychoanalysis, in the theory and treatment of mental illness. "The dream is a censorship of the wish so that it cannot appear in clear light," just as "psychoanalysis" and "neurosis" were the censorship of real palpable concerns presented not in clear light but rather in code, as a psychology and science concerned with a medical disease. "We are therefore justified in asserting that *a dream is the (disguised) fulfillment of a (repressed) wish,"* just as we are justified in asserting that psychoanalysis was the fulfillment of the culture's unadmitted but palpable wish for a satisfying, diversionary answer to exploding needs, wishes, and anxieties. Dreams and neurotic symptoms, constructed in the same way according to Freudian theory, "are equally unintelligible and stand in equal need of interpretation." The same was true of psychoanalysis for a hundred years.[12]

"There is no difficulty in discovering the general function of dreaming," Freud confidently asserted, and that is equally true of psychoanalysis. Dreaming "serves the purpose of warding off, by a kind of soothing action, external or internal stimuli which would tend to arouse the sleeper, and thus of securing sleep against interruption." If "psychoanalysis" is substituted for "dreaming," and "social stability" is substituted for "sleep," the meaning of psychoanalysis comes clear. As a soothing belief, its purpose was to keep social and historical stimuli from arousing despair and reaction, allowing the culture to proceed as smoothly as possible. "External stimuli" in dreams, Freud rightly says, unwittingly describing his system, "are warded off by being given a new interpretation and by being woven into some harmless situation. . . ." Freud had in just this way reinterpreted the dangerous, external stimuli of his age as personal and therefore relatively harmless problems from the political point of view. The crisis of the fin de siècle was converted into the "harmless" (indeed beneficial) study and practice of psychology, rather than the study of the history, culture, economics, and politics of the time.[13]

Internal stimuli "caused by the pressure of instincts are given free play by the sleeper and allowed to find satisfaction in the formation of dreams, so long as the latent dream-thoughts submit to the control of censorship." The uncoded meaning here is that as long as psychoanalysis, Freud's censorship of reality, was believed, Western culture could have free play in its thoughts. In following Freudian beliefs it would be censoring its thoughts without knowing it. "But if they [the internal stimuli] threaten to break free and the meaning of the dream becomes too plain, the sleeper cuts short the dream and awakens in terror."[14] That is, if dissatisfaction threatened to break free, and the meaning of psychoanalysis as a displacement of real needs and desires came clear, people would realize that the new belief system was designed to lower anxiety in lieu of achieving practical goals. The accomplishment of real goals might require action against the present order of things, a realization bound to induce anxiety, even terror. The actions usually proposed by the hellions of radical politics were, from the liberal point of view, unwholesome and unappetizing.

The utility of psychoanalysis and neurosis as symbolizations and displacements comes clear in these Freudian meditations on dreams. As long as real needs are clouded by convincing beliefs (especially convincing when presented as scientific), they cannot become plain. Therefore (it must be hoped) they cannot become dangerous, because attention and energy will be absorbed by the belief instead of the reality. Psychoanalysis, constructed like a dream, was a symbolical, deflective tale about the mysterious workings of the mind (which was really the quite puzzling and often irrational social order), told with a seeming reason and logic that many found believable. What the Freudians hoped for their society was the function they assigned to dreams: "We dream in order not to have to wake up, because we want to sleep."[15]

As with wish fulfillment, there was another side to dreaming in psychoanalysis, and that was its positive suggestiveness. Encouraging dreams produced a social benefit in the same sense that the irrational unconscious was to be recognized in the dullest of souls and wish fulfillment was to be recognized as the dream of the culture. It added spice to modernity and suggested that in the society where one lived, the unattainable just might be achieved (with patience and perseverance—the reality principle). That suggestion fortified hope and enterprise.

The cleverness of Freudianism in silently, latently, touching so many bases and performing so many, often disparate, functions was the equivalent to what Freud saw as the cleverness of dreams: "All dreams are equally insufferably witty and they need to be because they are under pressure and the direct route is barred to them."[16]

FREUD INFORMED his Clark University audience that after the patient's repressed memories were identified, the therapist introduced them "into the patient's consciousness" so they could be acknowledged, no longer feared and no longer desired.[17] Psychoanalysis did the same, we saw, with memories that were unconscious in the sense that history had left them behind. These memories—of the family, personal identity, community, emotional ties, and the morality of the Bible—were brought back to consciousness in psychological theories and practices so that the patient and the culture could see them as missing and now accept them in revised form. In bringing them back, therapy was not releasing repressed "material" from the unconscious, as the theory held, but reinserting it in the mind.

What Freud sought most to return to memory and a place deep in the psyche was the Father, his iron rod, and the fear he aroused. In the new age they were represented by the laws of the state, the prime minister or president, and psychoanalysis. The patient had to fear and believe in the legitimacy of the new Father, the new time, and its supporting belief, psychoanalysis. By putting the Father and old world institutions back in the mind, Freud obscured (repressed) the loss of the old world, which could not be admitted was wanted, and the reality of the new world, whose emptiness and materialism, anxiety and instrumentality, could not be admitted. He also repressed the experience of most people in the new culture; it could not be candidly recognized but could be normalized through the reality principle and therapy's claim to a timeless, universal knowledge: this is the way it has always been—some lead, others follow.

By returning some elements of the past and repressing others, Freudianism sought to prevent a very real "return of the repressed" that was most to be feared in the new age. The longings expressed by the critics of modernity were those that psychoanalysis attempted to forestall by returning the old world in images, its own version of the return of the repressed. The patient—the culture—would have to admit for sanity's sake that there could be no living in a dream, a fantasy, a past. That was wrong, unhealthy, and had to be exorcised while the new conditions were accepted.

Repression occurs, Freud explains, when "the demands of the sexual instincts . . . seem to the ego to constitute a danger menacing his self-preservation or his self-respect. The ego then takes up the defensive, denies the sexual instincts the satisfaction they claim and forces them into those by-paths of substitute gratification which become manifest as symptoms of a neurosis."[18] For Freud and the latent functions of his work, it was important to underscore that desire is repressed because it is a threat to self-preservation, self-respect, and sanity. After all, the desires of mass populations and the programs of radical politicians threatened the new European order.

Economic desire was castigated by both the right and the left for destroying social justice, one reason they sought to end the new social system. The nostalgias for God, family, community, the old certainties, a more ordered life, what the present had left behind, were equally destabilizing because they could not be fulfilled, providing more fodder for the radical fanatics. All of this and more had to be exorcised if Europe was to appear healthy. It was accomplished in part *not* by releasing repressed feelings of shame and fear but by *inculcating* them through Freudian theories of desire and repression. What was missing in the new age had to be returned to the singular patient but also and mainly to the larger patient, Western culture.

A symptom, Freud said, was "both a gratification and a punishment for that gratification."[19] Psychoanalysis, a symptom of social hysteria meant to be its cure, punished in the sense of being an imposition upon individuals, making them decoys, treating them, charging them. It punished also in the sense of disallowing the truth to a population judged too immature for it. Should anyone steal the truth, here was a means to bind him—just as the gods denied fire to Prometheus.

REGRESSION, Freud informed his readers, revives "the forces which protected [the neurotic's] infancy."[20] For just this reason psychoanalysis regressed to the past for images of comfort, ironically expressed in the theory as regressing to an individual's past in order to find the site of conflict. The valuable past was still with the individual—and the culture—therapy said. The terror of the present had been eclipsed by the theoretical revival of the old world or any Garden of Eden the patient—and the culture—might be dreaming about.

Regression took the patient and the culture back to a desirable but never-never land of the past, planted in the mind as still existing. That was the first movement of therapy, the recollection of the past and the certainty that it was still present in its most valuable essentials. Then came regression to the time of the trauma—but not a personal one, rather the world-historical one of loss and gain. That was the second movement of therapy, when the "inessentials" lost during the trauma were damned and converted into a memory, ultimately replaced by acceptance of the new age.

Cure came with the realization that there was no loss through the Fall in the Garden, or the fall of the old world, or the fall into neurosis. The old world still existed, and the old *you* still existed; you could find them and be cured. In a certain way, at least in the therapy situation, the old world and the old *you* did still exist, as a picture placed before the patient at the beginning of each session. And the picture, like the therapy situation, was "modern," an improvement. It was about freedom, achieved in part through symbols of the restraining past, not least of all the father.

Therapy gave a false surety about the past, now a "clarified" past whose best elements had been retained. It also offered a false analysis of the present, in which one was asked not to see that he was a mere cipher in a mass society, something like Kafka's bug (hence the tremendous attraction of the romantic radicals, who raised humans to the status of rebellious Fausts). In therapy at least, the individual was *somebody*. For all its false coats, therapy thus made a contribution, possibly inadvertent, to the creation of somebodies, which was one of the promises of democracy.

TWENTY-TWO

The Triumph of Suggestion

Now I beseech you, brethren, mark them which cause
divisions and offenses contrary to the doctrine which
ye have learned; and avoid them.
—Romans 16:17

No one thought of looking for the promised land
where it is, and yet it lies so nearby. There it is: inside
ourselves!
—Theodor Herzl, *Old-New Land*

FREUD'S CONCENTRATION on the past implies that he neglected the present. For many reasons he focused on the past, but the past was only half the curriculum of psychoanalysis as he established it. The other half was justifying the present. Symbolically reintroducing the past as nostalgia and revival, Freud also criticized it and told how its dream had to be dissolved so that the patient—the culture—could live in the present. Remember! was therapy's injunction, and then bring to mind the present as an advance upon the past that you remember.

The process of replacing the past with the present took place on the famous Freudian couch, an object that suggests seduction and thus continued the Freudian sex theme. Its imagery of comfort and relaxation also counterbalanced the stress of therapy.[1] But these were not its chief utility. It functioned as part of a seduction, a mental one, by which the past was excised and the present installed.

The couch was the invitation to a mental "surgical operation," and it was at the same time the operating table and the anesthetic for the operation. On that table an old heart (the old world) was removed and a new one (the new world) was substituted. On the couch, presumably, the patient lay, but it was a body altogether larger and more imposing: the culture of the West—"like a patient etherized upon a table" (in the words of *Prufrock*).

After the "surgical procedure," repression of facts was no longer needed: the patient—the culture—had a new view of the facts, having adopted the therapist's suggestions that the old world was mostly bad and best discarded, and the new world should be accepted as superior. "The repression must be got rid of—after which the substitution of the conscious material for the unconscious can proceed smoothly." The patient and the culture were reprogrammed with a new understanding. To use the term Freud employs, they received and accepted an "after-education."[2]

The location of the therapist, out of sight behind the couch, and the projection of his disembodied voice to the patient, questioning but rarely stating directly, symbolized the suggestive means by which this operation was accomplished. The location of the therapist bore the message that he was "not in the picture"; he was like a voice of conscience, the patient's voice of conscience. This was necessary because in the scheme of therapy one cured oneself, which was to say, he convinced himself of the right representations or ideas that were curative and should be in his mind (even though they were suggested by the therapist). Had the therapist done the convincing directly by command, it would have ruined the effect. Therapy had to be, from first to last, a suggestion system, not a *dictat* system. It had to be, from first to last, democratic, and as secretive as possible.

Like the couch, all of psychoanalysis employed simple means—household means, household truths, what was available and did not need elaborate manufacture. Freud's was the layman's viewpoint, as he said. At the level of suggestion the couch and the process performed on it must have been understood by patients in the same way as the deftly hidden but not entirely unrecognizable appropriations from Schopenhauer, the Bible, sociology, and so much more. In his dream book Freud told of "the principle of *Gschnas*. It consists in constructing what appear to be rare and precious objects out of trivial and preferably comic and worthless materials (for instance, in making armour out of saucepans, wisps of straw and dinner rolls)—a favorite pastime here in Vienna."[3] That was what hysterical neurotics did, according to Freudian theory, in creating fantasies out of "innocent and everyday material." It was also what the theorists did in creating psychoanalysis, not because they were hysterical neurotics but because they were somewhat hysterical citizens of modernity like millions of their contemporaries, and justifiably so. Freud's example of *Gschnas* is what the pioneers were doing: armoring democracy and freedom against their enemies, and doing so with *Gschnas,* bits and pieces found around the house of Western culture.

That the couch connoted seduction leads to the final meaning of Freud's two successive theories of the etiology of neurosis. One theory concerned seduction in childhood, and the other the child's fantasy wish to seduce a parent. In Freudian theory, youth had two latent historical meanings: the Middle Ages as the youth of modern Western man, and the nineteenth century as the youth of liberal democracy. In both cases seduction applied. The Middle Ages saw the seduction of the mass by the nobles and the church; the nineteenth century saw the seduction of the mass by democratic politics against its seductive competitor, romantic politics. But the new age also saw inferentially the seduction of the mass by the theories and practices of psychoanalysis. That is why, in the period 1895–1897 when Freud was developing his basic principles, seduction was much on his mind and played a central role in his theories.

"And false Christs and false prophets shall rise, and shall shew signs and wonders, to seduce, if it were possible, even the elect" (Mark 14:22). If the new prophets were false, their goal was not.

THE COUCH and almost all the substance of psychoanalysis had to do with suggestion, which had entered therapy through soul psychology, hypnosis, the practices of Liébeault and Bernheim, and the Suggestion Clinics. From the beginning the pioneers realized they were offering ideas to the patient, which he was apt to accept as true and then confirm by "material" supposedly brought up from the unconscious. Eeden (of the Amsterdam Suggestion Clinic) said this was precisely what therapy should do—place in the patient's mind good ideas that would drive out bad ones. But Freud, feeling keenly the need to justify psychoanalysis as science, pleaded embarrassment at the thought he might be feeding his patients the ideas they later fed back to him. (Regardless of what they told him, he urged them to look for sexual material.) Therapists of other schools similarly urged their patients to look for material that fit their particular theories, similarly made suggestions along the lines of what they considered reality, and similarly publicly deplored the use and effect of suggestion in their work.

The hope that suggestion could be eliminated from therapy, since it seemed unscientific, was ironic, impossible, and undesirable. Suggestion was therapy's entire modality, just as Puységur, Bernheim, Eeden, and many others recognized.[4] This was true as much for the treatment as for the theory. Born out of nineteenth-century suggestion theory, psychoanalysis was created to suggest and to inculcate on a broad scale what normative middle-class liberal democracy wanted for the new order and the new legitimacy. Without the willingness to do that under the guise of science and objectivity, Freudianism would have lost its glamour, unable to outlast its refusal to perform its cultural function, the weaving of a new mythos, a contemporary integration that strengthened the present against its myriad enemies.

Therapists, patients, and an entire culture came to believe through suggestion in a system of psychology that was a convincing reflection—an elaborate symbolization—of the time and culture in which they lived, angled so as to accomplish certain goals. "Psycho-analysis . . . learnt to recognize the power of memories," Freud wrote. It learned too—already believed from the beginning—the magical power of suggestion in treating the memory (the idea reservoir) of a whole society. Le Bon had explained (as Freud did later, in *Group Psychology*) that groups are like hypnotized subjects; the Freudians viewed the whole culture in the same way (as did Le Bon). That was the significance of romantic soul psychology and psychoanalysis having arisen from hypnosis through Mesmer, Puységur, Charcot, Liébeault, and Bernheim, and the contemporaneous use of suggestion in art and advertising. (Freud's nephew, Edward L. Bernays, introduced modern public relations in America.)[5]

The popular perception that therapy was designed to adjust the individual to the self and/or society was a deep misconception encouraged by the pioneers themselves. Therapy was a belief system about right and wrong, past and present, enemies and friends, meant for Western culture as a whole, like commandments blasted on new tablets, but conveyed subtly, through suggestion.[6] It was created to facilitate the acceptance of new conditions by means of the carrot and the stick. The carrot was the image of comfort and success supplied by the new psychology; the stick was madness.

Because the Freudians suggestively conveyed a psychology of the normal for the new age, they drew a bright line between psychosis and neurosis. Some of the leading lights, such as Jung and Bleuler in Switzerland, came out of asylum experience, working with psychotics. But once the Freudian system was under way, psychotics were given short shrift. Freud said he avoided them because they resisted treatment that required some recognition of reality and the common meaning of words and concepts, and because it was apparent that talk therapy could not make a dent in the armor of psychosis, no less offer a cure. That was paradoxically fruitful for the movement because psychosis touched few and was most difficult to treat.

Neurosis, on the other hand, could be read into everyone. Freud had made it a cardinal principle that the normal and the neurotic were wedded at the point of "the psychopathology of everyday life." Using the new diagnostic keys, anyone was—or could be made to seem—a potential or actual neurotic. They could absorb the norms spread by theoretical psychology, and since they were normal they could be cowed (Freud thought they wanted to be because they were preternaturally dependent, feared independence, and craved leaders to tell them what to do and what was right). They were society at large, where lay psychoanalysis's destiny, the normal in an abnormal time (abnormal by contrast with the past). Freudianism meant to help shape the normals, just as market forces were doing, just as nationalism was doing, just as liberal politics was doing. As psychology had rescued Freud from the blood and guts of the medical wards, which he admitted he disliked, so it rescued the majority of mental practitioners from the frustrating care for psychotics, leading them to the far more attractive roles of manifest magi and latent social arbiters.

As to the proof of the pudding being in the eating (that is, in cures achieved), that was no danger to psychoanalysis. Just as it could be demonstrated by the selection of diagnostic keys that individuals were neurotic, it could just as readily be shown that they were cured or much improved. Through the suggested belief in psychoanalysis as a true, scientific system, cures were as believable as diagnoses.

AS A SUGGESTION system, psychoanalysis is best construed latently. *Psycho* refers to the mind and more particularly to the images, ideas, and beliefs that inhabit the mind. *Analysis* was in practice the bringing to light of ideas the pioneers disliked, identifying them for the patient, and then characterizing and annihilating them by interpretation. As soon as the pioneers saw ideas they disliked, they wiped them out by demonstrating them to be scientifically unhealthy, as before priests had shown certain ideas and impulses to be impure and therefore incorrect. Then they replaced those ideas with new and better representations. And all of this was done by suggestion.

Given the proliferation of psychoanalytic organizations, theories, treatments, and publications, the effort of the pioneers to save the new liberal democratic culture may have been more extravagant than conditions warranted. It is well to remember that Freud was a hypochondriac in the period in which he settled on the basic tenets of psychoanalysis, exaggerating his illnesses and fearing an approaching death. When something bad happened he had thoughts of dying, one supposes as punishment for something he had done or as escape from the consequences. Along with physical symptoms, the cocaine he was taking induced delusions of grandeur, certainty, and salvation. He may well have applied these personal penchants for dread, exaggeration, and salvation to the European condition. But then, the European condition may have been as dangerous as he thought: others with different temperaments and without, we might presume, hypochondria or cocaine, were doing the same work or were soon attracted to it. So it is likely that Freud's predilections at the time furthered his concentration on the true illness he and the other pioneers had come to understand—the illness of Western culture after its spectacular first hundred years. It is likely that Western culture, too, was hypochondriacal and "high" on hysteria, its passionate fears fueling the hysteria. The fin-de-siècle themes of degeneration and decadence were themselves hyperbole, but not without content.

When the pent-up social trauma and hysteria of the nineteenth century burst forth in World War I, engaging all the conflicts of the twin revolutions at maximum energy and intensity, it was not so much proof of the failure of psychoanalysis as it was the final evidence of its need. In the next century more evidence accumulated as communism, fascism, and Nazism reacted against liberal democracy and modernity by regressing to old ideals in new garb, in the process giving a fair imitation of madness. What needed treatment was that reaction, clearly evident already in Freud's time. The treatment he provided proved its value to liberal democracy in the twentieth century.

Part VII

RESISTANCE:
HIDING THE TRUTH

... The human intellect errs very easily without
suspecting it at all, and ... nothing is more readily
believed than what—regardless of the truth—meets our
wishes and illusions half-way.
—Sigmund Freud, *Moses and Monotheism*

... Our work has had the result of driving out one
form of illness with another.
—Sigmund Freud, *An Autobiographical Study*

Casuistry of Psychologists. This man knows human
nature; why does he really study people? He wants to
seize little advantages over them—or big ones,
for that matter—he is a politician.
—Friedrich Nietzsche, *Twilight of the Idols*

... Any decision about whether something is
unpolitical is always a political decision. . . .
—Carl Schmitt, *Political Theology*

Or-der! Or-der!
—The cry of the speaker of the
House of Commons during debates

TWENTY-THREE

The Camouflage of Authority

Of its nature, camouflage is a reality which is not what
it seems. Its appearance, instead of declaring, conceals
its substance. Hence the majority of people are
deceived.
    —José Ortega y Gasset, *The Revolt of the Masses*

In my opinion, attack is the best defense.
    —Sigmund Freud, *Freud/Jung Letters*

A SYSTEM so questionable and audacious, so disguised in its methods and goals, needed protections, even from the self-awareness of the
theorists and therapists, so that it could perform its latent functions.
It needed, most of all, credibility and authority. The obvious defense
was to affirm the work as medical practice and deny that it was anything but what it said it was, as in the typical rebuttal by the American psychoanalyst A. A. Brill to what many sensed at the time: "The
main aim of psychology is to adjust the individual to his environment.
It is no more a philosophy of morals than any other branch of medicine."[1]

All the pioneers claimed that psychoanalysis was science, believable because most of them held medical degrees. And the practice of
intellectuals at the time was to give the label of science to beliefs in the
most diverse fields.[2] The claim to science was further supported by the
pioneers' assertion that they were treating patients for, and curing
them of, mental illnesses. Considering the pain caused to sufferers of
real mental illnesses and their families, and the long mystery associated
with these conditions, great regard and confidence were extended to
the analysts. They were believed to have the cure for one of the oldest
scourges of mankind. This basis for authority lent prestige to wide-

ranging commentaries by the pioneers and their followers on the most diverse subjects. Without belief in their first calling, healing, there would have been little regard for their second calling, cultural commentary.

Presented as scientific, psychoanalysis was by definition true, universal, timeless, objective, and value-free—claims that most of the intellectual clerks also made for their work. Purely at the practical level, these claims were necessary for the pioneers to justify fees for a medical practice as opposed to a religious or philosophical therapy.

Karl Popper, the noted philosopher of science, called attention to the unprovability of psychoanalysis (and by extension the other main therapeutic systems), a point on which Freud was sensitive. Unprovability might have disarmed psychoanalytic claims to science, but in fact it strengthened the authority of Freudianism in a way common to mass beliefs. Viable social beliefs are rarely tested, for if they are disproved they are lost. They are best when they can be argued but not disproved. Mass beliefs do not operate in the province of proof and disproof; they operate in the realm of persuasion and therefore are believed as long as a considerable body of opinion says they are true and as long as they demonstrate their social benefits to those who approve them. This psychoanalysis did. Considering the many benefits psychoanalysis provided, Freud would have been justified in crying out to the culture of his day, "Why do you want proof? Look what I'm doing for you!"

BEYOND CLAIMS to science and the echoes of past beliefs, psychoanalytic authority was built right into Freudian theories and practices. A formidable protection, lending immeasurable authority, was the questioning method, which Joe Kennedy Adams, perhaps alarmingly, relates to the Inquisition and witch trials. During the Inquisition, questioning was carried on in strict secrecy, often with torture. The burden of proof was on the accused, the accuser was not named, and there was no right to counsel—standards lower than those of the secular courts of the time. This was necessary for the work to be performed effectively, since it had no basis in logic or law. Similarly, Adams observes, psychoanalysis provided none of the usual protections to questioning. The process was private, the burden of proof was on the accused (who, according to theory, was guilty before the process started), the accuser was not named (the therapist stood in his place), and there was no right to counsel. The only counsel available was from the "accuser," the therapist, who went under a variety of names, one of them being counselor.

Therapy replaced physical torture with psychological and emotional discomfort, dredging up past failures and hurts and lingering on them, and assuring the patient that he had made mistakes in the past (of which he was unaware) which led to mental illness. The patient had acted badly, done wrong, was guilty. This form of "torture" reinforced the authority of the therapist, since the therapy was condoned on good authority and practiced in Freud's day almost exclusively by medical doctors. With this warrant, the therapist struck fear in the patient and offered hope: fear if the patient refused to take the right path, hope if the patient agreed, just as religion had done in the past.[3]

The inquisitor and the therapist had much in common to rely on for authority, Adams points out. Christian theology was a complex subject requiring years of study and a special language, Latin, not widely understood outside priestly circles. Similarly, psychoanalysis required years of study and the acquisition of a special, quasi-medical language. Christian theology was made to seem objective by means of logical conclusions based on biblical premises. Similarly, the doctrinal base of psychoanalysis had the appearance of objectivity while addressing interests that transcended the patient. The inquisitor maintained that he could detect true motivations even when they were the opposite of what appeared in surface behavior; this was mirrored in a cardinal principle of therapy, which asserted the ability to see into the hidden psychology of the patient. With his armory, the inquisitor could accuse anyone who differed from the norm of being in rebellion against the church; what differed from the norm in styles of living, dressing, and believing could be interpreted as heretical.[4]

Quite aside from its sinister historical connotations, questioning has the psychological effect of establishing authority. It teaches who is in command (the normal therapist, the normative society) and who is subservient (the patient, the citizen). As Elias Canetti, a Nobel laureate and student of the psychology of power, explains:

All questioning is a forcible intrusion. When used as an instrument of power it is like a knife cutting into the flesh of the victim. . . . On the questioner the effect is an enhanced feeling of power. He enjoys this and consequently asks more and more questions; every answer he receives is an act of submission. Personal freedom consists largely in having a defense against questions. The most blatant tyranny is the one which asks the most blatant questions.[5]

Early Freud patients walked out on him when the questioning grew too intimate and, to some of them, too absurd. But soon the prestige of therapy compelled the patient to remain, and to answer.

"The power of remaining silent," Canetti points out, "is always highly valued. . . . To the silent man is attributed the power of self-sufficiency. . . . The taciturn person has the advantage that people wait for his utterances and attach special importance to them. When they come they are terse and isolated and sound like commands." Thus the therapist was in a position of command without having to give commands. Freud was aware of the authority granted to therapists by peering into another's private life, and the loss of authority suffered by patients in this process. In 1909 he and Jung psychoanalyzed each other on their trip to America. At one point Jung asked for more personal details from Freud in order to test a theory he held about his colleague's mental life. Freud refused the request, protesting, "But I cannot risk my authority!"[6]

Questioning also protected the therapist from inconvenient reactions and challenges. With the patient kept busy answering questions, the therapist did not have to explain or justify himself. A patient might think the emphasis on sex or powerlessness or individuation beside the point, but the therapist need offer no explanation. A patient who glimpsed through the lattice of theories and practices and saw the tenets of Judeo-Christian theology or Schopenhauerian philosophy, might mentally question the proceedings. Or he might find the quest for minuscule clues hidden in memories rather quaint, in the style of Sherlock Holmes. He might wonder about a system in which the crime is already known but the criminal, the patient, is unaware of having committed it. He might wonder how it came to be that the therapist was in a position to define and designate crime (sin, neurosis). Why should the crime be rebellion? Against whom was the rebellion directed? No answers were forthcoming.

AS EFFECTIVE for maintaining authority was the "accusation" by the Freudian therapist that the patient wished to kill his father and have sex with his mother. The theoretical basis for this accusation was that this secret had to be revealed and made conscious in order to enable a cure. The methodological reason, however, was that the analyst had to be in place of the father, in order to lay down the law. The analyst was the father who was not to be killed, wronged, or defied. Better take his or her direction, which was the way to health, just as incorporating the father's *You must not* was the way to maturity. In this manner the therapy method replicated the authority of the father.

Two other accusations were routinely cast at the Freudian patient. One, explicit, was that the patient was resisting therapy in order to hide the horrors of the unconscious. *You are defending!*, therapists accused patients, when the true case was the other way around. Therapists were defending their practice and its latent meanings and functions. They wanted to break down resistance to their work while concealing its true nature. So they attacked in place of defense, fearing that any revelation of the latent meanings and functions of therapy would dissolve its authority and credibility.[7]

Having placed on patients the burden, and in people's minds the idea, of neurosis and madness, as diversions from reality, psychoanalysis proposed that those who did not believe in it were neurotics or psychotics, defending against their own unconscious horrors. To think that therapy was not science or medicine but a subtle form of politics would be accounted clinical resistance by the analyst, confirming the diagnosis of mental illness. The diversion away from the political, the social, the external, and onto the individual's interior needed to be hidden at all costs, and the doctrine of resistance furthered that endeavor.

The doctrine of resistance also stated concisely why the beliefs of a culture were composed and promulgated as scientific psychology. Those same beliefs conveyed as politics or economics could run into heavy resistance; resistance was mollified when the beliefs were presented as science. This at once disguised them, made them less of a target, and pronounced them as unavoidable truths. By displacing beliefs onto science (in the way Freud said patients displaced memories and feelings onto objects unconnected to them), the pioneers and the culture had an easier time of it. The substitute was more acceptable than the real thing.

"Transference," Freud asserted, "emerges as the most *powerful resistance* to the treatment." It too protected psychoanalysis. The patient's ill feelings that might be induced by the therapist, for whatever reason, the therapist could assign to transference. Thereby he was absolved of blame and maintained his authority as the one who is "right" as against the patient who is "wrong."[8] If the therapist verbally or emotionally abused the patient, and the patient reacted negatively, the judgment would be the same. If the patient disbelieved the therapist, also the same.

In the transference concept, as in other aspects of therapy, the methodology was so constructed that the therapist could not lose. Thus he consistently reinforced his superior position, his authority, and the correctness of his practice. Transference, like resistance, kept doubting and questioning at bay, not just in the therapy situation but in a sense as a public pronouncement that psychoanalysis was impregnable and must be believed.

A further use of transference was in emphasizing the past, the infantile, which was a function of the latent therapy enterprise. Further, it removed the interpretation of human relations from social sources, whether past or present, and diverted them back to personal, intrapsychic sources. Thus the patient could not escape the closed circle that had been constructed by theory and practice. With the concept of transference, psychoanalysis sought to keep the world firmly bottled up in the mind of the patient. In all these ways transference was a "powerful resistance," to use Freud's phrase, to challenging the therapist, and thus another self-protective device of psychoanalysis.

Over the years Ferenczi and other colleagues pressed on Freud the efficacy of dropping the superior position of the analyst. They suggested revealing some of the analyst's personal shortcomings to the patient, so that the analyst would not remain an ideal individual. This would help, some of the analysts thought, in eventually breaking the transference when the time was right, ending dependence on the analyst and allowing the patient to emerge from infantile regression. Freud refused to consider this approach: "You mean to show not only that the patient is a swine, but I too?"[9] The analyst was to be presented always as a scientist, above personal and perceptual sway, viewing the patient with total objectivity, just as analysis was to be presented as a science.

Together with resistance and transference was the accusation, this time implicit, that the patient was guilty—in Freudian doctrine of harboring the fantasy Oedipus complex and of retreating to a dreamland of the past as an escape from mature responsibilities. Again this turned reality around. It was the therapist who could be accused of practicing a form of indoctrination and social control under the guise of science. Wittingly or vaguely, therapists labored under a burden of guilt for performing work far removed from its stated purposes. *You feel guilty!* was the therapist's accusation—as he deflected guilt onto the patient. In this way the need to confess, presupposed by the theory, was fulfilled by therapists confessing in the way Freud said patients confessed, by saying No when meaning Yes.

The theoretical doctrine of anxiety had the same latent source. Therapists could not fail to be anxious that they would be found out. A recent study by John Farrell, *Freud's Paranoid Quest,* claims that Freud was wracked by suspicion.[10] Freud's theories reflected the suspicion rampant in his culture, which he may have felt all the more keenly because in his false position he may often have feared that his true work might be uncovered.

WARY OF "judgments on psychoanalysis from people who . . . demand with apparent scorn that we shall prove to them the correctness of our findings," Freud developed a series of rationales for these doubters, among them medical doctors and scientists. The first was that psychoanalysis was never rationally rejected; its disturbing truths reached down to the emotions of its critics and compelled rejection. Nonbelievers, he said, "behaved to psycho-analysis in precisely the same way as individual neurotics under treatment for their disorder": they resisted the truth. The second rationale was that people were hurt by the thought of life not being under conscious control, just as they were hurt when Darwin gave them an animal ancestry and Copernicus took them from the center of the universe. The third was that those who had no experience of analysis could not be expected to understand it. The fourth, he implied, was anti-Semitism: the fact that he was a Jew could make his system unacceptable to many.[11]

Of all the methods of hiding the truth and maintaining credibility and authority, by far the most thorough was appearing to do the work of physicians. This included the treatment of patients for mental illness; a vast publishing effort in books and professional journals given over to the discussion of diagnosis, treatment, and theory (Freud alone contributing more than three million words); and attendance at conferences and seminars dealing with these subjects. These activities, giving verisimilitude to the claims of healing and science, made it difficult to believe that the work was not as stated. This was reinforced by the recurrent claim of the pioneers that their theories were confirmed by clinical experience with patients—even though it was clear that Freudian patients confirmed Freudian theories, Jungian patients Jungian theories, and so on.

THE CHALLENGE to perform a false work and hide the real work is what may have led to the much-discussed "creative illness" of Freud and Jung at the beginning of their definitive careers. This illness was supposed to have been their entree to the truth of human psychology. Freud's self-analysis was said to have been undertaken to cure this illness. Jung's cure came with dream messages and visions that strengthened his resolve.[12] In both cases the illness may have represented a personal crisis: whether to do real psychology or serve the needs of Western culture under the guise of medical science. Both men were cured when they resolved to take the latter course, which promised more than a life in science or medicine could offer.

After the death of his father in 1896, Freud had a dream in which he saw an instruction printed on a placard: "You are requested to close an eye," that is, to "wink at or 'overlook.'" Ambiguously, the placard also seemed to read, "You are requested to close the eyes," that is, both eyes, not just one. The eyes might be the father's, to be closed by the loving son after death, in which case, Freud said, the meaning was "one should do one's duty toward the dead" in two senses: by "an apology (as though I had not done it and were in need of leniency) and the duty itself. The dream thus stems from the inclination to self-reproach that regularly sets in among the survivors. . . ."[13] This rich statement is directly applicable to his hidden duties in creating psychoanalysis without giving clear-sighted testimony of what he was doing. The new world, having made no apology for killing the old, had not done its duty to the dead either, and, as Freud's second meaning indicates, that duty should be done. Psychoanalysis was an outlet for the feeling of self-reproach the new world felt for its deed, and at the same time was the performance of that duty. It was also a wink of the eye, an overlooking of the truth of what it really was.

The differences between the two placard messages conveyed to Freud a certain "vagueness. . . . The dream-work failed to establish a unified wording for the dream-thought which could at the same time be ambiguous, and the two main lines of thought consequently began to diverge even in the manifest content of the dream." For good reason, I suggest, because the two main lines of thought were (a) consciously knowing what he was doing in creating psychoanalysis and (b) not consciously knowing it or rejecting clear knowledge of why and what he was doing. The situation was vague and ambiguous, as it was for all the pioneers. They knew and winked an eye at the latent work, and at the same time they did not know. The placard, in either version, did not ask Freud to keep both eyes open. He was instructed never to know clearly, never to let the right hand (to change the image) know what the left was doing. As Philip Rieff notes, Freud's "sense of guilt . . . appears to enliven his work." The obscured sight "tells us what he [Freud] did not know of his own highest sensibility. That sensibility, in its negational image of looking away from something too vital for direct sight, is often disclosed uncontrolled in the work of other theorists who aim to see what is highest."[14] Other pioneers did not disclose the latent work in an uncontrolled fashion, but over time they and later followers revealed more than Freud would countenance for most of his career.

Rieff comments, "Especially in our dreams, we know that we are all generously endowed, as if artists and scientists, with striking powers of evasion." That was the challenge of Freudianism, to keep an evasive, creative, mythopoetic work secret. The residue of truth in this dream of Freud's, says Rieff—as may be seen in Freud's work as a whole—was the sense of guilt,[15] in part guilt over his father, but far more significantly Europe's guilt over the old world it had abandoned and the new one it instituted, and Freud's guilt in creating latent psychoanalysis.

Wilhelm Stekel, one of the original members of Freud's Wednesday Psychological Society—forerunner of the Vienna and then the international psychoanalytic movement—recalled the excitement of the early meetings. "There was complete harmony among the five, no dissonances; we were like pioneers in a newly discovered land, and Freud was the leader. A spark seemed to jump from one to another, and every evening was like a revelation."[16] The pioneers warmly agreed on the latent work that needed to be done. The spark that jumped between them was the realization of how appropriate that work was to the needs of the time and how effectively formulated for that purpose. The movement may not have had the courage to be so audacious on its own, but with Freud as their leader, a "conquistador" who provided them with formulations measured to the needs of the time, they found it.

Not only did they mutually understand the need they filled, but they must have sensed their work would be amply accepted. By this means they could achieve a great work of and for civilization as they conceived it. The pioneers fit the very old mold of mythmakers, a function they performed obliquely.

TWENTY-FOUR

The Politics of Concealment

. . . In order to penetrate camouflage an oblique glance
is required, the glance of one who is translating a text
with the dictionary by his side.
    —José Ortega y Gasset, *The Revolt of the Masses*

You cannot understand something by using concepts
that contribute to its camouflage.
        —Sherry Turkle, *Psychoanalytic Politics*

FREUD WAS sensitive into old age over "the secession of former
pupils . . . often brought up against me as a sign of my intolerance
or . . . as evidence of some specific fatality that hangs over me."
Among the disciples with whom he quarreled and whom he expelled
from his movement were such luminaries as Jung, Adler, Rank, Ferenczi, Stekel, and Reich. At one time or another he called them all
paranoiac and *mishugah* (Yiddish for crazy), flinging demeaning
curses at them.[1] Earlier he broke with Fliess and parted company with
Josef Breuer, his first associate in psychoanalysis. He fought too with
other practitioners who were not part of his movement but were engaged in similar work, such as Pierre Janet.

Varying explanations have been proposed for these internal struggles. Thornton thinks they were caused by Freud's clinical paranoia induced by cocaine. Van den Berg blames Freud's emphasis on the past
as against those who were more concerned with the present. Some
think Freud was protecting his proprietary claim to psychoanalysis,
which he feared others wanted to usurp, or that he saw himself as a
high priest and the offending disciples as heretics. Some of the partic-
ipants viewed Freud as a bully who would not countenance opposition. Many more causes have been adduced to explain the repeated

splinterings, including Freud's defense that his heretical disciples were altering his theory "with the object of mitigating its repellent features," in the process mangling his ideas and harming psychoanalysis.[2]

A more persuasive argument can be made for Freud's desire to hide the latent sources and functions of psychoanalysis, which if revealed were potentially ruinous. The main charge against the movement was that psychoanalysis was unscientific and was in fact philosophy, religion, sociopolitics, or all three.[3] Freud had to deny this charge, excoriate it, just as he did those heretical followers whose divergent beliefs risked revelation.

Freud and Fliess came to see themselves as rivals and argued toward the end of their relationship over the priority of the bisexuality theory in Otto Weininger's *Sex and Character.* By the time Freud had gone fully in the direction of psychogenesis, Fliess was coming to feel more strongly that biological rhythms were the main determinants in sickness and health, physical and mental. These conflicts might have put distance between them in any case, but the more substantial cause of the break was that Fliess was something like the sound of his name—flighty. He was never pinned down to reality, as indicated by his surgery on Emma Eckstein. His ideas and practices, often on the wild side, threatened to sink the new psychology right at the start by associating it with quack medicine. Fliess was too heady an example of that to be tolerated, just at the time Freud had finished formulating the troubles and cures of modern Europe in a disguised psychological system. While Fliess retained regard for some of Freud's theories and cited them in his own work, he finally could not believe that psychoanalysis could cure people or even understand their problems. He told Freud that "the reader of thoughts merely reads his own thoughts into other people," a view which Freud said "renders all my efforts valueless."[4]

The break with Breuer came from a similar direction, only here the flighty one was Freud. Freud considered Breuer's treatment of Anna O. a clear proof of his theory: identify the patient's sexual trauma, bring it to consciousness, and the cure will follow by catharsis. Breuer suspected that this was not the case with Anna O., his doubts indicating that he was not a friend of the Freudian enterprise. Moreover he found Freud's general approach to science unscientific and more akin to religion. Breuer's concern over Freud's monomania about sex led Freud to fear that "According to him, I should have to ask myself every day whether I am suffering from *moral insanity* or *paranoia scientifica*."[5] They ended their partnership and their cordial relations on the day Freud passed Breuer on the street and refused to greet him.

Freud later declared that Breuer was not part of the fold because his early relations with his mother discouraged his relish for discovery. Freud also questioned Breuer's self-confidence and ability to handle criticism, which "were not so fully developed as the rest of his organization"; and he felt that psychoanalysis was leading in a direction to which Breuer "found it impossible to reconcile himself." Part of that direction was the sexual etiology of neurosis, which he thought Breuer "shrank from recognizing."[6] But the main problem, which Freud never mentioned, was that Breuer viewed himself as a medical doctor while Freud was only outwardly a physician. Breuer must have perceived where Freud's latent work was taking him, as did others. After the two had collaborated on their book, Freud's references to Breuer are humorously belittling or hostile. A physician above all, Breuer had seen that psychoanalysis was bad medical science and bad medical treatment. He was out to cure patients, not a culture. That Freud perhaps chafed at being financially indebted to the generous Breuer may have spiced their disagreements; but it could only be incidental to two basically different views of science, healing, and the truth.

FREUD SIDESTEPPED a damning association with philosophy at every turn. If psychoanalysis were thought to be philosophy, the claim of science would be undermined. If it were thought to have its source in specific philosophers such as Kant, Schopenhauer, and Nietzsche, its claim to originality would be disputed. Accordingly, when a disciple pointed out the similarities between psychoanalysis and Schopenhauer's beliefs, Freud claimed never to have read that philosopher closely. But in 1917 he gave credit to

> renowned names among the philosophers who may be cited as . . . predecessors, above all the great thinker Schopenhauer, whose unconscious "Will" is equivalent to the instincts in the mind as seen by psychoanalysis. It was this same thinker, moreover, who in words of unforgettable impressiveness admonished mankind of the importance of the sexual craving, still so depreciated.[7]

When the comparison with Nietzsche was called to his attention, Freud claimed never to have read him closely either. There was just too much there, he said, that took his interest; it was better if he got on with his own work or he would become more interested in Nietzsche's psychology than in his own.

The philosophical anti-Semitism of Schopenhauer and Nietzsche may have convinced Freud to keep his distance from them. Schopenhauer contrasted what he thought was practical and optimistic Judaism with ascetic and pessimistic Christianity. He thought Europe was dominated by Jewish ideas, the common plaint of nineteenth- and twentieth-century anti-Semites, and that Judaism was worse than Hegelianism, which for him constituted a mighty curse. According to Leon Poliakov, "Schopenhauer initiated his public into anti-semitism. . . ."[8] By the end of the nineteenth century, anti-Semitism was linked to racism, volkism, anti-modernism, and proto-fascism, all forces which Freud's system was designed to combat. Both because he was a loyal Jew and because of the political aspects of anti-Semitism, Freud was not pleased to hear such sentiments from any source.

The Nietzsche connection was particularly revealing because of the disguised politics in psychoanalysis. As far as can be determined, Freud never mentioned Nietzsche in a political context or alluded to his anti-democratic apostrophes. Nor did Freud speak of Nietzsche's diatribes against Judaism; but such remarks could not have escaped him, though they apparently made little impression on his disciples. Similarly, Nietzsche's *Genealogy of Morals* is so deeply insightful of what the Freudians would seek to accomplish—a pacification between the high and low in society, and the acceptance of modernity—and was so knowing about the therapeutic methodology they would adopt, that Freud could not have failed to be anxious that Nietzsche had given away the entire enterprise. Freud, however, remained ever delicate on the subject of Nietzsche, keeping a respectful distance. To have been openly opposed to Nietzsche might have revealed Freud's aims.

Before his career as a psychoanalyst began in earnest, Freud wrote Fliess: ". . . I must secretly nourish the hope of arriving . . . at my initial goal of philosophy. For this is what I wanted originally. . . ." But later, any linking of psychoanalysis with philosophy brought his ire. When an American disciple, James Jackson Putnam, urged the blending of psychoanalysis with Hegelianism, Freud shrank back in horror.[9] In his works he cites Kant's categorical imperative seven times, each time taking care to draw a distinction between that idea and the Oedipus complex. His justification for putting aside the influence of the metaphysicians was that philosophy was speculation and intuition while psychoanalysis was science. Moreover philosophy was a symptom of neurosis, like religion. Only before he became a psychoanalyst and after he retired from practice did Freud admit that philosophy had been his main interest, beginning in his youth, and that he had abjured it because its prospects were too uncertain (the same reason he gave for not entering politics). Beginning in his university days he was ready to dissemble about philosophy, writing a friend, "I am joining in the first year the faculty of philosophy. Accordingly, if anybody asks me (or asks you about me) what I intend to do, refrain from giving a definite reply and say merely—'Oh, a scientist, a professor, something like that.' "[10]

Jung similarly rejected the association of philosophy with psychoanalysis, as did the other disciples. Since philosophy was secular (though in its romantic branch was eminently spiritual), the pioneers could dismiss critical commentaries on this matter without much rancor. They could view the association with philosophy as a misapprehension by the public and certain critics. While anyone at the time could have checked the philosophical sources—and Freud and his disciples knew them well—the pioneers encountered little embarrassment on this score.

RELIGION was another matter, and here Freud gave no quarter. From the beginning he painted it as a false belief and a neurosis, a manifestation of infantilism. He went so far in old age as to tailor his memory of his extensive religious studies by stating that he was "brought up without religion."[11] Perhaps without faith, but his education in religion was wide and deep, as we have seen. When Putnam added to Hegelianism the recommendation that Freud incorporate religion as a positive element in his theory, he shot back that religion would only complicate the matter and chose not to hear of it again. Never during his active career would he welcome a good word on the subject. The religious accusation, if established, would reveal his work as pseudoscience and indicate its sociopolitical functions. And yet it kept seeping in, the worst offender being Jung, who while insisting he was a scientist could not keep the image of a religious seer sufficiently distant.

Jung assigned his break with Freud to the latter's sexual theory, which he considered overemphasized. This is usually taken to be the chief disagreement. Van den Berg assigns the break to Jung's emphasis on the patient's present rather than his past, also opposed to Freud's theories. These no doubt contributed to a loss of mutual sympathy, but a case can be made that the essential cause of the break was over religion. Jung, the minister's son, willingly became a fountain of religious beliefs expressed in their own right or in his jargon. The frequency of the word "God" in his writings and interviews is astonishing. "It makes little difference what I call it: God, Tao, the Great Voice, the Great Spirit," he once remarked. "But for people of our time God is the most comprehensible name with which to designate the Power beyond us." Recognizing the death of the Christ myth, "Jung viewed his career, at its end," Rieff remarks, "as a successful search for a functional equivalent in psychotherapy to what he assumed must have been the therapeutic effect of Christian imagery and institutions."[12] As he aged, his mind turned ever more firmly toward mysticism and religion, concentrating "in the clear" on what the enterprise of therapy had been about from the beginning.

Richard Noll believes Jung and Freud parted ways because Jung was more interested in religion and Freud in science.[13] That does not appear to be the case, for both were evidently interested in religion. Jung's crime in Freud's eyes was that he was always more obvious in his enterprise; Freud hid more securely behind science, jargon, and anti-religious rhetoric. For Freud, concealment—especially of the religious side of therapy—was a necessary part of the prescription for the new psychology. As revivified religion, psychoanalysis might attract a cult following; as science it could attract the entire Western world.

Jung had the decided disadvantage, in Freud's eyes, of actually believing in God. "I *know*," Jung said. "I don't need to believe. I know"—an attitude which for Freud had to be unforgivable. Freud had placed God as the Oedipus complex inside the psyche, following the example of the German Idealist philosophers who had similarly placed God in the mind. Having accomplished this, he would not countenance a God beyond the mind, a separate presence. For him there could be no greater heresy than believing in a transcendent God when he had provided a materialistic, natural one inside the psyche. Jung, by not following this line of thought, proved he was not sufficiently modern and too obvious, leaving little doubt that psychology was religion. It was only a false sense of maturity in the modern age, encouraged by Freud, he wrote, that led people to reject religion as the way to mental health: "religions are systems of psychic healing." Therapists are occupied, Jung said, "with problems which, strictly speaking, belong to the theologians."[14]

Jung told Freud in a letter of February 11, 1910, that he wanted psychoanalysis to "absorb those ecstatic instinctual forces of Christianity for the *one* purpose of making the cult and the sacred myth what they once were—a drunken feast of joy where men regained the ethos and holiness of an animal. . . . Yet what infinite rapture and wantonness lie dormant in our religion, waiting to be led back to their true destination." Freud must have been stunned. He responded two days later, "unable to restrain my own precipitate reaction." He warned his estimable disciple that "you mustn't regard me as the founder of a religion." Moreover, Jung was a Nietzsche enthusiast, and anyone who held Nietzsche in high regard had to be suspect to Freud.[15]

Pierre Janet was Freud's most direct and independent rival. Freud was hurt by "the glib repetition of the view that whatever is of value in psychoanalysis is merely borrowed from the ideas of Janet."[16] Both were neurologists and psychotherapists who had studied with Charcot (Janet staying on to run his own ward at the Salpêtrière), and both laid claim to discovering psychoanalysis. Janet's chief fault, in Freud's eyes, had to be that he was candid about psychotherapy as a substitute for religion. Like Jung, Janet did not pay sufficient heed to mystification. Surely Freud did not like a competitor laying claim to psychoanalysis; but he liked even less a presentation of it in the context of religion, and that is what Janet provided. Further, in characterizing religious zeal, Janet succeeded in painting a revealing portrait of Freud.

Religion, according to Janet, is a self-induced delusion, performing psychological functions for the believer. The value of its rituals is that they are performed, not that they are understood (which can be said to be one source of the ritualistic therapy session). Religion often engenders fanaticism, Janet thought, so that the believer cannot admit error, must scorn the adversary, and may exhibit intellectual dishonesty while impugning the honesty of the other party (all traits exhibited by Freud on different occasions in vehemently supporting his theories). Religion, Janet noted, usually evidences a proselytizing impulse, employing fear and the seductive promise of benefits. The highest degree of proselytism is religious persecution, which is a demand for mastery and intellectual unity. The highest point of religious feeling is ecstasy, providing a sense of absolute conviction that one's belief is maximally valuable and immutable. The connections here with Freud's methods and outlook need scarcely be elucidated. He was the greatest of all the psychological proselytizers, offering a system that induced fear and seduction. He demanded uniform adherence to his ideas and his alone, and never wavered. Was Janet indirectly commenting on his great competitor?

A chief virtue or function of religion, according to Janet, was to provide a basis for morality that was superior to secular law. Religion broke down, he said, when after many millennia it spawned the seeds of rationalism, science, education, and philosophy (logic, he thought, was a form of intellectual morality). Since religion had provided so many benefits, what would happen, he wondered, if it died? A substitute would have to be fashioned, and several were available, he believed. Philosophy was a means of seeking and finding answers, but it was not entirely satisfactory. Spiritualism seemed able to respond to the need to hear God speak, but it appeared to many as a cheap, weak substitute. Romanticism was a substitute, providing intimations of the divine. But the best substitute, Janet thought, lay with himself and other therapists. "Scientific psychology" was "destined to . . . put religion out of style" by "applying scientific principles to states of mind and personal needs previously served by religion."[17]

Freud seems to have had an unerring sense of where his wayward colleagues were headed, and it proved out in Janet. Like Freud, Janet was determinedly unidealistic, not inappropriate in the age of science and materialism. He thought that love and like feelings were abnormal manifestations. Later, however, he came around to a view closer to Jung's, honoring a reality beyond the empirically known. He came to think that mystics appeared to be misplaced in a practical society because they carried messages from the future. While the beliefs and methods of both Freud and Janet were more akin to mysticism than to science, Janet came to honor mysticism; Freud continued to see it as an illness while regarding it highly in himself.

Unlike Freud, Janet possessed an even temperament and faced professional disagreements with equanimity. He had a firmer scientific outlook and evidently lacked the fervor of his great competitor. He lost the race so thoroughly to Freud that when one of his former publishers was asked in 1970 if his books would ever reappear, the response was: "No, sir, Janet's works will *never* be reprinted." Freud's opinion was that "Janet's works would never have had the implications which have made psychoanalysis of such importance to the mental sciences and have made it attract such universal interest."[18] In large measure that was vitally true about the latent work of psychoanalysis which assured Freud's fame. As an allegorist and symbolist, condenser of what was important to embody and project, synthesizer of meanings and functions that would attract universal interest, Janet and no one else was the equal of Freud.

ADLER, Rank, and Ferenczi were problematic for Freud at the level of social concern (and Adler to some degree because of religion). As with Jung and Janet, his break with them concerned obviousness—revealing the hidden. Adler came closest to the sociopolitical meanings of psychoanalysis by transposing sex to power, an unwelcome translation of the Freudian endeavor. "Isn't this what you really mean?" Adler was asking his mentor. And Freud's reply could only be, "Perhaps so, but I don't want to say it." Early on Adler wrote about the plight of the poor and their consequent feelings of inadequacy and lack of power. He began with the idea of organic diseases caused by poor working and living conditions, later extending this to mental illness, which he also came to see as a social disease arising from a frustrated drive for power. In contradistinction to Freud, he felt that insight was not sufficient for a cure; action was needed, and action required courage. This took light away from the purely mental activity with which Freud concerned himself, and was a partial corrective to the Freudian diversion of the social to the personal.

Adler had another demerit against his name related to social outlook. He was influenced by Marx, so that his version of psychoanalysis could be seen, in the words of Ellenberger, as "a tedious psychological appendix to socialist doctrine." For a time he was a member of the Social Democratic party in Vienna. As with Nietzsche, Freud recognized Marx as an enemy of his program. Marxism attacked the middle class and therefore Freud's own system which supported the society, politics, and economics of the middle class. Nor would he have appreciated Marx's early anti-Semitism (the Jew as representative of capitalism). Marxism, by its own account, sought a better world, and Adler, with a strong messianic streak, thought along the same lines. To Freud this was intolerable. There could be no better world than the present one; its faults were timeless and unavoidable in civilization. He offered, in the manifest version of psychoanalysis, a messianic vision for the individual in place of social, political, or economic messianism, just as Luther had done when he made personal salvation the issue and goal of religion. When Adler was expelled from the movement he was joined by four or five other analysts, all Social Democrats, who became the core of his new school of individual psychology. As their reason for leaving they claimed that Freud violated the "freedom of science"[19] by not allowing open discussion and disagreement.

Even as Adler expressed socialist leanings in his work, he did not leave Nietzsche behind, as Freud recognized. Adler, he said, "turned away from the unconscious and the sexual instincts, and endeavored to trace back the development of character and of the neuroses to the 'will to power.' "[20] Adler was again blasphemous from Freud's point of view when he converted to Christianity in 1911, the same year he was expelled from the movement. He converted, he said, in order to show social solidarity with the majority of Europeans by sharing their religion. Freud probably did not mind Adler's particular choice of an alternative religion; it was the choice of any religion that he found deplorable, since he had replaced traditional religion. Adler maintained that religion was a manifestation of community feeling and therefore positive. Extensive conversations with a Protestant minister, the Reverend Ernst Jahn, led him to view the insights and functions of religion as similar to those of psychoanalysis, the main difference being that psychoanalysis was science. Together they wrote a book on the subject which was banned by the Nazis.

To Freud, "the world really rewarded [Adler] richly for his service in having contradicted psychoanalysis." But of course Adler did not contradict it, he revealed it. Freud charged Adler with putting "so much stress on his almost unintelligible theories that the readers must be utterly confused." The problem was just the opposite: Adler's theories were highly intelligible and far closer to the surface of everyday life than Freud's. Freud went on in his complaint against Adler: "He is always claiming priority, putting new names on everything," when that is precisely what Jung later charged Freud with doing and what they all were doing.[21] In breaking with Adler, Freud was once again trying to plug leaks from the Kingdom of Psychoanalysis. Not unlike Freud, Jung, and other pioneers, Adler was messianic, believing that his insights into mental health and education would transform the world. In that, all the pioneers traded on the religious impulse of psychoanalysis.

When the controversy with Adler was at its height, Freud also broke with Adler's closest ally in the group, Wilhelm Stekel, who suggested that Adler was not contradicting Freud because their ideas were extremely close. Such association could not have pleased Freud. He was doctoring, not saving the world, was his official stance. Stekel in some of his theories characterized Freud's messianism, and that too would not have been appreciated. To Stekel, the neurotic believes in a great mission. Everyone starts out with that in life, he thought, but gradually gives it up. What induces neurosis, or is a symptom of it, is not giving it up. Nor would Freud have liked the theory of repression and the unconscious held by both Adler and Stekel—that repression was a trick representing something the neurotic might consciously know but not want to admit. Freud would have likewise winced at Stekel's notion that neurosis arises from repression of religion or morals. Freud was about the business of burying traditional religion, which was a competitor to his system, replacing it with his substitute premises based on religion, and preaching situational ethics bounded by the reality principle. Stekel also practiced, overtly, emotional re-education, something concealed in the Freudian system. For all these reasons Stekel was not a friend in the Freudian court. He was vilified as a "louse" guilty of "terrorism," "*Sadismus,*" and "moral insanity."[22]

Otto Rank's theories were marked by two features, birth trauma and the struggle of the creative individual against society. Birth trauma as a cause of neurosis was a repeat of Original Sin and a reaffirmation of Schopenhauer's belief in inborn human corruption. But in Rank's formulation it said something distinctly unpleasant about society: it was traumatic merely to be born into it, for society, unlike the womb, was not designed for care but rather to undermine, and to abandon upon provocation. According to Rank, the unpleasantness of the world produced a nostalgia for the womb. The sin was the world's, not the child's.

The second half of Rank's formula was equally unwelcome. He was among the first to view the patient's conflicts as being not with the self but with society, which Rank believed was a force against creativity, difference, whim. It wanted something like a lockstep affirmation of its ways, not rebels or free-thinkers, and for this reason had an undying suspicion of creativity. The goal of therapy for Rank was to confront society and stare it down (not unlike Adler's concept of the need for courage).

Another Rankian deviation was to give as much or more psychological importance to the mother as Freud gave to the father. Freud could not allow this because his entire system was based on replacing the transcendent Father with a new internal Father for the benefit of his culture. Neither Judaism nor Christianity allowed for a female as the object of veneration and fear, and neither would Freud. Such a theory would have brought home to him that his disciples did not understand the absolutely essential functions of his movement. They were not as secure as he in sticking to the point and never deviating.

Rank was another enthusiast of Nietzsche and Schopenhauer. It was he who had shown Freud the passage in Schopenhauer that described what became the Freudian theory of the etiology of neurosis; and it was he who pressed on Freud the relevance of Nietzsche for psychoanalysis. These would have been missteps in Freud's eyes. Bringing forward the connection with philosophy would not have been appreciated, nor the source in Schopenhauer and regard for Nietzsche. Rank was expelled from the club and labeled, in what was by then routine fashion, a paranoiac. Freed from the Freudian movement, he developed a school of therapy that reflected his admirations and confirmed Freud's fears. His school of psychoanalysis was called Will Therapy and advocated short treatment of a few months. In his posthumous book, *Beyond Psychology,* Rank spoke of the roots of Freudianism in politics and the rule of the middle class.

Ferenczi is thought to have broken with Freud over the caveman story, which he doubted; short therapy, which he encouraged; the importance of the present as against the past; and childhood sexual abuse as the etiology of neurosis. But he too paid a price for spying out the social in psychoanalysis and favoring it. He came to realize the force of society in fighting against the individual, in whittling him or her down to size, and to see Freudian psychoanalysis in service to that work. He wanted to support the individual and, rather than to criticize, to love. This was uncongenial to Freud, as was Ferenczi's idea of short therapy which elided a primary function of therapy as the replication of the family. When Ferenczi was dying, the word was passed around the movement that he had gone mad, although his friend and fellow analyst Michael Balint, who was present during the final illness, saw no such signs, finding Ferenczi as acute as ever. Ferenczi was a seducer of his female patients (which is what Freud feared Ferenczi meant by giving love to his patients); nevertheless he also, in a disinterested way, stood for personal and social lovingkindness, something in which Freud had little faith. Only fear would work.

Eugen Bleuler, who after his university education had studied, like

Freud, with Charcot in Paris and Bernheim in Nancy, was the most doctorly of the pioneers. Throughout his career he was closest to the clinical situation in its most demanding form, the asylum. All the elements in Freudianism that covertly revived religious premises and bore on social conduct, to the degree that he could make them out, must have been unappealing to him, even though he found Freud of interest. Of all the pioneers, he seemed to have been most aware that the mind doctors around Freud and Jung had a different agenda, and it was not his. For this reason, no doubt, Freud found him a "cool . . . partisan" who "strove too eagerly for the appearance of impartiality." Bleuler apparently could not, or was unwilling to, put into words his objections to joining the Freudian movement. "He has not given one reason for unwillingness to join," Jung reported in 1910 to his chief in Vienna, to whom he was still loyal. "The 'tone' gets on his nerves, he 'just can't,' 'not yet' at least. He has no *conscious* reason. . . ."[23] Bleuler probably did not pierce the curtain of latent psychoanalysis, only sensing what was going on. Jung and Freud, meanwhile, agreed on the explanation for Bleuler's reluctance: latent homosexual longings for Jung. Bleuler finally joined the movement in January 1911 and abruptly resigned in November of that year.

The same aspersion was cast on Bleuler as on Adler—that he possessed a "mania to make the terminology as different as possible" from Freud's.[24] Bleuler's view that mental illnesses had an organic base must also have been uncongenial to Freud, since the work of most pioneers was primarily mental in outlook and had to be in order for it to perform its latent tasks. A doctor of the insane, like Bleuler, was not the best sort to be a doctor of culture. In the 1920s, however, Bleuler returned to romantic psychology in some of his writings. The war might have impressed him with the efficacy of psychology as a cultural belief system.

The last member to be expelled from the movement while Freud was still alive was Wilhelm Reich, whose blatant mixture of psychoanalytic theory and left-wing politics, which he called Sexpol, Freud found intolerable. For some years in the 1920s Reich was a member of the Communist party in Austria and an active community organizer in the poorer quarters of Vienna, establishing clinics concerned with the nexus of politics and psychological states. He had realized the inherent latent content of psychoanalysis and was pulling it toward the causes in which he was interested.[25] In 1934 he was expelled at the instigation of Freud and with the concurrence of Jones and other leading members of the movement. Freud, by then an old man, still had his antennae intact.

Fear that their latent work might be revealed led many of the pioneers to the projective defense that everyone else was paranoid, one of their favored attacks. Jung complained: "I try to be as amiable with people as I can. But to get any results I would have to be on duty day and night. Hardly is my back turned than they start getting paranoid."[26] Such free use of the terminology of madness was common among the group and is no evidence that any of them was psychotic or "latently" so; it was simply their way of expressing disapproval.

If paranoia is taken not in the sense of a mental illness but as extreme fear, it was certainly very much a part of Freud's movement and indeed sparked it. The Freudians had mounted a covert attack on myriad political enemies whom they feared might end their whole world; so it can be said that paranoia was a symbol or jargon term for what the Freudians were feeling and acting on: palpable political fears. When Freud said about the infighting among psychologists that his enemies would tear the shirt off his back if they could, we can believe he had more on his mind than professional enemies. Freud was in a high-stakes game of European politics; somewhere in his mind he would have known it.

No wonder Freud pushed so hard for his views as against all others, and that he was led to form his own organization and to exclude heretics who threatened to reveal the true nature of psychoanalysis. What he and his colleagues were doing was not being done elsewhere in science and medicine, and for good reason: it was separate and different. Freud vaguely recognized this throughout his career, and orthodox psychiatrists, by rejecting his work, reminded him of it. He and his colleagues had left the doctoring of individuals far behind in order to doctor modern culture. Although they squabbled, although some revealed more and others less, they all persevered in their chief work. Freud had conceded early on "that we shall go along with the doctors on the first stage of our journey, but we shall soon part company with them. . . ." It had been an advantage, he said, "to accompany the doctors but the moment of parting is at hand."[27]

Each of the leading pioneers who broke with Freud established his own school of therapy with a distinctive brand name. It might be thought they did so just as companies jump on a marketing bandwagon by manufacturing copycat products. But it makes no sense to think that was their main motivation. Each was making a course correction, moving closer to the original latent impulses of psychoanalysis as a social utility, without giving away the keys to the kingdom by nakedly revealing those impulses. The changes they wrought benefited psychoanalysis: as it lost credibility as a medical or scientific treatment, it gained acclaim for its philosophical, religious, and sociological insights, precisely what Freud was keen to hide in the early years.

FREUD EVENTUALLY allowed himself to do what he discouraged others from doing. His later works were overtly sociopolitical, though still offered as psychology. Now he said openly that social psychology was the main psychology and individual psychology was only a branch of it (a lesson taught long ago by Feuerbach). *Totem and Taboo* is a parable of the destruction of the old world and acceptance of the new age. It shows how to absolve the guilt of the new middle-class rulers through deferred obedience to the murdered father (the old world), that is, through psychoanalysis, which represents that deferred obedience.

Group Psychology and the Analysis of the Ego rationalizes the acceptance by the lower classes of the leadership of their betters. It is, further, Freud's explanation and apologia for having been instrumental in the creation of psychoanalysis. As the reader will recall, he speaks of the poet who disguises the truth with lies in order to satisfy the group's longings, which are identical with the longings of their heroes. The longings Freud is speaking of in this parable are those he dealt with from the Oedipus complex right through his late works—the return of the primal father (the old world). Europe, the "poet's" audience, longed for the primal father it had loved and killed. Freud himself is the poet and the hero who returned the primal father as an image in the mind, in deferred obedience. The great deeds performed by heroes, Freud says, are not primarily their work but the work of the poet's audience, and that is why the poet's sagas are so readily accepted. The poet uses the hero as a stand-in for the whole society, which is the real hero—one of Freud's many parables about the invention of psychoanalysis. It appeared to be the work of an individual or a group but was actually the combined effort of Western culture which, having helped fashion it, readily accepted it. *Group Psychology* is also a detailed retelling of how psychoanalysis was made by the use of suggestion, which Freud associates in the book with hypnotic suggestion, his inheritance from Mesmer, Charcot, Bernheim, and the Suggestion Centers. It is his way of urging that Europe agree to become a "psychological group" and to do so in part by adopting his psychology of suggestion, fashioned for welding individuals into a new group in the same sense as Durkheim's *représentation collectiv* and Sorel's myths.

The Future of an Illusion, which treats religion as a consoling fantasy, makes the point that ideals, arts, and most especially religions convince the masses to work, attend to duty, and accept the social order, which they would otherwise prefer not to do—the opposite of the attitude of the masters of society, who are eager to manage affairs. Again, the book is a disguised commentary on his work as a substitute religion, a presentation of ideals, and an aesthetic achievement. *Civilization and Its Discontents* says, in effect, do not look for satisfaction from the social order. The social is always necessarily restrictive. You are to accept that; it is in the nature of things, which was Freud's message of social stability from the Oedipus complex forward: Follow the way of restraint, do not rebel; civilization is a constant, rebellion against it is the way of madness.

Moses and Monotheism is a parable about Freud as Moses—the outsider Egyptian as leader of the Hebrews, the outsider Jew as leader of Christian culture, the outsider psychologist as leader of the politicians, with a new salvational testament in hand. This work is the *summa* of Freud's explanations of the creation of psychoanalysis, almost every line pregnant with his latent vocation. He is the bearer of a new religion for his people (the people of modernity), compounded from the old religion; the people kill Moses (Freud's imagined martyrdom for science), but then they turn to his beliefs so that in the end he triumphs. Their adoption of his religion is again, he explains, deferred obedience (to the past), just as psychoanalysis and its acceptance were. Understood culturally and not psychoanalytically, the situation Freud allegorized was simply this: cultures move slowly; culturally, people are not terribly creative; deferred obedience copies the past precisely because the mass mind is not creative and is afraid to abandon the known (the past), so it keeps repeating it; in its repetitions under new conditions it creates originality, incrementally. All of which is not psychoanalysis but merely, perhaps majestically, human history.

It is poetic justice that Freud began *Moses* before he was expelled from Austria by the Nazis and completed it in sanctuary in England, his lifelong dreamland of liberal democratic freedom. In this little book he reaffirmed for the last time why he struggled his entire life to safeguard the new age against the enemies he had perceived from early on, the romantic, radical madmen who by the time he was composing *Moses* looked like they would at last conquer Europe, repeal the Enlightenment, and replant barbarism.

These books probably had a confessional value, allowing Freud in old age to relate what he had actually been doing throughout his career without saying so directly. All his works conceal and reveal his latent concerns and methods; they are usually read as literal accounts of his thoughts on human psychology when in fact they are figurative analyses of modern European culture and its needs. The same can be said for the works of the other leading pioneers; but Freud is the best example of this because he so clearly produced veiled parables. Usually critics got only so far as to accuse him of publishing scientific fantasies, when in fact he was composing cultural fantasies.

In commenting on the theorists who succeeded Freud, the psychologist Philip Cushman draws a distinction between Harry Stack Sullivan, who was concerned with the interpersonal, social world of the patient, and Melanie Klein, who emphasized the self in conflict with itself and therefore not with society. The therapists who took Sullivan's path, Cushman says, were led to "political marginality and a less lucrative economic future." Klein's path assured "power, influence, and financial success," becoming the better-traveled road.[28] But, he asks, was the choice made by most therapists for the Kleinian way the right one? It was, we can see, the continuation of Freud's path. Any greater incursion into the social, which he feared in his heretical disciples, would deplete the resources of psychoanalysis and eventually lead away from it. Klein made Freud's choice. Sullivan was an American example of the impulse of Adler, Stekel, Rank, and Ferenczi, which was later taken up by Erich Fromm, Karen Horncy, Abraham Maslow, Rollo May, cognitive therapists, and a long list of others who eventually privileged the social over the psychic. Their path broadened the appeal of psychoanalysis and at the same time weakened its defenses by further revealing its sources and impulses.

TWENTY-FIVE

Reasons of State

... Thou shalt be called The repairer of the breach,
The restorer of paths to dwell in.
                                        —Isaiah 58:12

The mere refusal of a truth ... is in itself no wrong;
but every imposing of a lie is a wrong. The person who
refuses to show the right path to the wanderer who has
lost his way, does not do him any wrong; but whoever
directs him on a false path certainly does.
        —Arthur Schopenhauer, *The World as Will and
                                        Representation*

THE LIBERAL ELITES of the new age needed little prompting to realize that psychoanalysis provided a new justification for law and
order that was removed from the authorities and placed in the hearts
of the people. This was surely appropriate for a democratic society
that had to believe that as law was *for* all, it was *by* and *from* all, not
just the powerful. Moreover, while destroying the last vestiges of the
gemeinschaft, the elites could hold out the promise of reconstituting
the people who were affected by this loss. Their message: Western culture, in its methods of harnessing history, could not be blamed for the
reactions of individuals. The blame, or at least the cause, was to be
found in individuals themselves, according to timeless scientific psychological principles.

   Ameliorative social considerations, new and different public policies, were less urgent when the products of every social mess had
somewhere to go, something to do—therapy, for example. Therapy
promised to treat the individual, thus obviating the need to treat the
culture that had undergone trauma and hysteria. Even more effective

about the new psychology were the beliefs that resided in the theories and the hope that resided in the practice, available to all.

Mass man had reason to love the messages of the new psychology as much as the elites. There were rules to follow, there was some certainty in life: it was colder and lonelier without them. The rules were all the more comfortable because they contained their own justification—science, which was objective, not something you could overlook or had to decide about. You might not like the rules, but as they were established by science you could not avoid them. You could not live outside science, the new source of truth in the modern world. If the rules were true, you did not have to trouble your head about rebelling against them; it would be like rebelling against nature. And if you took the way of not rebelling, you had a reason anyone could understand.

The formula you could lean on was that rebellion equaled not only sin and political disobedience, but madness. Thus mass man had a rationale for living with his conditions, just as the Reverend Wilberforce had provided a religious rationale for forbearance: the game was not in this world, it was in heaven. Now mass man could believe the game was not in the outside world, in society, in the life he lived; it was in the soul, the unconscious, mental health—and considering the state of the outside world, mental health was nothing to sneer at. The primacy of inner life was comforting because modern culture with its disciplined work did not leave much time for the outside world; work and family were enough of a chore without thinking about other things. Now you had been told that you were on the right course: the outside world was not the game, the inside world was—Wilberforce had reappeared in Freud.

Mass man also loved the concept of therapy for putting him at the center, for concentrating on him as an individual, for expressing care and promising a cure. Mass man needed guidance in the new world, and here was an approved, authoritative source, somewhere to go with your hurts. There was success to be had, because lack of success was only an illness, something that could be cured.

Mass man derived benefits from the mere existence of modern psychology, without any reference to its use in therapy, just as the culture did. By providing a new source of certainty, it helped institutionalize the new social order, and order was much prized by mass man, even if the price was high. Further, it supported the belief that the new social order was right and just. "Human beings," says the historian Theodore von Laue, "need the psychic reinforcement derived from the conviction that life as they know it is universally the best life; any suggestion to the contrary is subversive."[1]

When the new culture, looking for firmer foundations, saw that psychoanalysis revivified the Judeo-Christian tradition of ethics; made madness the fearful consequence of disobedience; put God-fear back in the mind under a new name; gave the appearance of adjusting citizens to the loss of the old world and the new tempo without referring to these changes, and could therefore direct concern away from social policies, social structures, or "the quality of life" and onto individuals; and contained such fanciful elements as sex, so attractive for so many reasons—it lifted therapy high and gave it long life. The new psychology became a cornerstone of Western democracy, with a varying quotient of importance in each nation. It was Western culture's secret weapon, its Potemkin Village.

Liberal democracy needed an affect, an emotional base, which traditional religion and a disappeared king and dynasty and family focus could no longer provide. John Locke had said that "all the power of civil authority relates only to men's civil interests." That was not enough after the old world died. Perhaps more wisely, Robert Musil in Freud's Vienna found that "feelings are just as important as constitutional law, and . . . regulations are not the really serious things in life." "Traditionally," Paul Roazen writes, "it has been the political reactionaries who have sat in judgment on men's hearts."[2] That changed when it became the task of liberals to shape a new model of governance through much hidden reliance on the old model. By a rocky course, feudalism and then absolute monarchy had become democracy; by a somewhat less rocky course, Judeo-Christianity and philosophy became psychology.

Classically, religion functioned in two ways simultaneously: managing common, universal conditions of life—fear, illness, death, the lot of all; and supporting the political arrangements of the day and in this way upholding the nation under the rubric "God with us." Theoretical psychology did the same, providing a means to face the conditions of modernity and to support the political arrangements of the day; only this time it was rationalism and science that were "with us." The substitution, while perhaps unnoticed for a time, was an affective, effective, parallel source of state support, especially as it came equipped with the scent of the old God.

Alexis de Tocqueville thought he saw budding in America "a society in which all men would feel an equal love and respect for the laws of which they consider themselves to be the authors; in which the authority of the government would be respected as necessary, and not divine; and in which the loyalty of the subject to the chief magistrate would not be a passion, but a quiet and rational persuasion."[3] By 1900 that was not enough. Conditions for many were still tyrannical, unjust, and unfair, and wild and woolly in their social manifestations for all. In the democracies there were intimations of revolution, bomb-throwing anarchists, and a great many bloody unionizing efforts. Frustrations were relieved, in part, by transferring the emotions of the past onto the chief magistrate. That will give him a new aspect, it was thought, and it did: in the nations of autocracy there came revolution, but not in the democracies.

Freud was much concerned with screens in his theory, those psychological fallacies whose unconscious function was to hide the truth. They were the false, manifest material of the psyche as opposed to the true, latent material. He was also much concerned with "contracts," that is, giving up something to get something else—for example, giving up the free play of the libido for rules and socialization and ultimately for civilization. These two concerns together are sufficient to solve the mystery of the origins and acceptance of psychotherapy.

Democracy wanted order, not too much questioning, an appearance of normality, and the popular sense that its citizens were in control. The new hierarchical system was like none seen before: a system not supported by family ascendance or family ties; or by caste as in other cultures; or by exclusion of certain sectors of the populace, as in Greece and Rome; or by an official external structure or a traditional internal religious one—and yet one that would hold. It needed a new internal structure to support the subtle external one that could not legalize the hierarchy, could only legalize the operations of society based on property and competition. It needed theoretical psychology and its punishments and rewards, its fears and guilts, its strictures and allowances. A new formulation based on new conditions was needed and supplied.

"It is an immensely complicated problem to distinguish how modern civilization, the first of which we have knowledge which does not have some formal structure of religious belief at its heart, came into being," wrote J. M. Roberts in his *History of the World*.[4] The role religion played in the old world, psychology attempted to play in ours, down to its consoling public terminology. (In private, in the office or hospital, the language was sometimes scathing and demeaning, and in asylums not infrequently accompanied by knocks, straitjackets, and numbing drugs.) The modern world, working in ways beyond the wildest expectations, revealed broken parts never fixed. Where it was going, no one knew, and if it could get to wherever with its broken parts, no one knew. The psychoanalytic pioneers were *fakirs* in this busy and colorful bazaar. What the wonder and amazement of the *fakirs* meant to Indian culture long ago, the work of the pioneers meant to ours: talismans of the sublime and a call to social order.

The abiding mystery of how psychoanalysis came to be so accepted and so influential is solved by turning the mystery around: it was culture and history that were influencing everyone, including the pioneers. The influence of the Freudians was the influence of the culture in another form, and the Freudian message was the main cultural message in another form. Freud was not separate from the culture, no more than were the other intellectual clerks; he was one of millions working for it. But he worked at an elevated level, and that is why he became not merely professionally famous but culturally famous. By working in code he could be seen as independent of his culture, operating in an objective, scientific sphere and therefore worthy of separate praise or blame. But the separateness was an illusion created by the pioneers and fostered by the culture. Freud was a decent, middle-class citizen who saw the need to support the middle-class values of liberal democracy in his day. To carry off its methods, the culture needed persuasive rationales and convincing deflections. Freud provided them insofar as he could through his "science" and practice. He was cast in bronze, cast in stone, a monument of the new social order; his image, if not on the wall of every home, was yet more or less inside the mind in every home, and in that way all the more powerful.

When the poet W. H. Auden spoke of Freud as a "whole climate of opinion," he picked up the argument at the wrong end, not realizing the full force of the actual climate of opinion in which both he and Freud lived. Similarly with Edith Kurzweil, who observed that "our entire culture is infused with Freud's ideas, and is beholden to his genius." But it was middle-class culture that infused Freud's ideas. Wherever it went, Freudianism followed. Freud was a capsule of the culture, not a shaper of it in his time; it shaped him to be its messenger. The power perceived in his utterances was actually, and not independently, the power of middle-class liberal democracy. Freud contributed a script, a narrative, a symbolic representation to bolster the European middle class; he was its poet and hero. We were beholden not to *his*

genius but to the genius of liberal democracy, which adopted the
Freudians and a good deal more in order to settle accounts with internal and external enemies. When Freud said that "totemism
is . . . both a religion and a social system," he was describing with accuracy psychoanalysis.[5]

John Updike wrote of certain American impressionist and realist
painters in the years 1885–1915 that they were "guilty of genteel eu-
phemism," presenting "the grim facts of an America in the throes of
urbanization, industrialization, and mass immigration" while shelter-
ing "the viewer from the true hardness of the case"; pioneering pho-
tographers and muckraking journalists did a better job of telling the
truth.[6] Freud and his culture similarly worked in tandem to create a
"genteel fallacy" that things were otherwise all right, but you as an individual might be suffering from one of the newly discovered mental
illnesses, and that was the problem. As for society, there was a root,
fundamental, scientific truth—the Oedipus complex—that held us all
to morality in the face of a complete breakdown of faith and belief.

"In a universe suddenly divested of illusions and lights," Albert
Camus perceived, "man feels an alien, a stranger. His exile is without
remedy since he is deprived of the memory of a lost home or the hope
of a promised land. This divorce between a man and his life, the actor
and his setting, is properly the feeling of absurdity."[7] That is what it
meant to become modern; that rent in human experience is what the
Freudians hoped to heal or hide—or heal by hiding.

Freud came near the truth some years before his death, but in-
verted it. "I perceived ever more clearly that the events of human history, the interactions between human nature, cultural development
and the precipitates of primaeval experience (the most prominent of
which is religion) are no more than a reflection of the dynamic conflicts between the ego, the id and the super-ego. . . ." For talking about
society and culture as though he were talking about individual psychology, Freud was thought to be a genius—"a great figure in intellectual history" in the judgment of Paul Roazen (and many others). So
powerful is a culture in creating the knowledges and "knowledgizers"
it wants. Freud provided a halfway house between the religion no
longer believed and some new testament based on a world without
God and with science. He could not find the new testament nor a basis
for it, so he projected the old testaments through philosophical arguments disguised as science. "In the genesis of every State we see or
guess at the figure of a great 'company-promoter,'" wrote Ortega y

Gasset.[8] Liberal democracy found among its greatest promoters the psychological theorists, and among them a promotional wizard, Sigmund Freud.

If it seems peculiar to the reader that modern psychology should have lodged within it commanding impulses about religion, ethics, politics, economics, and nostalgia, consider the explanation of Michel Foucault. Power's style, he said, when it does not wish to confront you with a gun (as it does not in democracies), displaces itself into other things, keeping the gun hidden. It inhabits those other things so subtly that often it cannot be found in them, just as power wishes it to be. One of the things in which power hides is belief systems. Since psychoanalysis was not recognized as a belief system or as the message being given out by social power, and since the message was so desirable, it was inordinately successful.

"Society," writes John P. Carse, "is a manifestation of power";[9] modern psychology was a manifestation of social power delivered as a theory and a therapy. For that reason it was able for a century to maintain itself against all vicissitudes. When it lost its reputation as science, it was still considered effective, and when it lost that, it was still considered valuable. It was hard to give up because successful beliefs are too valuable to the receivers and senders, who believe they are involved only in truth. In this transaction between receivers and senders, Freudianism was in no sense a conspiracy. Protestantism was a parallel development to capitalism, Max Weber explained. Freudianism was a parallel development to liberal democracy.

Notes

FREUD'S WORKS CITED ARE ABBREVIATED AS FOLLOWS

Works on Psychoanalysis:
SE *Standard Edition of the Complete Psychological Works of Sigmund Freud*, ed. and trans. James Strachey, 24 vols. (London, 1953–1974)
CP *Collected Papers of Sigmund Freud*, trans. under supervision of Joan Riviere, 5 vols. (New York, 1959; orig. 1949–1950)

Works in the American printing of the Standard Edition:
AS *An Autobiographical Study* (New York, 1952; orig. 1925)
CD *Civilization and Its Discontents* (New York, 1961; orig. 1930)
FI *The Future of an Illusion* (New York, 1961; orig. 1927)
FL *Five Lectures on Psycho-Analysis* (New York, 1961; orig. 1910)
GP *Group Psychology and the Analysis of the Ego* (New York, 1959; orig. 1921)
IL *Introductory Lectures on Psycho-Analysis* (New York, 1966; orig. 1915–1917)
NIL *New Introductory Lectures on Psycho-Analysis* (New York, 1965; orig. 1933)
OP *An Outline of Psycho-Analysis* (New York, 1949; orig. 1939)
TT *Totem and Taboo* (New York, 1950; orig. 1913)

And:
ID *The Interpretation of Dreams*, trans. and ed. James Strachey (New York, 1965; orig. 1900)
MM *Moses and Monotheism*, trans. Katherine Jones (New York, 1967; orig. 1939)

Letters:
F/F *The Complete Letters of Sigmund Freud to Wilhelm Fliess, 1887–1904*, trans. and ed. Jeffrey M. Masson (Cambridge, Mass., 1985)
F/J *The Freud/Jung Letters*, ed. William McGuire, trans. Ralph Manheim and R. F. C. Hull (Princeton, 1979, abridged ed.; orig. 1974)
F/P *Psychoanalysis and Faith: The Letters of Sigmund Freud and Oskar Pfister*, eds. H. Meng and E. L. Freud, trans. E. Mosbacher (New York, 1963)

LSF *The Letters of Sigmund Freud,* ed. Ernst L. Freud, trans. Tania and James Stern (New York, 1975; orig. 1960)

Preface: The Hundred-Year Mystery

1. On Freudianism as hoax, charlatanry, and myth see, e.g., Frederick Crews, *The Memory Wars: Freud's Legacy in Dispute* (New York, 1995) and *Skeptical Engagements* (New York, 1986); Robyn M. Dawes, *House of Cards: Psychotherapy, Psychology Built on Myths* (New York, 1994); Hans J. Eysenck, *Decline and Fall of the Freudian Empire* (Washington, D.C., 1990; orig. 1985); R. M. Jurevich, *The Hoax of Freudianism* (Philadelphia, 1974); Jeffrey M. Masson, *Against Therapy: Emotional Therapy and the Myth of Psychological Healing* (Monroe, Me., 1994; orig. 1988); P. B. Medawar, "Victims of Psychiatry," *New York Review of Books,* January 1, 1975, p. 17; Nat Morris, *A Man Possessed: The Case History of Sigmund Freud* (Los Angeles, 1974); E. R. and Cathy Pinckney, *The Fallacy of Freud and Psychoanalysis* (Englewood Cliffs, N.J., 1986); Thomas Szasz, *The Myth of Mental Illness: Foundations of a Theory of Personal Conduct* (New York, 1974) and *The Myth of Psychotherapy: Mental Healing as Religion, Rhetoric and Repression* (Syracuse, N.Y., 1988; orig. 1978); E. Fuller Torrey, *Freudian Fraud: The Malignant Effect of Freud's Theory on American Thought and Culture* (New York, 1992)—this is only his latest on the subject, see bibliography for others; J. H. Van den Berg, *The Changing Nature of Man: Introduction to a Historical Psychology,* trans. H. F. Croes (New York, W. W. Norton, 1961); Bernie Zilbergeld, *The Shrinking of America: Myths of Psychological Change* (Boston, 1983).

2. For the influence of cocaine, see, e.g., E. M. Thornton, *The Freudian Fallacy: An Alternative View of Freudian Theory* (Garden City, N.Y., 1984); Peter J. Swales, "Freud, Cocaine, and Sexual Chemistry: The Role of Cocaine in Freud's Conception of the Libido" (privately published, 1983); Sigmund Freud, *Cocaine Papers,* ed. and intro. Robert Byck (New York, 1974). Thornton believes that the damaging effects of cocaine might well have influenced Freud long after he stopped using the drug. On the issue of delusion, see most of the works cited in note 1, which argue it as a possible alternative to conscious hoaxing. A work that makes the case specifically is Morris's *A Man Possessed,* which argues that Freud was self-hypnotized and went on to hypnotize the world.

3. On Freud's Jewish heritage, see John Murray Cuddihy, *The Ordeal of Civility: Freud, Marx, Levi-Strauss, and the Jewish Struggle with Modernity* (New York, 1974); Dennis B. Klein, *Jewish Origins of the Psychoanalytic Movement* (Chicago, 1985); Marthe Robert, *From Oedipus to Moses: Freud's Jewish Identity,* trans. Ralph Manheim (Garden City, N.Y., 1976); Carl E. Schorske, *Fin-de-Siècle Vienna: Politics and Culture* (New York, 1981); Murray H. Sherman, ed., *Psychoanalysis and Old Vienna: Freud, Reik, Schnitzler, Kraus* (New York, 1978). The literature on this subject is voluminous; see, e.g., the works cited in Sander L. Gilman, *Freud, Race, and Gender* (Princeton, 1993), pp. 201–206, which scarcely exhaust the matter.

4. Most studies of the Freudians cite their reaction against Victorianism. For Vienna's influence on Freud, see, e.g., Billa Zanuso, *The Young Freud: The Origins of Psychoanalysis in Late Nineteenth-Century Viennese Culture* (New York, 1986) and the excellent background in Allan Janik and Stephen Toulmin, *Wittgenstein's Vienna* (New York, 1973) and William M. Johnston, *The Austrian*

Mind: An Intellectual and Social History, 1848–1938 (Berkeley, 1976). There are many other studies of Vienna and Austria's "decadence," decline, and collapse, all of which, whether stated to be or not, are background to the Freudians. On the influence of Austrian politics, in addition to Schorske, see Peter Homans, "Disappointment and the Ability to Mourn: De-Idealization as a Psychological Theme in Freud's Life, Thought, and Social Circumstance, 1906–1914," in Paul E. Stepansky, ed., *Freud: Appraisals and Reappraisals,* 3 vols. (Hillsdale, N.J., 1988), 2:3–101, and William J. McGrath, *Freud's Discovery of Psychoanalysis: The Politics of Hysteria* (Ithaca, N.Y., 1985). On Freud's father- and mother-obsession, see, e.g., Marie Balmary, *Psychoanalyzing Psychoanalysis: Freud and the Hidden Fault of the Father,* trans. Ned Lukacher (Baltimore, 1982), and Marianne Krull, *Freud and His Father,* trans. Arnold J. Pomerans (New York, 1979); to which can be added the theory, in Nicholas Rand and Maria Torok, *Questions for Freud: The Secret History of Psychoanalysis* (Cambridge, Mass., 1997), that a family secret—an uncle's conviction for counterfeiting and the possible involvement of relatives of Freud in England—determined the course of Freud's theorizing and its vacillating structure. On the influence of detective stories, see Robert Wilcocks, *Maelzel's Chess Player: Sigmund Freud and the Rhetoric of Deceit* (Lanham, Md., 1994) and Michael Shepherd, *Sherlock Holmes and the Case of Dr. Freud* (London, 1985). There is also a growing literature on Freud's effectiveness as a writer and fictionalist, e.g., Richard E. Geha, "Freud as Fictionalist: The Imaginary Worlds of Psychoanalysis," in Stepansky, *Freud: Appraisals and Reappraisals,* 2:103–160; Stanley Edgar Hyman, *The Tangled Bank: Darwin, Marx, Frazer and Freud as Imaginative Writers* (New York, 1962); Patrick Mahony, *Freud as a Writer* (New York, 1982); and Alexander Welsh, *Freud's Wishful Dream Book* (Princeton, 1994). On Marxism, see, e.g., the discussion of Georges Politzer in Sherry Turkle, *Psychoanalytic Politics: Freud's French Revolution* (New York, 1978). On social reform, see E. Fuller Torrey cited above. For Michel Foucault, see his *Madness and Civilization: A History of Insanity in the Age of Reason,* trans. Richard Howard (New York, 1988; orig. 1961) and *The Birth of the Clinic: An Archaeology of Medical Perception,* trans. A. M. Sheridan Smith (New York, 1994; orig. 1963).

5. Such comparisons are often made by those who think the Freudians borrowed from these sources or were their descendants. On philosophy, see, e.g., Patricia Herzog, "The Myth of Freud as Anti-philosopher," in Stepansky, *Freud: Appraisals and Reappraisals,* 2:163–189; Sidney Hook, ed., *Psychoanalysis, Scientific Method and Philosophy: A Symposium* (New York, 1964; orig. 1959); Thomas Mann, "Schopenhauer" and "Freud and the Future" in *Essays,* trans. H. T. Lowe-Porter (New York, 1957; orig. 1929); Paul Ricoeur, *Freud and Philosophy: An Essay on Interpretation,* trans. Dennis Savage (New Haven, 1970); Robert C. Solomon, *Continental Philosophy Since 1750: The Rise and Fall of the Self* (New York, 1988). On religion, see, e.g., Hans Kung, *Freud and the Problem of God* (New Haven, 1979); H. L. Philip, *Freud and Religious Belief* (Westport, Conn., 1974); Reuben B. Rainey, *Freud as Student of Religion: Perspectives on the Background and Development of His Thought* (Missoula, Mont., 1975); Josef Rudin, *Psychotherapy and Religion* (Notre Dame, Ind., 1968); Richard Webster, *Why Freud Was Wrong: Sin, Science, and Psychoanalysis* (New York, 1995); Victor White, O.P., *God and the Unconscious* (London, 1960; orig. 1952); Benjamin B. Wolman, ed., *Psychoanalysis and Catholicism* (New York, 1976). Books, articles, and references to philosophical and religious themes are extensive in Freudian commentary.

6. These explanations of success, in the order given, are by Jerome D. Frank, *Persuasion and Healing* (Baltimore, 1961; rev. ed. 1973); Peter L. Berger, "Towards a Sociological Understanding of Psychoanalysis," *Social Research* 32, 1 (Spring 1965), 26–41; Peter L. Berger and Thomas Luckmann, *The Social Construction of Reality* (New York, 1966); Ernest Gellner, *The Psychoanalytic Movement, or the Coming of Unreason* (London, 1985); M. Munawar Butt, *Psychology, Sin, and Society: An Essay on the Triumvirate of Psychology, Religion, and Democracy* (Lanham, Md., 1992); Philip Cushman, *Constructing the Self, Constructing America: A Cultural History of Psychotherapy* (Reading, Mass., 1995). Gullibility and yielding to authority are argued by virtually all the works cited in note 1 above.

7. LSF, p. 346.

8. On the science question, see, e.g., Frank Cioffi, "Freud and the Idea of a Pseudo-Science," in Robert Borger and Frank Cioffi, eds., *Explanation in the Behavioral Sciences* (Cambridge, England, 1970); Allen Esterson, *Seductive Mirage: An Exploration of the Work of Sigmund Freud* (New York, 1993); Adolf Grunbaum, *The Foundations of Psychoanalysis: A Philosophical Critique* (Berkeley, 1984) and *Validation in the Clinical Theory of Psychoanalysis* (Madison, Conn., 1993); Malcolm MacMillan, *Freud Evaluated: The Completed Arc* (Cambridge, Mass., 1997; orig. 1991); Frank Sulloway, *Freud, Biologist of the Mind: Beyond the Psychoanalytic Legend* (New York, 1979); Hans J. Eysenck and Glen D. Wilson, *The Experimental Study of Freudian Theories* (London, 1973); Paul Kline, *Fact and Fantasy in Freudian Theory* (London, 1972); Karl R. Popper, *The Logic of Scientific Discovery* (New York, 1965; orig. 1935), which lays out his views on scientific method, and *The Open Society and Its Enemies,* 2 vols. (Princeton, 1962), in which Freud is classified with Hegel and Marx as an "oracular philosopher" in revolt against reason; Barbara von Eckardt, "Why Freud's Research Methodology Was Unscientific," *Psychoanalysis and Contemporary Thought* 5 (1982), 459–474. On the question of the therapeutic efficacy of psychoanalysis and related therapies, see, e.g., Allen E. Bergin and Michael Lambert, "The Evaluation of Therapeutic Outcomes," in Sol L. Garfield and Allen E. Bergin, eds., *Handbook of Psychotherapy and Behavior Change: An Empirical Analysis* (New York, 1978); Marshall Edelson, *Hypothesis and Evidence in Psychoanalysis* (Chicago, 1984); Seymour Fisher and Roger P. Greenberg, *The Scientific Credibility of Freud's Theories and Therapies* (New York, 1977); Jonathan Lieberson, "Putting Freud to the Test," *New York Review of Books,* January 31, 1985, pp. 24–28; Leslie Proileau, Martha Murdock, and Nathan Brody, "An Analysis of Psychotherapy Versus Placebo Studies," *Behavioral and Brain Sciences* 6 (1983), 275–310; S. Rachman and G. T. Wilson, *The Effects of Psychological Therapy* (London, 1980); R. R. Sears, Social Science Research Council Bulletin 51, *Survey of Objective Studies of Psychoanalytic Concepts* (New York, 1943). Studies of efficacy by those outside the therapy profession tend to be negative while those inside the profession are positive. Frank, among many others, argues for the close relationship of the varying schools of analysis (e.g., those of Freud, Jung, and Adler) and concludes that all contemporary therapy methods, including those introduced by the pioneer psychoanalysts, are equal in their effect, producing improvement in the early stages of treatment as the result of novelty, after which the patient usually slips back to the original condition; and that they are in any case equal to the improvement shown in individuals who consult a priest, rabbi, or other trusted acquaintance.

9. Popper, *The Open Society,* p. 200.

Chapter 1. Before 1800: The World We Lost

1. Peter Laslett, *The World We Have Lost* (New York, 1984; 3rd ed.), pp. 79, 52, 7–8. This work focuses on England, where the old world died first and the new one was born. It also makes reference to the Continent. What it describes is applicable, with variations, to most of Europe.

2. Ibid., p. 78.

3. Ibid., p. 24.

4. Ibid., p. 4.

5. Ibid., pp. 74, 79.

6. Marc Bloch, *Feudal Society,* trans. L. A. Manyon, 2 vols. (Chicago, 1961), 1:77.

7. Marcel Proust, *Remembrance of Things Past,* trans. C. K. Scott Moncrieff and Frederick A. Blossom, 2 vols. (New York, 1927), 2:1124.

8. In E. P. Thompson, *The Making of the English Working Class* (New York, 1966; orig. 1963), p. 92.

9. Laslett, *World,* p. 221.

10. Ibid., pp. 214, 222, 218.

11. In Bloch, *Feudal,* 2:417.

12. Thompson, *Working Class,* p. 67; G. G. Coulton, *The Medieval Village* (New York, 1989; orig. 1925), p. 139.

13. Bloch, *Feudal,* 1:73, 82.

14. Laslett, *World,* pp. 5, 16; A. Gallinek, "Psychogenic Disorders and the Civilization of the Middle Ages," *American Journal of Psychiatry* 99 (1942), 42.

15. Peter N. Stearns, *European Society in Upheaval: Social History Since 1750* (New York, 1975; orig. 1967), p. 14.

16. Thompson, *Working Class,* p. 272.

17. Laslett, *World,* pp. 177, 192; Robert B. Edgerton, *Sick Societies: Challenging the Myth of Primitive Harmony* (New York, 1992), p. 87.

18. See Thompson, *Working Class,* p. 269; Modris Ecksteins, *Rites of Spring: The Great War and the Birth of the Modern Age* (Boston, 1989), p. 69; Carl G. Jung, *Modern Man in Search of a Soul,* trans. W. S. Dell and Cary F. Baynes (New York, 1933), p. 204; Peter Kropotkin, *Mutual Aid: A Factor of Evolution* (London, 1908), p. 282.

19. CP, 2:290; Stearns, *Upheaval,* p. 2.

20. Marshall Berman, *All That Is Solid Melts into Air: The Experience of Modernity* (New York, 1982), p. 60.

Chapter 2. To 1850: The World We Gained

1. Michel Foucault, *The Order of Things: An Archaeology of the Human Sciences* (New York, 1994; orig. 1966), p. 50.

2. Karl Marx, *Communist Manifesto,* in *The Portable Karl Marx,* ed. and trans. Eugene Kamenka (New York, 1983; orig. 1848), p. 207; Marx, "The Poverty of Philosophy," in Marx-Engels, *Collected Works,* 6 vols. (New York, 1976), 6:113.

3. Laslett, *World,* p. 245. The lords wanted to use the land for sheep, in order to provide the wool industry with more raw materials to meet an ever-rising demand. The lords might also have wanted to build a factory on some of the land, or lease the land and thereby raise capital for investment in other ventures.

4. Laslett, *World,* p. 18.

5. Thompson, *Working Class,* p. 401.

6. Ibid., pp. 229, 232, 832.

7. Ibid., pp. 446–447, 445; Jacques Ellul, in *Propaganda: The Formation of Men's Attitudes,* trans. Konrad Kellen and Jean Lerner (New York, 1968; orig. 1962), comments about work in the new age: "Never have men worked so much as in our society. Contrary to what is often said, man works much more nowadays than, for example, in the eighteenth century. Only the working hours have decreased. But the omnipresence of the duties of his work, the obligations and constraints, the actual working conditions, the intensity of work that never ends, make it weigh much more heavily on men today than on men in the past. Every modern man works more than the slave of long ago . . ." (pp. 140–141).

8. Thompson, *Working Class,* p. 137.

9. In Paul Johnson, *The Birth of the Modern: World Society 1815–1830* (New York, 1991), p. 880; George Dangerfield, *The Strange Death of Liberal England, 1910–1914* (New York, 1961; orig. 1935), p. 441.

10. Thompson, *Working Class,* p. 93.

11. Johnson, *Birth,* p. 880.

12. Ibid., p. 754. Hannah Arendt observes that loneliness "became sufficiently great to be noticed by others and recorded by history only in the nineteenth century." This loneliness was unbearable, she says, because it was "the loss of one's self." See her *Origins of Totalitarianism* (New York, 1975), pp. 476–477.

13. Thompson, *Working Class,* pp. 446–447, 632, 746–747; in Eugene Kamenka, *The Philosophy of Ludwig Feuerbach* (New York, 1970; orig. 1969), p. 13.

14. Thompson, *Working Class,* p. 746; in George Duveau, *1848: The Making of a Revolution,* trans. Anne Carter (New York, 1967), p. 197.

15. Thompson, *Working Class,* pp. 402, 401.

16. His message was considered so subversive that rather than placing him on trial he was declared insane (as he may well have been) and removed to an asylum for the remainder of his days.

17. In Elizabeth L. Eisenstein, "The End of the Book?," *American Scholar,* Autumn 1995, p. 542.

18. Harriet Beecher Stowe, *Uncle Tom's Cabin* (New York, 1985; orig. 1852), p. 551.

19. Laslett, *World,* p. 193.

20. Michel Foucault, *Power/Knowledge: Selected Interviews and Other Writings, 1972–1977,* ed. Colon Gordon, trans. Colon Gordon, Leo Marshall, and Kate Soper (New York, 1980), p. 211.

21. Thompson, *Working Class,* p. 402.

Chapter 3. The Philosophy of Pleasure

1. In Robert M. Heilbroner, *The Worldly Philosophers: The Lives, Times and Ideas of the Great Economic Thinkers* (New York, 1992; orig. 1953), p. 40.

2. Ibid., p. 37.

3. Arthur Schopenhauer, *The World as Will and Representation,* trans. E. F. J. Payne, 2 vols. (New York, 1969; orig. *Die Welt als Wille und Vorstellung,* 1818–1844), 1:3. An earlier translation by R. B. Haldane and J. Kemp renders the title *The World as Will and Idea* and the opening sentence, with perhaps greater simplicity and directness, as: "'The world is my idea':—this is a truth which holds good for everything that lives and knows. . . ."

4. In Isaiah Berlin, *The Magus of the North: J. G. Hamann and the Origins of Modern Irrationalism,* ed. Henry Hardy (New York, 1993), p. 100.

5. In Graeme Garrard, "Joseph de Maistre's Civilization and Its Discontents," *Journal of the History of Ideas* 57, 3 (July 1996), pp. 443–444.

6. In Berlin, *Magus,* p. 96.

7. In Robert H. Greene, "Instinct of Nature: Natural Law, Synderesis, and the Moral Sense," *Journal of the History of Ideas* 58, 2 (April 1997), p. 174.

8. Schopenhauer, *World,* 2:513.

9. In Thomas Mann, *Essays,* p. 297.

10. In Will Durant, *The Story of Philosophy* (Garden City, N.Y., 1926), pp. 355, 358–359, 374.

11. In Kamenka, *Feuerbach,* p. 138.

12. In Fritz Stern, *The Politics of Cultural Despair: A Study in the Rise of the German Ideology* (Berkeley, 1974), pp. 40, 60.

13. In Hans Barth, *Truth and Ideology,* trans. Frederic Lilge (Berkeley, 1976), p. 176. Nietzsche's harsh language is sometimes taken as a metaphor for the quest for spiritual nobility, and that often seems to be the case; but that is not the way a good deal of his philosophy reads or what many thought it meant. It was not difficult to take alarm at his strident deprecation of democracy, the "little man," and the bourgeoisie, or his particular brand of anti-Hebraism (if it was not anti-Semitism).

Chapter 4. Riding for a Fall

1. Eugen Weber, *France, Fin de Siècle* (Cambridge, Mass., 1986) pp. 117, 119.

2. In John Weiss, *Ideology of Death: Why the Holocaust Happened in Germany* (Chicago, 1996), p. 163.

3. In E. J. Hobsbawm, *The Age of Capital, 1848–1875* (New York, 1975), p. 267.

4. Ibid., p. 268.

5. In Weiss, *Ideology,* p. 185.

6. Thomas P. Neill, *Modern Europe: A Popular History* (Garden City, N.Y., 1970), p. 107.

7. In Schorske, *Vienna,* p. 156.

8. Neill, *Europe,* p. 111.

9. Weber, *France,* p. 127.

10. Ecksteins, *Rites,* p. 83.

11. See, e.g., Nicholas Goodrick-Clarke, *The Occult Roots of Nazism: Secret Aryan Cults and Their Influence on Nazi Ideology; The Ariophists of Austria and Germany, 1890–1935* (New York, 1985).

12. Schopenhauer, *World,* 2:311, 503.

Chapter 5. Crisis

1. Max Nordau, *Degeneration* (Lincoln, Nebr., 1968; orig. 1892), p. 2.

2. The full title in English: *Treatise of the Physical, Intellectual, and Moral Degenerations of the Human Race and of the Causes That Produce These Maladive Varieties.*

3. The theory of degeneracy was apparently making two social claims by

means of a medical one. On the one hand, the lower classes were being observed closely for the first time, since in the past they had not counted as members of society, and under the conditions of urbanization and mass poverty they were shocking to the better class of people such as Morel. On the other hand, tarring the aristocracy with the brush of degeneracy, as Nordau did, recognized that the aristocracy—not its individual members—was degenerating, which it was (that is to say, it was disappearing as an institution). Both claims flattered the "healthy" middle class.

4. Nordau, *Degeneration,* p. 557. Since Nordau identified himself proudly as a Jew and a Zionist, it is worse than ironic that degeneration theory was seized upon by racism and eugenics. The "degenerate" cranium these theorists identified, and the "degenerate" face, nose, lips, palate, eyes, ears, and teeth, would later be found in Jews, Gypsies, homosexuals, and others that some groups disliked. There would be "sense" as well as madness to Hitler's exhibition of works by masters of modernism under the title "Degenerate Art."

5. Jules Renard, *The Journal of Jules Renard,* eds. and trans. Louise Bogan and Elizabeth Roget (New York, 1964), p. 129—a thorough modernist, he found that "the world makes no sense" (p. 206), and "The word that is most true is . . . 'nothing'" (p. 192); in Francis Haskell, "Art and Apocalypse," *New York Review of Books,* July 15, 1993, pp. 27, 26; in Vladimir Dedijer, *The Road to Sarajevo* (New York, 1966), p. 232.

6. In Haskell, "Art," p. 27.

7. In Paul Johnson, *A History of the Jews* (New York, 1988), p. 421.

8. In *New York Times Book Review* (May 30, 1993), p. 6; José Ortega y Gasset, *The Revolt of the Masses* (New York, 1957; orig. 1930), pp. 189–190.

9. In Van den Berg, *Changing,* p. 65

10. In Andrew Delbanco, "John Dewey's America" (review of Alan Ryan's *John Dewey and the High Tide of American Liberalism*), Partisan Review 3 (Summer 1996), p. 515.

11. Arendt, *Totalitarianism,* p. 147.

12. In the Great War the troops condemned to live in the mud of the front lines for four years gained the admiring title *Frontschwein* (front pigs) from the Germans and *poilus* (the hairy ones, suggesting unkempt and also animal-like) from the French. See Ecksteins, *Rites,* p. 146.

13. In Henri F. Ellenberger, *The Discovery of the Unconscious: The History and Evolution of Dynamic Psychiatry* (New York, 1970), p. 321. Ellenberger's monumental study of psychoanalysis is indispensable as background to the major pioneer theorists (Freud, Jung, Adler, Janet). Schreber published a famous account of his insanity and mission, *Memoirs of My Nervous Illness* (1903), still considered by modern psychiatry to be the most detailed rendering of psychosis ever written. At Jung's suggestion, Freud studied it and "analyzed" its author, reaching the conclusion that Schreber suffered from a repressed homosexual desire for his father (see CP, 3:387–470, "Psycho-Analytical Notes Upon an Autobiographical Account of a Case of Paranoia (Dementia Paranoides)"). Schreber, by his own account, feared that evil forces were plotting to murder his soul.

Chapter 6. The Freudians: The Liberal Imagination

1. Ellenberger, *Unconscious,* p. 463. Whyte sees Freud as a middle-class Victorian who "spent most of his life afraid of his own fancy, and sought security in

a stern moralism, a naive rationalism, an exact materialistic physiology, and a psychology based on the attempt to eliminate complexity" (p. 179).

2. Ibid., p. 465.

3. Otto Rank, *Beyond Psychology* (New York, 1958; orig. 1941), p. 28.

4. Erich Fromm, *Crisis of Psychoanalysis: Essays on Freud, Marx, and Social Psychology* (New York, 1991; orig. 1970), pp. 17–18.

5. When surrealism hailed Freud as its founding spirit, he rejected the proffered honor. Had it ever come to his ears that André Breton, the founder of the movement, described the perfect expression of surrealism as a person going out into the street with a gun and firing at people at random, he might well have been deeply shocked.

6. Max Horkheimer, *Critique of Instrumental Reason: Lectures and Essays Since the End of World War II* (New York, 1974; orig. 1967), p. 104.

7. ID, p. 230.

8. AS, p. 7.

9. Schorske, *Vienna*, p. 189; Rainey, *Religion*, p. 23; Philip Rieff, *Freud: The Mind of the Moralist* (New York, 1959), pp. 247–248.

10. Schorske, *Vienna*, p. 185.

11. ID, p. 242.

12. Ibid., p. 251, note 3.

13. *Leonardo*, SE 11:123.

14. Rainey, *Religion*, p. 19. Freud associated two Jewish figures with this dream: Victor Adler, his fellow student at university who also became a physician and later head of the Social Democrats, and Adolf Fischhof, a medical student of an older generation who had helped lead the student uprising during the Revolution of 1848. Freud's ambitions were apparently in conflict between his early goal in life, politics, and the one he settled on, medicine. There was a link between the two in the dream, for in the preceding year he had proposed the grand theory of the Oedipus complex, whose central idea concerned *lèse-majesté* against the father, whom to Freud was the symbolic representation of the king.

15. ID, pp. 175–176; in Max Eastman, *Great Companions: Critical Memoirs of Some Famous Friends* (New York, 1959; orig. 1926), p. 178; William M. Johnston, *The Austrian Mind* (Berkeley, 1983; orig. 1972), p. 240; Schorske, *Vienna*: "patricide replaces regicide; psychoanalysis overcomes history" (p. 197). The Freudians were somewhat opaque regarding practical politics, in contrast to cultural politics. Freud had good things to say about Mussolini and Stalin before the drift of events indicated that he should retract his statements. When Hitler was in the driver's seat, Jung found good things to say about him. In 1944, with the war obviously lost, Jung collaborated with the U.S. spy mission in Zurich. In 1938, by which time many leading Austrian Jewish intellectuals had already fled, Freud escaped Vienna at the last minute and only through the intervention of President Roosevelt and the American ambassador to France.

16. ID, p. 244 (italics in original). Acting under the guise of thinking is one of the main themes of *Totem and Taboo*. That there was a duplicity involved in doing so—i.e., operating under a disguise—apparently did not go unnoticed by Freud. In an 1898 dream he is questioned regarding a theft, cleared, and dismissed, but he cannot leave because he cannot find his hat. "My not being able to find my hat meant accordingly: 'After all, you're *not* an honest man'" (ID, p. 372).

17. FI, p. 8; in Schorske, *Vienna*, p. 156. The Jewish Freudians and other middle-class Jews often extended their elitism to their poor brethren in whom they

saw crudity and other gauche traits. Freud's occasional comments about poor Jews are scathing. One reported comment may have been as much about himself: "Jews have less self-confidence but more chutzpah" (in Joseph Wortis, *Fragments of an Analysis with Freud* [New York, 1954], p. 145).

18. In Rainey, *Religion*, p. 46.

19. Ibid., pp. 38, 15.

20. In F/F, p. 271.

21. LSF, pp. 18–19, 367.

22. Rainey, *Religion*, p. 143.

23. AS, p. 7.

24. Ibid., p. 32.

Chapter 7. In the Shadow of Decline: Freud's Miraculous Years

1. Robert C. Solomon, *Continental Philosophy Since 1750: The Rise and Fall of the Self* (New York, 1990; orig. 1988), p. 139; in Paul Roazen, *Freud: Political and Social Thought* (New York, 1986; orig. 1968), p. 258.

2. Janik and Toulmin give as an example of this ability to disguise reality the case of Alfred Redl, deputy director of Austrian Army Intelligence, a secret homosexual and spy for Russia who "succeeded *precisely because* he could assume a mask that completely veiled his real personality" (*Vienna*, p. 61); Johnston, *Austrian*, p. 240; in ibid., p. 206.

3. Schorske, *Vienna*, p. 185.

4. In E. James Lieberman, *Acts of Will: The Life and Work of Otto Rank* (Amherst, Mass., 1993), p. 14; McGrath, *Discovery*, p. 231. Commenting on a study of the influence of Hasidic mysticism on psychoanalysis, Ellenberger writes that the author "considerably exaggerated the intensity of anti-Semitism in Vienna in Freud's youth and mature years" (*Unconscious*, p. 544). Just limiting the focus to the period surrounding the turn of the century suggests that Ellenberger miscalculated on this point.

5. Michel Foucault, *The History of Sexuality*, trans. Robert Hurely, 3 vols. (New York, 1978–1985), 1:130.

6. F/F, pp. 129, 133. Already in 1888 Freud was searching for the singular key to human psychology, telling a journalist, "Mankind has always harbored the longing to be able to open all secrets with a single key" (F/F, p. 25).

7. Ibid., p. 184.

8. Ibid., pp. 181, 146, 169.

9. Ibid., pp. 180, 95, 398.

10. Ibid., pp. 219, 220, 224.

11. Ibid., pp. 283, 285, 286.

12. Ibid., pp. 95, 389, 403. About poverty, Freud told Fliess, "My mood also depends very strongly on my earnings. Money is laughing gas to me. . . . I came to know the helplessness of poverty and continually fear it" (F/F, p. 374). Later he told him of "my one weak point, my fear of poverty. . . ." (F/F, p. 412).

13. Nordau, *Degeneration*, p. 555.

Chapter 8. A Climate of Ideas

1. Schorske, *Vienna*, p. 120; McGrath, *Discovery*, p. 314.

2. Schorske, *Vienna*, pp. 165, 172.

3. Ibid., pp. 174, 175; McGrath, *Discovery,* pp. 315, 316.

4. Schorske, *Vienna,* p. 146.

5. Ibid., p. 164.

6. Ibid., p. 186.

7. Like the psychopoliticians, most of the clerks were right wing, anti-Semitic, and violently nationalistic. There were also centrist clerks upholding the liberal interests of the bourgeoisie. Some, like Marx and Péguy, were socialists. Still others, like Nietzsche, were not nationalists but culturalists, crossing all geographic borders; they wanted to shore up the new age or tear it down. "For half a century" the intellectuals, "whose function was to thwart the realism of nations . . . have labored to excite it with all their power and with complete decision of purpose. For this reason I dare to call their attitude 'The Treason of the Intellectuals.' If I look for its causes, I see profound causes which forbid me to look upon this movement as a mere fashion, to which the contrary movement might succeed tomorrow." Julien Benda, *The Treason of the Intellectuals,* trans. Richard Aldington (Boston, 1959; orig. 1927), p. 158. Several years before *Treason,* Benda published *Belphegor,* an echo of Weininger, in which Jews and women were the problem for the French; they were at the heart of romanticism, which was against the virile manliness of the French nation. In *Treason* Benda turned away from these views, casting suspicion on the peddlers of anti-Semitism, false science, practicality, materialism, and all the other attitudes of the new clerks.

8. Benda, *Treason,* pp. 45, 47, 39, 107, 167.

9. Ibid., pp. 75, 108–109, 103, 125, 5, 150, 57. To the clerk, group, race, and nation were practical synonyms, all referring to the interest with which the clerk aligned himself. The clerks were "religious realists" whose practical interests "assume the character of mysticism . . . of a religious adoration." Visionaries irritated them, and they hurled "anathemas at every sort of idealism," attacking "the religion of the Infinite with a precision of hatred, a skill in depreciation, unparalleled even in the Church." For them, "God must affirm a physical and not a metaphysical existence," and must be the means of securing "practical advantages" (Benda, *Treason,* pp. 22, 43, 176, 165, 155).

10. In Ecksteins, *Rites,* p. 194; Fritz Stern, *The Politics of Cultural Despair: A Study in the Rise of the German Ideology* (Berkeley, 1974), p. 126; Ecksteins, *Rites,* p. 194.

11. Benda, *Treason,* pp. 154, 164, 147, 153.

12. Ibid., p. 234; Nordau, *Degeneration,* pp. vi–vii; Benda, *Treason,* p. 76.

13. Ibid., p. 234; in Stern, *Politics,* p. 125; Benda, *Treason,* pp. 234, 107. "These men claim . . . the most purely scientific spirit. And they owe the special attention with which they are listened to by men of action entirely to this claim that they are men of learning, men who are fighting for a truth discovered in the austerity of the laboratory" (Benda, *Treason,* p. 50).

14. Ibid., pp. 123–124, 62, 64.

15. Ibid., pp. 144, 169, 174.

16. F/F, p. 251.

17. For Freud's use of cocaine and its derivative ecgonine, see, e.g., Thornton, *Fallacy,* who argues that Freud's abuse of cocaine was largely responsible for the creation of psychoanalysis, inducing sexual mania, manic certainty, the physical symptoms that led to his self-analysis, and a mild psychosis as the result of permanent brain damage. She gives as an example of the manic certainty induced by cocaine the case of a British colonial officer who under the influence of cocaine had a dream in which he discovered the answer to the riddle of the universe. He

roused himself to write it down and went back to sleep. In the morning he discovered what he had written: "The banana is great, but the skin is greater." Another man, under the influence of nitrous oxide (laughing gas) expressed the ultimate truth as: "Well, it's sort of green light" (Thornton, *Fallacy*, p. 123).

18. She later became a psychoanalyst under Freud's guidance. Fliess did not practice his theories only on others; he had surgery along the same lines performed on himself, and he performed similar surgery on Freud, all of it conforming to his theories about the importance of the nose in organ function. Victorian medicine, rife with these bizarre surgical procedures, was just as prodigal with novel medical theories, as for example Fliess's idea that labor pains would disappear with the application of cocaine to the nasal mucosa (which a medical writer checked and found to be without foundation), and the notion of Samuel Schenk, director of the Embryological Institute in Vienna, that diet could assure women having male babies. See F/F, pp. 310, note, and p. 313, note 1.

19. F/F, p. 310, note 4; several other medical men were dealing with this theory at the time, but it never acquired any utility in medical practice as far as can be determined. Fliess published his notions at least as early as 1893, so I am not suggesting that his ideas were known only to Freud; only that Freud's intense personal and professional relationship with Fliess over a period of seventeen years yielded something not available to his other colleagues in the movement.

Chapter 9. Soul Psychology: Mind over Matter

1. In a typical trick the shaman would place a bloody worm in his mouth, suck the patient's diseased area, and then draw out the bloody worm from his mouth as evidence of having extracted the foreign element that was upsetting the patient's equilibrium.

2. I am indebted to Ellenberger's researches into romantic soul psychology for these summaries.

3. E. J. Hobsbawm, *The Age of Capital, 1848–1875* (New York, 1975), p. 169.

4. In Ellenberger, *Unconscious,* p. 751; in F/F, p. 26.

5. AS, pp. 15, 16, 18.

6. Ibid., pp. 37, 75. The theme of the "omnipotence of thoughts," Freud's version of mind over matter, runs through his work to the very end.

7. In McGrath, *Discovery,* p. 159. When in August 1893 Charcot died, the obituary in a Paris newspaper spoke of his "inordinate pride, absorbing egoism, and self-aggrandizement verging on histrionics" (in Ellenberger, *Unconscious,* p. 769). These same terms critics would apply later to Freud, whose own obituary of Charcot called the Frenchman an Adam who named the animals in Eden (i.e., defined the mental diseases). Although Freud studied with Charcot for only four months (but kept up with his work before and after their meeting), he forever after considered him not only a medical but a spiritual guide, valuing him, he said, as "a worldly priest" (in McGrath, *Discovery,* p. 158).

8. GP, p. 58.

9. In Ellenberger, *Unconscious,* p. 765. Since most psychic treatments at that time owed a debt to suggestion and therefore to hypnotism, when one of Charcot's pupils, Joseph Babinski, investigated the nature of hypnotism in order to demystify it, he created an uproar among soul psychologists. In 1913 Babinski put Charcot's theories of hysteria to the test and disproved them, with, however, little effect on what had become the conventional psychological wisdom.

10. In ibid., p. 757.

11. Ibid., p. 773.

12. The idea of an unconscious travels through the Hindu Vedantas, Plato, Greek mystics such as Plotinus and Dionysius Areopagita, medieval mystics and alchemists, later mystics such as Boehme, philosophers such as Leibniz, Herbart, Kant, Schelling, and the philosophers of nature, and then Schopenhauer, C. G. Carus, and Hartmann, among many others. Despite this long history, the power of conventional wisdom can be seen in the blurb on the back cover of an edition of Freud's papers, which states that Freud "built his science on the basis of hypotheses that were contradictory to many scientific views then current. For example, he *assumed* the presence of the unconscious mind—an underworld that only a few poets had hinted at. . . ." See Philip Rieff, ed., *Freud: General Psychological Theory* (New York, 1963). Similarly, a short survey of Freud's life and work—Penelope Balogh's *Freud: A Biographical Introduction* (New York, 1971)—begins: "Until Freud published *Studies on Hysteria* in 1895, the idea that there was an unconscious part of the human mind attracted only an occasional philosopher or poet" (p. 7). Whyte notes that in 1868, when Freud was twelve years old, Hartmann had already delineated twenty-six characteristics of the unconscious. The year before Hartmann's book, Henry Maudsley declared that "The most important part of mental actions, the essential process on which thinking depends, is unconscious mental activity" (in Lancelot L. Whyte, *The Unconscious Before Freud* [New York, 1960], p. 162). Schopenhauer had said the same a half-century before. Freud would state that the conscious grows out of the unconscious, which was Schopenhauer's formulation. Sometimes Freud was more modest than his champions, referring, e.g., to what "psychoanalysis has discovered, or, if it is preferred, has deduced or conjectured" (CP, 5:327, note 2).

13. Ellenberger, *Unconscious,* p. 314.

14. Stern, *Politics,* p. 146. Whyte points out that by the 1870s such ideas were common in the intellectual salons of Europe.

15. Gustav Le Bon, *The Crowd* (Dunwoody, Ga., 1968; orig. 1895), pp. 20–21.

Chapter 10. Theory and Practice: Desire's Vicissitudes

1. FL, p. 44. I employ the word "theory," in this chapter and elsewhere in my study, for convenience, because it was so much a part of Freudian usage, but the reader should be aware that Freudian theories were at best hypotheses. In science, theories are a step beyond hypotheses, after a threshold amount of validated evidence has been collected. Occasionally Freud used the term "hypothesis," but usually he referred to his concepts as theories, his justification being his belief that evidence was supplied by his clinical practice rather than laboratory experiments or the accumulation of quantified data.

2. NIL, p. 111. This idea went back to the beginning of Freud's thought on neurosis, repeating the soul-psychology theory of unconscious danger signals.

3. The course of mental illness from trauma to repression, latency period, and the return of the trauma in the form of symptoms, was borrowed from Charcot, who probably adopted it from Schopenhauer. The belief that a traumatic idea or representation in the mind can produce mental illness was borrowed from nineteenth-century soul psychology, and is again an adaptation of Schopenhauer. Sensitive to the Schopenhauer connection, Freud wrote in one of his lectures, "You

may perhaps shrug your shoulders and say: 'That isn't natural science, it's Schopenhauer's philosophy!'" (NIL, p. 134).

4. In Armand M. Nicholi, Jr., ed., *The New Harvard Guide to Psychiatry* (Cambridge, Mass., 1988), p. 211. Freud spoke of this concept as "the splitting of the mind and dissociation of the personality," and as "hysterical dissociation (the splitting of consciousness)" (FL, pp. 18–19).

5. F/F, pp. 37, 215, 51; NIL, p. 112. While from the beginning there was no scientific proof of the power of mind over matter producing mental illness, it remained the psychoanalytic basis for attempting to relieve mental illness by changing biochemistry through a therapy of words that theoretically changed ideas or representations in the mind. This lack of a scientific basis did not change over all the years in which psychoanalysis gained acceptance as a therapeutic methodology. But in the loose way the clerks used the term, and in the loose way figures such as Morel, Lombroso, and Nordau practiced it, the pioneers can be said to have been doing science. On the point of mind over matter, which Freud often referred to as the "omnipotence of thoughts," there is a close connection between nineteenth-century suggestion theory, what Freud understood as primitive magic, what he called obsessional neurosis, and psychoanalysis. In several places he speaks of the "omnipotence of thoughts" (which by the fin de siècle was a soul-psychology doctrine) as the kernel of primitive magic and obsessional neurosis, without acknowledging that it was the basis for psychoanalytic theory and practice (belief in the omnipotence of ideas or representations, i.e., *Vorstellungen*). See his discussion of the connection between primitive magic and obsessional neurosis in TT, p. 107ff. See also below, note 15.

6. FL, p. 54.

7. For years after announcing the Oedipus theory, Freud continued to give attention to sexual seduction in youth as a viable etiology for neurosis.

8. CP, 1:125; FL, p. 51. Displaying his collections of Shakespeare and the Greek tragedies to a local playwright, Freud exclaimed, "Here are my masters," explaining that the true source of his theories was the intuition of the great poets (in Ellenberger, *Unconscious,* p. 460).

9. CD, p. 90. This was what Kant was reflecting, Freud believed, in the categorical imperative.

10. FL, p. 51; F/F, p. 272. Freud used the phrase "family romance" in correspondence with Fliess and in 1909 contributed a long note to Otto Rank's *The Myth of the Birth of the Hero* under the title "Family Romances," by which time it was one of his names for the Oedipus complex. Freud also used the term "father complex" with the same meaning.

11. FL, pp. 54, 58. Determinism was a philosophical doctrine from at least the time of Spinoza, who was reflecting the much older religious view that a higher power, God, determined all. It was subsequently a doctrine of deism.

12. CP, 2:279; FL, p. 55; FL, p. 13; MM, p. 89.

13. CP, 2:252, 280.

14. TT, p. 178.

15. MM, p. 169. He had a similar response to the charge that Lamarckian biology was a discredited scientific theory. To the contrary, he said, it was an example of "the power of unconscious ideas over one's own body, of which we see the remnant in hysteria, in short the 'omnipotence of thoughts.'" For Freud, Lamarckism confirmed the soul-psychology idea of mind over matter, and he maintained this position to the end: "The present attitude of biological science . . . refuses to hear of the inheritance of acquired characteristics by succeed-

ing generations. I, however . . . cannot do without this factor in biological evolution" (from a letter to the Berlin psychoanalyst Karl Abraham, quoted in J. N. Isbister, *Freud: An Introduction to His Life and Work* [Cambridge, England, 1985], p. 226).

16. Over time, different views were taken of the problem of neurosis. To some theorists, the id was too strong and had to be tamed; to others, the superego was too strong and had to be reined in; to others, the ego was not strong enough and had to be reinforced.

17. FL, p. 33.

18. ID, p. 382.

19. Freud sometimes meant symbols to be understood in relation to a particular patient and the theories of psychoanalysis; they did not have absolutely fixed meanings. At other times he meant them to have the same meanings in the case of all patients. See, e.g., his vacillation in the many editions of the dream book and commentary on it by Rand and Torok in their Chapter 3, "Dream Interpretation: Free Association or Universal Symbolism?"

20. NIL, p. 85.

21. Ibid., p. 179.

22. FI, p. 63; CP, 5:74.

23. AS, pp. 54, 56: "At Easter 1908, the friends of the young science met at Salzburg, agreed upon the regular repetition of similar informal congresses and arranged for the publication of a journal. . . . At the second Congress, held at Nuremberg in 1910, they formed themselves, upon the proposal of Ferenczi, into an 'International Psycho-Analytical Association' divided into a number of local societies but under a common president."

24. GP, p. 3; "The Question of Lay Analysis," SE, 20:253; AS, p. 82: "My interest, after making a lifelong detour through the natural sciences, medicine and psychotherapy, returned to the cultural problems which had fascinated me long before, when I was a youth and scarcely old enough for thinking."

Chapter 11. The Art of the Symbol

1. FL, p. 55.

2. ID, p. 528. Freud theorized that the unconscious does not know No, it only knows Yes. Following this line of reasoning, he decided that the unconscious does not know contraries or contradictions: "The way in which dreams treat the category of contraries and contradictions is highly remarkable. It is simply disregarded. . . . They show a particular preference for combining contraries into a unity or for representing them as one and the same thing" (ID, p. 353). He says again: "The logical laws of thought do not apply to the id, and this is true above all of the law of contradiction. Contrary impulses exist side by side, without cancelling each other out or diminishing each other, at the most they may converge to form compromises under the dominating economic pressure toward the discharge of energy" (NIL, p. 92). Psychoanalysis, in the contradictions which have been found in it, followed this law, which has an analog in the contradictions that appear in systems of thought and in society without ever being harmonized but sometimes softened by compromise formulations and methodologies. There is of course a contradiction in Freud's very theory of contradiction in that in anticathexis, for example, the unconscious knows what it does not like and knows what it wants to reject, i.e., what it says No to.

3. CP, 3:457.

4. CP, 2:282; GP, p. 96.

5. In his dream book Freud drew the parallel between mental illness and the Fall (which is contained in the psychoanalytic model of mental illness, whether he referred to it or not) when he gave the example of Faust telling of the dream of "a lovely apple-tree/ on which two lovely apples shown," to which a witch responds, "Apples have been desired by you,/ Since first in Paradise they grew . . ." (ID, p. 321). In adopting Schopenhauer's theory of mental trauma, Charcot like Schopenhauer was also recalling the Fall.

6. Jerrold Seigel, *Bohemian Paris: Culture, Politics and the Boundaries of Bourgeois Life, 1830–1930* (New York, 1987), pp. 174–175.

7. CP, 2:279; FL, p. 56. In contrasting the neurotic, the psychotic, and the healthy person, Freud lays out the situation of the Freudians with some exactitude: "In psychosis, flight at the beginning is succeeded by an active phase of reconstruction, while in neurosis obedience at the beginning is followed by a subsequent attempt at flight. Or, to express it in yet another way, neurosis does not deny the existence of reality, it merely tries to ignore it; psychosis denies it and tries to substitute something else for it. A reaction which combines features of both these is the one we call normal or 'healthy'; it denies reality as little as neurosis, but then, like a psychosis, is concerned with effecting a change in it. This expedient normal attitude leads naturally to some active achievement in the outer world and is not content, like a psychosis, with establishing the alteration itself; it is no longer *auto-plastic* but *allo-plastic*" (CP, 2:279–280).

8. In Whyte, *Unconscious*, p. 165.

9. F/F, pp. 109–110, 112; see also note 7 above. In Jones's biography Freud speaks of Jesus as quite possibly "an ordinary deluded creature" (3:377).

10. In Webster, *Wrong*, p. 545.

11. F/F, p. 255.

12. In Andrew Fitzmaurice, "Classical Rhetoric and the Promotion of the New World," *Journal of the History of Ideas* 58, 2 (April 1997), 228–229; NIL, p. 90. A reading of Fitzmaurice's article reveals the elements of rhetoric adopted by the Freudians in their efforts at persuasion: familiarity (to set the audience at ease and enhance comprehension), strangeness (to add bite, avoid boredom, and weld the familiar with the strange), involvement of the emotions, moralism (to assure the audience that they were being persuaded to the right course), and benefits. J. H. Elliott is quoted to the effect, "It may be that the human mind has an inherent need to fall back on the familiar object and the standard image, in order to come to terms with the shock of the unfamiliar" (p. 222). The utility of rhetoric as not just words but action is registered by John Donne in a sermon on the Apostles: "There are reckoned in this booke, 22 sermons of the Apostles; and yet the booke is not called the Preaching, but the Practice, not the Words, but the Acts of the Apostles" (p. 242).

13. MM, p. 170. The nineteenth century presented a notable case of the symbolic representation of a desired achievement. Maelzel's Chess Player was an automaton that seemed to be playing winning chess when in fact it contained, hidden from view, an expert chess-playing dwarf to whom positions on the board were conveyed by a clever arrangement of mirrors. The simple and true explanation of the matter having been rendered invisible, the automaton created a sensational illusion that for a time was believed to be fact, a wonder of nineteenth-century science and engineering. A similar wizardry—if I am not stretching the parallel too far—was practiced on another level by such figures as Morel, Nordau, and Lom-

broso, who rendered social and political opinions in medicalese, and by Hegel and Schopenhauer before, the one supporting Germany's monarchy by reinventing Christianity under the guise of philosophy, and the other criticizing the new age's freedom and competition by reinventing Christianity and Hindo-Buddhism under the same guise. (Modern technology actually produced the automaton envisioned in Maelzel's Chess Player: the IBM computer in a laboratory of the Massachusetts Institute of Technology that in 1997 defeated the reigning world chess champion, Gary Kasparov.)

Chapter 12. The Old in the New

1. ID, p. 294; in Jeffrey M. Masson, *Final Analysis: The Making and Unmaking of a Psychoanalyst* (Reading, Mass., 1990), p. 173. Mothers remain a favorite target. See, e.g., Rozsika Parker, *Mother Love/Mother Hate: The Power of Maternal Ambivalence* (New York, 1996), and Diane Eyer, *Motherguilt: How Our Culture Blames Mothers for What's Wrong with Society* (New York, 1997).

2. Jacques Ellul, *The Technological Society,* trans. John Wilkinson (New York, 1964; orig. 1954), pp. 82–83.

3. Freud recreated a family in the psychoanalytic movement; he was the father, the disciples were the children. Disobedient members such as Adler, Jung, and Ferenczi left, "rebelling" against the father. For a discussion of these rebellions, see Chapter 25. By the time of the *Introductory Lectures* (1915–1917), Freud had expressed the clear case about transference: "We suspect . . . that the whole readiness for these feelings is derived from elsewhere, that they were already prepared in the patient and, upon the opportunity offered by the analytic treatment, are transferred on to the person of the doctor." Therefore "a transference is present in the patient from the beginning of the treatment and for a while is the most powerful motive in its advance" (ILP, pp. 550–551). Therapy began where the old family left off; refinding the family was, truly, a powerful motive in the patient and in the culture—in the patient for seeking and continuing treatment, and in the culture for valuing therapy as valid. The *Introductory Lectures* also reveal another significance that transference held for Freud: he considered it an assist to suggestion. Under the influence of positive feelings for the therapist transferred from the family, the patient, Freud theorized, was more open to ideas the therapist thought correct and helpful. In this way suggestion became an integral part not only of the theory but of the therapy process itself; it was a prime aspect of the methodology, little different from what the Suggestion Centers proposed and practiced.

4. His story has attracted considerable attention, not only because of the length of the treatment but because of the strained interpretations on which the treatment was based. See Patrick Mahony, *Cries of the Wolf Man* (New York, 1984); Muriel Gardiner, ed., *The Wolf-Man by the Wolf-Man* (New York, 1971); Karin Obholzer, *The Wolf-Man: Conversations with Freud's Patient—Sixty Years Later,* trans. Michael Shaw (New York, 1982). The Wolf-Man told his own story in Sergius Pankejeff, *The Wolf-Man* (New York, 1991).

5. Only in recent years, as the result of efficiencies imposed by medical insurance plans, has short therapy, which elides a basic element in the romance of the process, become a prominent approach.

6. A recent approach moves parent guilt to the level of biology by using data that seem to suggest that mental illness may run in families (a reactivation of

nineteenth-century degeneration theory). This does not change the concept of parent responsibility for mental illness, only its rationale. Psychiatry continues to want to say, from its Freudian legacy, that the parents did it, even though the patient is also responsible—an ambiguity of therapy theory.

7. CP, 3:457.

8. MM, p. 167.

9. While individual therapy reproduced the old family, group therapy later reproduced the old community.

10. GP, p. 88.

11. Otto Rank, *Beyond Psychology* (New York, 1958; orig. 1941), pp. 36–37.

12. Rank, *Psychology,* p. 39.

13. Gellner, *Movement,* p. 40.

14. In Daniel G. Brenner, ed., *Baker Encyclopedia of Psychology* (Grand Rapids, Mich., 1985), p. 353.

15. In Thomas Johnston, *Freud and Political Thought* (New York, 1965), p. 116; MM, p. 172.

16. Freud tells the story of a legendary doctor whose invariable diagnosis, whatever the patient's complaints, was: "bewitched." Did patients look down on the doctor for this? No, they were pleased, indicating to other patients that this "was a fellow who understood things" (NIL, pp. 174–175). Freud used this story to illustrate Adler's inadequacy in adopting the one-note theory of inferiority, without mentioning that he had adopted the same approach with his theory of sexual etiology.

17. Cuddihy, *Ordeal,* p. 136.

18. F/F, p. 169.

Chapter 13. Themes

1. NIL, pp. 78–79.

2. *The Portable Nietzsche,* trans. and ed. Walter Kaufmann (New York, 1968), pp. 95–96; TT, p. 180.

3. MM, pp. 89–90.

4. CP. 4:349; CP, 5:128; CP, 5:316; Rank, *Psychology,* p. 46.

5. Rank, *Psychology,* p. 35.

6. "The Claims of Psycho-Analysis to Scientific Interest," SE, 13:186; in Ecksteins, *Rites,* p. 117.

7. V. N. Voloshinov, *Freudianism: A Critical Sketch,* trans. I. R. Titunik, ed. with Neal H. Bruss (Bloomington, Ind., 1987; orig. 1927), p. 75.

Chapter 14. The Return of God and King

1. *The Portable Nietzsche,* p. 501. Nietzsche's grandfather, Friedrich August Ludwig, was given an honorary degree by the University of Koenigsberg in 1796 for *Gamaliel,* a book that tried to respond to the spiritual unrest stemming from the French Revolution.

2. As a Jew and an apostate from religion, Freud would have been impressed by an earlier attempt to render the principles of the Bible natural and rational— the one by Spinoza. But the example most prominent to Freud and his age was

Kant, at the head of German Idealist philosophy, and the more general Enlightenment movement of deism.

3. Philip Rieff, *The Triumph of the Therapeutic* (New York, 1966), p. 306; F/F, p. 249. Freud neglects the commandment against lying (bearing false witness) for reasons discussed in Chapters 18 and 19.

4. In Balmary, *Psychoanalysis,* pp. 170–171. In the same place she quotes Michel LeBris: "Modern Barbarism began when the intellectual pretended to have done with God—one will think what one wishes of that, but it is a *fact.*" This bitter complaint was not without justice, but the old religious world was not without barbarism, and it was not only intellectuals who had rejected the old God, it was the whole culture of the West—the same culture that was playing a role in the Freudian revival of a Godly morality without God.

5. In Ecksteins, *Rites,* p. 118. For the relationship of law and psychoanalysis as rhetorics of defense and denunciation in support of a social order, see Peter Goodrich, *Oedipus Lex: Psychoanalysis, History, Law* (Berkeley, 1995). One of Goodrich's conclusions, echoing Szasz, is that "rhetoric is the premodern form of psychoanalysis" (p. 181); but Szasz believes it remains the modern form.

6. Freud charged Marx (in NIL, pp. 220–223) with diverting internal aggression to the outside, without acknowledging that he himself was diverting external aggression to the inside.

7. Against great odds he labored tirelessly to improve the working, living, and educational conditions of the poor. In the long run he and the other critics of the liberal order contributed to many changes.

8. Szasz, *Myth of Mental Illness,* p. 7.

9. Gellner, *Movement,* p. 143.

10. FL, p. 59.

11. F/F, p. 268; Gellner, *Movement,* p. 128.

12. NIL, p. 208.

13. What Freud sought is what he said Moses achieved when "the decision was made to concede all power to one God only and not to suffer any other gods beside him" (MM, p. 171).

14. Foucault, *Power/Knowledge,* pp. 94–95.

15. *The Portable Nietzsche,* p. 515.

16. Peter Murphy, "The Birth of Humanism," *Thesis Eleven* 40 (1995), 45.

17. F/P, p. 61.

18. Jacques Ellul, *Propaganda: The Formation of Men's Attitudes,* trans. Konrad Kellen and Jean Lerner (New York, 1968; orig. 1962), p. 152.

19. Schopenhauer, *World,* 1:523, 525.

20. Eysenck, *Decline,* p. 203.

21. ID, pp. 295–296.

22. Ibid., p. 295.

23. For a discussion of Jarry against the backdrop of the fin de siècle, see Seigel, *Paris,* pp. 310–322.

24. CD, p. 84 (italics added).

Chapter 15. That Old-Time Religion

1. While religion was ostensibly distant from their scientific work, the pioneers were not unaware of what they were doing. Jung infused a religious outlook into his work almost from the start; Adler regarded the cosmic order as the guide

to psychic health; Janet recognized psychoanalysis as a substitute for religion. Freud recalled, with a good deal of self-awareness, that "My deepest engrossment in the Bible story (almost as soon as I had learned the art of reading) had, as I recognized much later, an enduring effect upon the direction of my interest" (AS, pp. 6–7). In the preface to the Hebrew translation of *Totem and Taboo* he gave assurance that while he was an atheist, the essence of Judaism remained with him. Although it might be difficult to discover in his work, he hoped that one day it would become accessible to the "scientific mind" (TT, p. xxxi).

2. AS, p. 77: "man's sense of guilt ('original sin')"—Original Sin in relation to guilt, the caveman killing, and the Oedipus complex is also discussed by Freud in TT, GP, FI, and CD; Thornton, *Fallacy,* p. 122.

3. Howard Gardner, *Creating Minds: An Anatomy of Creativity Seen Through the Lives of Freud, Einstein, Picasso, Stravinsky, Eliot, Graham, and Gandhi* (New York, 1993), p. 72. Adler thought the Oedipus theory was a remote, artificial interpretation of the role of sex in psychology. Consider power, the community feeling, and the cosmic order, he urged. "It is extremely doubtful whether Oedipus, who came to Thebes as a young man, sought the fulfillment of his sexual desires in the aging Jocasta," Joseph Rattner pointed out in his *Alfred Adler,* trans. Harry Zohn (New York, 1983), p. 193. (Rattner's objection is ahistorical if not amythical; sexual attraction was rarely first on the list of factors in royal marriages.) Breuer, Jung, and James similarly thought Freud's emphasis on sex queer, mistaken, obsessional, which must be taken as further examples of how Freud, working to establish beliefs for the new world by reinventing beliefs of the old world, was met by misunderstanding from colleagues and critics.

4. Freud may have been groping for a structural explanation here: an action and its consequences built into the human condition and therefore not inherited but always repeated. That is perhaps what he meant by using Lamarckism and what Christian theology actually meant by Original Sin.

5. The psychoanalyst Gregory Zilboorg, in his *Psychoanalysis and Religion* (New York, 1962), p. 45, explains that the "concept of original sin or of the original fall of man finds its empirical counterpart in the findings of psychoanalysis," when what the Freudians were actually seeking were empirical (really symbolical) counterparts to their biblical source. Zilboorg refers to the "findings of psychoanalysis," but it was replication that was in progress, so that a fresh belief system could at the same time be familiar. That we are all a little neurotic was expressed in the Old Testament in such a passage as Ecclesiastes 9:2–3, in which we are pictured as all more or less evil: ". . . as is the good, so is the sinner. . . . The heart of the sons of men is full of evil, and the madness is in their heart while they live, and after that they go to the dead." Paul Roazen (*Freud: Political and Social Thought* [New York, 1970], p. 128) thinks Freud used psychoanalysis "to extend our understanding of religious phenomena," when Freud used it, rather, to *reproduce* religion as science. Jung, Janet, and Adler, and sometimes Fromm, similarly clung to the religious model, but they often wandered into obscure corners of the East, myths, and shamanism. With indomitable concentration, Freud focused on what was best known: the Judeo-Christian tradition, which was rich enough to form the basis of his entire system and subsequently the main lines of all psychoanalytic psychology. He received the palm over his competitors in part because he took the trouble to give careful attention to the conceptual selections he made so that they would have maximal effect through maximal familiarity.

6. In Rainey, *Religion,* p. 147.

7. As in John 6, where eating the flesh of Christ and drinking his blood are

the way to salvation. AS, p. 77: "The ceremony of the totem-feast still survives with but little distortion in the form of Communion," an observation Freud said he "found in the works of Robertson Smith and Frazer." The Viennese audience, so Catholic, was prepared to understand the totem meal as Holy Communion, and so were the other societies of Europe so firmly based in the past on Catholicism. It was easy to find in it the retelling of sin and salvation, which is why, we must believe, Freud was right in thinking that it fit firmly within the total construct he was forming, even if Robertson Smith's scholarship was wrong.

8. MM, p. 153. This parable, presented as a scientific hypothesis, was first stated in *Totem* and then repeated in *Group Psychology* and *Moses*.

9. Ibid., p. 175.

10. FL, p. 59.

11. Another Christian cure method embedded in psychoanalysis is exorcism, whose great period was the Middle Ages. The exorcist does not speak in his own name but in the name of a higher power (in Freud's case, science; in the case of later therapists, in the name of Freud, Jung, Adler, etc.). He must have absolute confidence in this higher power and in his own abilities (which the pioneers invariably expressed). He presents himself as a threat to the intruder spirit (in therapy, the intruder is the unconscious or the mental illness) while encouraging the possessed (replicating the ambiguous theory that the mental illness is not the patient's fault but the "fault" of the unconscious). The exorcism takes place in a structured environment (the Freudian treatment session), with sometimes a few onlookers (in the case of teaching hospitals and other training institutions, by means of two-way mirrors allowing students to view the proceedings). The exorcist seeks to make the intruder (the unconscious, the neurosis) speak. The process may take days, weeks, months, years. (See Ellenberger, *Unconscious,* p. 145.) And still deeper in the European imagination were the magical cures of shamanism, a primordial root of religion, which psychoanalysts and all soul psychologists reflected in an age when European imperialism was rediscovering shamanism among colonized peoples.

12. Joe Kennedy Adams, *Secrets of the Trade: Madness, Creativity and Ideology* (New York, 1971), p. 75.

13. LSF, p. 390; in Gardner, *Minds,* p. 76.

14. In Peter Gay, *A Godless Jew: Freud, Atheism, and the Making of Psychoanalysis* (New Haven, 1987), p. 145. Paraphrasing Le Bon, Freud observed that a leader "must himself be held in fascination by a strong faith (in an idea) in order to awaken the group's faith; he must possess a strong and imposing will, which the group, which has no will of its own, can accept from him" (GP, p. 17).

15. In Rainey, *Religion,* p. 69; F/F, p. 111.

16. F/F, p. 356.

17. Alasdair MacIntyre, *A Short History of Ethics* (New York, 1966), p. 111. A recent study by Suzanne R. Kirschner finds that contemporary post-Freudian psychoanalytical theory is founded on cultural and religious sources; but that was always the case, starting with Freud, as I have been demonstrating. See her *The Religious and Romantic Origins of Psychoanalysis: Individuation and Integration in Post-Freudian Theory* (New York, 1996).

18. Fredric Jameson, *The Political Unconscious: Narrative as a Socially Symbolic Art* (Ithaca, N.Y., 1982), p. 69.

19. CD, pp. 65–67.

20. F/F, p. 112; MM, p. 133. Typical of many commentators who believed that Freud had discovered a new science of the mind, Paul Roazen summarized

Freud's main insights in this way: "The notion of a human nature in conflict with itself, disrupted by opposition of social and asocial inclinations, the view that the social self develops from an asocial nucleus . . . and finally the conception that reason's control can be extended by a detailed knowledge of repressed asocial tendencies—all this was not known before Freud" (*Freud*, pp. 249–250). This passage scarcely needs rewriting to conform to religious wisdom: The notion of a human nature in conflict with itself (Original Sin), disrupted by opposition of religious and irreligious inclinations (to do good or to do bad), the view that the religious self develops from an irreligious nucleus (Original Sin again), and finally the conception that God's control can be extended by detailed knowledge of irreligious tendencies—all of this was Judeo-Christianity and Schopenhauer, long before Freud gave thought or set pen to paper. All of it, one could say, is ur-religion, revived by the Freudians to give new resolve and comfort to an age without traditional religion and prone to hysteria. Neill, in his *Modern Europe,* conveys the conventional opinion that "Freud . . . remains the originator of a new science that has taught men much about themselves that they never knew before" (p. 160). But they knew it all before, when they called it religion.

Chapter 16. Infantilism: Heroes, Villains, Sermons

1. In Ernest Jones, *The Life and Work of Sigmund Freud,* 3 vols. (New York, 1953–1957), 3:205.

2. In Webster, *Wrong,* p. 327; in CP, 5:122 Freud gave *"The Cornerstones of Psycho-analytic Theory.* The assumption that there are unconscious mental processes, the recognition of the theory of resistance and repression, the appreciation of the importance of sexuality and the Oedipus complex—these constitute the principal subject-matter of psycho-analysis and the foundations of its theory. No one who cannot accept them all should count himself a psycho-analyst."

3. FL, pp. 44, 56; CP, 1:289.

4. CD, p. 22; in NIL religion is "the counterpart to the neurosis which individual civilized men have to go through in their passage from childhood to maturity" (p. 208).

5. *The Basic Writings of C. G. Jung,* ed. Violet Staub de Laszlo (New York, 1993), p. 248. "Infantile" was the second most common insult the pioneers flung at colleagues with whom they were dissatisfied, the first being "paranoid."

6. In Masson, *Therapy,* pp. 49, 51.

7. Michael Crozier commenting on "the owner of capital" beginning in the eighteenth century, in "The Civic Paradigm and Shaftesbury," *Thesis Eleven* 40 (1995), 73.

8. FL, p. 55.

9. Rank, *Psychology,* p. 283.

10. Ibid.

11. FI, p. 30. Not for nothing Freud told Fliess, "The ancient gods still exist, because I obtained a few recently, among them a stone Janus who looks at me with his two faces in a very superior manner." And a bit later he told Fliess about "my double-wish theory of the neuroses . . ." (F/F, pp. 361, 375). Like everyday reality, Freud had in mind the unruly child, and what could be—the trained, obedient child. This was an example of how, in Freudianism, the same symbol can have two, opposite meanings: things can be "reversed into their negative" (TT, p. 161) and/or into their positive. The unconscious, says Freud, does not know con-

tradition. The double vision of the child as good and bad paralleled the nine-teenth-century public idealization of the sweet, pure child and the private practice, noted by Billa Zanuso, of subjecting the child to "corporal punishment," "the withholding of pleasures," and "a systematic reign of terror as a means of enforcing parental discipline" (Zanuso, *Freud,* pp. 14, 16).

12. CP, 5:284.
13. FL, p. 60.

Chapter 17. More Heroes, Villains, Sermons

1. CP, 3:470; in Paul H. Ornstein, "Heinz Kohut's Legacy," *Partisan Review* 4 (1996), 616.
2. Stern, *Politics,* p. 129.
3. FL, p. 49.
4. Ibid., p. 53.
5. Roazen, *Freud,* pp. 230, 207, 231.
6. FL, p. 19.

Chapter 18. The Lessons of Sex

1. ILP, p. 443; Peter J. Swales, "Freud, Cocaine, and Sexual Chemistry: The Role of Cocaine in Freud's Conception of the Libido" (privately published, 1983), p. 19.
2. CP, 1:193; ID, p. 149.
3. FL, pp. 61–62.
4. CP, 5:171, 170.
5. FL, p. 43; Herman Nunberg and Ernest Federn, eds., *Minutes of the Vienna Psychoanalytic Society* (New York, 1967), 2:89; FL, p. 61.
6. CP, 5:92.
7. In Kamenka, *Feuerbach,* p. 143; LSF, p. 341. It was on this point that in the early years of the movement Jung and Adler began to diverge from Freud. Jung, with a deeply religious outlook, could not give up what Freud called illusion. Adler, with a deeply socialist outlook, looked forward to a better day for all through political change, and Freud could not forgive that either. The last disciple expelled while Freud was yet alive, Wilhelm Reich, was a Communist. Those who sought to revive old beliefs or better the world in some other way found themselves inevitably in conflict with Freud, who accepted the inward sense of a spiritless humanity which was the "discovery" of the modern West. For more on this, see Chapter 25.
8. Guy Debord, *The Society of the Spectacle,* trans. Donald Nicholson-Smith (New York, 1995; orig. 1967), p. 18.
9. ILP, p. 61.
10. In Webster, *Wrong,* p. 404; in Ellenberger, *Unconscious,* p. 576.
11. Exemplified by Filippo Maria, last of the Visconti dukes of Milan, who was "unequalled in his capacity to disguise his thoughts. He never said openly what he wanted, but veiled everything by his peculiar way of expressing it." Elias Canetti, *Crowds and Power,* trans. Carol Stewart (New York, 1962; orig. 1960), p. 293. In the first quarter of the twentieth century, Carl Schmitt found "distrust of the world and every man"; a "feeling of eternal deception"; doubt "whether Christ and the Antichrist are distinguishable" (in John P. McCormick, "Nietzsche,

Schmitt and the Antichrist," *Philosophy & Social Criticism* 21, 3 [July 1995], 71). In a national survey conducted by the *Washington Post,* Harvard University, and the Kaiser Foundation, reported in January 1996, two-thirds of those surveyed said that most people can't be trusted.

12. CP, 4:355.

13. Whyte, *Unconscious,* p. 179. Commenting on the competing therapy systems, Paul R. McHugh writes: "Now that the end of the century approaches and much of the dust of controversy among the followers and the independents has settled, it is clear that the great protagonists of psychodynamics, Freud, Jung, Adler—like Baskin-Robbins ice cream—differ in flavor but not in essential ingredients." See his "Jung at Heart," *American Scholar,* Autumn 1995, p. 617.

Chapter 19. The Uses of the Unconscious

1. OP, p. 87; NIL, p. 91.

2. Whyte, *Unconscious,* p. 71.

3. CP, 5:297.

4. AS, p. 64.

5. Rank, *Psychology,* p. 15.

6. FL, pp. 26, 30; FI, p. 15 (italics added).

7. The British psychoanalyst R. E. Money-Kryle gives this example of political "psychopathology" in his *Psychoanalysis and Politics: A Contribution to the Psychology of Politics and Morals* (London, 1951); see his Chapter 9, "On the Analysis of Political Motives."

8. Friedrich Nietzsche, *The Birth of Tragedy* and *The Genealogy of Morals,* trans. Francis Golffing (Garden City, N.Y., 1956; origs. 1872 and 1877), p. 228 (italics added).

9. Andrew Samuels, *The Political Psyche* (New York, 1993), pp. 90, 99, 102.

10. Otto Rank, *Truth and Reality,* trans. Jessie Taft (New York, 1978; orig. 1936), p. 43.

11. Roazen, *Freud,* pp. 24–25.

12. CP, 5:277.

13. ID, p. 654.

Chapter 20. Neurosis: Diverting Social Hysteria

1. IL, p. 319.

2. NIL, p. 106.

3. Ibid., pp. 105, 114.

4. AS, p. 26.

5. AS, pp. 14–15. Freud's further comment on Erb is instructive in view of his own case: "The realization that the work of the greatest name in German neuropathology had no more relation to [medical] reality than some 'Egyptian dreambook,' such as is sold in cheap bookshops, was painful, but it helped to rid me of another shred of the innocent faith in authority from which I was not yet free."

6. Ibid., p. 60.

7. FL, p. 55.

8. F/F, p. 109.

9. Ibid., p. 108.

10. Ibid., p. 109.

11. GP, p. 87.

12. Rieff, *Freud,* p. 355.

13. Joe Kennedy Adams, *Secrets of the Trade: Madness, Creativity, and Ideology* (New York, 1971), p. 92.

14. GP, p. 28.

15. Karl Kraus proposed how to deal with the psychoanalytic denigration of genius: "Nerve doctors who ruin genius for us by calling it pathological should have their skulls bashed in by the genius' collected works . . ." (in Janik and Toulmin, *Vienna,* p. 77).

Chapter 21. Wishes, Dreams, Repression, Regression

1. For this, among other reasons, Jung and Adler began to diverge from Freud. They admitted the substantiality of survival needs in human psychology. Freud did that in his own life too, but very little in his theories; e.g., he told Fliess that his mind was strong enough to face anything except the prospect of poverty.

2. F/F, p. 251.

3. CP, 1:281; FL, p. 10.

4. CP, 2:254. Freud was used to employing economic analogies for psychic energy, a practice he shared with several other soul psychologists in Europe and America. There was a certain amount of this energy, he theorized, which he viewed as psychic capital, and the question was always how and on what it was to be spent.

5. Ibid.

6. Ibid.

7. CP, 3:139.

8. C. G. Jung, *Modern Man in Search of a Soul,* trans. W. S. Dell and Cary F. Baynes (New York, no date; orig. 1933), p. 33. Freud commented frequently on the biblical connections of dream interpretation, as for example in ID, p. 129.

9. Ellenberger, *Unconscious,* p. 311.

10. F/F, p. 255; ID, pp. 128–129.

11. AS, pp. 47, 48.

12. Ibid., p. 49.

13. Ibid., p. 50.

14. Ibid.

15. F/F, p. 354.

16. Ibid., p. 371.

17. FL, p. 21.

18. CP, 4:328–349.

19. F/F, p. 252.

20. FL, p. 10.

Chapter 22. The Triumph of Suggestion

1. F/F, p. 251. Rank thought Freud used the couch as an aid to recovering memory, encouraging regression back to the trauma. At the personal level, Freud admitted to using it because he did not like patients looking at him. At the therapeutic level, he introduced it when he replaced hypnotism with free association, relaxation on the couch serving as a substitute for the relaxation of the conscious mind induced by hypnosis. Freud also thought the couch encouraged the trans-

ference process. In what they thought the function was, both Rank and Freud were right as far as latent psychoanalysis was concerned.

2. ILP, pp. 543, 561. In a near-perfect social analysis in the guise of an individual analysis, Freud writes further about the success of treatment—that is, when the operation I have described achieves its goal: "We have succeeded in reviving the old conflict which led to repression and in bringing up for revision the process that was then decided. The new material we produce includes, first, the reminder that the earlier decision led to illness and the promise that a different path will lead to recovery, and, secondly, the enormous change in all the circumstances that has taken place since the time of the original rejection. Then the ego was feeble, infantile, and may perhaps have had grounds for banning the demands of the libido as a danger. Today it has grown strong and experienced, and moreover has a helper at hand in the shape of the doctor. Thus we may expect to lead the revived conflict to a better outcome than that which ended in repression, and, as I have said, in hysteria and in anxiety and obsessional neuroses success proves us in general to be correct" (ILP, p. 545). In other words, he has said that under the cultural doctor's guidance, ideas about the past and present are revised, making the patient—the culture—stronger. Then Freud turns to the cases he says psychoanalysis cannot handle—paranoiacs, melancholics, sufferers from dementia praecox. They fit those recalcitrant segments of the population (the romantic radicals) which the Freudian belief system cannot reach because the radicals are armed with a belief system stronger than democracy, Christianity, or psychoanalysis, based on fanatical fantasies and nostalgias. That gap in the psyche which psychoanalysis was designed to fill was in the radicals already filled.

3. ID, p. 251.

4. Freud's longest explication of psychoanalysis, the *Introductory Lectures,* concludes with a justification of suggestion (from which I quoted earlier). Psychoanalysis, he says, does not use direct suggestion (hypnosis); it employs, rather, the more subtle form of indirect suggestion. Direct suggestion, he argues, may have some effect on symptoms but cannot probe the cause and motive of the illness, an achievement possible only by using indirect suggestion.

5. CP, 5:92. The intellectual kinship between Freud and his nephew is usually traced in ambiguous, tangential terms, as, e.g., in Stewart Justman, "Freud and His Nephew," *Social Research* 61, 4 (Summer 1994), 457–476. At the level of culture, not clients, Freud's work was closely related to his nephew's, which he always denied, seeing Bernays's work as low and his as high, just as he saw religion as false and psychoanalysis as science, separated by an unbridgeable gulf. How easily the transition could be made from one to the other is illustrated by Bernays asking Freud's American disciple A. A. Brill what would be a good public relations theme for promoting cigarette smoking among women. Brill was quick with his response: freedom. Smoking could symbolize liberation from the bonds of male domination.

6. Freud objected to "the magic word 'suggestion'" (GP, p. 27) and Le Bon's term "contagion" as too indefinite and ill defined, preferring instead "libido" and "identification." He did not doubt there was an irrational power of persuasion that swayed the citizenry, but he understood it as love and imitation of the loved one, which he said were the main factors in hypnotism, suggestion, and therapy (see Chapter 4, "Suggestion and Libido" in GP).

Chapter 23. The Camouflage of Authority

1. In Ronald W. Clark, *Freud: The Man and the Cause* (New York, 1980), p. 371. Among vociferous doubters was Gustav Aschaffenburg, a psychiatrist who was a constant thorn in the side of the movement. In 1906 he proclaimed "that the doctrines of so-called psychoanalysis are well-founded neither theoretically nor empirically, that its therapeutic effect is unproved, that its permanent gain for clinical psychiatry is nil, that it conveys the impression of unscientific method, that its pursuit is dangerous for the patient and compromising for the physician, and finally that its only permanent interest is in the field of the history of Kultur." An American psychiatrist, Samuel A. Tannenbaum, no less unequivocal, declared that "Psychoanalysis is a pseudoscience like palmistry, graphology and phrenology. It has enough of a foundation in fact to deceive the uncritical and, as in Christian Science, there is a certain modicum of truth in it" (in Clark, *Freud,* pp. 371, 414–415). When a certain Dr. Hoche, also a psychiatrist, spoke on psychoanalysis at a medical congress in 1910, he titled his paper "An Epidemic of Insanity Among Doctors." According to Jung, Hoche charged the pioneers with "mysticism, sectarianism, arcane jargon, epidemic of hysteria, dangerousness, etc." (F/J, pp. 147, 150). Freud's essay on Leonardo, in which he portrayed the painter as a latent homosexual, was greeted by a review entitled "Genius Spat Upon."

2. Rank remarks that "epoch-making theories, whether they deal with biology, sociology or psychological phenomena, owe their popular appeal to the ideological concept of universality . . . project[ing] specific conditions of a certain time and age . . . into a timeless and placeless universe" (*Psychology,* pp. 33–34). The claim to psychoanalytic universality possessed a hidden viability which is not often considered. Machiavelli had dealt with rulers not only as a class but as individuals, with their differences of style and approach to their role; Shakespeare did the same, passing over the psychology of the groundlings in silence, disgust, or jokes. At that time only a psychology of the nobleman was required. A universal psychology was needed only when the groundlings entered history after the twin revolutions. The new psychology, democratically recognizing all individuals as it could not fail to do in the new age when all individuals constituted the sovereign of the state, proclaimed a generalized psychology of *all.* In this narrower sense Freudianism was universal. Further, to be functional socially and politically, it had to include all, else its theories, messages, and instructions would not be seen as applicable to all. Universality in a Western context was also relevant to the latent themes of psychoanalysis: family, community, identity, motivation, belief, religion and the state, the power of the past, the power of mass fantasies, social and political order, freedom, modernity, the modern flight of morality, the death of God, the relation of classes.

3. Thought reform as a model for psychotherapy, Frank notes, "illustrates the use of detailed reviews of the sufferer's past history, with special emphasis on guilt-arousing episodes, followed by the opportunity for confession and atonement, as a means of producing attitude modification" (*Persuasion,* p. 105). In the secular state, where God was dead or no longer knowably present, the therapy session remained the elemental situation of sinfulness in which the patient was to answer for a crime. Freud usually warned his patients before the start of therapy that they were in for an ordeal.

4. Adams, *Secrets,* p. 74. Freud told Fliess (F/F, p. 227) that he had ordered a copy of one of the medieval tomes designating the signs of witchery and heresy, the famous *Malleus Maleficarum* or *The Hammer of Witches.* If one looks at the 374 mental disorders described in the fourth edition of *Diagnostic and Statistical*

Manual of Mental Disorders, published by the American Psychiatric Association, it becomes apparent that one is studying an equivalent tome. Critics charge the *DSM* with supplying diagnoses for the convenience of payment by health insurance companies and adding new "conditions" in order to increase business. See, e.g., Herb Kutchins and Stuart A. Kirk, *DSM: The Psychiatric Bible and the Creation of Mental Disorders* (New York, 1997). In outlining the margins within which the "well"—as before the faithful—may operate, the *DSM* can be read as a cool, suave alternative to Nordau's hysterical medicalizing of social issues and a continuation of Morel's concepts of degeneration and stigmata.

5. Canetti, *Crowds,* pp. 284–285.

6. Ibid., p. 294; F/J, p. 246.

7. The pioneers were not chary of using attack-as-defense on each other, as Jung noticed. When established theories were questioned or new ones proposed, the movement's reaction was to attack in defense of the established order by wielding the cudgel of mental illness. New ideas, said Jung, were written off as the product of complexes. "The protective function of [psychoanalysis]," he urged, "badly needs unmasking," for he had arrived at "the painful conclusion" that the majority of analysts were misusing their discipline "for the purpose of devaluing others and their progress by insinuations about complexes (as though that explained anything. A wretched theory!)." Jung was taken care of by the rumor that "my libido theory is the product of anal eroticism. When I consider *who* cooked up this theory [probably Freud, who manufactured mental diagnoses for most of his dissenting disciples] I fear for the future of analysis" (F/J, p. 247). Here, attack-as-defense swung back to hit some of the pioneers.

8. In Rieff, *Freud,* p. 151. The patient was always in the position of having made a Jungian psychological "mistake" or, in the words of Freud, being "psychologically wrong" (CP, 5:171).

9. In Paul Roazen, *Freud and His Followers* (New York, 1975), p. 153.

10. John Farrell, *Freud's Paranoid Quest: Psychoanalysis and Modern Suspicion* (New York, 1996).

11. FL, p. 41; CP, 5:172–174. Freud would not allow the thought that it could be disturbing for physical scientists to see pseudo-scientific theories purveyed as empirical science, and that this alone could make them critical to the point of anger. Nor would he concede that the Oedipal conflict was any more disturbing than Original Sin, and that whatever anxiety it invoked was caused first by the repetition that it was anxiety provoking (said to be so by his scientific psychology), and second by its echoing timeless invocations against murder and incest and timeless messages from authority to follow along and not rebel, making it a powerful accusation. Further, he failed to consider that professional murderers, bearing a far greater burden of guilt than the Oedipal fantasy, often showed no outward signs of mental disturbance and justified their crimes as work (one need only offer members of the Cosa Nostra as evidence). The saliency of the Oedipal crime for mass society was that a "crime" was needed that it could be said innocent people were thinking of unconsciously.

12. See, e.g., Gardner, *Minds, passim*; Ellenberger, *Unconscious,* also deals with this subject, pp. 39, 210, 216, 447–448, 672–673, 713, 736, 889–892.

13. ID, pp. 353–354; F/F, p. 202; Rieff, *Freud,* p. 364.

14. Rieff, *Freud,* p. 366.

15. Ibid., p. 273.

16. In Webster, *Wrong,* p. 305.

Chapter 24. The Politics of Concealment

1. AS, p. 59. Privately the pioneers were not delicate in their language. When a skeptical psychiatrist visited Freud to discuss psychoanalysis, Freud admitted to treating him to "the most insulting remarks," telling him that he was "essentially a brute, a retarded guttersnipe (this in more polite language, to be sure)." Jung commiserated with Freud on this encounter, referring to the visitor, who was known to him, as "a slimy bastard." He went on: "I hope you roasted, flayed, and impaled the fellow. . . . Such is the nature of these beasts. Since I could read the filth in him from his face I would have loved to take him by the scruff of the neck. I hope you told him all the truths so plainly that even his hen's brain could absorb them. . . . Had I been in your shoes I would have softened up his guttersnipe complex with a sound Swiss thrashing." Denigrating speech was not reserved for critics only. Speaking of his patients on his return from vacation, Freud told Jung, "Today I resumed my practice and saw my first batch of nuts again" (F/J, pp. 150, 151, 160).

2. CP, 5:123.

3. A fourth accusation that was potentially disturbing but did not trouble Freud (or Jung) was that psychoanalysis was occultism. Both Freud and Jung were attracted by the occult and saw nothing shameful in it; they thought it contained truths not yet accessible to science. Freud favored soothsaying, clairvoyant visions, numerology, and mental telepathy. Once, he arranged a séance in his home. He published papers on "Psychoanalysis and Telepathy" and "Dreams and Telepathy" (both appear in SE, p. 18), "The Occult Significance of Dreams" (in SE, p. 19), and in NIL included a chapter on "Dreams and Occultism." The occult had the same general mass appeal, I suggest, that dream interpretation did: it harked back to the superstitious peasant past of Europe and in that way was attractive. Ernest Jones, afraid that Freud's interest in the occult, once known, would harm psychoanalysis, recommended keeping it secret. Jung, a true adept of the occult, ultimately went beyond Freud to visionary conversations with spirits and communion with the dead (see Noll, cited below). Among the insiders, Ferenczi was known as "The Court Astrologist."

4. F/F, p. 447.

5. Ibid., p. 175. A recent study by Mikkel Borch-Jacobsen, *Remembering Anna O.: A Century of Mystification* (New York, 1996), maintains that she feigned a mental condition. But Thornton, Webster, and others argue for a physical condition which affected her brain and accounted for her symptoms, probably tuberculosis of the brain contracted while taking care of her tubercular father, though its exact nature may never be known. Recognizing that her illness persisted despite his efforts, Breuer sent her to a sanitarium in Switzerland where her physical symptoms were treated. She finally revived and from that time forward never had a good word to say about psychotherapy.

6. AS, pp. 23, 26.

7. CP, 4:123.

8. Leon Poliakov, *The Aryan Myth: A History of Racist and Nationalist Ideas in Europe* (New York, 1996; orig. 1971), p. 247.

9. F/F, p. 159. In 1911 Putnam, a professor of neurology at Harvard, delivered a paper at the psychoanalytic congress in Weimar entitled "The Importance of Philosophy and the Further Development of Psychoanalysis."

10. In Herzog, "Myth of Freud," in Stepansky, *Freud: Appraisals and Reappraisals,* 2:175.

11. LSF, p. 366.

12. *C. G. Jung Speaking: Interviews and Encounters,* eds. William McGuire and R. F. C. Hull (Princeton, 1977), p. 419; Rieff, *Triumph,* p. 108. "Among all my patients in the second half of life . . . ," Jung lamented, "every one of them fell ill because he had lost what the living religions of every age have given their followers, and none of them has been really healed who did not regain his religious outlook" (in Victor White, *God and the Unconscious* [Cambridge, England, 1960; orig. 1952], p. 69). He later defined a "religious outlook" as a view of life in its wholeness, containing both a philosophical and ethical component; in short, the *gemeinschaft* outlook. "Christian doctrine has lost its grip to an appalling extent," he said, and could no longer manage "our restless and crazy time" (in an article about Jung, *New York Times* [December 18, 1994], p. 8).

13. See Richard Noll, *The Jung Cult: Origins of a Charismatic Movement* (Princeton, 1994).

14. *Jung Speaking,* p. 428; Jung, *Modern,* p. 240.

15. F/J, pp. 136–137. Between 1935 and 1939 Jung conducted a series of Nietzsche seminars. In the years leading up to World War II he, like many German-speaking Nietzsche admirers, cooperated with the Nazis, finally achieving leadership of psychiatry in German-speaking Europe (to which he had once aspired as Freud's heir). The excuse he gave later was that he was protecting psychiatry from the Nazis. Jung's Nietzsche side appears in a letter to Freud in which he feels "precariously on the fence between the Dionysian and the Apollonian" and wonders, "must we not love evil if we are to break away from the obsession with virtue that makes us sick and forbids us the joys of life?" Ethics, he says, must be infused with an "archaic-infantile driving force," which was the cry of romantic German proto-fascists from early on. See F/J, p. 135. Jung's later blatant occultism also had to be unappealing to Freud, who insinuated his occultism but never trumpeted it.

16. AS, p. 33.

17. In Ellenberger, *Unconscious,* p. 400.

18. Ibid., p. 417, note 177; AS, p. 33.

19. Ellenberger, *Unconscious,* p. 646; Clark, *Freud,* p. 310.

20. CP, 5:123.

21. In Clark, *Freud,* p. 311. In the period of the break, Freud professed cordial feelings for Adler, characterizing him as a "very decent and highly intellectual man," but in the next breath revealed a harsher attitude, labeling him, as was common in that period, "paranoid" (in Clark, *Freud,* p. 307). Nor was it kind of Freud later, never forgetting his enmities, to say of Adler that for a "Jew boy" from Vienna to die in the streets of Aberdeen showed how far he had come in the world. Ellenberger wonders why Freud won out over Adler. The answer is to be found in the fact that Adler's individual psychology was so much a practical philosophy of life that his disciples called him the Confucius of the West. Freud's was also—and eminently—a practical philosophy, but his was hidden, presented as mysteries of biology first and then of the psyche. Freud's victory validated the approach of keeping the system hidden and mysterious. Ellenberger thinks the contrast between these two figures is to be found in Adler being like a stoic when that was out of fashion, and Freud being like an epicurean when that was in fashion. But the contrast seems to be between a philosophy (Adler) and a religion (Freud). Freud's psychoanalysis gave the impression of possessing infinite depth, like religion, while Adler's individual psychology was like a philosophy, with rational borders. While Jung lost out to Freud just as Adler did, he may have attained the

second position because his system also gave the impression of unfathomable depth.

22. Webster, *Wrong,* p. 365.

23. CP, 5:122; F/J, p. 166.

24. F/J, p. 167.

25. Later, Reich's Orgone Box for the accumulation of orgasmic energy was barred by the U.S. Food and Drug Administration as a fraudulent medical device.

26. F/J, p. 156.

27. FL, pp. 4, 6. Freud manifestly meant that psychoanalysis was parting company from conventional neurology and psychiatry, but his words accurately reflected the direction he and his colleagues had taken.

28. Philip Cushman, *Constructing the Self, Constructing America: A Cultural History of Psychotherapy* (Reading, Mass., 1995), p. 159.

Chapter 25. Reasons of State

1. Theodore von Laue, *The World Revolution of Westernization: The Twentieth Century in Global Perspective* (New York, 1987), p. 7.

2. In Roazen, *Freud,* p. 59; in Janik and Toulmin, *Vienna,* p. 36; Roazen, *Freud,* p. 58.

3. Alexis de Tocqueville, *Democracy in America* (New York, 1990; orig. 1835), p. 9.

4. J. M. Roberts, *The Penguin History of the World* (New York, 1990), p. 659.

5. W. H. Auden, "In Memory of Sigmund Freud," in *W. H. Auden: Collected Poetry* (New York, 1945), p. 166; Edith Kurzweil, in "Letters," *Partisan Review* 4 (1996), 710; TT, p. 129.

6. John Updike, "Beyond the Picturesque," *New York Review of Books,* June 23, 1994, p. 21.

7. Albert Camus, *The Myth of Sisyphus,* trans. Justin O'Brien (New York, 1955), p. 6.

8. AS, pp. 82–83; Roazen, *Freud,* p. 322; José Ortega y Gasset, *The Revolt of the Masses* (New York, 1957; orig. 1930) p. 154.

9. John P. Carse, *Finite and Infinite Games: A Vision of Life as Play and Possibility* (New York, 1986), p. 53.

Bibliography

Adams, Joe Kennedy. *Secrets of the Trade: Madness, Creativity, and Ideology.* New York, Viking Press, 1971.

American Psychiatric Association. *Diagnostic and Statistical Manual of Mental Disorders.* 4th ed. Washington, D.C., 1994.

Anderson, Lorin. "Freud, Nietzsche." *Salmagundi* 47–48 (Winter–Spring 1980), 3–29.

Arendt, Hannah. "Some Questions of Moral Philosophy." *Social Research* 61, 2 (Winter 1994), 739–764.

———. *The Origins of Totalitarianism.* New York, Harvest Book Edition, 1979; orig. 1951.

Aschheim, Steven E. *The Nietzsche Legacy in Germany 1890–1990.* Berkeley, University of California Press, 1992.

Auden, W. H. *W. H. Auden: Collected Poetry.* New York, Random House, 1945.

Balmary, Marie. *Psychoanalyzing Psychoanalysis: Freud and the Hidden Fault of the Father.* Trans. Ned Lukacher. Baltimore, Johns Hopkins University Press, 1982.

Balog, Penelope. *Freud: A Biographical Introduction.* New York, Scribner's, 1971.

Barth, Hans. *Truth and Ideology.* Trans. Frederic Lilge. Berkeley, University of California Press, 1976; orig. 1945.

Barthes, Roland. *Mythologies.* Trans. Annette Lavers. New York, Hill and Wang, 1972; orig. 1957.

Benda, Julien. *The Treason of the Intellectuals.* Trans. Richard Aldington. New York, W. W. Norton, 1969; orig. 1927.

Berger, Peter. "Towards a Sociological Understanding of Psychoanalysis." *Social Research* 32, 1 (Spring 1965), 26–41.

Berger, Peter, and Thomas Luckmann. *The Social Construction of Reality.* New York, Doubleday, 1966.

Bergin, Allen E., and Michael Lambert. "The Evaluation of Therapeutic Outcomes." *Handbook of Psychotherapy and Behavior Change: An Empirical Analysis,* eds. Sol L. Garfield and Allen E. Bergin. New York, John Wiley & Sons, 1978.

Berman, Marshall. *All That Is Solid Melts into Air: The Experience of Modernity.* New York, Simon and Schuster, 1982.

Bernays, Edward L. *Propaganda.* New York, H. Liveright, 1928.

————. *The Engineering of Consent.* Norman, University of Oklahoma Press, 1955.

Bernheim, Charles, and Claire Kahan, eds. *In Dora's Case: Freud-Hysteria-Feminism.* New York, Columbia University Press, 1987.

Bersani, Leo. *Baudelaire and Freud.* Berkeley, University of California Press, 1977.

Bettelheim, Bruno. *Freud and Man's Soul.* New York, Alfred A. Knopf, 1982.

Borch-Jacobsen, Mikkel. *Remembering Anna O.: A Century of Mystification.* New York, Routledge, 1996.

Bower, Bruce. "Oedipus Wrecked." *Science News* 140 (October 19, 1991), 248–250.

Bowie, Malcolm. *Freud, Proust and Lacan: Theory as Fiction.* Cambridge, Cambridge University Press, 1987.

Brandell, Gunnar. *Freud: A Man of His Century.* Trans. Iain White. Atlantic Highlands, Humanities Press, 1979.

Brenkman, John. *Straight Male Modern: A Cultural Critique of Psychoanalysis.* New York, Routledge, 1993.

Brenner, David G., ed. *Baker Encyclopedia of Psychology.* Grand Rapids, Baker Book House, 1985.

Bronowski, J., and Bruce Mazlish. *The Western Intellectual Tradition.* New York, Dorset Press, 1986; orig. 1960.

Butt, M. Munawar. *Psychology, Sin, and Society: An Essay on the Triumvirate of Psychology, Religion, and Democracy.* Lanham, University Press of America, 1992.

Camus, Albert. *The Myth of Sisyphus.* Trans. Justin O'Brien. New York, Vintage International, 1955.

Canetti, Elias. *Crowds and Power.* Trans. Carol Stewart. New York, Viking Press, 1962; orig. 1960.

Carroll, David. *French Literary Fascism: Nationalism, Anti-Semitism, and the Ideology of Culture.* Princeton, Princeton University Press, 1995.

Carse, John P. *Finite and Infinite Games: A Vision of Life as Play and Possibility.* New York, Ballantine Books, 1986.

Castel, Robert, *et al. The Psychiatric Society.* New York, Columbia University Press, 1982.

Cioffi, Frank. "Freud and the Idea of a Pseudo-Science." *Explanation in the Behavioral Science,* eds. Robert Borger and Frank Cioffi. Cambridge, Cambridge University Press, 1970.

————. "Freud—New Myths to Replace the Old." *New Society* 50 (1979), 503–504.

————. "Psychoanalysis, Pseudo-Science and Testability." *Popper and the Human Sciences,* eds. G. Currie and A. Musgrave. Dordrecht, Nijhoff, 1985.

Clark, Ronald W. *Freud: The Man and the Cause.* New York, Random House, 1980.

Cooper, I. S. *The Victim Is Always the Same.* London, Paladin Books, 1982.

Corsini, Raymond J., ed. *The Handbook of Innovative Psychotherapies.* New York, John Wiley & Sons, 1981.

Crews, Frederick. *The Memory Wars: Freud's Legacy in Dispute.* New York, New York Review of Books, 1995.

————. *Skeptical Engagements.* New York, Oxford University Press, 1986.

Crozier, Michael. "The Civic Paradigm and Shaftesbury." *Thesis Eleven* 40 (1995), 68–92.

Cuddihy, John Murray. *The Ordeal of Civility: Freud, Marx, Levi-Strauss, and the Jewish Struggle with Modernity.* New York, Dell Publishing, 1974.

Cushman, Philip. *Constructing the Self, Constructing America: A Cultural History of Psychotherapy.* Reading, Addison-Wesley, 1995.

Dahl, Robert A. *Democracy and Its Critics.* New Haven, Yale University Press, 1989.

Dawes, Robyn M. *House of Cards: Psychology and Psychotherapy Built on Myth.* New York, HarperCollins, 1994.

Debord, Guy. *The Society of the Spectacle.* Trans. Donald Nicholson-Smith. New York, Zone Books, 1995; orig. 1967.

Dedijer, Vladimir. *The Road to Sarajevo.* New York, Simon and Schuster, 1966.

Delbanco, Andrew. "John Dewey's America." *Partisan Review* 3 (1996), 515–520.

Deleuze, Gilles, and Felix Guattari. *Anti-Oedipus: Capitalism and Schizophrenia.* Trans. Robert Hurley, Mark Seem, and Helen R. Lance. New York, Viking Press, 1977.

Doctor, Roland M., and Ada P. Kahn. *Encyclopedia of Phobias, Fears and Anxieties.* New York, Facts on File, 1989.

Eastman, Max. *Great Companions: Critical Memoirs of Some Famous Friends.* New York, Farrar, Straus and Cudahy, 1959; orig. 1926.

Eckardt, Barbara von. "Why Freud's Research Methodology Was Unscientific." *Psychoanalysis and Contemporary Thought* 5 (1982), 549–574.

Ecksteins, Modris. *Rites of Spring: The Great War and the Birth of the Modern Age.* Boston, Houghton Mifflin, 1989.

Edelson, Marshall. *Hypothesis and Evidence in Psychoanalysis.* Chicago, University of Chicago Press, 1984.

Ellenberger, Henri F. *The Discovery of the Unconscious: The History and Evolution of Dynamic Psychiatry.* New York, Basic Books, 1970.

————. "The Story of 'Anna O.': A Critical Review with New Data." *Journal of the History of Behavioral Sciences* 8 (1972), 267–279.

Ellul, Jacques. *The Technological Society.* Trans. John Wilkinson. New York, Vintage Books, 1964; orig. 1954.

————. *Propaganda: The Formation of Men's Attitudes.* Trans. Konrad Kellen and Jean Lerner. New York, Vintage Books, 1968; orig. 1962.

Engelman, Edmund. *Berggasse 19: Sigmund Freud's Home and Offices, Vienna, 1938.* New York, Basic Books, 1976.

Entralgo, P. Lain. *The Therapy of the Word in Classical Antiquity.* New Haven, Yale University Press, 1970.

Esterson, Allan. *Seductive Mirage: An Exploration of the World of Sigmund Freud.* Chicago, Open Court Press, 1993.

Eyer, Diane. *Motherguilt: How Our Culture Blames Mothers for What's Wrong with Society.* New York, Times Books, 1997.

Eysenck, Hans J., and Glen D. Wilson. *The Experimental Study of Freudian Theories.* London, Methuen, 1973.

————. *Decline and Fall of the Freudian Empire.* Washington, D.C., Scott-Townsend Publishers, 1990; orig. 1985.

Fancher, Raymond E. *Pioneers of Psychology.* New York, W. W. Norton, 1979.

Farrell, John. *Freud's Paranoid Quest: Psychoanalysis and Modern Suspicion.* New York, New York University Press, 1996.

Feuerbach, Ludwig. *The Essence of Christianity.* Trans. George Eliot. Buffalo, Prometheus Books, 1989; orig. 1841.

Fish, Stanley. "Withholding the Missing Portion: Power, Meaning and Persuasion in Freud's 'The Wolf-Man.'" *Times Literary Supplement,* August 29, 1986, pp. 935–938.

Fisher, Seymour, and Roger P. Greenberg. *The Scientific Credibility of Freud's Theories and Therapies.* New York, Basic Books, 1977.

Fitzmaurice, Andrew. "Classical Rhetoric and the Promotion of the New World." *Journal of the History of Ideas* 52, 2 (April 1997), 221–243.

Forrester, John. *Dispatches from the Freud Wars: Psychoanalysis and Its Passions.* Cambridge, Harvard University Press, 1997.

————. *Truth Games: Lies, Money and Psychoanalysis.* Cambridge, Harvard University Press, 1997.

Foucault, Michel. *Madness and Civilization: A History of Insanity in the Age of Reason.* Trans. Richard Howard. New York, Vintage Books, 1965; orig. 1961.

————. *The Birth of the Clinic: An Archaeology of Medical Perception.* Trans. A. M. Sheridan. New York, Vintage Books, 1994; orig. 1963.

————. *The Order of Things.* New York, Vintage Books, 1994; orig. 1966.

————. *The Foucault Reader.* Ed. Paul Rabinow, trans. Josue V. Harari, et al. New York, Pantheon Books, 1984.

————. *Power/Knowledge: Selected Interviews and Other Writings 1972–1977.* Ed. Colon Gordon, trans. Colin Gordon, Leo Marshall, and Kate Soper. New York, Pantheon Books, 1980.

Frank, Jerome. *Persuasion and Healing.* New York, Schocken Books, 1973.

Freud, Sigmund. *An Autobiographical Study.* Trans. and ed. James Strachey. New York, W. W. Norton, 1952; orig. 1925.

————. *Civilization and Its Discontents.* Trans. and ed. James Strachey. New York, W. W. Norton, 1961; orig. 1931.

————. *Cocaine Papers.* Ed. Robert Byck. New York, Stonehill, 1974.

————. *Collected Papers.* 5 vols. Trans. under supervision of Joan Riviere. New York, Basic Books, 1959; orig. 1949–1950.

————. *Five Lectures on Psycho-Analysis.* Trans. and ed. James Strachey. New York, W. W. Norton, 1961; orig. 1909.

————. *The Future of an Illusion.* Trans. and ed. James Strachey. New York, W. W. Norton, 1961; orig. 1927.

————. *Group Psychology and the Analysis of the Ego.* Trans. and ed. James Strachey. New York, W. W. Norton, 1959; orig. 1922.

————. *The Interpretation of Dreams.* Trans. and ed. James Strachey. New York, Avon Books, 1965; orig. 1900.

————. *Introductory Lectures on Psycho-Analysis.* Trans. and ed. James Strachey. New York, W. W. Norton, 1966; orig. 1915–1916.

————. *Moses and Monotheism.* Trans. Katherine Jones. New York, Vintage Books, 1967; orig. 1939.

————. *New Introductory Lectures on Psycho-Analysis.* Trans. and ed. James Strachey. New York, W. W. Norton, 1964; orig. 1932.

————. *An Outline of Psycho-Analysis.* Trans. and ed. James Strachey. New York, W. W. Norton, 1949; orig. 1939.

————. *The Psychopathology of Everyday Life.* Trans. and ed. James Strachey. New York, W. W. Norton, 1965; orig. 1901.

————. *The Standard Edition of the Complete Psychological Works of Sigmund Freud.* 24 vols. Trans. James Strachey. London, Hogarth Press, 1953–1974.

———— and Joseph Breuer. *Studies on Hysteria.* Trans. and ed. James Strachey. Boston, Beacon Press, 1961; orig. 1895.

————. *Totem and Taboo.* Trans. and ed. James Strachey. New York, W. W. Norton, 1950; orig. 1913.

————. *The Complete Letters of Sigmund Freud to Wilhelm Fliess, 1887–1904.* Trans. and ed. Jeffrey M. Masson. Cambridge, Harvard University Press, 1985.

———— and C. G. Jung. *The Freud/Jung Letters: The Correspondence between Sigmund Freud and C. G. Jung.* Ed. William McGuire. Princeton, Princeton University Press, 1974.

————. *The Letters of Sigmund Freud.* Ed. Ernst L. Freud, trans. James Strachey. New York, Basic Books, 1975; orig. 1960.

———— and Oskar Pfister. *Psychoanalysis and Faith: The Letters of Sigmund Freud and Oskar Pfister.* Ed. Heinrich Meng and Ernst L. Freud, trans. Eric Mosbacher. London, Hogarth Press, 1963.

Fromm, Erich. *Sigmund Freud's Mission: An Analysis of His Personality and Influence.* New York, Harper & Brothers, 1959.

————. *The Revolution of Hope: Toward a Humanized Technology.* New York, Bantam Books, 1968.

————. *The Crisis of Psychoanalysis: Essays on Freud, Marx, and Social Psychology.* New York, Henry Holt and Co., 1991; orig. 1970.

Gardiner, Muriel, ed. *The Wolf-Man by the Wolf-Man*. New York, Basic Books, 1971.

Gardner, Howard. *Creating Minds: An Anatomy of Creativity Seen Through the Lives of Freud, Einstein, Picasso, Stravinsky, Eliot, Graham, Gandhi*. New York, Basic Books, 1993.

Gay, Peter. *Freud: A Life for Our Time*. New York, W. W. Norton, 1988.

————. *A Godless Jew: Freud, Atheism, and the Making of Psychoanalysis*. New Haven, Yale University Press, 1987.

Gelfand, Toby, and John Kerr, eds. *Freud and the History of Psychoanalysis*. Hillsdale, N.J., Analytic Press, 1992.

Gellner, Ernest. *The Psychoanalytic Movement, or the Coming of Unreason*. London, Paladin Books, 1985.

Gilman, Sander L. *Freud, Race, and Gender*. Princeton, Princeton University Press, 1993.

Goldenson, Robert M. *The Encyclopedia of Human Behavior: Psychology, Psychiatry, and Mental Health*. 2 vols. Garden City, Doubleday, 1970.

Goodrich, Peter. *Oedipus Lex: Psychoanalysis, History, Law*. Berkeley, University of California Press, 1995.

Green, Martin. *Prophets of a New Age: The Politics of Hope from the Eighteenth Through the Twenty-First Centuries*. New York, Macmillan, 1992.

Green, Robert H. "Instinct of Nature: Natural Law, Synderesis, and the Moral Sense." *Journal of the History of Ideas* 58, 2 (April 1997), 173–198.

Gregory, Robert L., ed. *The Oxford Companion to the Mind*. New York, Oxford University Press, 1987.

Grinstein, Alexander. *On Sigmund Freud's Dreams*. Detroit, Wayne State University Press, 1968.

Grunbaum, Adolf. *Validation in the Clinical Theory of Psychoanalysis*. Madison, International Universities Press, 1993.

————. *The Foundations of Psychoanalysis: A Philosophical Critique*. Berkeley, University of California Press, 1984.

Guattari, Felix. *Molecular Revolution, Psychiatry and Politics*. Trans. Rosemary Sheed. Harmondsworth, Penguin, 1984.

Gupta, R. K. "Freud and Schopenhauer." *Journal of the History of Ideas* 36, 4 (October–December 1975), 721–728.

Halleck, Seymour L. *The Politics of Therapy*. New York, Science House, 1971.

Haskell, Francis. "Art and Apocalypse." *New York Review of Books*, July 15, 1993, pp. 25–29.

Hayes, Paul. *Fascism*. New York, Free Press, 1973.

Hegel, G. W. F. *The Phenomenology of Mind*. Trans. J. B. Baillie. New York, Harper Torchbooks, 1977; orig. 1807.

Heilbroner, Robert L. *The Worldly Philosophers: The Lives, Times and Ideas of the Great Economic Thinkers*. 6th ed. New York, Simon and Schuster, 1992; orig. 1953.

Herzog, Patricia. "The Myth of Freud as Anti-philosopher." *Freud: Ap-*

praisals and Reappraisals. Ed. Paul E. Stepansky. 3 vols. Hillsdale, Analytic Press, 1988.

Hirsch, E. D., Jr. *Validity of Interpretation.* New Haven, Yale University Press, 1967.

Hobsbawm, E. J. *The Age of Capital, 1848–1875.* New York, Scribner's, 1975.

Hoffman, Frederick J. *Freudianism and the Literary Mind.* 2nd ed. Baton Rouge, Louisiana State University Press, 1967; orig. 1957.

Holt, Robert R. *Freud Reappraised: A Fresh Look at Psychoanalytic Theory.* New York, Guilford Press, 1982.

Holtzman, P. S., and S. Matthysse, "The Genetics of Schizophrenia: A Review." *Psychological Science* 1 (1990), 279–286.

Hook, Sidney, ed. *Psychoanalysis, Scientific Method and Philosophy: A Symposium.* New York, Evergreen, 1964; orig. 1959.

Hopkins, Jim. "Killing and Eating Father." *New Statesman* 98 (1979), 900.

Horkheimer, Max. *Critique of Instrumental Reason: Lectures and Essays Since the End of World War II.* New York, Seabury Press, 1974; orig. 1967.

Horney, Karen. *The Neurotic Personality of Our Time.* New York, W. W. Norton, 1937.

Hyman, Stanley Edgar. *The Tangled Bank: Darwin, Marx, Frazer and Freud as Imaginative Writers.* New York, Atheneum, 1962.

Isbister, J. N. *Freud: An Introduction to His Life and Work.* Cambridge, Polity Press, 1985.

Jacoby, Russell. *Social Amnesia: A Critique of Conformist Psychology from Adler to Laing.* Boston, Beacon Press, 1975.

Jameson, Fredric. *The Political Unconscious: Narrative as a Socially Symbolic Act.* Ithaca, Cornell University Press, 1981.

Janik, Allan, and Stephen Toulmin. *Wittgenstein's Vienna.* New York, Simon and Schuster, 1973.

Johnson, Paul. *The Birth of the Modern: World Society 1815–1830.* New York, HarperCollins, 1991.

———. *A History of the Jews.* New York, HarperPerennial, 1987.

Johnston, Thomas. *Freud and Political Thought.* New York, Citadel Press, 1965.

Johnston, William M. *The Austrian Mind: An Intellectual and Social History, 1848–1938.* Berkeley, University of California Press, 1983; orig. 1972.

Jones, Ernest. *Hamlet and Oedipus.* New York, W. W. Norton, 1976.

———. *The Life and Work of Sigmund Freud.* 3 vols. New York, Basic Books, 1953–1957.

Jung, C. G. *C. G. Jung Speaking: Interviews and Encounters.* Ed. William McGuire and R. F. C. Hull. Princeton, Princeton University Press, 1977.

———. *Modern Man in Search of a Soul.* Trans. W. S. Dell and Cary F. Baynes. New York, Harcourt Brace & Co., no date; orig. 1933.

———. *Psychology and Religion.* New Haven, Yale University Press, 1937.

————. *The Basic Writings of C. G. Jung.* Ed. Violet Staub de Laszlo. New York, Modern Library, 1993.

————. *The Undiscovered Self.* Trans. R. F. C. Hull. New York, New American Library, 1957.

Jurevich, R. M. *The Hoax of Freudianism.* Philadelphia, Dorrance, 1974.

Justman, Stewart. "Freud and His Nephew." *Social Research* 61, 2 (Summer 1994), 457–476.

Kamenka, Eugene. *The Philosophy of Ludwig Feuerbach.* New York, Praeger Publishers, 1970; orig. 1969.

Kant, Immanuel. *Prolegomena.* Trans. Paul Carus. Chicago, Open Court Press, 1902; orig 1783.

Kerr, John. *A Most Dangerous Method: The Story of Jung, Freud and Sabina Spielrein.* New York, Knopf, 1993.

Kirk, Stuart A., and Herb Kutchins. *The Selling of DSM: The Rhetoric of Science in Psychiatry.* New York, A. de Gruyter, 1992.

Klein, Dennis B. *Jewish Origins of the Psychoanalytic Movement.* New York, Praeger, 1981.

Kline, Paul. *Psychology and Freudian Theory: An Introduction.* New York, Methuen, 1984.

————. *Fact and Fantasy in Freudian Theory.* London, Methuen, 1972.

Krista, Alix. "Honor Thy Father and Mother: No Way." *Observer* (London), September 15, 1991, p. 52.

Kropotkin, Peter. *Mutual Aid: A Factor of Evolution.* London, Heinemann, 1908.

Krull, Marianne. *Freud and His Father.* Trans. Arnold J. Pomerans. New York, W. W. Norton, 1986.

Kung, Hans. *Freud and the Problem of God.* New Haven, Yale University Press, 1979.

Kuper, Adam. *The Invention of Primitive Society: Transformations of an Illusion.* New York, Routledge, 1988.

Lakoff, Robin Tolmach, and James C. Coyne. *Father Knows Best: The Use and Abuse of Power in Freud's Case of "Dora."* New York, New York Teachers College, 1993.

LaPiere, Richard Tracy. *A Theory of Social Control.* New York, McGraw-Hill, 1954.

Laslett, Peter. *The World We Have Lost: England Before the Industrial Age.* 3rd ed. New York, Scribner's, 1984.

Lasswell, Harold D. *Psychopathology and Politics.* New York, Viking Press, 1960.

Laue, Theodore von. *The World Revolution of Westernization: The Twentieth Century in Global Perspective.* New York, Oxford University Press, 1987.

Le Bon, Gustav. *The Crowd.* Dunwoody, N. S. Berg, 1968; orig. 1895.

Levin, Kenneth. *Freud's Early Psychology of the Neuroses: A Historical Perspective.* Sussex, Harvester Press, 1978.

Lieberman, E. James. *Acts of Will: The Life and Work of Otto Rank.* Amherst, University of Massachusetts Press, 1985.

Lieberson, Jonathan. "Putting Freud to the Test." *New York Review of Books*, January 31, 1985, pp. 24–28.

Lomas, Peter. *The Limits of Interpretation: What's Wrong with Psychoanalysis?* Harmondsworth, Penguin, 1987.

MacIntyre, Alasdair. *A Short History of Ethics*. New York, Macmillan, 1966.

———. *After Virtue: A Study in Moral Theory*. Notre Dame, University of Notre Dame Press, 1982.

Mackay, Charles. *Memoirs of Extraordinary Popular Delusions and the Madness of Crowds*. London, Office of the National Illustrated Library, 1852.

Macmillan, Malcolm. *Freud Evaluated: The Completed Arc*. Amsterdam, North-Holland, 1991.

Mahony, Patrick. *Freud as a Writer*. New York, International Universities Press, 1982.

———. *Cries of the Wolf-Man*. New York, International Universities Press, 1984.

Mann, Thomas. *Essays*. New York, Knopf, 1957.

Marx, Karl. *The Portable Karl Marx*. Ed. and trans. Eugene Kamenka. New York, Penguin Books, 1983.

Masson, Jeffrey M. *Final Analysis: The Making and Unmaking of a Psychoanalyst*. Reading, Addison-Wesley, 1990.

———. *Against Therapy: Emotional Tyranny and the Myth of Psychological Healing*. Monroe, Common Courage Press, 1994; orig. 1988.

———. *A Dark Science: Women, Sexuality, and Psychiatry in the Nineteenth Century*. New York, Farrar, Straus and Giroux, 1986.

———. *The Assault on Truth: Freud's Suppression of the Seduction Theory*. New York, Farrar, Straus and Giroux, 1984.

McCormick, John P. "Nietzsche, Schmitt and the Antichrist." *Philosophy & Social Criticism* 21, 3 (July 1995), 55–92.

McGrath, William J. *Freud's Discovery of Psychoanalysis: The Politics of Hysteria*. Ithaca, Cornell University Press, 1985.

McHugh, Paul R. "Psychotherapy Awry." *American Scholar* 63 (Winter 1994), 17–30.

———. "Psychiatric Misadventures." *American Scholar* 61 (Autumn 1992), 497–510.

———. "Jung at Heart." *American Scholar* 64 (Autumn 1995), pp. 617–622.

Medawar, P. B. "Victims of Psychiatry." *New York Review of Books*, January 23, 1975, p. 17.

Money-Kryle, R. E. *Psychoanalysis and Politics: A Contribution to the Psychology of Politics*. Westport, Greenwood Press, 1973; orig. 1951.

Morris, Nat. *A Man Possessed: The Case History of Sigmund Freud*. Los Angeles, Regent House, 1974.

Mowrer, O. H. *The Crisis of Psychiatry and Religion*. Princeton, Van Nostrand Publishers, 1961.

Munson, Edward L. *The Management of Men: Handbook on Systematic*

Development of Morale and Control of Human Behavior. New York, Henry Holt, 1921.

Murphy, Peter. "The Birth of Humanism." *Thesis Eleven* 40 (1995), 44–67.

Nagel, Thomas. "Freud's Permanent Revolution." *New York Review of Books*, May 12, 1994, pp. 34–38.

Neill, Thomas P. *Modern Europe: A Popular History*. Garden City, Doubleday, 1970.

Neu, Jerome, ed. *The Cambridge Companion to Freud*. Cambridge, Cambridge University Press, 1995; orig. 1991.

Nicholi, Armand H., Jr., ed. *The New Harvard Guide to Psychiatry*. Cambridge, Harvard University Press, 1988.

Nietzsche, Friedrich. *The Portable Nietzsche*. Trans. and ed. Walter Kaufmann. New York, Viking Press, 1968.

———. *The Birth of Tragedy* and *The Genealogy of Morals*. Trans. Francis Golffing. Garden City, Anchor Books, 1956; orig. 1872 and 1877.

Noll, Richard. *The Jung Cult: Origins of a Charismatic Movement*. Princeton, Princeton University Press, 1994.

Nordau, Max. *Degeneration*. Lincoln, University of Nebraska Press, 1968; orig. 1892.

Nunberg, Herman, and Ernest Federn, eds. *Minutes of the Vienna Psychoanalytic Society*. New York, International Universities Press, 1967.

Nyberg, David. *The Varnished Truth: Truth Telling and Deceiving in Ordinary Life*. Chicago, University of Chicago Press, 1993.

Obholzer, Karin. *The Wolf-Man: Conversations with Freud's Patient— Sixty Years Later*. Trans. Michael Shaw. New York, Continuum, 1982.

Ofshe, Richard, and Ethan Watters. *Making Monsters: False Memories, Psychotherapy, and Sexual Hysteria*. New York, Scribner's, 1994.

Ortega y Gasset, José. *The Revolt of the Masses*. New York, W. W. Norton, 1957; orig. 1930.

Packard, Vance O. *The Hidden Persuaders*. New York, Pocket Books, 1957.

Pankejeff, Sergius. *The Wolf-Man*. New York, Hill and Wang, 1991.

Parker, Rozsika. *Mother Love/Mother Hate: The Power of Maternal Ambivalence*. New York, Basic Books, 1996.

Pendergrast, Mark. *Victims of Memory: Incest Accusations and Shattered Lives*. Hinesberg, Upper Access, 1995.

Philip, H. L. *Freud and Religious Belief*. Westport, Greenwood Press, 1974.

Pinckney, E. R., and Cathy Pinckney. *The Fallacy of Freud and Psychoanalysis*. Englewood Cliffs, Prentice-Hall, 1986.

Poliakov, Leon. *The Aryan Myth: A History of Racist and Nationalist Ideas in Europe*. New York, Barnes and Noble Books, 1996; orig. 1971.

Popper, Karl. *The Logic of Scientific Discovery*. New York, Basic Books, 1958.

———. *The Open Society and Its Enemies*. 2 vols. Princeton, Princeton University Press, 1962.

Porter, Roy. *A Social History of Madness: Stories of the Insane*. London, Weidenfield & Nicholson, 1987.

Powell, Russell A., and Douglas P. Boer. "Did Freud Mislead Patients to Confabulate Memories of Abuse?" *Psychological Reports* 74 (1994), 1283–1298.

Proileau, Leslie, Martha Murdock, and Nathan Brody. "An Analysis of Psychotherapy Versus Placebo Studies." *Behavioral and Brain Sciences* 6 (1983), 275–310.

Proust, Marcel. *Remembrance of Things Past*. Trans. C. K. Scott-Moncrieff and Frederick A. Blossom. 2 vols. New York, Random House, 1932; orig. 1913–1927.

Rachman, S., ed. *Critical Essays on Psychoanalysis*. London, Pergamon Press, 1963.

―――― and G. T. Wilson. *The Effects of Psychological Therapy*. London, Pergamon, 1980.

Rainey, Reuben B. *Freud as Student of Religion: Perspectives on the Background and Development of His Thought*. Missoula, American Academy of Religion and Scholars Press, 1975.

Rand, Nicholas, and Maria Torok. *Questions for Freud: The Secret History of Psychoanalysis*. Cambridge, Harvard University Press, 1997.

Rank, Otto. *Beyond Psychology*. New York, Dover, 1958; orig. 1941.

――――. *Truth and Reality*. Trans. Jessie Taft. New York, W. W. Norton, 1978; orig. 1929.

Rattner, Josef. *Alfred Adler*. Trans. Harry Zohn. New York, Frederick Ungar Publishing Co., 1983.

Renard, Jules. *The Journal of Jules Renard*. Trans. and ed. Louise Bogan and Elizabeth Roget. New York, George Braziller, 1964.

Ricoeur, Paul. *Freud and Philosophy: An Essay on Interpretation*. Trans. Dennis Savage. New Haven, Yale University Press, 1970.

Rieff, Philip. *Freud: The Mind of the Moralist*. New York, Viking Press, 1959.

――――. *The Triumph of the Therapeutic*. New York, Harper & Row, 1966.

Riesman, David, with Nathan Glazer and Reuel Denney. *The Lonely Crowd*. New Haven, Yale University Press, 1961.

Roazen, Paul. *Freud: Political and Social Thought*. New York, Vintage Books, 1970.

――――. *Freud and His Followers*. New York, Knopf, 1975.

Robert, Marthe. *From Oedipus to Moses: Freud's Jewish Identity*. Trans. Ralph Manheim. Garden City, Anchor Books, 1976.

Roberts, J. M. *The Penguin History of the World*. New York, Penguin, 1980.

Robinson, Paul. *Freud and His Critics*. Berkeley, University of California Press, 1993.

Rubinstein, Benjamin B. "On the Clinical Psychoanalytic Theory and Its Role in the Inference and Confirmation of Particular Clinical Hypotheses." *Psychoanalysis and Contemporary Science* 4 (1975), 3–57.

Rudin, Josef. *Psychotherapy and Religion.* Notre Dame, University of Notre Dame Press, 1968.

Rudnytsky, Peter L. *Freud and Oedipus.* New York, Columbia University Press, 1986.

Samuels, Andrew. *The Political Psyche.* New York, Routledge, 1993.

Schact, Richard. *The Future of Alienation.* Urbana, University of Illinois Press, 1994.

Schatzman, Morton. "Freud: Who Seduced Whom?" *New Scientist,* March 21, 1992, pp. 34–37.

Schopenhauer, Arthur. *The World as Will and Representation.* Trans. E. F. J. Payne. 2 vols. New York, Dover, 1969.

Schorske, Carl E. *Fin-de-Siècle Vienna: Politics and Culture.* New York, Vintage Books, 1981.

Schreber, Daniel Paul. *Memoirs of My Nervous Illness.* Trans. and eds. Ida Macalpine and Richard A. Hunter. Cambridge, Harvard University Press, 1988; orig. 1903.

Schur, Max. *Freud: Living and Dying.* New York, International Universities Press, 1972.

Sears, R. R. *Bulletin 51. Survey of Objective Studies of Psychoanalytic Concepts.* New York, Social Science Research Council, 1943.

Sedgwick, Peter. *Psycho Politics.* London, Pluto Press, 1982.

Seely, John R. *The Americanization of the Unconscious.* New York, International Science Press, 1967.

Seigel, Jerrold. *Bohemian Paris: Culture, Politics and the Boundaries of Bourgeois Life, 1830–1930.* New York, Penguin Books, 1987.

Sharkey, Joe. *Bedlam: Greed, Profiteering, and Fraud in a Mental Health System Gone Crazy.* New York, St. Martin's Press, 1994.

Shepherd, Michael. *Sherlock Holmes and the Case of Dr. Freud.* London, Tavistock, 1985.

Sherman, Murray H., ed. *Psychoanalysis and Old Vienna: Freud, Reik, Schnitzler, Kraus.* New York, Human Sciences Press, 1978.

Shorter, Edward. *The Making of the Modern Family.* New York, Basic Books, 1975.

Simmel, George. *Schopenhauer and Nietzsche.* Trans. Helmut Loiskandl, Deena Weinstein, and Michael Weinstein. Amherst, University of Massachusetts Press, 1986; orig. 1907.

Slater, A. *A Case Against Psychoanalysis.* New York, Henry Holt, 1972.

Solomon, Robert C. *Continental Philosophy Since 1750: The Rise and Fall of the Self.* Oxford, Oxford University Press, 1988.

Stannard, D. E. *Shrinking History.* Oxford, Oxford University Press, 1980.

Stearns, Peter N. *European Society in Upheaval: Social History Since 1750.* New York, Macmillan, 1975; orig. 1967.

———, ed. *The Impact of the Industrial Revolution: Protest and Alienation.* Englewood Cliffs, Prentice-Hall, 1972.

Steedman, Carolyn. *Strange Dislocations: Childhood and the Idea of Interiority, 1780–1930.* Cambridge, Harvard University Press, 1995.

Stepansky, Paul E., ed. *Freud: Appraisals and Reappraisals*. 3 vols. Hillsdale, Analytic Press, 1986–1988.

Stephens, W. N. *The Oedipus Complex Hypothesis: Cross-Cultural Evidence*. Glencoe, Free Press, 1962.

Stern, Fritz. *The Politics of Cultural Despair: A Study in the Rise of the German Ideology*. Berkeley, University of California Press, 1974.

Sternhall, Zeev, Mario Sznajder, and Maia Asher. *The Birth of Fascist Ideology: From Cultural Rebellion to Political Revolution*. Princeton, Princeton University Press, 1994.

Stone, Lawrence. *The Family, Sex and Marriage in England 1500–1800*. New York, Harper & Row, 1978.

Stowe, Harriet Beecher. *Uncle Tom's Cabin*. New York, Modern Library, 1985; orig. 1852.

Strouse, Jean. "Freud Without Myths." *Newsweek*, October 29, 1979, pp. 98–99.

Strupp, H. H., S. W. Hadley, and B. Gomes-Schwartz. *Psychotherapy for Better or Worse: The Problem of Negative Effects*. New York, Jason Aronson, 1977.

Sulloway, Frank. "Reassessing Freud's Case Histories: The Special Construction of Psychoanalysis." *Isis* 82 (June 1991), 245–275.

———. *Freud, Biologist of the Mind: Beyond the Psychoanalytic Legend*. New York, Basic Books, 1979.

Sutherland, Stuart. *The International Dictionary of Psychology*. New York, Continuum, 1989.

Swales, Peter. "Freud, Cocaine, and Sexual Chemistry: The Role of Cocaine in Freud's Conception of the Libido." Privately published by the author, 1983.

———. "Freud, Fliess, and Fratricide: The Role of Fliess on Freud's Conception of Paranoia." Privately published by the author, 1982.

———. "Freud, Minna Bernays and the Conquest of Rome: More Light on the Origins of Psychoanalysis." *New American Review* 1 (1982), 1–23.

Szasz, Thomas, M.D. *The Myth of Psychotherapy: Mental Healing as Religion, Rhetoric and Repression*. New York, Syracuse University Press, 1988.

———. *The Therapeutic State: Psychiatry in the Mirror of Current Events*. Buffalo, Prometheus, 1984.

———. *The Myth of Mental Illness*. Rev. ed. New York, Harper & Row, 1974.

———. *Karl Kraus and the Soul-Doctors: A Pioneer Critic and His Criticism of Psychiatry and Psychoanalysis*. Baton Rouge, Louisiana University Press, 1976.

Tannenbaum, Edward R. *1900: The Generation Before the Great War*. Garden City, Doubleday, 1976.

Thompson, E. P. *The Making of the English Working Class*. New York, Vintage Books, 1966.

Thornton, E. M. *The Freudian Fallacy: An Alternative View of Freudian Theory*. Garden City, Doubleday, 1984.

Tocqueville, Alexis de. *Democracy in America.* New York, Vintage Books, 1990; orig. 1835.

Toffler, Alvin. *Future Shock.* New York, Random House, 1970.

Torrey, E. Fuller. *Freudian Fraud: The Malignant Effect of Freud's Theory on American Thought and Culture.* New York, HarperCollins, 1992.

———. *The Death of Psychiatry.* New York, Penguin Books, 1975.

———. *Witchdoctors and Psychiatrists: The Common Roots of Psychotherapy and Its Future.* New York, Harper & Row, 1986.

Toulmin, Stephen. *Cosmopolis: The Hidden Agenda of Modernity.* New York, Free Press, 1990.

Turkle, Sherry. *Psychoanalytic Politics: Freud's French Revolution.* New York, Basic Books, 1978.

Updike, John. "Beyond the Picturesque." *New York Review of Books,* June 23, 1994, pp. 21–23.

Van den Berg, J. H. *The Changing Nature of Man: Introduction to a Historical Psychology.* Trans. H. F. Croes. New York, W. W. Norton, 1961.

Voloshinov, V. N. *Freudianism: A Critical Sketch.* Trans. I. R. Titunik, ed. with Neal H. Bruss. Bloomington, Indiana University Press, 1987; orig. 1927.

Waldron-Skinner, Sue. *Dictionary of Psychotherapy.* London, Routledge and Kegan Paul, 1986.

Wallace, E. R. *Freud and Anthropology: A History and Reappraisal.* New York, International Universities Press, 1983.

Weber, Eugen. *France, Fin de Siècle.* Cambridge, Harvard University Press, 1986.

Webster, Richard. *Why Freud Was Wrong: Sin, Science, and Psychoanalysis.* New York, Basic Books, 1995.

Weiss, John. *Ideology of Death: Why the Holocaust Happened in Germany.* Chicago, Ivan R. Dee, 1996.

Welsh, Alexander. *Freud's Wishful Dream Book.* Princeton, Princeton University Press, 1994.

White, Victor. *God and the Unconscious.* Cambridge, England, Fontana Press, 1960; orig. 1952.

Whyte, Lancelot L. *The Unconscious Before Freud.* New York, Basic Books, 1960.

Wilcocks, Robert. *Maelzel's Chess Player: Sigmund Freud and the Rhetoric of Deceit.* Lanham, Rowman and Littlefield, 1994.

Woodward, William R., and Mitchell G. Ash, ed. *Psychology in Nineteenth-Century Thought.* Cambridge, Cambridge University Press, 1982.

Wortis, Joseph. *Fragments of an Analysis with Freud.* New York, Simon and Schuster, 1954.

Wrong, Dennis H. *The Problem of Order.* New York, Free Press, 1994.

Yerushalmi, Yosef. *Freud's Moses: Judaism Terminable and Interminable.* New Haven, Yale University Press, 1991.

Zanuso, Billa. *The Young Freud: The Origins of Psychoanalysis in Late Nineteenth-Century Viennese Culture.* New York, Blackwell, 1986.

Zilbergeld, B. *The Shrinking of America: Myths of Psychological Change.* Boston, Little, Brown & Co., 1983.

Zilboorg, Gregory. *Psychoanalysis and Religion.* New York, Farrar, Straus and Cudahy, 1962.

Index

A NOTE ON THE AUTHOR

Martin Wain was born in Brooklyn, New York, and studied literature at Long Island University and at Queens College. His writings on politics, history, philosophy, and culture have appeared in *New Political Science*, *Intellect*, *Puck*, and *Exquisite Corpse*; his books include *The Last Word* and *Vietnam Essays*. Mr. Wain has also written professionally on matters of science and technology. He lives in Glen Cove, New York.